Frontiers and Sanctuaries

*A Woman's Life in
Holland and Canada*

MARIANNE BRANDIS

McGill-Queen's University Press
Montreal & Kingston · London · Ithaca

© McGill-Queen's University Press 2006
ISBN 13: 978-0-7735-2968-7   ISBN 10: 0-7735-2968-3

Legal deposit second quarter 2006
Bibliothèque nationale du Québec

Printed in Canada on acid-free paper that is 100% ancient forest free
(100% post-consumer recycled), processed chlorine free

McGill-Queen's University Press acknowledges the support of the Canada
Council for the Arts for our publishing program. We also acknowledge the
financial support of the Government of Canada through the Book Publishing
Industry Development Program (BPIDP) for our publishing activities.

LIBRARY AND ARCHIVES CANADA CATALOGUING IN PUBLICATION

Brandis, Marianne, 1938–
Frontiers and sanctuaries : A woman's life in Holland and Canada /
Marianne Brandis.

Based on the diaries, letters and other writings of Madzy Brender à Brandis.
Includes bibliographical references and index.
ISBN 13: 978-0-7735-2968-7   ISBN 10: 0-7735-2968-3

1. Brender à Brandis, Madzy, 1910–1984.   2. Authors, Canadian (English)
– 20th century – Biography.   3. Dutch Canadians – Biography.
4. Immigrants – Canada – Biography.   1. Brender à Brandis, Madzy,
1910–1984   11. Title.

PS8553.R38Z54 2006   C818'.5409   C2005-906670-9

Set in 10.8/13.4 Adobe Caslon Pro
Book design & typesetting by Garet Markvoort, zijn digital

For my father, Bill, and my brothers, Gerard and Jock,
my companions on this journey

❧ CONTENTS

Appendices

MY MOTHER, Madzy Brender à Brandis-van Vollenhoven, was born in Holland in 1910, the third of four children in an upper-middle-class family. Her privileged childhood did little to prepare her for the varied and often difficult life she was to live. The protected existence did not, in fact, suit her: she rebelled against its restrictions, discovering in herself a great need to be free, a hankering for adventure, and a drive for self-fulfillment that were to last life long.

As a young woman, despite her mother's disapproval, she studied law in Leiden, planning to practise in what was then the Dutch East Indies, but shortly before obtaining her degree she married. With her new husband, Wim Brender à Brandis, she lived for several years near New York City. On the eve of the Second World War, she and Wim returned to Holland. In 1942 Wim was sent to a prisoner-of-war camp, and Madzy was left, in a time of great danger and hardship, to care for two small children. The reunited family emigrated in 1947 to Canada to homestead on a farm in northern British Columbia. After selling the farm nine years later, both Madzy and Wim returned to university and earned Canadian degrees.

Throughout all this, and for the rest of her life, Madzy was writing, in both Dutch and English. She contributed columns to four different newspapers in Holland and Canada. Her book about our life on the farm was published in English as *Land for Our Sons*; she was asked to translate it into Dutch, and the translated and revised edition, *Land voor onze zonen*, sold widely in Holland. She also wrote short stories and a quantity of material that was never published or was printed only for the family: diaries, memoirs, historical works, and innumerable letters. When she was no longer able to write by hand or to type, she made tapes. Her last important work was a chronicle, *Memories*, dictated when the arthritis had damaged her hands so badly that she could hardly hold a pen.

The extent of Madzy's surviving work is among the factors that make her story important. She was only one of many thousands who emigrated from Holland to Canada, but few leave such detailed records of their outer and inner lives. Besides dealing with the universal aspects of human existence, she wrote about the issues that immigrants face, the long-continuing sense of displacement and alienation, the conflicts between the old country and the new, the relationships between the immigrating generation and their children. She also wrote about the surge of freedom and delight that she often experienced in her new country. Her writings illuminate the lives of all newcomers, not only those from Holland.

Because Canada is a nation of immigrants, her story is part of Canadian history; she speaks not only *to* immigrants but also *for* them. It is also part of Dutch history, providing for Dutch readers a detailed picture of one such life, both typical and unique.

On a more personal level, hers is a story of survival through war, terror, and near-starvation, a gruellingly hard pioneer existence, physical handicaps, and chronic pain. It is a story of an intensely creative personality interacting with those limitations, as well as with the move from one language and culture to another, finding expression in every way possible, in living as well as writing and the visual arts.

An important part of my mother's creativity was her ability to make a home wherever she went – and the list of her addresses in Holland, the United States, and Canada is a very long one. Furthermore, in the years in Canada she created the environment that nurtured the interests and talents of her children. I became a writer; my brother Gerard Brender à Brandis is a wood engraver and maker of handmade books; and my youngest brother, Jock Brandis, is a film technician and inventor of devices to improve life in the Third World.

In writing my mother's life, I have tried as much as possible to allow her to speak for herself. I wanted to make all of her voices heard, the inner and outer, the public and private. She had a strong drive to write autobiography: almost all of her writings, published and unpublished, have an autobiographical element. What she never did, however, was to make one unified account of it, and therefore she never dealt with the contradictions, inconsistencies, paradoxes, and ambiguities in the fragmentary but copious record. In this book I am exploring them, delighting in them – and never, I hope, ironing them out into a generalized greyness. I am writing the biography of the many different people she was, the many different lives she led.

Names

Like many immigrants of our generation, we anglicized our names when we arrived in Canada. Our surname, Brender à Brandis, was for daily use shortened to Brandis, though we use the full name for official purposes, and Gerard always uses the complete form. I have business cards for both.

When *Land for Our Sons* was accepted for publication, the publisher objected to the name Madzy and persuaded her to use "Maxine." Although she never liked it, she continued to use it for the stories that appeared in the *Atlantic Advocate*, but she used Madzy for almost everything else.

Bill is the anglicized form of Wim (William). Forced to choose between several possible causes of confusion, I decided to call my father Wim in the chapters that deal with the Dutch part of his and Madzy's lives (which included the two years in the United States, because they regarded themselves as expatriates rather than immigrants) and Bill for the Canadian part.

Gerard was for some years Gerald, and then went back to the Dutch form. I was christened Marie Anna, became Mary Anne in Terrace, and evolved into Marianne after that. Jock was christened Joost after his grandfather but in Terrace found the teasing intolerable and became Jock.

In *Land for Our Sons*, Madzy gave most of us fictional names. To avoid further confusion, I silently replaced them with our real ones.

Terms of Address

In her writings, Madzy was inconsistent in her use of the Dutch and English versions of terms such as "uncle," even within the same memoir. In speech she almost always used the Dutch forms. I have kept her originals, except where the shift from one form to another was very obvious. The Dutch forms are *moeder* (for mother), *vader* (for father), *oom* (for uncle), and *tante* (for aunt).

Cast of Characters

I have identified people in the text, but a brief list of the fairly immediate family might help. Ancestors who died before the story begins are mentioned in appendix 2, "Ancestry."

Marianne, Gerard, Jock: Madzy and Bill's children. Jock is the only one who married. His wife (deceased) was Suzanna; their son, Darwin William Taylor, was born four years before Madzy's death, daughter Maaike in the year after her death.

Iete (Moeder): Mother of Madzy.

Joost (Vader): Father of Madzy.

Hans (Moeder): Mother of Bill (Wim).

Gerard (Vader): Father of Bill (Wim).

Jet: Stepmother of Bill (Wim).

Hansje: Madzy's younger sister. After we left Holland, she married Wiet van Lanschot, and they had five children: Muike, Cathrien, Miriam, Cunera, and Wiet.

Joost: Madzy's older brother, who had Down Syndrome.

Paul Adama van Scheltema: Madzy's older half-brother; his wife was Mita. They had four daughters: Mill, Marlieke, Madzy, and Janneke.

Lies: Sister of Bill (Wim). Her daughter is Monica.

Juus(je): Long-time nanny in Madzy's family, and a member of Madzy's household during the three war years when Bill (Wim) was in the prisoner-of-war camp.

A Note about This Book and *Finding Words*

A few years ago I wrote *Finding Words: A Writer's Memoir*, which covers some of the same ground as this present book, though from a very different angle – more personal, subjective, and selective – and with a totally different focus. In the course of researching the present book, I obtained documents and information that made it clear that some of my memories were inaccurate or my information incomplete. For instance, Madzy earned only one university degree in Canada, not two, and when she worked at the library at the Extension Department of St Francis Xavier University, she was not a volunteer but a paid employee. In cases where such inconsistencies occur, the present book is the more authoritative one.

❦ ACKNOWLEDGMENTS

MANY OF Madzy's relatives and friends contributed information and memories to this book, in conversation with me or in letters and e-mails, or by lending or giving me tapes she made, letters she wrote, photographs, or other material. Because of lack of space, I have not quoted or specifically referred to all of this material, but every bit of it contributed to my understanding of Madzy and her life.

My thanks go to Freules Mechteld and Catherine Sandberg, who returned the survivors of the many tapes Madzy had sent to their sister, Tini; and to Ineke de Vries for remembering and collecting information. Monica Ellis shared memories of the war years and e-mailed a short piece of Madzy's writing that was new to me, as well as tracking down what had become of the publisher of *Land for Our Sons*. Madzy's sister, Hansje van Lanschot–van Vollenhoven, provided memories from their childhood, and Madzy's nieces Madzy Boonacker-Adama van Scheltema and Janneke Adama van Scheltema provided memories, information, photographs, and insights that were invaluable. Madzy's niece Marlieke Adama van Scheltema gave me a copy of a story she had written that illuminated conditions in the Dutch East Indies at the beginning of the Second World War. Charlotte Boon-Mees and Hester Hoogenraad-Laman Trip, two of the survivors of Spuit Elf at the time of writing, contributed memories of Madzy's time in Leiden.

For throwing light on the early years in Canada, I am grateful to the help of Enid van Stolk, Mien van Heek, and Rein Doorman. Besides sharing her memories with me, Enid also gave me a poem Madzy wrote for the first "Sinterklaas" we celebrated in Canada. I am especially grateful to Just Havelaar, our neighbour in Terrace and author of an unpublished memoir, "Jumping and Landing," which provided me with information and revived memories of my own. Bob van der Hoop's picture of our family as we were in 1955 was extremely useful.

Hubert and Gillian Bunce shared with me the tapes and letters they had received from Madzy during the Brandstead years, and Hubert wrote a vivid short sketch of Madzy and Brandstead as they were when his family visited. Elisabeth C. Salm Young lent me tapes Madzy had sent to her and her mother. Don Bragg provided a negative answer to a question I asked him – but a negative answer is also information. John Kneale had an illuminating memory of Madzy. Cal and Fay Whitehead provided several interesting stories.

Very special thanks go to Ina and Freek Vrugtman, friends and neighbours, who not only saved and cherished Madzy's letters and gave them to me but also responded to a number of the tiresome questions to which a biographer would like to find answers.

When I was in the Netherlands in the spring of 2001 to do research, I stayed with my aunt Greet Blijdenstein-de Beaufort in Maarn, and she drove me around the neighbourhood. She also arranged for me to meet with Jim van Notten and his wife, Emilie. My warmest gratitude goes to her, and also to Jim, for allowing me to read and make notes from the diary that his aunt, Dientje Blijdenstein, wrote during the last year of the war. I also visited Annetje and Floris Kool in Oestgeest, near Leiden; they had memories of my mother during the war. Chris de Rooij looked up a piece of information for me. Other family members, already named, were always ready to answer my questions.

Special help came from yet another group of people. Frank Steensma provided information about his father's experiences during the war and related matters, and was also of great help in finding information about the government agency under whose auspices *Land voor onze zonen* was published. Rom Steensma sent me information about the publisher of the book. My thanks go to them both. Addison Worthington provided information about his grandmother, Virginia Donaldson, and his aunt Elise; he also gave me the letters Madzy had written to his grandmother and mother, as well as information about the way in which our two branches of the family are related. Cathrien and Carel Beynen supplied me with books about Rotterdam that enabled me to reconstruct the world from which Madzy's family came and also provided information about the impact of the war on Holland in general and Rotterdam in particular. Mirjam and Hein Bloemen gave me tapes that Madzy had made. My good friend Anne Eyolfson returned letters I had written to her during the years 1971 to 1996; because of her affection for Madzy, I reported regularly on Madzy's health, and the information proved to be very valuable. Barb Wintar explained how she worked with Madzy and also provided glimpses of Madzy as a person. Arnold Goldberg supplied some medical information; Alexandra van Hout-van Tuyll van Serooskerken contributed the spelling of a name, and Edward Baxter translated the epigraph that Madzy used in *Land for Our Sons*.

Archivists and librarians were unfailingly helpful. My special thanks go to Kathleen MacKenzie, archivist at St Francis Xavier University, and Erwin Woderczak at the Archives of the University of British Columbia. I am very grateful to George Granger, registrar at McMaster University, for making Madzy's McMaster transcript available to me. Linda McKnight provided important guidance in the matter of obtaining permissions. In the course of searching for copyright information, I had special help from J.S. Blick at the Ministerie van Sociale Zaken en Werkgelegenheid in the Netherlands, and from Anry van Esch-Staal at Uitgeverij Het Spectrum, Utrecht, the Netherlands.

This book would never have come into existence without the support and help of my father, William Brender à Brandis, and my brothers Gerard Brender à Brandis and Joost Brender à Brandis. Bill and Gerard helped me at every stage; I drew extensively on the genealogical information that Bill had already collected and also asked him further questions about his and Madzy's ancestry. Both Bill and Gerard ransacked their memories for recollections and for the answers to my interminable lists of questions, and both of them read each chapter in semi-final form and provided comments and further information. For their tireless help and support I am more grateful than I can say.

Bill and Gerard and I made every attempt to be accurate, but memory is seldom completely reliable. Madzy's writings about her past may also have contained small errors of fact, and everything comes through the screen of perception, interpretation, and all the other filters.

AS REGARDS copyright, *Land for Our Sons* is long out of print. J.S. Blick at the Ministerie van Sociale Zaken en Werkgelegenheid, the ministry under which the Emigratiedienst (which bought the copyright for *Land voor onze zonen* and then sold it to the publisher Het Spectrum) functioned, contacted Het Spectrum on my behalf and obtained permission for me to quote from the book.

MY FAMILY and I are deeply grateful to those who have helped to finance the publication of this book. As a token of our thanks, Gerard created this

Madzy's writing place, Terrace, B.C. Wood engraving, © Gerard Brender à
Brandis, 2005

engraving, a copy of which was offered to each of them. It depicts the Marketing Board office in Terrace, Madzy's first real writing room, where she wrote *Land for Our Sons*.

Contributors

J. Adama van Scheltema

Cathrien Beynen-van Lanschot

Greet Blijdenstein-de Beaufort

Mirjam and Hein Bloemen

David Bohme

Madzy Boonacker-Adama van Scheltema

Don Bragg

Gerard Brender à Brandis

W. Brender à Brandis

Hubert and Jill Bunce

Robin and Monica Ellis

Anne Eyolfson

Ellen and John Frei

Audrey and Paul Grescoe

Just and Hanneke Havelaar

Cunera and Toine Huenges Wajer

Janice Kneale

John Kneale

J. Bryce Lee

Mary Jane Mossman and Brian Bucknall

Ninette Prociuk

Ellena Raffan

Sheila Russell

Freules M. and K. Sandberg van Leuvenum

Muike Sandberg-van Lanschot and Germain Sandberg van Oudshoorn

Bern Slavin

J. Roy Smith

Carel Steensma

Frank Steensma

Betty Syed

Robert van der Hoop

Hansje van Lanschot-van Vollenhoven

Wiet and Pietie van Lanschot

Enid van Stolk

Cal and Fay Whitehead

Barb Wintar

Addison and Frances Worthington

FRONTIERS AND SANCTUARIES

My aim is to be as free and uninhibited in putting down my very inner thoughts knowing that no one will read them as long as I live. After my death I do not care what one thinks or knows of me; the more of me and my thoughts the better, for then they won't put me on an unearned pedestal. Rather let my real self appear, something I so often try to hide. For they often think or pretend to think that I am a better or more honest person than I am. This really bothers or worries me.

MADZY BRENDER À BRANDIS-VAN VOLLENHOVEN
30 APRIL 1982

CHAPTER ONE

The Child Madzy, 1910–1923

WHEN MY mother, Madzy Brender à Brandis-van Vollenhoven, was about seventy, she dictated stories about her parents and ancestors and her own youth into a tape recorder and hired a typist to transcribe rough drafts, which she then revised and had retyped. The version we have contains a few further corrections in her by-then painful and shaky handwriting.

In the first part, she sets out to describe the house in which she was born, but the memoir actually begins: "We are standing in front of a house about one mile away from the spot where, exactly 250 years before, Samuel Pepys put foot on land on the beach near the fishing village which he called Scheveling but which, in reality, is called Scheveningen."

Madzy's linking of private and public events is half whimsical, half serious, wholly characteristic. Pepys, the seventeenth-century diarist and naval administrator, was one of a party of Englishmen who went to Holland in 1660 to escort the about-to-be-restored Charles II to London. In his diary he describes their landing in Scheveningen, near The Hague.

She depicts the area as it was in 1660, then as it looked in her youth. When she lived in The Hague in her late teens, she went regularly to concerts at the big Kurhaus hotel. She describes the wheeled bathhouses pulled into the water by horses; later, these bathhouses were replaced by little cabins. Her mother always treated her to a subscription, so she and her friends swam in the sea summer after summer.

She describes the pier projecting out into the ocean, rented one night by the University of Delft for a student ball that she attended. The party continued until the sun came up. After the orchestra played the national anthem, the girls threw their bouquets into the sea and watched them bob away.

Then she returns to Samuel Pepys and the house in which she was born.

AT THE TIME of Madzy's birth, her parents, her half-brother, Paul, and her brother, Joost, had just returned from the Dutch East Indies. Madzy's father, also Joost, had been living in Sumatra for twenty-five years, and her mother, Iete, for twelve years. During her third pregnancy Iete returned to the Netherlands, and Joost joined her in time for the birth of their daughter on 25 August 1910.

Joost van Vollenhoven had been born in Rotterdam in 1866. After finishing school, he was made a partner in his father's lumber-importing company. However, at age nineteen – being, as Madzy says, a restless, unconventional person – he went to the Dutch East Indies. The Deli Tobacco Company employed him to work as a supervisor on a plantation in the thinly populated country beyond Medan, on the island of Sumatra.

In later life Madzy told many stories of life in the Dutch East Indies. She had never been there, but her parents and visitors returning from the colony often talked about it. The Dutch East Indies (now Indonesia) was a rough place in the late nineteenth and early twentieth centuries. Relations between the local population and the European rulers were strained – in fact, war was raging at the western end of the island, in Atjeh. For Madzy, however, the place and time formed the background for an almost mythologized family history that helped to shape her ideas and imagination.

In his position as local supervisor, Joost worked from four in the morning until dark, every day of the week: strenuous work in the tropical heat. Each month he had four or five days of leave, which he spent in the town of Medan.

At some point during that period, his mother in Holland became worried because she had had no news of him in a long time. She boarded a ship – on which another son of hers was first mate – and went to Sumatra to assure herself that Joost was all right. Finding that he was, she continued on to Java and stayed for a few days with other relatives, then took the same ship home.

In 1902 Joost was promoted to the position of chief administrator of that division of the company and lived in a large house in Medan, with a summer home in the mountains where it was cooler. Medan was a company town, and his position made him a prominent citizen. Once established there, he was joined by his unmarried sister, Johanna, twelve years his junior. In 1905 she married Professor Dr Wilhelm Schüffner, a German doctor and researcher working in Medan. Both were to become important people in Madzy's life.

Madzy's mother, Iete, was born Marie Louise Rochussen in 1878 in Lochem in the Netherlands. Iete's mother came from a noble Prussian family; Iete always took great pride in this. Iete had a twin sister; "Mother was the prettier and the smarter of the pair,"[1] Madzy wrote. When the

Joost van Vollenhoven as a young man. The photo was taken in Medan.

twins were six, their father died, leaving his widow with them and an eight-year-old daughter, to live on a fairly small income.

Madzy tells a story from her mother's girlhood about swimming in the Berkel River: "Mother and her girlfriend went there before school, but since it was such a big job to put on your corset and then take it off and, after swimming, put it on again, they bicycled with their corsets under their arms to the pool. I am sure her mother never knew that! I thought this was rather a funny story – that girls of the age of twelve, thirteen, fourteen already wore tightly laced corsets in order to have a slender waist."

When Iete was about twenty – intelligent and beautiful but not well off – she went to Rotterdam to study to be a teacher. Apparently she did not relish the prospect of teaching, and when she met Johannes Adama van Scheltema, a man of thirty-seven and a captain in the Netherlands East Indies Army, she married him, against her mother's wishes. Immediately after the wedding they went to the Dutch East Indies and lived in a fortified compound in Atjeh, where Captain Adama van Scheltema's unit was engaged in the war. It was a big adventure for a young woman from a sheltered family; Madzy says that there was only one other European woman there at that time. The Europeans occupied houses outside the compounds but at the first sign of danger would flee to safety within the palisades.[2] Iete's first child, Paul, was born there in 1900.

Iete was distantly related to Joost van Vollenhoven. In 1903, when she had to undergo kidney surgery, she and her husband and little son went to stay with him and Johanna in Medan. Early on the morning of 23 October,[3] Johanna and the captain went out riding. A man leapt out of the bushes wielding a long knife; the captain's horse startled and threw him. His neck was broken and he died.

It was impossible for Iete, a widow with a small child, to return to the fortified camp where she had been living, nor did she want to go back to her staid and rather narrow life in Lochem. She remained with Joost and Johanna, and in 1904 she and Joost married.

In 1907 a son was born and was christened Joost. He was later diagnosed as having Down Syndrome. In 1910 the family moved back to the Netherlands.

This was a permanent return. Work in the tropics was considered so physically stressful for Europeans that, when calculating retirement age, each year spent in the tropics counted as two. However, Joost was only forty-four, and he had no intention of idling away the rest of his life.

The family was now affluent. Madzy writes: "My father had worked very, very hard and had invested his money in all kinds of enterprises, which did

In Medan. Those present are, from left to right around the semi-circle, Paul
Adama van Scheltema, Willy Schüffner, Johanna, Joost van Vollenhoven, Iete
van Vollenhoven; the lady at the right and the two children can not be identified.
The date is probably 1906 or 1907.

very well in those days. So he had become a wealthy man and my mother could have whatever she wanted, really until the end of her life. Although she had spells of economizing ('Turn the light off when you leave, then we can have cookies with our tea!') they never lasted long, thank goodness."

Madzy was born in a rented house in Scheveningen. Six weeks later, Iete, the baby, and a nurse went to Wiesbaden in Germany. When they returned a month later, it was to a different house in Scheveningen, bigger and more suitable for the van Vollenhoven family:

> It was a large house and had a big garden, around which was a fence of black wrought iron with spears and an opening for cars; we had a garage separate from the house. The chauffeur and his wife and one child lived above the garage.
>
> The house had a basement. I still remember the kitchen with a large kitchen stove, and next to it an equally large kitchen where the servants ate and spent their free time. There were many cellars including a well-stocked wine cellar.
>
> On the ground floor were a parlour, a dining room, and a large study for my father. Attached to the dining room was a large veran-dah at the south side. We sat there quite often in the summer, a very nice place with windows leading into the garden ...
>
> We couldn't do with less than a cook, and an assistant cook who also served at the table, a butler, one or two servants who lived in for cleaning the house; then we had the chauffeur, and a charwoman or two who came in to help with the cleaning. We also had a man who came once a week to wind the clocks and set them. I still remember how I loved those days, because as soon as he came, I followed him everywhere. He took along a chair to climb on in order to reach the grandfather clock and the "golden sun" clock. I chatted and talked with him all the time while he went through the whole house and serviced the clocks. I don't know how long it lasted, but to me it was a special event and I enjoyed it tremendously.
>
> We also had a man who came once a week to polish the silver. When he was there, I was allowed to sit in the little room in the basement and to play with all the silver, among which was the large replica of my father's house in the Dutch East Indies, a wonderful thing with endless windows and little doors I could open and close. (I think you children must remember that house. We still had it at the time you folks visited Grandmother.) There was also a ship. I was intrigued by all the tiny little additions, cables, and even sails, little doors, and little men on deck, all in silver.

There was a room on the same floor where our nursery was, which was used as the everyday living room, cosy with leather easy chairs, and a couch, many books, many interesting objects, and a balcony. It was there that most of the family congregated, and we always had visitors. As soon as a new person whom we knew slightly returned from the tropics, he was not allowed to go to a hotel but was invited to stay for as long as he wished.

One of the servants, Justine Egner, became a permanent member of the family. Juus (or Juusje, the diminutive form) was in her early twenties when she was hired, the third of three sisters who served the family successively as nannies, beginning in Medan. They were of French Huguenot descent. Juus never married and, from the time she joined us, lived and worked with one or another branch of the family almost until her death more than fifty years later. During the Second World War she lived with our immediate family, and I remember her well. She was spare and upright, with a bush of (by then) grey frizzy hair tucked more or less into a bun, and she was usually rather stern in her demeanour, but she and we were immensely attached to each other. After we came to Canada, Madzy corresponded with her – tried to write every week – and when we went to Holland, we visited her in the seniors' residence where she was then living.

Upon his return from the Dutch East Indies, Joost ran for a seat in the Tweede Kamer, equivalent to the House of Commons. He campaigned vigorously. Madzy writes: "My father had placards made and stuck to the windows of our car, and the chauffeur had to travel with the car through The Hague and surroundings. On those placards was written 'Vote for the Liberals.' The chauffeur didn't like it very much, but it had great success for Father was elected and remained a member of Parliament until, in 1916, during the First World War, he became managing director of the Bank of the Netherlands."

Madzy's parents frequently entertained and went out:

> I didn't see much of my mother except when she went to a party; then she always came and said good night to us in her party dress to show it to us. And that is why I remember my mother always as a beautiful woman out of a fairytale. She was beautiful. Her background, partly Dutch, partly Prussian, accounted for her high cheekbones, slightly hollow cheeks, her deep blue eyes and her wavy black hair. She was a lively woman and always on the go.
>
> I remember one time when she came in and I was already in my cot wearing a little nightie made of a stretchy material. Her dress

Juus Egner as she was in 1945

must have been fairly low cut – *décolleté*, as it was called (a child picks up words like that in no time). My mother asked me, "What do you think of my dress? Do you like it?"

I said, "Yes, I like it very much and when I am grown up I am also going to have a *décolleteetje* like you." At which I stretched my nightie down to my navel.

My mother really laughed about that and, although she wasn't usually very talkative, she suddenly asked me, "Whom do you love better, me or Juusje?"

Juusje was standing a little bit behind my mother and pointed at my mother very fiercely because she wanted me to say, "You, of course," to my mother.

For a moment I hesitated. I was a very truthful child and I felt that I could not lie; so I said, "Juusje, of course."

At that my mother turned around and walked away.

I got a scolding from Juusje, but I said, "I can't help it. It's the truth." Then Juusje turned away with a little smile.

My father, on the other hand, was fond of children, and his greatest joy was to come home, go upstairs, take off the bothersome stiffly starched collar (which was, of course, attached by studs to the neck of his shirt), take off the stiffly starched cuffs, and without his coat, still having his vest on, go to the nursery. He had his own armchair there, and as soon as he had sat down he took Joost, my brother, on his knee and I leaned against his other knee. He would take his golden watch out of the pocket of his vest and press the button on the top. This was a very remarkable watch because it not only chimed the hour but also the quarters, and sounded like Big Ben. So in the night when Father wanted to know the time he didn't have to light the candle. He could just press on the button of the watch and count first the hours and then the quarter-hours and know exactly what time it was. He held the watch against Joost's ear, and Joost thought this was wonderful. But that was all the reaction Father could create in Joost. He just waved his hands and sort of jumped up and down on Father's knee with pure glee.[4]

Madzy was aware that in her taped narrative she did not portray her mother as "a nice, friendly person":

A warm personality she didn't have, but she was always ready to help and she was a very interesting person. When I went to Holland for

Iete, circa 1905

her funeral [in 1963], Hansje [Madzy's younger sister] went with me into Mother's room and looked down upon her there lying on her bed, surrounded by an enormous amount of flowers. Afterwards when we left the room we said to each other, "*Elle était une grande dame.*" That's what she was – "*une grande dame*," a Victorian lady. She was brought up in a Victorian age and her mother had grown up under the German system of "*gerade halten*" which means "keep a stiff upper lip." That is what my mother had, a stiff upper lip, and that's what she gave to us. I think that this made me more sensitive and more secretive than I otherwise would have been.

There were so many things that I wanted to do and wasn't allowed to do – also, of course, for health reasons. There were many things that I would do secretly because I knew that if I would tell her, she wouldn't approve. Moreover, she always wanted to lead my life. She never left me free, and I suppose this created in me a sort of antagonism, and that comes out in my stories. But this is unfair because she was a very interesting person, and she really cared very much for other people.

I still remember the story about our bookkeeper who once came and told my father that his wife was sick with scarlet fever. The very next day my mother went with all kinds of food and medicines to the woman and made her comfortable. Perhaps she didn't realize how contagious this disease was, but she always said, "Oh, I don't catch any diseases." This was true, but she might have brought it home to us. None of us got it. She went and looked after this woman several times.

She was also very good as the mistress of the home, which shows through the fact that our servants stayed with us for years and years. Juusje stayed for fifty years and that was the longest by far, but when the other servants left, it was not because they didn't like us but because we moved, or they got married.

Hansje, with whom I discussed this, agrees that in later years Iete became very conventional and was certainly so in her way of bringing up Madzy. It's possible that her inherited family pride, together with Joost's prominent social position, reinforced the conventional elements in her personality. But in her earlier years she was, for her times, adventurous and even rebellious. She was slender and vigorous, and in the years after her return from the Dutch East Indies she and three women friends went on walking tours.

MADZY WAS four years old when World War I broke out. During the first days of the war, the Germans invaded Belgium and left the Netherlands neutral. Many Belgians fled over the border into Holland:

My mother and many of her friends immediately set up a committee to find homes for these people, and I remember that one day when I woke up Juusje told me that during the night a family of eight or nine had moved into our basement. I was, of course, very excited. I wanted to go and see them, but first Mother came into the nursery and said, "We are going to sort out your clothes and see what you can spare, because these children have only the clothes they are wearing."

Now there was one piece of clothing I loved most of all, and that was a sailor suit. Of course Joost had a sailor suit – all boys of that age wore them – but the girls, some of the girls anyway, had them too. Instead of short pants they had pleated skirts. This was my pride and joy.

Mother didn't like it very much. When she sorted out my clothes, she said, "Of course that sailor suit of Madzy's is just right for that girl who came."

I pulled at Juusje's skirt and said, "Juusje, not my sailor suit!"

Juusje shook her head and said that I shouldn't say anything and pushed me aside. I tried it once more but she really was firm and said, "The children downstairs need clothes." So I manfully rubbed my tears away and saw the sailor suit go on Juusje's arms with a lot of our clothes.

My mother said, "Juusje, bring them to the people downstairs," and then walked away.

Juusje looked down at me and said, "I know you like your sailor suit, but if Mother says that it has to go, we can't do anything against it." And I knew that. Mother's word was law.

To make it a little easier for me, Juusje said, "But come on, let us bring it to them. And haven't you got some toys to give?"

Now I loved giving things to people, and I rummaged and found dolls and animals; even if they were dear to me, I wanted to do my part in the war. So we walked down all the stairs into the basement.

Here we found – in the linen room, as we called it – a large family consisting of a grandfather, a grandmother, a father and a mother and something like five children. They spoke French, I think, for we couldn't understand them; if they had spoken Flemish, we could have talked with them. When I saw the girl who was to have my

Madzy as a child

sailor suit, I think I forgot my tears right away, for her own dress had been torn during their hurried departure and escape over the border through a barbed-wire fence.

WHEN MADZY was about four, she had frequent colds and fever, and it was feared that she had tuberculosis. In Scheveningen, the illness was fairly common among the fishermen. Normally, people suspected of having TB were sent to a sanatorium in Switzerland, but because the war made that impossible, Madzy had to lie on a chaise-longue and was not allowed to play. "Rather a dull time for me," she recalled.

Then she and a nurse went to stay for five months with "Oma Lochem," Madzy's grandmother Rochussen in Lochem, the only one of her grandparents she ever knew. Oma Lochem's house was inland and had a better climate. It had a lovely garden, including a kitchen garden. Madzy was allowed to eat five strawberries or other small fruit and then had to report to her grandmother. She would not have dared to eat more.

Stiff and formal, priding herself on her noble German ancestry, Oma Lochem always spoke German and was very firm with herself and everyone else. No one was permitted to be shy or afraid. There is a story from the time when she and her one yet-unmarried daughter (Iete's twin sister, Marta) were together. During the night there was a suspicious sound from downstairs, and Oma Lochem sent Marta down to investigate. As Marta did so, timorously, Oma Lochem admonished her from the top of the stairs, "*Marta! Gerade halten!*" – "Hold yourself up straight!"

Madzy was not happy there. On one occasion her mother, young Joost, and Juus came to visit; when they left, she ran after the car, crying "Take me home!"

Several years later, when Oma Lochem was dying, Madzy went with Iete to visit her.

> On a certain afternoon (we must have been staying there for a couple of days) my mother wanted to go and visit someone, and she told me to go and sit in the bedroom with my grandmother, who was partially paralyzed and couldn't speak much anymore.
>
> She was lying in bed, and my mother told me that whenever my grandmother would call me I should go downstairs and call the nurse, who was sitting downstairs talking with the maid. Well, I was sitting there with a book and I was simply scared to death, because I thought, "She's going to die any moment. She's lying there and she's mumbling to herself and I just don't know what she's saying."

She was saying something in German. I thought she was just mumbling and talking to herself. In fact she was asking me to ask the nurse to help her on the bedpan, but I didn't know that. Later on, when the nurse came upstairs, my poor grandmother had made her bed wet, and the nurse was cross with her. I never have forgotten that bad feeling that went over me when I noticed this – that the last thing that I had been able to do for her, I hadn't done.

In 1916, Madzy's father was asked to resign his seat in parliament to become managing director of the Bank of the Netherlands. The family moved out of the large, comfortable home in Scheveningen and into a hotel in Amsterdam until a suitable house was found.[5]

It was a large hotel and very near the bank, so that my father could walk to his work. At that time, he had already had his first heart attack, and a daily walk was good for him.

The hotel was built against one of the canals of Amsterdam. Every week, or maybe twice a week, there was a flower market there. Flower growers would come with their barges and moor them at the side of the Singel and sell their goods from the ships; these were the flower shops then. We stayed eight months in the hotel before we found a home in the Vondelstraat, with a large garden right against the Vondel Park.

I don't think I minded very much living in the hotel, although it wasn't very cosy. We children had to have our evening meal before the rest of the guests, so we sat in an empty large dining room full of empty tables beautifully laid with silver and glasses, and were served by the head waiter. He was an Italian, and he liked Juusje very much so when we had our dinner he never left our table but talked with us and Juusje. But Juusje was not very impressed by him. He told us stories about his native land and about his travelling from hotel to hotel, but Juusje ate and helped us with our meal and never showed any appreciation for all his efforts. He really was very nice and always asked us what we liked to eat best. Then he ordered the cook to prepare it for us.

An odd life for children, you would say. Indeed, it was at that time, too.

I went to a private school. Juusje brought me in the morning at nine o'clock, and got me at twelve. We had two hours for lunch. At two o'clock I was at school again, and at four o'clock she came and got me. I loved school, but because I seem to have been a delicate child, I often caught cold, and I remember that I spent more time in bed with a cold than in my classroom. The first year at school I was only allowed to go in the mornings, which was rather tough because in the mornings we were taught the three R's, and in the afternoon we were brought into the basement of the school and learned all kinds of handicrafts with clay and sewing and drawing. And I missed out on that because I had to stay home and take my nap.

Luckily, when I went to grade two I could go to school the whole day, but then the handicraft lessons stopped because we were too old for that and had to work in the morning and in the afternoon to learn our three R's and geography and history. Fairly soon we were started on French.

Joost sometimes took Madzy and her brother to walk in the park. In the winter, he took them to the zoo and the museum. When other people stared at her brother, Madzy dropped back and made faces at them. In those days, no one knew what to do for children with Down Syndrome. When he was about nine years old, Joost was enrolled in a special school. But he had no experience of playing with other boys; his only playfellow had been Madzy. Madzy wrote in her memoir that boys at the school "knocked him down, sat on him, kicked him, and rubbed mud in his face." After a week, he was removed from the school and kept at home with a governess.

When they moved to a house in the Vondelstraat, Juusje still brought Madzy to school and home again. Because the house was further from the school than the hotel had been, Juusje's walks were longer:

She was very philosophical about it and said she had never had such a good figure as during those years. When I was about nine or ten years old, I was finally allowed to walk alone back and forth to school.

Sometimes Father took me along if he felt like walking to work. He could always ask for a car, and he did that when he was tired or in a hurry. But he loved to walk, and then he would take me along. He was always entirely involved in his own thoughts, so as soon as we started to walk, he folded his hands on his back, his eyes staring at the ground. He forgot me entirely. I grabbed his sleeve and ran and hopped beside him because he took long strides and didn't consider that I had shorter legs. But I didn't mind it because I thought it was great to go with Father.

When we came to the end of the Vondelstraat, we came to a very busy intersection where there was a policeman directing the traffic. As soon as he saw my father, he stopped all the traffic because he knew that my father wouldn't even stop at the edge of the sidewalk but just go on without stopping. Father and I walked through the empty lane the policeman had made for us towards the other side. However, when we passed the man, Father would lift his head to say, "Good morning, Jansen." The policeman would touch his cap and say, "Good morning, *mijnheer.*" I thought that it was always very remarkable that this traffic was stopped entirely for us two – something like the Red Sea opening for Moses and the Jews to escape the Egyptians.

Not long after this, Madzy was given a bicycle. I remember her telling me how cold bicycle riding was in winter. She wore lisle stockings, but there was always a gap between the tops of the stockings and the bloomers, and the cold air came up her skirt.

In 1919 another child was born – a daughter, christened Johanna, always called Hansje. Iete, then forty or forty-one, was ashamed of being pregnant and laced herself very tightly to conceal her condition. On the day when her labour pains began, Joost had to attend a very important meeting of economists to discuss the rehabilitation of the world economy after the war. It was hard for him to leave her, but he went to the meeting.

Juusje fetched Madzy from school as usual. There would be a surprise waiting for her, Juusje said. Once they got home, Madzy was allowed to go into the guest room to see her mother and to hold Hansje.

When her father arrived, Madzy ran to tell him, but he had already heard the news. Madzy writes: "I wanted to follow him into the guest room but he was firm: 'No, no, I am going alone first.' He tiptoed into the room and closed the door. When he came out, the tears were running down his cheeks and we looked at him in awe. We had never seen tears on Father. I said, 'Aren't you happy with our little sister?' And he said, 'Yes, but sometimes when you are very happy you can't help crying.'"

It may have been the nine years' difference between Madzy and Hansje that prevented them from being very close when they were young, but in later years they were extremely good friends. Hansje came to Canada a number of times to see Madzy, especially after worsening rheumatoid arthritis kept Madzy from travelling to Holland.

Because of the spacing of the siblings, Madzy may have felt almost like an only child. Her half-brother Paul was ten years older. Young Joost was

Madzy, her brother Joost, and her sister, Hansje. This was a postcard sent by Iete from Bad Nauheim in Germany; it was dated 4 July 1922, so the children were, respectively, eleven, fourteen, and two.

three years older than Madzy but must always have seemed younger. Madzy loved and protected him. In his adult years he lived mostly in the home of elderly ladies who were paid to look after him, but for a few months towards the end of the Second World War he lived with us. He died in 1966 at the age of fifty-eight. I remember him as being always dressed in a suit and tie, very much a gentleman.

IN *Land for Our Sons*, Madzy compared our life in northern British Columbia with her own childhood, reflecting on the very different ways in which children in the two eras were brought up and expected to behave. She writes about herself in the third person:

> She was a girl of [eleven] years old, dressed in a red woollen dress with long sleeves and a white starched collar. She had on long black stockings and high black shoes polished until they shone. Her blond hair hung in corkscrews around her face with its large blue eyes: the curls were not natural, but every night before bedtime the hair was carefully parted in five parts by Juusje, and combed with a wet comb, then turned up in white rags. It was not very comfortable in bed, until Madzy found a way to lay her head just so, so that none of the tightly wound balls would hurt. Her hair now was held together with a red bow. She had entered the breakfast-room quietly, careful not to make unnecessary noise.
>
> She walked over to where her father sat, reading his morning paper while finishing his meal. He was a heavy-set man of fifty, looking much older and tired. He was dressed in a dark grey business suit and black tie. His long moustaches curled up at the ends, and his side-whiskers made his face broad looking. His bushy eyebrows above the blue eyes, the same blue as the girl's, were frequently drawn together in a deep frown, the frown of a man who carries the heavy weight of important decisions. The butler was hovering near the mahogany sideboard, trying to guess every wish of his master.
>
> The father lowered the morning paper and looked over his pince-nez with a kind smile at his little daughter. They loved each other, as far as they *could* love each other through the barrier of distance that separated parents and children in those days.

Father says that he will take Madzy to school that day, and Madzy runs upstairs to get her coat and hat and gloves. As they walk, he asks her to recite the French lesson she had to learn for that day, though before long he is lost in his own thoughts.

At noon Juusje fetches her home for lunch. The children eat with their parents, Madzy sitting on one side of Juusje, her little sister in her high chair on the other side.

> "How was school, darling?" Mother asked. She was sitting at the foot of the table, opposite her husband. The butler was serving the lunch. Madzy was allowed to help herself.
>
> "I knew my French lesson well, Mother," she answered.
>
> "I'm glad," her mother said. "It is very important for girls to learn foreign languages. Especially for little Dutch girls," she added with a smile. Madzy wanted to go on talking, but Mother began a conversation with Father, and children were not allowed to speak if not spoken to.[6]

THE HOUSE in the Vondelstraat also proved to be a temporary residence. Joost had a larger project in mind: he and a partner financed the building of an apartment house in the de Lairessestraat,[7] on the outskirts of Amsterdam. In 1920 the family moved into the ground floor, and they also had the basement for the kitchens and the servants. They lived there until early 1924.

This was a luxurious apartment, as befitted the managing director of the Bank of the Netherlands. To the left of the marble foyer, three steps led down to the kitchens and the servants' quarters; eight steps up, straight ahead, was a sexagonal or octagonal reception room. From it opened a long corridor with bedrooms and bathrooms, including several rooms for guests. Also straight ahead were a cloakroom and powder room, and on the right the butler's pantry, the dining room, the family room, and an enormous hall used for receiving company and, frequently, for afternoon tea. Beyond the hall were Iete's salon and Joost's study, with wide picture windows overlooking a park-like landscape.

In the basement were living and working quarters for a cook, a housemaid, Juus, a butler (who was also Joost's valet), Iete's maid, young Joost's governess, and a registered nurse who lived with the family for half a year after Hansje's birth. In addition to the live-in staff, a man came to polish shoes and silver, another to clean stoves and refill coal shuttles, and one to wind and set the clocks. Several charwomen came in by day. Also living out were the gardener and the skipper for Joost's yacht; a mate for the yacht was hired during the sailing season.

During this time, Joost formed a connection that proved to be extremely long lasting. Mr Giebel was a bookkeeper at the bank and also looked after Joost's personal finances. He adored Joost, and after his death continued to handle Iete's finances until her death in 1963; Gerard and I saw some of his immaculate old-fashioned letters at that time. Madzy and Hansje regarded him as an old family retainer.

Because of his position at the bank, Joost became involved in international trade negotiations during the First World War:

> My father took rather an important part in the actions when Holland was neutral. Holland's resources and food supplies were becoming very scarce, especially in the later years of the war. Through the blockade the Allies had formed around Germany, Belgium, and other countries, England couldn't allow much import of food into Holland. Moreover, the seas were full of mines. The food shortage in Holland became very dangerous, and in 1917 a group of businessmen created the Netherlands Overseas Trust Company. They put up a large sum of money, including their own private funds, to guarantee that whatever food the Allies would allow into the Netherlands would not go on to the enemy.

Joost was one of the committee of three who negotiated this arrangement and put up funds. The negotiations required him to make "many dangerous trips to England through the waters full of mines." (In fact, he spent so much time in England that he and Iete took an apartment in London.) Young as she was, Madzy knew that her father was in danger and worried about him constantly.

> My father made a trip with the ship *Tromp* to America to arrange with the firm of van Stolk to have enough grain at hand for shipment as soon as the war was over. On their return across the Atlantic, they suffered seven big storms, and the ship was badly damaged. At the same time, the northern part of Holland suffered greatly from floods. The dykes broke through, and large stretches of agricultural land stood under water. In these cases where her people suffered, Queen Wilhelmina inspected the destruction herself and visited the people who suffered, dressed in gumboots and a thick coat, with a scarf over her head. That was why she happened to be in the neighbourhood of the navy base where my father's ship was to dock. Just before the ship reached safety – they had already lost the lifeboats through the storm

– the rudder broke, and only with the help of several tugboats were they able to bring the ship safely into the harbour. My mother, who had heard of the arrival of the ship, had gone to Den Helder [the navy base] and was standing alone on the quay when a little further on she saw two little ladies standing. My mother was wondering who these ladies were. The storm howled around and the rain slashed in their faces.

When the ship was moored and the gangplank was out, my father came down in his heavy duffel jacket and old sailing cap. He directed his steps immediately towards my mother, when he suddenly turned to meet the two ladies, to the great astonishment of my mother. Then she saw that one of the ladies was Queen Wilhelmina who had heard about the dangers the ship had gone through. She wanted to meet my father to thank him personally for all he had done for the country while risking his life.[8]

For his work in setting up the Netherlands Overseas Trust, Joost was knighted by King George V of England. As Knight Commander[9] of the Most Excellent Order of the British Empire, he became Sir Joost van Vollenhoven – an unusual honour for someone who was not a resident of the British Empire. He was also made a member of the Order of the Lion of the Netherlands, Holland's highest order.

MADZY ALWAYS loved music. She was enthralled by the barrel organ that came down the street playing melodies from operas, and by the gramophone that the butler, Christiaan, kept in the linen room. It stood on the blue chest in which the dirty linen was kept. Christiaan would play the three gramophone records that he owned, while he and Madzy listened.

The family had a player piano that even the children could play if they could reach the pedals:

It was a long time before I had long enough legs so Juusje, who loved music too, was the one who played. But since the piano was in the salon, we only could do it when our parents were out. As soon as they were out and we knew that they wouldn't come back soon, we said, "Juusje, come on! Let us go and play some music." Juusje was always keen on playing, especially in the afternoon when she had done most of her work. So she played and Joost and I danced or sang and again, these were mostly opera.

Joost van Vollenhoven in later life, wearing his orders

I know that my mother thought that it was a horrible thing,[10] so when we knew when to expect her, we closed everything and ran upstairs.

At school I received singing lessons in a little choir under the direction of a certain Miss Gleichman. She was very nice to me and I loved her dearly because I loved to sing. I was always one of her best pupils, she said. (When I left elementary school, I got piano lessons, which I hated, so we won't mention them.)

Once there was an occasion where I had to sing a solo while the choir sang the refrain. My solo came, I think, four times. I must have mentioned this sometime or other during our supper, but no one asked about details. When the time came for this event, we were all set up in our places, and this time there was a man who played the piano so that Miss Gleichman could direct the choir. So we all started to sing; and just before my solo part came, the door opened and, although it was already quite crowded in the room with parents, they all made room for two people. And who entered? Tante Johanna and Father!

For a moment I was so taken aback that I hardly knew if I would be able to sing. Then I thought, "Now I am going to sing the best I ever can." Miss Gleichman gave me an extra nod and smile. So I really came through this rather stiff ordeal, but I was so proud that my father and Tante Johanna had come especially to hear me sing for this occasion. When it was over, I heard some shuffling and when I looked around I saw that Father and Tante Johanna had left again. Obviously, Father had phoned the school and asked at what time it was. He had so little time to spare that he had just enough time to come and listen to my solo. I shall never forget that feeling!

IN 1920, the household in Amsterdam had been increased by two: Johanna, Joost's sister who had lived with him in Medan, and her husband, Dr Willy Schüffner. Because of a severe housing shortage in Holland, on their return from the Dutch East Indies the Schüffners lived in the family apartment for about three years.

Willy and Johanna had an important influence on Madzy. Johanna was a lively, intelligent woman, with a light-heartedness much like Joost's. She filled the gap left by the remoteness of Iete, who was more interested in clothes and social life than in children. Furthermore, both Johanna and

Willy loved music: "Oom Willy was so musical that if he went with Tante Johanna to one of the Mengelberg concerts [at the Concertgebouw], he would come back, sit down at the piano, and play parts of the symphony he had just heard for the first time. He always said to me, 'Madzy, come and listen. This is Schumann' – or Mahler or whatever it was. In that way, I learnt a lot of music."

One day when Willy was unable to attend the Mengelberg concert, Johanna took Madzy, then twelve or thirteen. Beforehand, Willy took her to the piano and played for her a theme from the Schubert Ninth Symphony, which was on the program, and repeated it until she knew it: "That's so that you won't feel so strange." It was the first concert she attended, and she was bemused by the wonder of it and glad that she knew that one bit of music.

AFTER THE end of the First World War, Joost's youngest sister, Rietie, came to live with them as well.

> Tante Rietie had been in Germany for years singing in operas, and got stuck there during the war. I can't tell you very much about her except the vague stories I heard told among the servants. I only know that she had an excellent contralto, and that she sang in an opera company in Germany. What I remember of the stories is that she lived with a German man there but was not married.[11] This man was killed during the war.
>
> After the war, Tante Rietie, very sad and underfed, came to stay with us. Now this was of course something that happened constantly. In a family like ours, an unmarried daughter or sister came automatically to one of the relatives. There was always an aunt or a cousin or a friend who didn't have a home for a while staying with us, sometimes for months on end. That was how it happened with Tante Rietie.

Rietie and Willy gave private concerts in the hall in the apartment:

> She had a real opera voice so we had to open the doors to the large hall, otherwise it would be too loud. We heard the most beautiful music – songs of Schubert ("The Shepherd on the Rock" was one), Schumann, Brahms. I could sit there for an hour or two and listen to a real concert.

Oom Willy took the time to train my voice. He would all of a sudden say, "Madzy, come. We are going to have a lesson." And then he showed me what I had done wrong and how I had to sing.

It was because of this training, Madzy conjectured, that she was later accepted into a concert choir when she was a student at the University of Leiden.

Willy Schüffner was a scientist of some stature. In Sumatra, where he lived for many years, he and several other doctors had set up hospitals and undertaken large research projects on tropical diseases. He and another doctor discovered that if native prisoners were fed white rice, they got beri-beri, whereas when eating their usual diet of brown rice, they did not. The word "vitamin" had not yet been invented,[12] but the concept was known – the English navy had long ago begun giving lime juice to sailors to prevent scurvy. Willy also did research into malaria, and he tested medications first on himself. Once or twice he was temporarily deaf because of the medications he was testing.[13]

After his return to the Netherlands in 1921, he became professor of tropical hygiene at the University of Amsterdam. There he had a large research laboratory, which Madzy often visited. He also invited her to see magic-lantern slides on medical matters: "When Oom Willy and his friends met in our home to discuss these subjects," Madzy recalls, "I was asked to serve tea and was allowed to stay and watch the slide show. On these slides I saw children who had malaria, who had skin diseases, or beri-beri which causes the terrible bloated stomach on the children. I was shocked but also a little proud that at least my uncle was doing something for these poor children."

AT SOME TIME before 1917, Joost bought a boat, which he called *Dolphijn*. It was a "*botter*" – a flat-bottomed Dutch fishing vessel converted into a pleasure yacht. Madzy went sailing on it from the time she was seven. On one sailing expedition (or perhaps more than one), they went to the chain of islands skirting the northern coast of the Netherlands. When she came to write her account of her seventeenth-century ancestor Isaac Rochussen, who towed a captured English ship from the Scilly Isles to Norway, then to a port near Hamburg, and finally (between those islands) to Amsterdam, she mentions having sailed in that area with her father.[14] Prince Hendrik, Queen Wilhelmina's consort, was sometimes a guest on *Dolphijn*. He would ask to be taken to the area to hunt seals.

The first surviving piece of Madzy's writing is an account of a day's sailing on *Dolphijn*. It consists of photographs, typewritten rhyming verses,

De Dolphijn

Madzy on board *de Dolphijn*, on the day memorialized in her photo essay. She was probably thirteen.

and lively line drawings, all in a photo album. She cannot have been more than thirteen when she made it,[15] but the style of the verses and the look of the project suggest an older child.

On the boat that day were Madzy, her father and mother, Willy, and an unnamed aunt, probably Johanna. There were also Uleke, the full-time skipper-caretaker, and a part-time mate called Jan. Madzy probably took most of the pictures, but she appears in some.

On the first page is an adroit sketch of a gentleman with a moustache, wearing a knitted tuque with a drooping point and tassel. The first verse makes it clear that it is Willy. Roughly translated:

> Oom Willy wanted to go sailing;
> And there he saw the *Dolphijn*.
> "Look at it lying there!
> It's just the boat for me!"

After a photo of the boat moored at the quay with sails raised, and then one of Uleke and Jan on board, there is another verse, supposedly spoken by Joost:

> "My brother-in-law
> Is a learned chap
> But on the subject of sailing –
> I don't think he's too well informed!"

Many verses contain dialogue. Madzy shows a neat ear for idiom and the slang appropriate to a girl in a family like hers. One of the verses says that Willy bought the tuque and a windbreaker in order to look casual, and Madzy pokes affectionate fun at this get-up as well as at Willy's idiom, in which German words are mixed with the Dutch. He seems to have wanted to go in swimming but to have fallen into the water together with the ladder that was lowered over the side. There are no photos of this incident, but it is recorded in sketches of stick figures and another drawing of Willy up to his nose in water, still wearing the tuque.

They go ashore in Alkmaar, and then pass an airfield: two small planes are sketched above the photos of people gazing skywards.

Madzy makes an amusing story of the fact that the boat's clock stopped. Willy tries unsuccessfully to mend it, calling for "a chisel, a hammer, and some grease." Madzy quotes a clockmaker to whom the timepiece was later taken as saying that he had never seen such a dirty clock in his life. Again there are drawings: clocks with stick arms and legs, making faces.

Finally, it appears, the ladies leave the boat while the gentlemen stay on board and go on to compete in a race. A photo shows the yachts at the starting line: "Good luck, *Dolphijn!*"

I first saw the album after I had been working closely with Madzy's later work. I delightedly recognized in it the creativity that I had already come across in many other forms – the same voice, the same perceptive eye, the same adroit way of telling a story.

DURING THE First World War, because it was impossible to travel abroad, the family spent their holidays in a rented house at the seaside at Noordwijk-aan-Zee. On the first of these, when Madzy was five, the family's chauffeur, Jan Hage, and his wife and child came with them. (It was Jan who, under protest, had driven the car covered with election campaign posters.) "My brother Joost had a dreadful terror of water so he never went along," Madzy recalled. "No one else went into the water except the chauffeur, so he took me along on his shoulders, and he jumped with me among the waves and we had a wonderful time."

Madzy mentions that her Tante To, Joost's oldest sister, Catharina Maria, was often at the seaside with them. To never married: in the late 1890s, Madzy writes, she "went off unannounced to the U.S. and found refuge with the Salvation Army before she was accepted as a student nurse in a hospital in New York." This likely helped to endear her to Madzy, who had a similar adventurous streak.

After the war the family spent vacations at Bad Nauheim in Germany, and also in Switzerland. Madzy describes the packing for such a vacation. One trunk was devoted entirely to four of Iete's hats, the enormous creations of that period, carefully placed in separate trays one above the other so that nothing would be crushed. Besides the family, Juus and "Miss Agatha," Iete's maid, went along, as did Christiaan the butler, to serve as Joost's valet.

Joost, who hated the afternoon socializing customary in spas, would instead rent a carriage and take Madzy and young Joost and Juus for drives. Then they would find a nice inn where they could drink lemonade and eat cookies. Because he was a boy, young Joost had to sit beside the coachman, while Madzy sat inside with her father and Juus. In fact, Joost would much rather have been inside, while Madzy would have loved to be beside the coachman.

SUDDENLY, on 26 November 1923, all this changed forever. At the age of fifty-six, Joost van Vollenhoven died of a heart attack. Madzy was thirteen. It was a terrible shock and a loss. Nearly half a century later, she recalled the day after the funeral:

> My mother said to Juusje, "Juusje, you take Madzy and buy her mourning clothes."
>
> Juusje looked at my mother and said, "All in black?"
>
> "Yes," Mother said, "all in black – stockings, dress, hat, coat – well, you know what she needs."
>
> So we went to the trolley car that would bring us to the store. A man who was sitting opposite me was reading a newspaper, and at a certain time he turned the page over and this whole page which was facing me was full of pictures of father's funeral. I just stared at it, wordlessly.
>
> Suddenly Juusje grabbed my hand and said, "Come on. We have to get out."

Madzy had loved her father devotedly and shared his taste for casual ways, his lightheartedness, his quick laughter. For the rest of her life she was drawn to people who reminded her of him – unconventional individuals, adventurers, artists, free spirits. His death marked one of the great turning points for her. Quite apart from the grief of losing him, her life became much lonelier.

With him gone, however, and with her mother having such different interests and ideas, Madzy had to begin designing her own life.

"Fledgling Oak," painted by Madzy in late middle age

fledgling oak

CHAPTER TWO

The Young Woman, 1923–1936

AT THIRTEEN, Madzy was left with her mother, her four-year-old sister, Hansje, and Juusje. Young Joost was living in the care of three single ladies in Driebergen, where he was to stay until early 1945. Willy and Johanna were in Hilversum, not far away but no longer part of the household. Tante To lived in Wassenaar, on the outskirts of The Hague. Paul, now twenty-three, was studying to be a shipbuilding engineer at the University of Delft; when the family moved back to The Hague, he lived with them.

The Hague was a more "aristocratic" city than the commercially oriented Amsterdam. Iete took a house in the de Riouwstraat, in a part of the city inhabited by many people who had been in the Dutch East Indies. This street had probably been built in the second part of the nineteenth century, a row of rather stately residences, their front doors opening onto the sidewalk. On the first floor, looking over the back garden, was a big veranda. It was a good location socially; Iete, as Lady van Vollenhoven, was someone of considerable social standing, though she now had fewer servants.

It was in this time that Madzy began to rebel against her mother. One disagreement was about Madzy's hair. Iete wanted it long; Madzy wanted it short. This was by all accounts quite a battle, and Madzy won.

Another disagreement was about Madzy's schooling. Upon their return to The Hague, Iete enrolled her in a girls' school, but after the first day or two Madzy came home and told her mother that she was not going back to that "nanny-goat affair." She insisted on being sent to a school that prepared students for university, and Paul supported her. Protesting but ultimately complying, Iete enrolled her in Het Haagsch Lyceum, which had a heavy program of classics and sciences. Madzy was good at languages and, besides Latin and Greek, studied French, English, and German. She enjoyed school. For recreation, she played field hockey, tennis, and golf, and skied in Switzerland.

She was now a tall young woman. When I was growing up, we both had trouble finding clothes to fit our long-legged, long-armed bodies and frequently resorted to wearing men's sweaters and shoes. However, until the later years of her life, Madzy stood straight. Gerard, my brother, records: "I never knew her to be in the least uncomfortable about being tall. On the contrary, she was pleased to be tall." She was *"sportief,"* a Dutch word that not only means athletic and physically active but indicates as well a love for casual dress.

She was also a beauty, though of an unconventional kind. A photograph taken after she had won permission to wear her hair short shows a face that is delicate and grave; there is a subdued tension in it, the watchfulness of being on a threshold.

IT WAS AT this time that she developed a strong connection with her Tante Louise Smit and her family. Louise, Iete's older sister, had married a shipbuilding engineer named Frits Smit who, with his brother, owned a large firm, known world-wide for the dredges it built, in Kinderdijk. From 1923 on, Madzy often visited the Smit family.

> They lived right next to the shipbuilding yard, which was about an hour's travelling by boat [a shuttle belonging to the Smits' shipyard] from Rotterdam up the River Lek. It was on a high dyke there, and the two houses of the two families [the partners in the firm] were built on the narrow top of the dyke. One side of the dyke went very steeply down into grasslands and farms; at the other side was the water, of course. The houses had no fence in between. There was the lawn which ran out to a wooden dock and, as one sees in every harbour in Newfoundland, with small ladders. There were all sorts of small boats. Many of the children had their own little yacht – one sail, some had two sails. It depended on how much money they had been able to save and get from uncles and grandparents and so on. Of course these children, who lived constantly near the water, knew how to swim like frogs.
>
> For me it was an absolute joy to go and stay with them. In the summer I sometimes stayed for several weeks and we swam and sailed in a side branch just off the main traffic of the big river.
>
> I had one problem. I had never had proper swimming lessons. When my father was alive, he had said, "Madzy should learn to swim," and so, dutifully, I was enrolled in a swimming class. First we started with three "dry" lessons – that meant that you were put on

Madzy, about fifteen

your tummy on a chair and you had to learn the motions of swimming. After three of these lessons I got an infection of the kidneys and was sick for a couple of months, and the swimming lessons were forgotten. I just pretended to know it. Not, I must say, that I ever felt as entirely at home in the water as my cousins felt – but I didn't show it, of course.

After my father's death I used to spend New Year's Eve there. My mother never liked New Year's Eve very much and always went to bed at ten or ten-thirty and forgot about it. But at my Tante Louise's, there was a big party, with lots of friends and family and all the goodies that the Dutch ate at that time. At twelve o'clock they all opened their doors and started big fireworks, tremendous! And you can imagine that on the dyke, over those low-lying lands and water, those fireworks were really a sight to be seen. I still remember the joy every New Year's Eve that I spent there.

The Smit family had five children; the oldest, a girl, was ten years older than Madzy, and another, Wies, was a year younger. One of the sons, Jan, was Madzy's particular friend.

Jan was the type who couldn't sit still, couldn't study, and wanted to go to sea. So he went to seaman's school, or whatever one calls that, and was rather a wild type. We have it in our family ... we always have a type that falls out of the solid Dutch character, and certainly Jan was one of those.

I loved Jan – he was my best friend, and he helped me and did things for me and sailed with me, took me out, taught me swimming more than I knew, and I really had a crush on him – let us call it that.

At a certain time he suddenly ran away and went to the United States. At that time the United States had a lot of attraction for people who didn't fit in Europe; Jan found a job and was very happy. Of course, Tante Louise was unhappy. I know that she must have missed him very much as he was the most cheerful person ever and, although he was the most difficult child, he was her darling. He found a job with a rich American – maybe a millionaire – who lived on Long Island and had a large yacht. At a certain time, the millionaire decided that the yacht had to be sailed, I think to Florida, and Jan wrote a letter home saying that he was going there and as soon as he arrived he would write. The letter never came, the yacht never arrived in Florida, and it has always been a mystery.

No doubt Madzy missed Jan too, first when he went to New York and then when he disappeared. She was in her mid-teens, and Jan was, so far as we know, the first young man she was attracted to. After her father's death, it was natural that she should attach herself to someone else, and a sailor would have enormous appeal – an imaginative appeal quite apart from his kindness to her. The loss of her sailor-cousin would have echoed the death of her sailor-father. Although in the memoirs she says nothing further about this, it must have been another great grief for her.

Some of Madzy's adventures in Kinderdijk would have horrified Iete, had she known of them:

> One of the attractions of staying with my aunt was a visit to the ship's wharf which was, as I told you, right next door to their house. We weren't allowed to go there alone, only with someone like a male cousin or my uncle. But of course it was far more fun to go "exploring" together. Wies and I often managed to slip away, and my aunt wasn't very careful in watching us.

> We could do it only on Saturday afternoons or Sundays when the men weren't working. There was a watchman who had a little cabin near the opening of the big fence surrounding the wharf on the side of the dyke – but we managed to go through the garden, and from the gate he could not see us come in. I loved to go into the workshops and nose around.

> It was a large wharf and we roamed around for quite a while among all those buildings and then at the end we always said, "And now we are going up the cranes." There were two large cranes. One was larger than the other and they were both rather daunting because you had to climb on ladders made of metal pipes ... Apart from being rather scary, it was also painful for the feet. Since I was a year older than my cousin, I couldn't for the life of me say, "No, I won't do that." She always climbed those ladders like a monkey while I followed more slowly, but we did it so often that I got used to it.

> We started with the lower crane ... ran around [the first] platform and then the second (and maybe there were four platforms) and came to the top. The view was absolutely stunning. Can you imagine all those waterways and those little Dutch houses clinging to the dykes, with their red tile roofs, like toy houses, and then behind the dykes the stretches of green pastures dotted with cows, black and white, red and white ... and the farms and their hay stacks? It was a really

beautiful sight and I loved to lean against the railing and forget all about the height.

Down was always worse than up. Up I always managed very easily because I looked up, but down you had to grope with your foot for the next lower rung and you had to look down ...

We never told anyone. If they had known, I think we would have been punished pretty severely. I still remember the feeling, and I still admire my own courage to be able to follow Wies on those cold, wet ladders; and what I remember the most is the feeling of relief I felt when we were safely back on earth again. Perhaps it must have been the same feeling that the men felt who flew to the moon, for the memory of those cranes always came to my mind when I watched the safe return of those astronauts to earth.

IN THE SUMMER of 1924, the first after Joost's death, Madzy and Iete, together with Tante Louise and Wies, took a holiday. It was Louise who suggested it:

"How would it be if [we] go together to the Ardennes Mountains in Belgium? There is a very nice little place called Houffalise. There is a river called the Ourthe and one can take lovely walks in the valley."

We enjoyed ourselves tremendously there. We often walked along the Ourthe over pastures.

One afternoon we sat down to rest near the bank of the river. We had taken a picnic with us. Of course Wies and I took our socks and shoes off and paddled in the shallow Ourthe full of rocks and fish. It was a hot day, and after some time my mother took off her shoes and her stockings, pulled up her long skirts, and went into the water too.

My aunt was highly indignant and said, "Iete, you can't do that! Fancy if someone passes by!"

"Well," my mother said, "no one is passing by at the moment; and last night I talked to that man who always brings his horse to the Ourthe and puts him in the river ... When I asked him, 'Why do you do that?' he said, 'It's good for his legs.' Well, if it is good for a horse's legs, it will certainly be good for my legs."

We were happily paddling in the water. After five minutes, what do we see? Tante Louise, who was rather buxom and round, waddling also very carefully on bare feet towards the Ourthe to join us! No one intruded and we had great fun.

Madzy and her mother, together with Hansje and Juus, also went in winter to Bavaria. Mostly, however, they went to Switzerland, both in summer and in winter. One of Madzy's most vivid memories is of attending the Fête des Vignerons [winegrowers] in Vevey; it must have been in 1927,[1] when she was almost seventeen.

> In the early morning at four o'clock, we left Champéry, changed trains in Montreux, and arrived in Vevey at eight o'clock! The Fête des Vignerons happens only once in twenty-five years,[2] and on the marketplace is built a background like a mediaeval wall of a city with towers and two large doors through which the participants enter. The large market square is surrounded by a large circle of bleachers for thousands of people. In the cobblestoned marketplace the people parade: the whole of Switzerland takes part in it which means that every canton sends representatives. They all come in their various colourful costumes ... They sing in groups – male choirs, mixed choirs, children's choirs – there were a few special opera singers. One little choirboy from Paris stood all alone in the middle of this enormous place with one little goat at his side and he sang a song. That little voice filled the whole arena. For the rest, it was a succession of groups of people who showed off their harvest – carts full – grapes, wheat, barley, oxen, horses, sheep, cheeses, milk ...
>
> It lasted four hours. We were sitting on those bleachers which were nothing but boards. We sat in the broiling sun. But we were spellbound. Now and then the church carillon told us the time. At the end, we walked through the little place of Vevey, and all the participants in this festival walked around too, so one could see the costumes better. Finally, we took the train back to Champéry and arrived there very late, the ragged tops of "les Dents du Midi" sharply outlined against the starlit night sky.

The tone of the writing indicates how completely she was reliving the event when she recorded this memory in old age.

WE DO NOT know when Madzy began to write fiction, but she records that when she was fifteen or sixteen she had her first story published and paid for. She sent it to a magazine called *Eigen Haard* [*One's Own Hearth*]. This was a well-established periodical; her great-uncle Charles Rochussen, before his death in 1894, had been on its board of governors. We don't know the title or subject of the story, or how much she was paid for it.

Her earliest surviving story (there is no indication whether it was the one published in *Eigen Haard*) dates from this period. It is written in a strong, round, mature handwriting that was to remain the same for decades. It is entitled "De Föhn." A *föhn* is a hot wind like a chinook, but what Madzy is dealing with is something different. The story describes a beach in Holland on a hot day, crowds sunbathing, the sky cloudless, the North Sea smooth. The pier is a huge centipede astride the water. Then, in the south, a dark mass of cloud pushes up. A change in the weather? Surely not.

Some people are gathering their belongings. Those who stay ridicule them. "Oh, maybe a bit of a thunderstorm tonight. The weather won't change."

The clouds block the sun. The sea is leaden. And then – what's that? In the distance is a cloud of sand, coming closer. Panic! People struggle to close parasols already "performing amazing dances." Suddenly everything is wrapped in flying sand. Cars race back and forth on the boulevard. People rush for the exit. Blinded by sand, they seek shelter in stores. Children scream. Sand cuts the skin, sweeps across the pavement, turns the blazingly bright day dark.

Then it starts to hail. The hailstones bounce on the pavement, making everything white in an instant.

A small sailboat, its sails down, bobs on the water, trying to stay away from the pier and the beach. The wave tops curl and fall roaring and frothing on the strand. They crash furiously against the piles of the pier, spitting foam high in the air.

The hail turns to rain. The ground is one huge puddle.

Suddenly it's over. The clouds rush away, the sun reappears. People venture back onto the beach. The lifeguard climbs his tower. "The sun sends scorching rays over the browned bodies. It appears as though it will always be fine weather."

It is effectively done, and the last words suggest that it is in some way symbolic. It might be too much to say that Madzy seems to be thinking of the clouds that were threatening Europe in the 1930s, but the trustful voices that deny that there could be a change in the weather seem to me to resonate with unspoken meanings. Madzy, remembering the First World War and her fears for her father, could hardly be unaware of what was happening in Germany, a few hundred miles to the east.

THE TEN-YEAR age gap between Madzy and her half-brother, Paul, must have been significant when she was a child. After 1923, however, he was one of the replacements for her father. Paul was one of the unconventional spirits to whom she was always attracted. He had wanted to be an artist, but his stepfather had advised him to train for a money-earning profession and paint in his spare time. So he studied marine engineering. He would eventually marry and go to the Dutch East Indies, but before then, he and Madzy often did things together:

> Since he was very adventurous and saw no danger in anything, I followed him. I sailed with him in a yacht he had built himself. The mast was far too high because Paul wanted more sail on it. He needed someone for balance and ballast, and I went along – although I couldn't swim well at all, and we never thought of life jackets in those days. I went on trips with him on his motorbike, clinging to him; but he looked after me very well.
>
> He had to do military training (this is compulsory in Holland) and he chose flying. Military aviation training had actually just started in Holland in 1924. Either his group or the group before was the first unit to be trained as flying officers. They had a wonderful time because there were no strict regulations yet ... Now and then he managed to fly over The Hague. Beforehand, he told me to climb on the roof with a sheet and wave. This climb onto the roof was not too easy. I could go to the top floor, then on the balcony, then climb from the balcony to the roof – which I did without thinking of any danger, although now I would get the jitters. Mother – who could not see me – would stand on the sidewalk and wave with her handkerchief.

WHEN MADZY was fifteen, her Tante Johanna died of cancer. Iete told Paul to take Madzy to the funeral: "Oom Willy likes her so much."

> The cemetery is a very special place. It lies on the coast, in the dunes, straight west of Haarlem, so near the sea that you can hear the waves. It is called Westerveld. Here and there a clump of stunted evergreens bends away from the prevailing winds. There are many winding, sandy paths, and on either side of the paths are graves.
>
> When we formed the procession, first came the coffin carried by the six men of the funeral home, in black with black top hats. Behind the coffin walked Oom Willy. He was alone. Paul said, "You go with Oom Willy." I grabbed Oom Willy's hand and we walked together slowly behind the coffin. We went a little dune up and a little dune down along many paths and past little woods until we climbed a fairly steep dune and reached the top of it.

There we stopped near an open grave. In order not to look at it, I turned around and I saw a stone erected at the head end of a grave with my father's name on it. There was no stone on the grave. My father had always said, "I do not want to be buried under a stone. I want to be buried where I can hear the wind through the trees and the waves of the sea." And I noticed, too, that there was a space for my mother and another space for my brother Joost.

When all was over, we walked back and Oom Willy climbed into the limousine of the funeral home to go home to Hilversum. Paul said, "We are not going to let you go alone, Oom Willy. We are coming along." And so we drove along with him. There were two very faithful old maidservants who would look after him with loving care.

[At a certain point] Oom Willy said, "You'd better go home now, it's getting late." We took the train. It was only then that I realized that it was Christmas Eve.

AFTER JOHANNA's death, Madzy's Tante To – one of those not very well off single women who, at that time, usually had to find a home with other people – went to share Willy's house. Madzy often spent vacations there. Willy arranged for her to have riding lessons; she did not enjoy them. Her horse ran away with her, and the scare lasted for the rest of her life (although she did come to feel fairly comfortable with the horse we later had in Canada for farm work).[3]

A YEAR BEFORE she would normally have finished her studies at the Lyceum, Madzy became very ill with a swelling of the thyroid gland (a goitre). She was at home for two years and became very weak. Fearing for her life, Iete contacted several doctors in Amsterdam. One of them told her to bring Madzy by ambulance to a well-known private hospital. For six weeks she was kept there to build up her strength. An operation – done under local anesthetic – was performed by a professor-internist and a surgeon, both famous. Because it was one of the first operations of its kind, many people came to observe, including Willy Schüffner. The operation was a success. After two weeks Madzy went to Willy's house to recuperate and then, with Iete, Juusje, and Hansje, to a spa in Germany.

AT EIGHTEEN Madzy was among the debutantes presented to Queen Wilhelmina at a lavish ball. This was the last such event held in the evening;

when Hansje was presented nine years later, it was an afternoon event and not nearly so formal.

At the time of Madzy's presentation there was a series of especially grand balls, because Crown Princess Juliana was also being formally presented to her mother, the Queen. Before the principal ball it was announced that the only dances would be old-fashioned ones such as the waltz and the quadrille. As a mere two weeks' notice of this had been given, dancing masters suddenly had to work overtime to teach the young ladies who were more familiar with the Charleston and the fox trot. No doubt dressmakers also worked overtime. Hansje remembers seeing Iete and Madzy setting off for the ball, both looking magnificent.

AT NINETEEN or twenty, Madzy spent nearly a year in England to perfect her English. She went to a small private establishment on the outskirts of London run by a Dutch lady, Miss de Lanoy Meyer, who took in girls of good family from Holland and the Dutch East Indies. She employed an Englishwoman, Miss Bain, to teach English language, literature, and history. The girls were taken to concerts, art galleries, and museums.

Before long Miss de Lanoy began asking Madzy to show new girls the ways of the house. Madzy also worked in the garden and enjoyed that. In fact, she seems to have loved the experience altogether and ever afterwards had a warm affection for England and the English.

In these years, at home as well as in England, she must have done a good deal of reading. She was always a reader, and in later years she showed herself to be very familiar with the work of John Galsworthy and other English writers of the early twentieth century. She read more books in English than in Dutch.

On her return from England, she had not yet done the final exams, the *staatsexamen*, needed for university entrance. She studied at home, with the help of her former mathematics and science teacher at the Lyceum, Mr Veldhuis, and a teacher of classical languages. In a tape made towards the end of her life, she talked about that time: "I worked in the mornings from eight to twelve, and then took an hour off, had a bite to eat, and went for a walk to get some exercise, because I am an athletic person, and then worked again till five or six. But I always ensured that I went to play golf or tennis one afternoon (summers tennis, winters golf) so that I kept on with sports."

Having earned extremely high marks in the *staatsexamen*, Madzy declared that she wanted to go to the University of Leiden to study law. Her

Madzy, about twenty, on a friend's yacht

mother opposed this plan, but Madzy had her way. It may have helped her case that a cousin of Joost van Vollenhoven's was professor of law there.

Madzy went to Leiden in 1931, when she was twenty-one. In later life she often talked about how much she had loved university life and the contact with other intelligent young women – women who were as independent and unconventional as she was. In her late forties she wrote an article for the *Nitor*, the publication of the Vereeniging Vrouwelijke Studenten Leiden (VVSL), the society of women students at Leiden, in which there are glimpses of this time. She had been asked to contribute something to a special issue marking a reunion of her year. Perhaps her name came to mind because a few months earlier the English version of her book *Land for Our Sons* had been published. Or the editors, researching the class whose reunion this was, may have noticed that she had been a contributor when she was a student.

In this article, written in 1959, she describes revisiting Leiden as an alumna. Our family of five had gone to Holland for Christmas 1958; my father and I cannot recall when, in those busy three weeks, she had time to go to Leiden, but it is not impossible that she did. In any case, the picture she draws – even if imagined rather than real – is a vivid one.

Wet snow was falling on the Rapenburg when I brought the car carefully to a halt alongside the sidewalk across from the VVSL building. The car windows were fogged over, so I rolled down the one beside me to have a better look at the spot where, twenty-eight years ago, I idled away so many delightful hours. Here we, the new members in the year 1931, had done a lot of laughing and singing, and the presence of Princess Juliana in our midst gave an additional glow to the company.

The building of the VVSL faced me, imposing and almost overwhelming – especially so because I had spent [eleven] years among the low wooden bungalows of Canada. At one time an uncle of mine had lived in this large house; now the door stood hospitably open to welcome the young women students. This house with its high rooms and maze of attics, with its atmosphere ripened during the years, surely must make an impression on those who spend time there. Had it left an impression on me? Did the VVSL have any value for me, a Dutch immigrant in Canada?

Without noticing that the wet snow blew in against my face, my thoughts slid backwards, just as one's eye will slide along a shelf of books in a library ...

The uncle she mentions was Jonkheer Nicholaas de Gijselaar.[4] When Madzy was a student, he had been mayor of Leiden for many years and was so still, though no longer living in that house.[5] He was the brother of Madzy's Tante Cor, the sister-in-law of Madzy's grandfather. Madzy knew the mayor and his wife, Anna, well enough so that as a wedding present Anna gave Madzy quite a lot of table silver with a "G" engraved on it.

The VVSL was important to Madzy, but she did not fit snugly even into an organization of independent and unconventional young women. All new women students were expected to join a club within the organization, but Madzy and ten other just-arrived women students decided to form their own. There were eleven members, and they called it Spuit Elf.

This expression is untranslatable, but it can be explained. In Dutch cities and towns in earlier days, fire-fighting was done by local citizens with hand carts – a barrel, hoses, a hand-operated pump. There were lots of these neighbourhood arrangements to ensure that help (however rudimentary) arrived quickly. Later there were also fire engines, but for many years the small carts still existed. Pulled by willing human hands, they could with luck reach a fire in a few minutes. One of these would, of course, always be the last, the latecomer, and the colloquial expression for that last arrival was *"spuit elf"* – sprayer number eleven.

This was the name Madzy and her friends chose for the club they formed, apparently because they were latecomers. In 2000, Spuit Elf was still holding its annual reunion; they had continued in unbroken succession from the 1930s, except perhaps during the war. Its members were from only that one year; it did not take in new recruits. I corresponded recently with two of the surviving members.

We also know that Madzy rowed on the canals, a common student sport in Leiden. In our archives is a certificate saying that she was "declared competent" to handle a scull.

ALONG WITH two other women students, Madzy lived in the home of Mrs van der Vlugt and her unmarried daughter. Madzy had a pleasant room on the top floor with some of her own furniture. Mrs van der Vlugt was the widow of a professor, a very respectable, stately lady and interested in young people. The young women ate with Mrs van der Vlugt and her daughter, waited on by two German maidservants. Hester Laman Trip, one of the other young women living in the house, remembers that Madzy told amusing stories at meal-times and wrote short pieces for the *Nitor*. It was through Madzy that Hester became a member of Spuit Elf.

Another member, Lot Boon-Mees, wrote to me: "I think [Madzy] was the most intelligent of us all – and always full of plans. She started very young writing – and I always thought she [might become] a journalist."

Every weekend Madzy went home to The Hague, taking "*de gele tram*" – "the yellow tram." When I spent two months in Leiden in 1961, I also took *de gele tram* to visit my grandmother Iete in The Hague – the same route, the same destination. It was definitely a tram and not a train, and it trundled along with many stops, covering the fifteen kilometres from Leiden to The Hague in leisurely fashion. I got off near my grandmother's house and walked up the street with my overnight bag to be welcomed with sherry and my grandmother's by-then old-fashioned hospitality. It startles me now to realize that in 1961 I was much closer to the 1930s when my mother was in Leiden than to now, the early twenty-first century.

EVEN WHILE Madzy was in Leiden, not all the battles between her and Iete had been fought and won. When Madzy wanted to join a concert choir, her mother objected, afraid that Madzy would end up like Tante Rietie, who had been an opera singer and lived an immoral life in Germany. Again Madzy persevered, and again succeeded. In later years she loved the recollection of having been part of a great chorus of voices singing Verdi's *Requiem* and Bach's *St Matthew Passion*.

DURING THESE years, in addition to holidays with her mother, she took two other trips. One was a walking tour in England, which she and a woman friend in Leiden organized. The friend suggested that they invite a third, Tini Sandberg, who was studying medicine at the University of Utrecht. The three women walked through Cornwall with their belongings in knapsacks, finding lodgings when they were tired. Again we do not know nearly enough about it, except that it confirmed Madzy's love for England and things English. It also initiated what was to be a close, lifelong friendship with Tini.

The other holiday was a trip by boat along the coast of Norway. Iete and Hansje were going to Switzerland in December, but Madzy had to do an exam in the middle of the month. They did not want to wait and asked her to join them later. Instead she got the idea of going to one of the Scandinavian countries. Scandinavia seems not to have been a regular tourist – or even travellers' – destination, but Iete managed through friends to get her a place on a Dutch freighter travelling to Norway. The boat went as far as Trondheim. Madzy was deeply impressed by the country. The mountains

Madzy hiking in Switzerland

were absolutely staggering, vertical right to edge of sea. The ship skirted so close to them that the passengers could almost touch the rock.

In what she wrote about this trip, she described Trondheim in some detail and said she was sorry that she did not travel more in that part of the world, but normally she travelled with her mother and Iete preferred to go to countries she knew.

MADZY RECORDED in her last years a memory dealing with this time.

> When one decides to emigrate and go to a new country and live a new life, one sometimes forgets that one leaves behind centuries of memories and heritage.
>
> As reward for their brave deed [defying the Spanish in 1574 by breaching the dykes and flooding the countryside], the town of Leiden was allowed to have the first university of Holland, which was very important, for now Holland could start training its own scholars. Law was one of the first disciplines that was taught there.
>
> ... My lectures were all in the oldest part of the university and were still conducted as they were when the university started ... We gathered in a large theatre-like hall and sat in the rows that formed a semicircle opposite the lectern. As soon as the door opened, we fell silent and stood up, and remained standing until the professor had ascended the platform, had put his papers in order, and had taken his cap off. Then we sat down and he began his lecture, while we took hasty notes. After 50 minutes he stopped, gathered his papers, put on his cap, and descended from the platform; and we all got up again until the door was closed behind him.
>
> We never had any personal contact with the professor during these lectures. The only time that we had contact with him was either when we asked for an interview or when we had to come to him for what we called a *tentamen*, a sort of trial exam for that one subject. We either learned everything by ourselves but usually we needed tutors, which is the same system as at Oxford or Cambridge.
>
> I had five subjects and passed all these *tentamina*, and then got the date for my exam. It was on a day that there were no lectures and the old big building was empty and sounded hollow when you walked over the tiled floors and then up the stone steps of the staircase. The usher[6] led you to what was called "the little sweating room." This was a smallish room with two tall windows and a few hard-backed chairs

and one little wooden table. On all the walls and the ceiling and even in the corners on the baseboards and the window sills the students had written their names and the date of their exam, and it was hard to find a place where you could still write your name. It was said that the walls were never painted over during all those centuries, but I don't think that can have been true. I think they must have sometimes been whitewashed. But I did see several signatures with dates from the beginning of the 19th century ...

The usher came to get me and led me to a door which he opened and I came into a large room. In the middle was a long narrow table covered with green baize cloth, and behind it were sitting five professors in their gowns and caps. One hard-backed chair was standing at the other side of the table facing the professors ... To my great dismay I saw that one of the five professors was Uncle Cornelis van Vollenhoven, a full cousin of my father's.

Then the exam began and one by one the professors asked me questions. At the end the president of the group asked the other professors if they still wanted to put a question to me. They all shook their heads. The president said to me, "Please will you leave the room."

So I went back to the little room to wait for the result of the exam. The usher had heard the door close and came again. After some time he came to me and said, "Please will you follow me," and opened the door for me and closed it behind me. The president said, "Miss van Vollenhoven, will you please take your seat." And then he looked at me and said with a smile, "We are very pleased to tell you that you are now a candidate in law." Then they all got up and the president took off his cap and shook my hand. Then I shook hands with the other professors, and when I shook Uncle Cornelis's hand I looked at him and saw that he took a fatherly pride in me. Then I walked away into the hall. It was very silent and my steps sounded very loud.

And suddenly I felt the importance of the fact that I had become a real particle, small as it was, in the long row of centuries of the history of Holland. Uncle Cornelis was one of the very first thinkers of the conception of a European economic community. When this conception became a reality, he had died already many years before but he was still remembered at the time when the EEC was opened.

There is little more about Leiden in Madzy's surviving writings. She did not draw on it for her short stories, though many of them have verbal snapshots of other real places or events in her past. The rest of my information about this period, therefore, comes from what my father and my brother Gerard and I recall of the stories she told.

WHEN MADZY first decided to study law, she had two possible careers in mind: joining the diplomatic service or becoming a magistrate in a juvenile court.[7] The choice of diplomacy would surprise no one who knew her. She was a natural diplomat, always interpreting between uncomprehending or opposing sides. This talent was very important in shaping our family atmosphere; we felt its fading and absence in the last months of her life and after her death. As a juvenile-court magistrate she could have drawn on this talent, but I have difficulty imagining her arriving at judgments. Judging was not her forte in the same way that understanding and mediation were.

She was at the University of Leiden for just over four years, until she was twenty-five. After two or three years she passed the "*candidaat*" stage – the examination described above – and went on towards the "*meester*" level that would make her a full-fledged lawyer.

IN 1933, MADZY's brother Paul came home from the Dutch East Indies on a year's furlough. Six years earlier he had married Mita de Veer and they had gone out to Batavia (now Djakarta) where Paul worked as assistant director of a shipbuilding firm. Now they returned with a family of three little girls. (A fourth was born later.) At first they stayed with Iete in The Hague, but before long they rented a house in Baarn. Madzy was often there, and we have a photograph of her pushing her god-daughter, Madzy, the youngest of the three little girls, in a wheelbarrow.

Madzy's strong bond with Paul included Mita, who was only two years older than her and shared her interest in music. Mita played the piano with great seriousness and dedication. She gave lessons and, though seldom performing in public, played for friends and sometimes accompanied other musicians. Her daughter Janneke suggests that she and Madzy may have played and sung together, at least for their own pleasure.

Madzy, who loved writing letters, had no doubt been corresponding vigorously with Mita and Paul while they were in the Dutch East Indies. It may have been during the visit home – but could just as well have been in the course of the correspondence – that the plan was formed for Madzy, when she finished her studies, to go to the Dutch East Indies to practise. Paul told her that there was a demand for young lawyers. By the time she was studying for her final exams, in December 1935, she had bought her tropical clothing.

But she never went.

Paul, Mita, and their children in December 1936 in the Dutch East Indies

IN JUNE OR July 1934, Madzy attended a dinner party given by Betsy de Beaufort, one of the ladies with whom Iete went on walking tours. The dinner was given in honour of Wim Brender à Brandis, Betsy's nephew, who was going to New York to work in the overseas branch of his firm. Madzy and Wim were seated together at the table. They knew each other slightly; Wim had spent a year in the Lyceum in The Hague, and they had played on the same field-hockey team. There were, in fact, several connections between their families: another of Iete's walking friends was Gusta Brender à Brandis, Betsy's sister and therefore also Wim's aunt, and the two families were distantly related.

Not long after, Wim's father, Gerard, told Madzy that he was worried about Wim being lonely in New York and asked if she would write to him now and then. She did so, and the correspondence flourished.

At Christmas 1935, Iete and Hansje went to Switzerland. Madzy, studying for an exam, did not go. Either for company during the holiday season, or because it was not proper for a young woman to be by herself in the house with only the servants, she went to stay with Gusta Brender à Brandis. Wim, home from New York on Christmas leave, went to visit his Tante Gusta. When he arrived at the house, his aunt said, "Guess who's upstairs! Madzy van Vollenhoven!" Wim and Madzy walked and talked; by the end of his ten days in Holland he had asked her to marry him, and she had accepted.

When Iete was told that Madzy had become engaged to "Wim," for once she was pleased with something her daughter had done – but she was thinking of a different Wim, someone in the diplomatic service. She had intended that Madzy would marry into the nobility. The Brender à Brandis family included professors and other professionals, and was as old and distinguished as those of the van Vollenhovens and Rochussens, but was not part of society as Iete knew it. Again, however, Iete was persuaded to consent.

By then, for unknown reasons, Madzy was having trouble with her studies. She failed the *tentamina* leading up to her final examinations and was given three months to study and try again. Then came Wim's visit; after he left, she did the *tentamina* again, and once more she failed. It may be that she could have tried yet again, but by then she was engaged and knew that she would be going to the United States. She withdrew from the university.

A letter survives from Mita, in the Dutch East Indies, to her parents in Holland (dated 12 January 1936) in which she writes how disappointed she is that Madzy will not be coming to them. Instead, in early September of 1936, Madzy went to New York to marry Wim.

Wim as a young man

MADZY'S REBELLION against her mother runs through this period of her life. Iete was in many respects very conventional (the young girl riding her bicycle with her corset tucked under her arm was far in the past) and extremely conscious of social class and propriety. In these years, and in opposition to her mother, Madzy developed the strong core of identity that would take her through the difficult times to come. It gave her a longing for freedom that may, in the end, have taken her further than she really intended.

Her rebellion against her mother was perhaps partly a means of perpetuating her father's ways and ideas, and to that extent it was a form of filial piety, nostalgia, grieving, something consciously adopted as well as a manifestation of her innate character. At the same time, however, she carried with her conventions, assumptions, and guidelines – many of them unexamined – that had their roots in the ways and ideas of her mother. Those two strands run through the rest of her life, sometimes in creative balance, sometimes in painful conflict.

She tried to be the sort of mother against whom I would not need to rebel – against whom I would not wish to rebel. In her adoption of that course, I can see a reflection of some of the pain those struggles with Iete must have caused her, though by the time she told the stories there was little of it left except occasionally some amused irritation.

Firethorn berries, painted by Madzy in late middle age

CHAPTER THREE

Newly Married in America, 1936–1938

IN HIS EIGHTIES Wim Brender à Brandis – his name by then anglicized to Bill – wrote about his youth and his early life with Madzy. In what follows, I use these writings, because Madzy's memoirs contain little about her early married life, though her journalism and fiction give glimpses.

Willem Jean Brender à Brandis was born in The Hague in 1911. His father was Gerard Brender à Brandis, born in 1881, and his mother was Anna Nancy Hoogewerff (always called Hans), born in 1883. They already had a daughter, Lies, aged three.

My parents lived in a modern, medium-sized house on the outskirts of The Hague. All houses were built in row-housing style ... We had a garden in the back which was long and narrow. Over the years I spent a lot of time there. My father was a good gardener, so there were a lot of flowers which he grew from seed. He also had a small greenhouse – heated by warm-water pipes from a coal stove outside – where he grew all kinds of plants, particularly chrysanthemums and azaleas. The garden had a high wooden fence around it, which gave it a privacy which I liked very much.

My father was a chemical engineer at the municipal gasworks where gas was produced from coal; natural gas had not yet been developed. This gas was used for lighting and cooking; houses were heated by coal stoves. Usually there was a stove only in the living room, leaving the bedrooms icy cold in winter.

... My father was a specialist in his field, and in 1923 he was appointed part-time professor in gas technology at the University of Delft, near The Hague, while remaining general manager of the municipal gas works. This gave him additional income, and he had two pensions after his retirement. He was always careful in spending money but could be very generous, as in the case of supporting a cousin who returned penniless from the Dutch East Indies ...

Except for meals, my father was seldom at home; and when he was, he was in the garden or his greenhouse. He worked on Saturday morning, and on Saturday afternoon and Sunday morning he went horseback riding along the beach or in the dunes. He had his own horse stabled at a small riding stable. This was one of the few luxuries he afforded himself. Every day in the late afternoon he went to his club, where he would meet his friends, many of them army officers.

My mother was much at home except when attending meetings of her Anthroposophical society, of which she was the librarian for many years. She was always studying and reading in her room, which was the cosiest one in the house. When my sister and I had tea with her in the afternoon and evening, she often read stories to us. She created a very nice atmosphere in the house, and I have the memory of a happy childhood. As was customary in our circles at that time, we had a maid so my mother did not have to do any housework.

Despite Wim's happy memories, his parents' marriage was not working. The Anthroposophical movement, in which Hans had become interested shortly after her marriage, held beliefs about science, medicine, and education that Gerard (the scientist) considered unproven. No doubt there were many other difficulties. In 1925, when Wim was fourteen, his parents divorced. Hans and the children moved to the other side of the city, where Wim was never happy.

FROM HIS early childhood, Wim was interested in horses. His favourite toys were two small horses. When he outgrew the toy horses, he had live rabbits and pigeons. He also liked working with wood and began to do carpentry, receiving some lessons from an elderly carpenter.

He loved gardening, a taste acquired not only from his father but also from his grandmother.

My grandparents on my mother's side lived in the country after the retirement of my grandfather as chemistry professor in Delft in 1906. My grandmother's brother, who was a rich merchant in Rotterdam, had a big estate just outside The Hague with a beautiful forest of old beech and oak trees. He had a house built for my grandparents with a view over small market gardens and, beyond that, dairy farms. There was a very large garden; my grandmother was a good gardener and botanist,[1] collecting many plants from friends and relatives. She had scrapbooks with clippings about plants all over the world. She was always telling us grandchildren about trees,

Wim in 1918, at age seven

plants, birds, and wildlife. I spent much time there as it was only half an hour by bicycle from our house, via a very quiet country road.

BESIDES THE house and garden of his grandparents, there was another "good place" in Wim's youth.

The eldest sister of my father was my Tante Betsy. She was married to Ferd de Beaufort, who was born in Woudenberg where his father was mayor. He came from a very large and well-to-do family; he was partner in a business firm in Amsterdam which had many enterprises and transactions in the Dutch East Indies ... They lived in an old patrician house on the Heerengracht in Amsterdam, a prime location; the house was narrow and high and beautiful.

Then he acquired, at the turn of the nineteenth to the twentieth century, a large area of land in Maarn which adjoined Woudenberg. It was located on sandy soil on the hilly ridge – the Utrechtse Heuvelrug – which separates the lowlands of Holland with the polders and windmills and ditches from the higher, wooded land away from the sea ...

Part of Oom Ferd's property was just about at the highest point of that ridge. He built himself a beautiful summer home, de Hoogt, designed by a very well-known architect of rural estate residences and homes, a man called Hanrath ...[2]

De Hoogt had a beautiful view overlooking a shallow valley, mostly wooded but with some grain fields. There were nice gardens laid out, rather sparse in the beginning because of the poor soil ... In the fall there were always shooting parties. As a matter of fact, Oom Ferd's father, the mayor, had much earlier had a hunting lodge built also on that high ridge ...

As soon as the summer vacation of the de Beaufort children began, the whole family moved to de Hoogt. They also often went there during Christmas. The house was rather cold, because the only heat came from open fireplaces. The house in Amsterdam, however, was also cold, with bad heating and high ceilings, so everyone was used to being cold.

Tante Betsy and Oom Ferd had five children, all in the same age range as my sister Lies and I ...

Probably from when I was one year old we spent two weeks every summer in Maarn ... Lies and I had meals in the nursery with the de Beaufort cousins and the nanny and the French governess ... There was a donkey carriage in which the governess took the five younger ones (Lies and me and the three youngest de Beaufort children) on picnics, etc. There was a

De Hoogt in 1929

small swimming pool, which was very unusual. In the late afternoon we went swimming.

In 1925 Wim's uncle had the house enlarged to double its size, with more salons and guest rooms, and it became a year-round residence.

> There was a large staff indoors, and outdoors a head gardener with assistants ... and a large vegetable garden. There were greenhouses with grapes, etc. A chauffeur. Two cars. A game warden who was also responsible for running the gasoline engines for pumping water ... There was a tennis court. In the evening, almost always, everyone changed for dinner. I was about six when I started eating with the family. I also had to change into a neat suit.

On the property was a small barn with stalls for two horses. It was almost always empty, but after about 1925 Wim's father, when he came for his summer holiday, would bring one or two horses by train – in boxcars – from The Hague.

> Later, when I was able to ride, my father and I sometimes rode all the way from The Hague to Maarn (about 120 km), taking one or two days for the trip. In the countryside, because there was no network of footpaths, we rode over gravel roads, which is not ideal. We went through the cities when necessary; for instance, we rode right through downtown Utrecht, through the market, among the trolleys, past the cathedral, right through the old city. We would pass through Gouda too, and I remember once spending the night there.
> At de Hoogt every morning, he and I would go to the stable and bring the horses out and groom them thoroughly, according to the rules. When I went as cadet to reserve-officer training for the field artillery, I was a good rider and knew about horses and the care of horses.

THE DIVORCE had badly disrupted Wim's education. He was shuttled from school to school, the choice made sometimes by his mother, sometimes by his father. In the end he lost two years. When he finished high school, he did not have the mathematics and science credits needed to go to university and study agriculture, which is what he would have liked to do, even though at that time there were very few careers for graduates in agriculture or forestry.

In any case he first had to do a year's compulsory military service. He was selected for training as a reserve officer in the field artillery. Because the regiments were equipped with horses – the guns were drawn by horses, and the officers were mounted – this was very much to his liking.

Following his military service, Wim had to find work. It was 1932, the Depression, and jobs were scarce, but he was able to get a junior office job in the grain importing firm in Rotterdam founded by his great-grandfather and now headed by his cousin Kees van Stolk.

Two years later, in 1934, he was sent to the very small New York office of the firm. At first he lived on Staten Island, boarding with Cornelius Kolff, an elderly Dutch gentleman who had emigrated as a young man and who had his unmarried daughter, Mimi, and a mentally disabled son living with him. The next winter Wim moved to the YMCA in downtown Manhattan, and the summer after that to Montclair, New Jersey, where he rented a room in an old house belonging to a widow with two sons.

He wanted to spend Christmas 1935 in Holland and booked a third-class passage on the fastest trans-Atlantic steamer, which made the crossing in six days each way, leaving him ten days in Holland. It was during these ten days that he met Madzy again, proposed, and was accepted. Two days later, he returned to New York.

TWO DAYS AFTER becoming engaged, therefore, Madzy was left alone. Probably she felt rather stunned. As we know, she tried her *tentamina* again, failed again, and withdrew from the university.

Twenty years later, in a fragment of a novel, she writes about the shape of women's lives, as seen retrospectively when their children are grown up: she contrasts those who marry young with those who marry a bit later. There is a brief reference to "the woman who had an interesting job, or was studying an interesting subject before marriage, and drops this completely at her marriage"; her focus is not on the moment of dropping the studies, however, but on how a woman like that designs her life after her children are grown up. If the repercussions of this radical change of direction were still with her twenty years later, how much stronger her disorientation must have been immediately after. Being Madzy, though, she probably buried it under a bustle of preparation for marriage and the move to the United States.

All the same, it meant a major shift. The Dutch East Indies were comparatively familiar: even though she had never been there, she had from her earliest childhood heard stories about them, and she would have been going to Paul and his wife and family. Instead she was marrying a man whom she did not know very well and moving to a country that at that time was extremely remote from Holland. Her whole image of who she was and what shape her life would take had to be changed.

She and Wim had decided that she would travel to New York in late summer and they would marry there. Wim would be unable to obtain leave to go to Holland again so soon, and Madzy wished to avoid the big wedding that would have been inevitable in Holland. Because of U.S. immigration regulations, the wedding would have to take place within a week of her arrival.

There were, of course, preparations to be made. Never having done any cooking or housekeeping, she took a cooking course. She learned how to make delicacies, but everyday cooking was something that she acquired by trial and error. She would, in fact, be the first woman in her family to do her own cooking and housework, so she had no tradition or experience to draw on.

She decided not to acquire her entire trousseau and household equipment before the wedding (as prospective brides at that time normally did) but to buy what she needed in the United States, using the gifts of money that she received. Because of customs restrictions on bringing in new merchandise, she asked people planning to give her presents to choose things from their own households. She probably had some trousseau already; I have a linen tablecloth and napkins with an "MV" embroidered on the corners.

She kept up a vigorous correspondence with Wim. Most letters went by boat, but at least one of hers went by zeppelin, and one was on the Hindenburg that burned. She remarked many years later that a courtship by correspondence is not a bad thing; she did not explain what she meant with this tantalizing remark.

She thought it might be a good idea to be examined by a gynecologist. This doctor told her that she might never have children because her uterus lay in an odd way. Madzy reported this to Bill and gave him a chance to cancel the engagement if he counted on having children. He wired back saying that the engagement was on.

Then there were a great many farewell visits to pay.

WIM TELLS the story of her voyage to New York.

> Madzy booked passage on the SS *Statendam* of the Holland-America Line. Neither her nor my relatives planned to attend our wedding. In those days America was such a faraway country, and the voyage was much more of an enterprise than now. My father brought Madzy to the ship, and the custom was that the family or friends would be allowed on board, to look at the cabin, have coffee in the lounge, and have a tour of the ship.

In the lounge there was a group of people who recognized my father and said, "Hey, Brender, what are you doing here?"

"I am seeing off my future daughter-in-law, who is going to marry my son in New York."

My father knew all of those men as they were professors and managers of utility companies, who with their wives were going to attend an energy conference in New York. Madzy was warmly received and invited to join their group as they were one lady short. That meant eating at their long table and playing games on deck. She had a marvellous trip.

The *Statendam* arrived in New York on 6 September 1936, a beautiful Sunday morning. Wim and Mimi Kolff had driven in Mimi's car from Staten Island to the Holland-America Line docks in Manhattan. As their ferry crossed the bay, they saw the *Statendam* come through the Narrows and head for the docks. Wim recognized Madzy among the crowd on deck, and he waved frantically.

For the week that was to elapse before the wedding, Madzy stayed with the Kolffs. Mimi had found a room for Wim nearby; of course it would never do for the bride and groom to be under the same roof immediately before the wedding.

Wim had arranged for the ceremony to be held at the Presbyterian Church in Montclair where he lived. He invited a few people he had met, including some from a folk-dancing group he had joined. Two of the people with whom Madzy had travelled came, as did two elderly friends of Iete's who had also been on the *Statendam*. On that important day, therefore, Madzy was surrounded by strangers or near-strangers.

She wrote an account of the wedding and honeymoon for relatives and friends. It is seven typed pages, single-spaced with only the narrowest margins and virtually no paragraph breaks. She typed on onionskin paper and made multiple carbon copies, a system that she was to use whenever she wanted to write the same story to several people. One copy she kept.

Having arrived only a week before, she was seeing everything with new and often astonished eyes. After a brief rehearsal for the ceremony, she and Wim went to a cafeteria to have a bite to eat – and there were the minister and his wife, so Wim and Madzy joined them: "slid ourselves in at their table." "Something like that happens only in a country like this, that before your wedding you sit cosily eating a meal in a cafeteria with the clergyman." When they were packing, Wim was his own valet (she is joking: Wim had never had a valet) and she her own lady's maid. On the morning of the wedding-day, travelling to the rectory (where she would change into her wedding gown), they stopped in at the gas and electricity company to arrange to have the utilities in their apartment connected by the time they returned from the honeymoon. The casualness of all this delighted her.

Other remarks remind us that she was embarking on marriage with a man she knew mainly through correspondence. They had never been on a car trip before: he drives, she navigates. It was a sufficiently novel experience to need mentioning. When she arrived in New York, Wim had taken all the cash she had with her – including what she had won on shipboard in games and betting on horse races – and put it in the bank. During the honeymoon, when she needed to go to the washroom, she did not have a single dime to pay the attendant.

WIM AND MADZY had not made definite plans for the honeymoon, but they had the use of Mimi Kolff's car. They first drove north, then (because the weather was cold) south. Madzy's account contains snippets about hotels good and bad, brief observations about American houses and the different driving habits of Europeans and Americans.

What she is totally silent about is the emotional and physical reality of marriage. Not until six years later, in the diary she kept during the war, did she write about it briefly and allusively:

> I think of how you, with a sigh of relief, put all my extensive wedding baggage in the back of the Ford we borrowed from Mimi Kolff. The bride in the front seat. You behind the wheel ... I think of the ride to the north to a little hotel on a lake. I think of the things we did *not* say on the way. How did you feel, young and inexperienced as you were yourself, with a young girl next to you who was so disoriented that she hardly knew what she did. Did you know that she knew absolutely nothing about what was going to happen to her but only was terribly scared, so scared that her teeth rattled?

Madzy was twenty-six at the time of the wedding; her referring to herself as a young girl is very revealing.

The highlight of the honeymoon was four days spent in Shenandoah National Park, in a resort with cabins scattered among the trees. They made their own breakfast and supper and fetched their midday meal from the dining room. Every day they went for walks. There was a porch with rocking chairs, and indoors a big fireplace with two easy chairs beside it.

> When you stepped through the screen-door (against the flies) onto the porch, you held your breath in wonderment at the panorama that

Madzy and Wim took pictures of each other while on their honeymoon in
Shenandoah National Park

lay before you, because the little chalet stood at the edge of the mountain ridge and looked out over the Shenandoah Valley. The whole valley lay before us with, beyond it, the mountains, three separate ranges one behind the other and constantly changing colour. The valley was a quilt of colours where in the evenings small lights shone, like a field full of diamonds. When the moon rose from behind the mountains and the stars glittered in the dark blue evening sky, we felt as though everything were a dream.

After leaving the park, they visited the Supreme Court Building in Washington, D.C. Wim discovered that there were wonderful washrooms, so he went to get cleaned up, pointing Madzy in the direction of the "Ladies." It was there that she found that she hadn't a dime to pay the attendant, so she sat in the entrance hall and waited for Wim. The commissionaire came twice to ask her if she was waiting for someone, and twice she said yes. Then it turned out that it was closing time (they were the last visitors in the building) so the commissionaire went to find Wim and the two of them were hustled out. She makes an amusing story of it but there is an edge of anxiety and certainly embarrassment.

They next went to visit Virginia Donaldson, a distant relative of Wim's who lived in Maryland.[3] Her ancestor, related to Wim's mother's side of the family, had come to America about 1812, and the two branches had maintained contact ever since. The visit to Mrs Donaldson renewed a contact that was to become important after the Second World War.

The following day they were back in Montclair, and it was then that Madzy's married life really began. Wim had rented a small apartment within walking distance of the railway station from which he commuted to his office in Manhattan. He left at 7:45 in the morning and returned home at 7:00 in the evening, sometimes 8:00, and then he was tired and soon ready for bed. On Saturday afternoons, after what was called a half-day's work, he arrived home at 4:00. On Sundays they went for walks in a nearby area of wooded hills.

Madzy spent the long days alone in a strange place, knowing no one. She had to learn how to shop for food, to cook and keep house, all things she had never done. Still it was not enough to keep her busy. Wim had chosen Montclair because he always wanted to live outside cities. For Madzy that was not a good arrangement: if she had been in New York she could have gone to museums and taken courses at Columbia University. She tried to find work, but it was the Depression. When she went to the local library asking if there was volunteer work available, she was told that they did not employ foreigners. At the end of her life she wrote that those two years in the United States were a nightmare of loneliness and idleness.

To fill some of her time, she began to write. Possibly the first of those writings (apart from letters) was an account, in Dutch, of how she and Wim had taken part in the New York celebrations of the wedding of Princess Juliana, the Dutch crown princess with whom Madzy had been acquainted when both were students in Leiden. The typescript is dated 7 January 1937, and the story was published in the January 20th issue of *Het Vaderland*, a prominent Dutch newspaper with a liberal bent.

On the day before the royal wedding, Madzy and Bill had attended a church service in New York honouring the occasion. New York had, after all, once been New Amsterdam; the city's Dutch roots were visible in place names such as Staten Island and Harlem. "When we emerged from the subway into Fifth Avenue and heard the bells of the St. Nicholas Church, where a service was being held in honour of the Princess's wedding," Madzy wrote, "it was as if the bells called to us, 'Come in and express all the suppressed feelings of longing and homesickness; everyone here understands it because they have come here for the same purpose. Come in and feel for a short time the bonds with your native land, which after all you never leave behind you.'"[4] The service was in English, but at least one of the hymns was Dutch, and the highlight of the ceremony was a presention of the Dutch and the American flags.

The next day they set their alarm clock for 5:30 when the live radio coverage of the wedding would begin. As the readers of *Het Vaderland* would have heard the broadcast themselves, or might even have been in the crowds in The Hague, Madzy's lengthy article deals mainly with the emotions that she and Wim felt – expatriates, exiles, in whom this unusual event set off a wave of homesickness. Moreover, they had lived in The Hague most of their lives; they could picture it all. The grey, rainy morning outside their windows in Montclair disappeared, and they were in spirit part of the crowd outside the church in Holland on that clear, cold, windy day with the flags snapping and the plumes waving.

The broadcast they heard was directed to the North American audience. To Madzy's disappointment, there was an English-speaking commentator; but fortunately his comments were brief, and for the most part what they heard was the sound of Holland, the sound of home.

She submitted the article, and it was immediately published (without byline) as a private letter. The editor evidently indicated that he would be glad to see more of her work, for in the following months she wrote a number of columns entitled "Impressions of a Dutch Housewife in America." We have eight of them, either the typescripts or the clippings. She wrote a few articles for other publications, and also fiction – most of it unpublished, so far as I can tell.

The columns describe her life in Montclair and later in Summit, N.J., particularly focusing on how she as a new arrival was learning what she needed to know and how American ways differed from Dutch ones. She describes an American drugstore:

> When I arrived here, I had an image of a drugstore formed by what I had seen in the movies, and I had connected it in my thoughts with gangsters. I was a bit disappointed to find that a drugstore was just an ordinary, everyday store – even though it was a bit different than the Dutch kind. In a drugstore here you can buy every kind of medicine that you can think of, and have all prescriptions filled. Then there are toilet articles, and everything to do with tobacco, and books and magazines. I don't know why, but books in a drugstore are much cheaper than they are anywhere else, and they are very good books: books about music, history, geography, and about the life of Plato, as well as novels and best-sellers ...
>
> And then there is a soda fountain – and for a Dutch person that is the odd thing, that a person can eat and drink in an apothecary's shop.[5]

The amount and choice of details makes us realize that her readers had never seen such a thing at first hand, and many had not even heard of it or seen it in films.

In another column she describes one of her first shopping expeditions, when she searched everywhere in the main street for the kind of butcher shop that she was used to. In the end a policeman directed her to the A&P. It had never occurred to her to look for meat in a grocery store.

She explains that, in Montclair, schoolchildren and working husbands do not come home for midday dinner, so housewives do not cook hot meals for themselves. In another column she remarks that it is the wives of commuting husbands who look after the family car, buy licences, and arrange for repairs.

She mentions that she has no live-in servant because she and Wim can't afford it; in Holland she certainly would have had one, or at least someone who came in during the day. In a short story dating from this time, published in *De Javabode*, a newspaper for the Dutch population in Java,[6] she explains that visitors, after ringing the doorbell, have to wait *outside* the house because there is no servant to admit them and allow them to wait indoors until the master or mistress of the house is able to see them. The subject would be significant to her readers: she wants to convey that in America not having a servant is the usual thing, not a sign of poverty or inferior social class.

MORE OBLIQUE, but more revealing in some ways, are Madzy's short stories. Except for two, there is no indication that they were even submitted for publication. Their private, inward tone does not suggest that they were directed to a particular audience – adapting to the audience's interests and needs was something Madzy was very good at – so perhaps they were written mainly for herself, to unburden her heart.

The three we have are in Dutch. One, entitled "Your Land Is My Land," is written from the point of view of a young Dutch woman named Annie who is living in New York with her husband. The first paragraphs set the scene:

> When you live in New York, you regularly receive a letter from Holland that says: "So-and-so is coming to New York. Maybe you could arrange to meet each other, do something nice together?"
>
> It's not only people you know who are shoved at you in that way, but also complete strangers, whom – from verbal descriptions that never match the reality, or photos that don't look a bit like the original – one has then to identify in the busy lobby of a hotel or in the huge crowd of people meeting an arriving ship.

Annie receives such a letter, from a university acquaintance writing to say that her friend Els, who has recently married an American, will shortly be arriving in New York on the *Nieuw Amsterdam*. Reluctantly Annie goes to meet the ship. There is no sign of Els, but Annie – although hampered by not knowing Els's married surname – finds out from the purser to which hotel she has gone. There she finds her.

The next Saturday afternoon Els and Martin, her American husband, come to the small town outside New York where Annie and her husband Bob live. Annie likes Martin, but she finds Els strangely subdued. She discovers why: Martin had expected to be located in New York, but just the previous day had heard that he was being sent to Denver.

Annie tries to comfort Els by pointing out that in Denver she will more quickly become accustomed to American ways. "'But I don't at all want to become American,' Els said, and there was an obstinate look in her eyes. I was silent, but I thought, 'Why, then, did you marry an American?'" The marriage does not last. After half a year Els turns up on Annie's doorstep on her way back to Holland. Annie drives her to the ship, and during the ride they talk about immigration and adaptation.

Madzy's sympathies are with Martin: she is critical of Els, who thought she could remain Dutch while being married to an American and living (as she had at first assumed) in New York. Though not a particularly good short story, it shows some of the underside of the experiences of adaptation that Madzy handled more lightly in her columns.

A story published in *De Javabode* – the 1937 Christmas issue – also begins with a young Dutch woman arriving in New York. This one is named Let; she is single, twenty-six, studying medicine. She has come to spend Christmas with her friends Miep and Bob, who are carbon copies of the Dutch couple in the earlier story. Miep, the wife, is the narrator.

During the visit Let meets Kees, a young Dutchman working in New York. The issue of exile comes up in connection with him: he also comes to stay with Miep and Bob for the holidays, and he and Miep talk about Christmas as he has experienced it – a single man, a foreigner with no family in New York. Madzy is clearly drawing on what she knew about Wim's life in the two years before she joined him, and what she had heard from other expatriates. Kees and Let marry and return to Holland. Miep is concerned about the speed of events, but not about the compatibility of the couple or their decision to return home.

A story entitled "Birthday" deals with a surprise birthday party given for a woman called Maya by a group of Dutch expatriates in New York. In the middle of the party she observes the gathering from outside the room, reflecting:

> There they all sat: Dutch people who had left their country to find their fortune. Had they succeeded? No, certainly not. Dick [her husband] wasn't where he wanted to be; she herself still had to learn not to yearn constantly for home, and to learn to make a home for herself – her own atmosphere – *here*. Everyone else no doubt was missing something. Even though they did not show it, deep in their hearts they longed for their homeland; and then they crept together, "the gang," and took every opportunity to have a party. A birthday or holiday in the royal family, the birthday of one of themselves, a housewarming, nothing went by without some party being made of it. And even if there was nothing, they gathered for a picnic and told each other stories about their lives in Holland, embellished by

distance and frequent retelling ... The gang crept together sometimes to conceal homesickness. Homesickness? But isn't this a better experience than to stay home and spend your life longing to leave your country and see new people, new countries, different conditions?

Clearly Madzy was giving a great deal of thought to the issues of exile, of isolation and loneliness, of marriage, of the connection between personal identity and nationality. They did have a circle of friends with whom they had regular parties on weekends, and the gathering in "Birthday" clearly reflects these occasions.

BESIDES THE stories and columns, we have in our files a piece written by Cornelius Kolff (in English) about early Dutch times in the New York area. With it is a Dutch version by Madzy, consisting of an introduction that describes Mr Kolff, and then a free translation of his work, followed by additional material. The piece is incomplete and unrevised. Translating Mr Kolff's stories about the early Dutch residents of New York, and analyzing the differences between Europe and North America, she strikes a note heard in her writings from now to the end of her life, that of explaining individuals and nationalities to each other.

IN THE EARLY summer of 1937, Madzy and Wim rented a house in Summit, New Jersey. It was further from the railway station, and Wim would have to pay an additional $3 per month in commuting costs; it is an indication of how tight their finances were that this was an important factor in deciding whether they could afford to move. But the house was pleasantly located on the edge of town, with a view over fields, and by now they had a car, a second-hand Ford coupé bought with some of the money Madzy had received by way of wedding gifts. She could now drive Wim to the station in the morning and pick him up in the evening. She had just learned to drive; on the day she got her licence, she drove into Manhattan to fetch Wim at his office!

In one of the columns for *Het Vaderland*, she describes the move to Summit, and the house.[7] The two things she likes most about it are the porch and the cedar closet for storing things that had to be protected from moths: blankets, coats, sweaters – all made of wool in a time before synthetic fabrics were readily available.

The house was built on an open-plan design, which was not common in Holland; Dutch houses had passages from which doors opened into separate rooms. In the house in Summit, Madzy writes, when you come in through the front door you find yourself immediately in the sitting room.

She describes the layout in such detail that it is clear that otherwise her readers would have no idea what she meant. She also describes the kitchen, and the basement, very different from the Dutch storage cellar. The bedrooms have no washbasins (as Dutch bedrooms do) – "much easier to arrange the furniture this way."

In another column she describes the arrival of her first American summer. "My sense of being an old-established resident has suffered a shock. After much muddling, I had begun to acquire a safe feeling in all this newness, and now I have to deal with countless new circumstances that upset my sense of safety." She explains that screens are installed in front of all the windows and around porches, for otherwise insects would make it impossible to keep the windows open or sit on a porch. In summer American families live – and, in a heat wave, even sleep – on their porches, an astonishing idea for the Dutch. Because of the screens, however, it is not possible to reach out through the window and shake a dustcloth or scatter crumbs for the birds. As so often in these columns, I catch a sudden glimpse of how things were done in Holland: I recognize these customs from my younger years there and from later visits. I *see* one of my aunts reaching out through a window to scatter the breakfast crumbs for the birds.

When there are visitors in hot weather, Madzy continues, it is one of the hostess's duties to invite the gentlemen to take off their suit jackets if they wish. She mentions, in passing, that in the Dutch East Indies, where it was even hotter, gentlemen visitors would arrive carrying their suit jackets neatly folded over their arms, to show that they actually did own such things.

In the house in Summit, the furniture has acquired cretonne summer covers. Dark winter-weight drapes have been replaced with light summer ones. For us, now, some of these customs are as strange as they would have been to Madzy's Dutch readers: by describing them so vividly, with such an eye for detail, she inadvertently bridges this gap too.

In all this there is a touch of naïve wonderment, an intense interest in what she was seeing and learning. Her attention is firmly focused on both the American and the Dutch ways. Her reference to having and then losing a "sense of safety" indicates that none of this learning was easy. In a humorous piece for the alumni magazine of the lyceum that she and Wim had attended, she writes that it is handy to have two countries because you can pick and choose whichever customs you like; but there is clearly a dark side to this as well.

The newspaper columns often allude to her isolation during the long days when Wim was at work, the lack of kindred spirits. This is late afternoon in the dormitory suburb:

Towards six o'clock the village, that by day slumbers sweetly, suddenly wakes up. The traffic is so heavy that three traffic policemen are required. They stand in the middle of intersections under a brightly coloured parasol (because of the hot weather) in blue shirts and no jackets. They know everyone and wave cheerfully at the passing cars. In the cities there is obviously also a rush of wives in cars to the parking places near the railway stations, unless husband and wife each own a car. Just notice, when you take a train past all the little stations: on every parking lot there will be 100 to 300 cars parked, depending on the size of the town and its surroundings.

Towards six o'clock this number doubles. At that time the parking lot consists of little "wreaths" of housewife-friends. Children play tag among the parked cars, other cars arrive and are parked beside those already there and the housewives join the circles.

Then the train whistles in the distance. The "wreaths" fall apart; everyone searches for her child or children from between or under the cars, here and there car doors slam and engines start. The train stops with squealing brakes. It's a competition to be the first to drive off, and the men jump from the train before it comes to a halt. In two minutes the parking lot is one tangle of cars moving forwards or backing out. One after the other shoots out of the tangle and heads for home.

Then the housewife faces her last task: to serve the meal hot out of the oven and then to wash the dishes.

Despite this cheerful passage, the reality was sadder and lonelier. Madzy would go to the station to meet the earliest train that Wim could possibly arrive on. At the end of the honeymoon, she wrote later, she "woke up as if out of a delightful dream into a terrible dark scary night when I went every evening in the dark from our little apartment to the bridge over the Lackawanna railroad to see if you were on this train, and to wait for the next, again and again. Oh, those lonely evenings in the dark when other couples walked arm in arm and I was still waiting for the next train, and the next."

She acquired a dog, Pandourijntje, who was some comfort. The days were still just as long, but her outward life went on. Besides the no-doubt frequent letters, they had visitors from Holland. Twice a year they saw a cousin of Wim's, Greet, one of the children with whom he had played at de Hoogt. Greet had married Jan Blijdenstein and they now owned an orange grove in Florida; they spent winters there and summers in Holland, leaving their car with Wim and Madzy in Summit.

Wim's mother came to visit them, which he recalls as rather a disaster:

> She had never been on a ship before and was completely out of sorts after the ten-day trip, ten days without feeling solid ground under her feet and the endless sea around her. She had to be kept busy by Madzy; also she endlessly told Madzy that her cooking was completely wrong. During that time also my sister Lies came on her way to our cousin Greet, who lived in Florida and who had invited her for the winter. Then, after probably a month, my grandmother Hoogewerff died and my mother returned to Holland in haste on a much faster German ship.

In 1938 Iete and Hansje came. Bill recalls that as a "nice visit" of a few weeks. They made a trip by car to Vermont and Quebec City, returning to Summit through Maine. In *Land for Our Sons*, Madzy recalls her first impressions of Canada: "I was enthralled with this place. After more than a year of pure Americana, Quebec had a European flavour that warmed my heart. The little restaurants with French food, the shops with French-speaking clerks, the old buildings and ruins, the historic atmosphere, I revelled in it. Canada to us meant a succession of nice little French cafés and charming curiosity shops."[8]

Later, Juus came as well. The plan had been that after a few days she would go to Brooklyn, where her brother was a clergyman. Then she would return to Summit to be with Madzy during the birth of her first child, expected in the fall. Events interfered with this, as we shall see.

With Madzy's encouragement, no doubt, Wim had left the job he'd always hated and found another, in the Freight Department of the New York office of the Holland-America Line. The hours were better though the work was dull and the pay somewhat lower. It still, however, did not have the kind of future Wim wished for, and they both disliked living in the crowded area around New York City. They were both homesick, and by the summer of 1938 there was a baby (me) on the way.

The pregnancy made Madzy feel ill, and she spent a good deal of time lying down. It was a very hot summer. She developed a skin rash that stayed until the day after I was born. She took a lot of showers, and her skin was "nothing but crusts and blood."

But it was public events that sealed their decision to return to the Netherlands. In later life, Bill wrote:

> In March 1938 Hitler invaded Austria, and the Dutch government started to incease their armed forces. [In August an announcement was made that] reserve officers could become active career officers. My time in the army

had been the best time in my life, and I had been sorry that my education did not qualify me for being a career officer.

I had been with the field artillery, but the shortage of officers was with the cavalry. My father applied for me ... I was accepted and we had to return as soon as possible ... It seemed foolish that with a war threatening one would leave the "safe" U.S.A. to go into the army, but being a reserve officer I would have had to go into active service anyhow in case of war.

Because I was an employee of the Holland-America Line, we got a very cheap rate for our passage and the lift van with furniture, so we decided to take most of it along, and also the car. Within a week we sailed on the *Statendam*. The ship's doctor was very cross that Madzy made the trip while being about eight months pregnant, but all went well.

AND SO IT was that in September 1938, with war looming, they returned to Holland. Madzy's need to move away two years before had had much to do with her desire to be free of her mother's convention-driven ways. What she discovered in America was that such freedom was immensely costly. To achieve it, she had to give up the supportive community she had had at home and the intellectually and culturally nourishing life of Europe. Wim, unhappy in the United States when he was there alone, had concluded that the solution was to marry. This, however, was not enough. Homesickness was one of the forces impelling them both to return to Holland.

But whatever the advantages of returning, the problems that Madzy had been running away from were still there. It seemed that she had to choose *either* freedom and individuality *or* a community of kindred spirits, and intellectual and cultural sustenance – that she could not find or create both together.

There was another, related conflict: her rebellious, independence-loving self was yoked with another that was self-sacrificing, submerging her moods and wishes in those of other people. Hansje told me that in her opinion Madzy took their mother too seriously. Madzy had shown that she could rebel against Iete; but clearly the rebellious part of her was often not strong enough: she allowed herself to be dominated, then became angry.

Those two selves, uneasily harnessed together, pulled her this way and that: two selves, two images that she valued, that she used to shape her identity. This shaping would in the next few years be influenced by the war that swept across her like a huge destructive wave before withdrawing and leaving her battered and traumatized. Thus the next time she confronted the same dilemma there would be, in addition to the earlier factors, a whole set of new ones.

A branch, drawn by Madzy in late middle age

CHAPTER FOUR

Return to Holland, 1938–1942

The photo album Madzy kept for this time begins with pictures taken on board the *Statendam*, showing the receding New York skyline. The captions give no hint of regret at leaving; a page or two later, there is distinct pleasure at returning to "the Fatherland." The coast of England evokes a delight in its "Europeanness." On the same page as her landing card for Rotterdam is mounted the visiting card that she and Wim used in the United States ("Mr. and Mrs. W.J. Brender à Brandis, 11 Iris Road, Summit, N.J.") and, handwritten next to it, "Exit Bill Brender and his bride!" They were once more Wim and Madzy.

As soon as she stepped on the quay in Holland, however, this enthusiasm was tempered by another reaction: "They took hold of me and my life as they had done before and I had no say in anything." The family had arranged everything: where she would live, where she would have the baby. She submitted to the behests of others for a few days, then began to arrange things to suit herself.

Wim went immediately to Amersfoort to join the training course for cavalry officers. He was with ten other men who had transferred from the field artillery, some of whom he knew well. He found two rooms in a boarding house at Prinses Julianalaan 15 where, for the three months it took him to complete the course, he and Madzy – and I, when I was born – lived.

Madzy gave birth to me in the Roman Catholic hospital in Amersfoort on 5 October 1938. In the album there is a photo of me lying in a travel crib; the caption says that on the trip home to the Netherlands, the crib had been packed full of cocktail glasses and beer mugs.

Amersfoort was in a familiar part of Holland, near Hilversum, where Oom Willy lived, and Baarn, where Paul and Mita had rented a house during their furlough. Maarn, where Wim had spent those enjoyable summer holidays during his youth, was ten kilometres away. Near Amersfoort lived Dick and Charlotte Kolff, who were to become very good friends.

At the end of the training course, when the officers chose the regiment with which they would serve, Wim selected a mounted cavalry regiment stationed in Amersfoort. He and Madzy and I moved to a small house in the Bisschopsweg, not far from the barracks. Madzy had a housemaid called Rika, who lived on a farm within bicycling distance. Rika was to be a resource for Madzy during the hard war years to come.

War was definitely threatening. In September 1938 Chamberlain met with Hitler at Munich, and in October Germany occupied Czechoslovakia. Among the baby pictures in the photo album are others of the cavalry regiment and Wim in uniform. Madzy includes an earlier one – of Wim in 1931 or '32, during his compulsory military service, standing beside a piece of field artillery. Another, probably from 1939, shows him on a horse named Turando, jumping a fence – a picture that gives me, looking at it now, a glimpse of an unfamiliar aspect of my father.

For a time yet, ordinary life continued. Madzy and Wim visited their parents and other relatives – there are pictures of family groups in gardens, and of me on the lap of one or another grandparent. In June 1939 the three of us spent ten days in a small cabin in Maarn, on the de Hoogt estate – "the only time that we really had fun" before war broke out. A photo shows a meal being cooked in a pan balanced on a little structure of stones, and the baby book records that I much enjoyed seeing ashes falling into my porridge. Madzy and Wim played tennis and swam. The weather was wonderful.

IN THE LATE summer of 1939, one of those incidents occurred in which personal and public events interact especially closely. Elise Donaldson, the daughter of Virginia Donaldson whom Madzy and Wim had visited in Maryland during their honeymoon, travelled to Russia as secretary to a Dr Yarros and her husband. Dr and Mr Yarros had been Jewish refugees from the Russian revolution, and she was now a prominent gynecologist. Elise had been a newspaper reporter specializing in medical matters before she became Dr Yarros's secretary.

Dr Yarros had been invited to lecture in Leningrad, but this turned out to be a dangerous time for such a trip. On the way home the party was unable to travel through Finland as planned but was turned back by the Germans. With difficulty they reached the Netherlands, where, with several days to spare before returning to the United States, they visited Madzy and Wim. A day or two before their departure, Dr Yarros suffered a serious heart attack; they were unable to sail as planned. Because every ship was packed with people fleeing Europe, they could not find space on another ship until Wim, using his connections with the Holland-America Line,

Madzy has been playing tennis; the child is Marianne. Summer 1939, just before the war began

found berths for them in a small and uncomfortable freighter. The ship was torpedoed in mid-Atlantic but did reach New York, and Dr Yarros recovered from her illness.

In a letter to Virginia Donaldson on 12 December 1939, Madzy refers to this incident: "You ought not to thank us for the very little we could do for your daughter. If only we had known beforehand, she could have come and stayed with us! As a matter of fact I hope fervently that she will cross the ocean again when times are more secure. We liked her so much and we liked her friends very much too and are anxious to know if Dr Yarros was very ill and whether he[1] will be better soon."

This incident strengthened the links with the Donaldson family – a contact that would later be enormously beneficial to us.[2]

A GROUP OF photos taken in August 1939 is headed "The last war-free days." By the time Madzy was mounting these pictures in the album, the war had evidently begun. I can imagine her, busy with glue and the white ink used to write captions on black paper, looking back across what must already have seemed like a great divide. She would have been doing this after 25 August, when the Dutch army was mobilized, and after 1 September, when Hitler invaded Poland, and after 3 September, when Britain and France declared war on Germany. Very suddenly, life had changed.

Upon the mobilization of the army, Wim's regiment was moved east to Vaassen, a small town near Apeldoorn, a front-line location. The unit was billeted on farms and in barns and schools because only in a rural area was there accommodation for all the horses.

On the eve of Wim's departure, photos were quickly taken "for Papa to take along ... where to? For how long?" Madzy writes, "We try to smile."

THE NETHERLANDS had been neutral during the First World War. Relations with Germany had always been close; the two countries had never been at war with each other. Queen Wilhelmina, who was on the throne of the Netherlands in 1939, had had a German consort (by then deceased) and a German mother; Juliana, the crown princess, had married Prince Bernhard, who was of German birth. But by the late 1930s the rise of Hitler caused uneasiness. Hitler's moves into the Rhineland, Austria, and Czechoslovakia seemed ominous developments.

The Netherlands relied on its ability to repel invaders by flooding the extensive stretches of the country that were below sea level. It had worked with the French invasion of 1672. This would leave the western and most heavily populated part of the country protected – or so the thinking went.

Wim in dress uniform, with Madzy and Marianne, 1939

The country also relied on its neutrality but hoped that in a pinch France and England would come to its aid. In the spirit of neutrality, however, it was denying permission to French and English troops to assess the Dutch defences. It was an uncomfortable situation.

The Netherlands' armed forces were sufficient in manpower but very badly equipped. As the project of flooding the low land indicates, the country's leaders still thought about warfare in terms of much earlier conflicts. Wim reflected many years later, "It is unbelievable that the cavalry and artillery still used horses, as these were slow and particularly vulnerable to bombing, and impossible to hide or camouflage from enemy planes. Our firing power consisted of rifles, a few light machine guns, and sabres. It was as if we were at war with Napoleon. Besides several mounted regiments, there was one cavalry regiment on bicycles and two newly created regiments of cavalry on motorcycles, and there were in total eight armoured cars. No tanks."[3]

When the war broke out at the beginning of September 1939, the Netherlands again declared neutrality, and the belligerents said they would respect it. At a secret conference with his military leaders in Berlin on 23 November, however, Hitler made it clear that the Netherlands would be invaded. The Luftwaffe needed the Dutch airfields.[4]

SHORTLY AFTER the transfer to Vaassen, Wim left the regiment to take charge of a group of about sixty staff personnel – cooks, chauffeurs, clerks, and the signal unit – in Apeldoorn. At first Madzy and I stayed in Amersfoort. In the baby-book entry for 5 October, my birthday, Madzy records that Wim came home every two weeks. On these occasions I was at first frightened, but soon, she writes, I recognized him, even after an absence of two weeks. Photos taken on my birthday show him in uniform.

About the end of October, Madzy was invited to come to Apeldoorn and stay with Thila Fabius, the wife of one of Wim's fellow officers. Thila was a friend of Madzy's from before her marriage. Madzy gladly accepted, because this meant that she would see Wim more frequently. She was in Apeldoorn by about the first of November.

On 11 November, there was a serious scare: the German army was massed on the Dutch border and an attack was rumoured to be imminent.[5] In fact a major assault was planned for the next day, but bad weather prevented it. On the night of the 11th to the 12th, Madzy drove to The Hague with Thila and their two small children. It was a frightening trip, partly because of the fear of attack, partly because, on account of the blackout, the car's headlights had been taped so as to leave only narrow slits to illuminate the road.

Madzy wrote about this in the baby book on 29 November, the first entry since 5 October: "Weeks have passed, weeks of mobilization, tension, and wandering. So far as I can remember: we stayed for a week in The Hague [with Wim's father and stepmother]. Then Wim was moved, and we went to stay near him in Apeldoorn. This lasted for just 10 days, and then the intense tension and anxiety began. Then we fled by night to The Hague. But after the easing of the tension we returned clandestinely to our dear Pappa."

In a letter of 12 December 1939 to Virginia Donaldson, she described that night's drive: "In the middle of November we really had very trying days, and I had to flee with Marianne in the car through a very dark foggy and rainy night to The Hague. It took me nearly five hours of driving very carefully, but we arrived safely at my mother's house. On the whole The Hague is not safe either, but nobody knows what is safe and so we just pretend to be safe anywhere!"

In the same letter she comments on receiving Virginia's letter: "I would not have thought it possible that a letter from across the Atlantic would have come over in safety. But when your letter, written Nov. 5, arrived this morning, I saw that although it took more than a month, it still came through, and so I shall try the same with this letter of mine."

Remarks like this about the uncertainty and slowness of letters crossing the Atlantic reveal something about what was actually happening: German U-boats attacked shipping between North America and Europe, communications were disrupted, and feeling safe was a matter of make-believe.

SHORTLY AFTER the crisis in November, Wim was moved to St Oedenrode, in Brabant, in the south of the country. He was billeted in a private house; Madzy and I often stayed there, though it was strictly forbidden for wives to be with their officer-husbands. The letter of 12 December to Virginia Donaldson was written from there. In it Madzy reports: "There is no shortage in food as yet. Only sugar and peas and beans are rationed, and several articles have gone up in price, but that is really all. Probably you should like to know what we think of everything. Well, we do not think much; we try to keep a merry face to all inconveniences and pray fervently that our neutrality will be considered. On the whole the outlook is not pleasant."

THE WINTER of 1939–40 was a very cold one. The mood in the country was quiet, watchful, anxious. Walter B. Maass, in *The Netherlands at War: 1940-1945*, briefly describes this time: "The war on the seas started claiming victims among the neutrals. The Dutch tanker *Sliedrecht* was sunk by a German submarine and 26 lives were lost. In November, the large liner *Simon Bolivar* struck a magnetic mine and sank with many of her passengers. Both British and German planes often infringed on Dutch air space, notwithstanding all protests."[6]

There was fighting in Scandinavia: the Soviet Union, with whom Germany had signed a non-aggression pact in August, had attacked Finland in November, and in April the Germans overran Denmark and Norway.

Wim was stationed in St Oedenrode until April 1940. Madzy seems to have been anxious and unhappy whenever she was separated from him. As an officer in the army, he might well, in spite of Dutch neutrality, see action of some sort. The time in the United States, with no other relatives or close friends nearby, had made them very interdependent, and now, though they were once more within easy reach of friends, the close relationship continued. Wim provided Madzy with a sense of emotional safety that she had probably not had since her father's death.

SOMEWHERE BETWEEN October 1938, when I was born, and September 1941, when she became pregnant with Gerard, Madzy miscarried of twins. She had not told Wim that she was pregnant, and she did not tell him of the miscarriage. Between April 1940 and February 1942 there are no entries in the baby book and, except for the letter to Virginia Donaldson, no other written records from this time. It was not until forty years later, when her daughter-in-law, Suzanna, had a miscarriage, that she spoke of it briefly to Gerard. He did not tell me about her revelation until after her death, and then we told Bill, who was stunned. It gave us much to think about, but mainly we speculated about the reasons for Madzy's not having told Wim when it happened. The pregnancy, however, must have been far enough advanced to show that it was twins. Of course the times were unsettled, and for nearly two years Madzy was moving from place to place to be near Wim, with intervals of staying with her mother in The Hague.

Madzy had a very strong maternal instinct, and on the one hand she may have welcomed the prospect of more children. But the anxiety surrounding the war must have cast a shadow over whatever pleasure there was in that prospect. Not telling Wim was certainly a way of sparing him worry. And so she went through it by herself. Did she confide in anyone? We have no way of knowing.

The pregnancy and miscarriage no doubt threw a cloud of apprehension over her next pregnancy, with Gerard, in the winter and early spring of 1941–42. As for the secrecy – perhaps it was the sort of secret that, once kept, could not be divulged. Until forty years later.

ALTHOUGH MADZY never wrote an account of this period, fortunately Wim did:

> On the first of May 1940, our secret service expected a German invasion and we moved to Oisterwijk, also in Brabant. Madzy knew a lady there, Mrs van Aken, who had been a friend of her parents in Indonesia ... So she welcomed me when I billeted myself in her house, and she invited Madzy and Marianne as her guests. The house was on a small lake, and the woods around it were known for the singing nightingales. In the beautiful night of May 9 to 10, with the birds singing, we were awakened by the roar of hundreds of war planes which flew over at 3:00 a.m. We were naïve and said, "They are going to England." However, a telephone call came to tell me that the Germans had invaded.

The regiment was ordered to move, but Madzy remained in Oisterwijk. The Germans simply overran the area, and there was no fighting. However, she and Mrs van Aken – having been warned that enemy soldiers, if they found wine, would get drunk and become dangerous – opened all the wine bottles in the cellar and, with great regret, poured the contents out in the garden.

Wim writes that he and two other officers still had three horses with them. On 10 May they sent them for safekeeping to the cavalry horse depot in The Hague. Wim's father, notified of this, found Wim's horse, claimed it on Wim's behalf, and rode it for a year until it was requisitioned by the Germans. Wim's comment was that it probably died in Russia.

ON 10 MAY 1940, the Germans attacked Holland, Belgium, and France with an enormous force of tanks, motorized infantry, and aircraft. The Allies had at this time no idea of the ways in which the German army would use tanks, or of the mobility they permitted. Paratroopers were used for the first time; some wore Dutch uniforms, causing great confusion and panic. The speed of the attack and the landing of paratroopers far inside Dutch territory showed the absurdity of relying on flooding to stop an enemy invasion.

The Dutch army put up as much resistance as it could, and there was serious fighting near The Hague and Rotterdam. The royal family and the cabinet were able to escape to England. Then, to quench the continuing fighting in Rotterdam, the Luftwaffe attacked it on 14 May and destroyed the centre, setting the entire city on fire. They also attacked the harbour. Other cities would be bombed if the country did not surrender. The Netherlands capitulated, and the fighting ended on 15 May.

During those few days, Wim came under fire at least twice. One bomb fell very close to him, and on another occasion he survived a bombing by sheltering in the cellar of a farmhouse while the entire village was destroyed. On 15 May, when the Dutch capitulated and the fighting stopped, he was able to phone his father to say that he was unharmed and to tell him where he was. When Madzy heard the news, Wim writes, "She, with the help of her friend, hired a man with a tandem bicycle and came all the way from Oisterwijk to see me."

The fighting continued elsewhere in western Europe. Another prong of the same German assault pinned the British Expeditionary Force and some French troops at Dunkirk. The evacuation from Dunkirk took place about two weeks after the fall of Holland, and Paris fell two weeks after that. As a result the Germans were able to use Dutch and French air bases for the attack on Britain, which began with fighting over the Channel in mid-July and continued with the bombing of the country itself (the Battle of Britain) until May 1941.[7]

When the Dutch surrendered in May 1940, the armed forces were demobilized. Wim writes: "Normally we should have been made prisoners of war, but the Germans, expecting Dutch cooperation in their war effort if they treated us well, allowed the entire Dutch army to go home. However, career officers had to sign a document saying that they would not engage in activities against the German army or their occupation of the country. Except for a few officers who considered that against their honour, we all signed."

In the photo album Madzy records these events briefly. There is a picture of Wim in uniform on his horse – the last of the military pictures – and then, by itself on a page, a tiny newspaper clipping noting that during the five days of fighting the Dutch army losses were 2,890 dead, 6,889 wounded, and 29 missing. "Let us forget the black pages in between," she writes grimly.

Very glad to be out of active service, Wim enrolled in an agricultural school in Leeuwarden, in the north-eastern part of the country. In a tape made late in life, Madzy said that they lived primitively; knowing that they would not be there for long, they unpacked only some of their furniture and hung a few curtains. They knew no one, and Madzy spent all her time with me. I had to be kept quiet so as not to disturb Wim, who was studying for exams; fortunately I seem to have been a quiet child. "We made it through that winter," she recorded, "but it wasn't a very enthusiastic winter, as you can imagine." We lived there from August 1940 to spring 1941, and then moved to Maarn, where Wim had spent those happy summer vacations at de Hoogt.

Recording his memories much later, Wim set the scene:

> In that general area, adjoining properties were owned by other prominent families. One of them was the Blijdenstein family, who had large properties, mostly wooded, with very little moor. There were two daughters in that family, Dientje and Christie, and two sons, Jan and Willem. Jan had married Greet de Beaufort [Wim's cousin], Willem married a Norwegian woman, Christie married Piet van Notten, and Dientje remained unmarried.
>
> Dientje and Christie managed the estate. I knew the family – not very well, but there were many connections. During the war, therefore, when I was demobilized and had spent one year at the agricultural school in Leeuwarden, in Friesland, and wanted to find a job, Madzy and I decided to move to Maarn. I asked Christie and Dientje if we could temporarily stay in a small apartment attached to the game-warden's cottage. They agreed. They didn't know Madzy before that, but it became a very close friendship. Dientje then asked whether Madzy and I were interested in living in the small gardener's cottage ("het Tuinmanshuisje") on the estate. It was very modest but had just been renovated and now had running water and indoor plumbing. Madzy and I gladly accepted the offer. And that's how Madzy and the children came to spend all those war years in Maarn.

Wim, who was still an army officer and received a portion of his salary, found part-time and volunteer work in forestry and estate management. He marked trees for cutting and thinning and did some surveying.

Madzy, on the tape just referred to, said: "I was a little bit afraid of it because it was again lonesome. It was again away from people and friends ... and with the Germans around and a depot of explosive materials not so very far away it was dangerous, but it was the right thing for Dad. He just loved it and I thought, 'I will love it too.' Finally, actually, in Maarn I had a fairly nice time because I made a lot of contacts."

We recognize the pattern: Madzy was not drawn to rural life as Wim was.

AT FIRST the occupation was not unduly severe.[8] The Germans, thinking of the Dutch as "cousins," expected them to be cooperative. But the Dutch are an independent-minded people and did not like living under enemy occupation, and relations rapidly became strained. Wim writes that he and Madzy were in no danger provided that they did not do anything to oppose the Germans – which has an ominous sound. So long as they kept their heads down, however, life was simple and peaceful.

The cottage in Maarn as seen from the road

The house had started out as a worker's cottage, consisting of one ground-floor room with a scullery off it and a bed built into the wall. Upstairs, under the sloping roof, was a small bedroom. Perhaps about the beginning of the twentieth century, an addition had been built of two rooms downstairs and two up (none of them large). Behind was a small barn with an adjoining pigsty that we used as a woodshed, and a vegetable garden. Along one side was an orchard, to the other side and behind were woods, and the area across the road was also wooded except for a long driveway leading to 't Huis te Maarn, the main house on the estate. No other houses were visible from it, and there was no telephone.

Madzy seems to have done no writing at this time, but on 15 February 1942, after a gap of nearly two years, she makes an entry in the baby book.

> Wars and misery passed over Marianne's head, and left no mark except that she is terrified of airplanes. The food-rationing problems don't affect her ...
>
> The war continues. This is the day of the fall of Singapore. Fear clenches our hearts for the Dutch East Indies, with all that is dear to us there.[9] But here we look out on peaceful woods decorated by snow and hoarfrost, and all we notice of the war is sometimes bombing either nearby or farther away and the rationing of food. What preoccupies us most is the coming of Marianne's little brother or sister in the beginning of May, and the exam that Papa has to write.

The combination of inner anxiety and cheerful faces continued. Madzy was always good at lifting the spirits of those around her. It is in her writings, sometimes, that it is possible to catch sight of the inner woman. She did have some reason to be cheerful. She and Wim were together and safe, Wim had work of a sort, and in Maarn they had found an agreeable home. They were living in a village surrounded by woods and farming country and had old friends nearby, as well as the new friends they were making. Wim's Tante Betsy, one of his favourite relatives, was at de Hoogt, a mile or two away. Dientje Blijdenstein and Christie van Notten were delightful people; the local doctor, Ad van Kekem, and his wife became very good friends. Others were within bicycling distance or a short train trip away. It was a circle of intelligent and congenial people, with similar interests and backgrounds.

However, there *was* a war on. Maarn, in the centre of the country, was close to major east-west roads and railways, which the Germans used for the movement of troops and materiel. It was also under the regular routes for bombers and fighters; during major raids, they flew over in massive concentrations, Allied planes on their way to Germany and German planes going to Britain. The Allies bombed the roads and railway lines. The woods surrounding Maarn were useful as camouflage: the German army built a major anti-aircraft battery in the forest close to de Hoogt, and for the rest of the war it was the target for Allied bombing. When its guns fired, our cottage trembled. The woods also concealed German armament depots, and provided hiding places for the Dutch underground.

All this was to get worse later, but already the war was a continuous presence and danger. The Netherlands was suffering the constrictions and shortages caused by the war. The rationing of food was a worry to Madzy as a housewife and the mother of one small child, with another on the way. There was the anxiety of living under enemy occupation, of identity papers, of uncertainty about what would happen next. The refusal of the Dutch to cooperate with the occupying forces led, before long, to friction. Friction led to repression, and then to what was in effect a reign of terror, with the German administration and several different police forces controlling almost every aspect of the Dutch people's lives and delivering arbitrary and brutal punishment.[10]

ON 18 MAY 1942, Madzy began a diary – writing it to deal with the shock of sudden and nearly unbearable disaster. At the instant she begins, a door opens and we are suddenly able to look into her life, the inner as well as the outer. For me as both daughter and biographer, the diary is immensely important, and the experience of reading that first page – that sudden opening of the door – is indescribable.

I draw on the diary extensively in the next chapter. But to sketch Madzy's life as it was in the spring of 1942, I am cautiously extrapolating backwards from the situation made visible when that door opens. If this is how things were on 18 May 1942, then in the preceding weeks ...

Wim planted an extensive vegetable garden, partly because he makes gardens wherever he lives and partly because food was scarce. I was three and a half, a sturdy toddler much attached to Pappa and helping him in the garden. I remember (or was that from after the war?) holding one end of the twine that he used to plant seeds and seedlings in a straight line. The twine was wound around two stakes. He would unroll as much as was needed for the length of the row, and we would hold it straight and steady, above the ground, and when he was satisfied that it was in the right place, we'd push the stakes into the soil.

Because of the fine weather, there might have been planes flying, especially at night, and I was frightened of them. But the garden was a good place for me, and the presence of Pappa and Mamma must have provided a considerable sense of security.

Wim did some of his paperwork at home, so in the living room there was a desk with ledgers and correspondence. In addition, he was taking courses that would qualify him for a diploma as an estate manager, and he was studying for another exam.

We had a goat and chickens. Wim ordered additional pullets; having one's own eggs was useful, though a certain number of eggs per hen had to be handed over to the Germans if one wanted to receive an allocation of poultry feed.

Madzy had part-time help in the house, but she did a good deal of the work herself. Wim's raincoat was sent to the cleaners. Preparations were made for the baby's arrival. She would give birth at home as was customary, with the local doctor officiating; a private nurse, the friend of a friend, came to stay. Other preparations for the birthing included having Madzy's bed put on blocks to make it easier for her attendants.

On Wednesday, 13 May 1942, Gerard Willem was born. Two days later Madzy was still in bed; it had been a difficult birth, and in any case it was the practice then for new mothers to remain in bed for about two weeks.

DURING THE preceding two years, Wim and Madzy had been reminded once a month that he was still an army officer. With other demobilized officers, he had to go to Amersfoort – ten kilometres away, cycling distance – to report to the German authorities. The official he reported to always asked what work he was doing. Wim's work in agriculture was acceptable, because indirectly it supported the war effort – which meant, of course, the German war effort.

But that May the pattern changed. Wim received notice that on Friday, 15 May 1942, his next scheduled reporting day, he was to go to a German army unit in Ede. This was twenty kilometres away and meant travelling by rail. It was lovely spring weather. Leaving Madzy still in bed after the birth, telling her that he would be back on the train arriving at six o'clock, he rode his bicycle to the station and took the morning train to Ede. He had with him a scribbler of notes; he would spend the short train trip studying for his exam. Because of the fine weather he wore his ordinary suit, with no coat.

It was more than three years before he returned.

White-pine cones, drawn by Madzy in late middle age

CHAPTER FIVE

Wartime, 1942–1945

18 May 1942
Maarn

My dearest,

[This book] will be a description of the life that I and the children lived without you while waiting for the happiest day of our lives – the day when you return to us and the champagne cork pops.[1]

I could write a thousand things of what happened during the first days, but let us skip over them quickly. It is still too difficult for me to write very much about it. I worried during the whole of Friday the 15th,[2] but when you didn't return at 6:30 and I didn't get a phone call I almost panicked. At 8:30 Wendela left me alone with the children and went to phone Amersfoort and came back with alarming news. At 9:30 Moeder Iete came from de Hoogt with the news that you all were detained. Dr van Kekem came at 10:30. Pankie slept that night with me.[3]

The next day was spent anxiously waiting for news. No letter. Moeder Hans came and stayed for the night. On Sunday Marietje[4] fetched the mail and we got your so-called letter.[5] Oh, my dear boy, when I got it I cried more than I had done during all the labour of giving birth. Let's not think about it ...

I thought only of you and of the moment when you had to choose between your conscience and your wife. I will never know how difficult that must have been.[6]

And then I worried about your well-being.

But I had to think of your son. I consider Gerard Willem more as your son than as mine – no, more as a gift from me to you, for whom I now have to care with my very best efforts in order to give him to you healthy and sound when you come home.

I will not talk about the countless signs of sympathy, the visits and the tears shed around the cradle. But I must tell that Kraaloogje [one of the hens] who had – out of grief – disappeared for two days, put in an appearance again this morning.

There were innumerable arrangements to make. I got Vlastuin [a neighbouring farmer] to fetch the goat; no one knew how to look after it. They asked me where the chicken feed was, etc. I didn't know anything. How unprepared we were!

I asked Oom Willy[7] to come in order to ask him if he could make personal contact with you in Ede to tell you that I was well, and Gerard Willem also – not knowing that you had already been for days in Germany. I also asked him if he would, if there was a chance, speak in connection with the possibility that some officers would be released because of work they did.[8] He said he would if he had a chance. "But not against our conscience," I warned him, and so he left again after five minutes.

Your suitcase had to be packed. I spent all day thinking what to include. Everybody helped, but I was unable to walk and check on everything.[9] Moeder Iete dived into the trunk of winter clothes and found your uniform. I selected the shoes and put new laces in them. Finally, in the evening, Wendela and I packed it with incredible care. On my behalf she walked all through the house, and she brought rolls of toilet paper, and your windbreaker. Moeder Hans packed your toilet articles. And in the evening at 9:30 came VaVa [a neighbour and close friend] begging to be allowed to add something: she brought chocolate and peanut butter and something else.

And now I realize that when I wrote the label I omitted a part of the address. Will you get the suitcase soon? I will be glad to hear that you received everything. Be sure to remember that we packed it with our best care and love.[10]

Oh! we forgot your slippers! That's terrible! But we included nine hard-boiled eggs, half a pound of butter, a tin of paté and pipe tobacco and cookies. Caspar weighed it. Tante Betsy gave labels to attach to it. Hester Laman Trip [a friend of Madzy's] soaked the dangerous labels off the suitcase.[11] Finally Tante Betsy's Piet [the house boy] brought it personally to Ede.[12]

Today Jet and Vader [Wim's father and stepmother] came; more tears around the cradle. The little one is really being sprinkled. We will never forget his first days, so full of sorrow and sadness about your departure. But nor will we forget the sympathy and help we received from everybody, even from Vlastuin, where the goat is staying.

This morning Mr. and Mrs. Stratenus came by in their car.[13] Moeder Iete received them. They remain loyal to you and told her, "We don't know how we will manage without your son-in-law."

It's now Monday evening. Juus came and the household is again running quite well. Gerard Willem is still drinking too much (150 grams each time) and he gets only five feedings. He slept all day, but Wendela says that that's because yesterday I took tranquillizers and sleeping pills.

Now I'm going to sleep with full faith that I can carry out the task which God has entrusted to me and that I can be proud to have such a courageous husband. May God bring us together again. We both will then have learned a lesson, namely that to earn happiness like ours we have to make a great effort, and that such a thing is not dropped in one's lap. We love each other so much that it can bridge the great distance from Linz[14] to Maarn. You have a heavy task – to keep up your spirits far from everything you love. I hope your friends will help you.[15] My task is, all of a sudden, to care for our two children, the house, the garden and the animals. I will try to do everything in the way you would have done it; the garden with help from a labourer, the animals with advice from Dick Kolff. In all this I will miss your help and advice, but I will have the feeling that I'm doing everything to the best of my ability. I will have to fill the days with this work, and it will indeed fill them. May it not last too long: that is my deepest wish and my intense and daily prayer to God. I am, after all, a soldier's wife and a Dutch woman. Now I have to show that I am worthy of it. You have bravely followed your con-science and mine. Now I have to show that I am brave also. I need this lesson badly as I have been till now too self-centred and selfish. From now on my thoughts and deeds will be only for you, Marianke, and Gerard Willem. I will count myself out and live only for the three of you. That will be my life. God will help me and I will pray every evening in Christ's name that you may be brought back healthy and safe as soon as possible. I leave everything in the house as it was, your coat and hat hanging in the hall, the books on your desk, your pipes in the rack. I still base my hopes on the one chance you have: that you will be released because of your work in agriculture. That hope supports me and makes me strong. One thing I have received already: my faith in God, which means a great deal. Up to now I hesitated, but now I know that there is a God and that everything has a purpose.

You may be safer where you are than here with us. Less danger of bombing there, and if there were an English invasion you would not have to fight. Prisoners of war don't have it too bad in general. We will try to send you as much food as possible. If you only can stand up to it in your spirit. If you are tough, I will be too.

My dearest, I hear the rain from a thunderstorm on the roof above my head. And fortunately it's becoming a little cooler, because I'm swimming in perspiration in bed. I am going to dream of your homecoming, as I will do every night and I will ask God to keep you safe for us.

THE DIARY is one long letter addressed to Wim. It is written in two large hardback notebooks. To save paper – no doubt rationed or unobtainable – she leaves no margins, and at times her writing is small and compressed, though her normal handwriting was bold and round. When she had filled the second notebook – but had to continue the diary because Wim was still away – she used loose sheets torn out of a school scribbler. The diary is about eighty thousand words long – a book-length work in itself.

On the back flyleaf of the first volume are gardening notes for the following year, and questions: "How do I do the hoeing under the strawberry net? Herbs and flowers take too much space from vegetables." There is a calendar on which she was crossing off the days (of Wim's absence, no doubt) in 1942 and again from September 1944 on. There are a few random notes: "Churchill says that it can still last months."

She writes that she intends to give the diary to Wim when he returns, but at times it reads like one half of a conversation with him: she asks questions as though expecting immediate answers. At other times the entries are like letters to which she will receive a speedy reply: she explains problems, asks for information and advice. Often, however, it is all inward turning, talking to herself, or talking into the emptiness where he used to be. Towards the end, when he has been away for so long that she feels as though he has completely disappeared (and when she does not know whether he is still alive), he is occasionally no longer "you" but "Wim."

In May 1976 she reread the diary. By then she was sixty-five years old, living in Canada, and crippled with rheumatoid arthritis. She was using audio tapes for correspondence and for recording her childhood memories. At Gerard's urging, she put on tape some of her memories of the years of her husband's absence, drawing on her "book" and providing additional details and comments. This narrative is in English, addressed to her children, and in what follows I use it from time to time.

She comments that the diary is written in pencil. "I usually wrote it at the end of the day in the bedroom, in my bed, where I was lying next to the empty bed of Dad and at that time of course we didn't have ballpoints but fountain pens and you never used a fountain pen in bed because you were sure to leave blobs of ink on your nice white sheets."

THE DIARY sounds at first like a totally uncensored outpouring, but as I worked with it and other materials and learned more about the conditions of the time, I came to realize that it is much more circumspect than it appears. Because Madzy was aware that it could fall into the hands of the Germans, it contains nothing that might endanger herself or her friends. The German police regularly raided private houses looking for stockpiles of food, for Jewish people in hiding, for men who should have gone to Germany to work in industries and labour camps but went underground instead, for any evidence of disobedience to their regulations. These "*razzias*," as the raids were called, were arbitrary, sudden, frightening. From what Madzy told us later, we know some of the things about which, in the diary, she was silent. We know that she lent books to a Canadian airman shot down nearby and hidden by one of her friends, or possibly even by herself. On tape and in a short story she mentions that in the area around Maarn – thickly wooded and, by Dutch standards, thinly populated – there were large numbers of men in hiding and much underground activity. A diary of the last year of the war by Dientje Blijdenstein refers to this, but, as she clearly states, she added this sensitive material only after the war. In the last winter of the war, Dientje reports that VaVa Hoogewegen, another neighbour, harboured two English officers and a secret radio transmitter, and that the Germans arrested three local leaders of the underground.[16] Madzy would have known about all this but does not mention it in her diary.

In daily life, fearful of endangering herself and the children, she kept as much as possible to the regulations. In a time and place where one's principles had become irrelevant or even dangerous, where any assertiveness or individuality was likely to be ferociously punished, she was extremely cautious. Her knowledge of German meant that in her contacts with officials and the police she could understand what they were saying and reply appropriately – which mostly meant carefully, submissively. She records things that happened to other people; some of these were rumours, as she makes clear, but they were frightening all the same. Dutch women were punished for singing the national anthem. A family was evicted and their house destroyed because nails had been scattered on the street in front of it to puncture German tires. (There was no danger of Dutch tires being punctured, because by then almost all Dutch vehicles had been requisitioned by the Germans.) The Germans took hostages from among the civilians to ensure the good behaviour of the rest of the population. An undetermined number of these hostages were shot.[17]

BUT THERE were ways of resisting. Many years later, Madzy wrote a story about one of those instances of the triumph of the underdog so crucial to morale in difficult times.

In May 1943[18] the Germans ordered the Dutch to turn in their radios, their daily link with the free world.

> Always, every day, promptly at ten o'clock,[19] the Dutch turned off the light and "went to bed." Then they gathered around their hidden radio set to listen to Radio Orange sent out from England with the latest news. It told us how to resist and how to disobey the invaders. Now and then Queen Wilhelmina talked to us, a special broadcast. Then her sympathetic, motherly but also firm and positive voice always brought the tears to our eyes; the broadcast ended with a few bars of the national anthem.
>
> "I'm not going to give up my radio," I muttered.

The decree ordered that radios had to be turned in that evening at the school gym. The narrator's friend Pete offers her an old radio – known in Pete's family as "Uncle Sebastian's Pet" – which she can turn in so as to pretend to comply with the regulations. She accepts.

> Later that afternoon, to my slight dismay, I watched Willem, the gardener's son, stagger up the driveway pushing a wheelbarrow with all his strength. From it protruded a bulk hidden under a potato sack. Uncle Sebastian's Pet certainly seemed voluminous to me. And, indeed, it consisted of two large wooden boxes. One is the radio, the other the batteries, explained Willem.
>
> That evening, I hoisted one of the boxes with great difficulty on the carrier of my bicycle, fastened it as well as possible with ropes to the saddle, and, holding it in place with one hand, pushed the bicycle with the other. Once I hit a pothole in the dark and it almost slid off but I just caught it in time.
>
> In the gym stood a long row of tables, a row of expectant German soldiers behind them, while the villagers (all wearing their familiar

poker faces) trooped in with the most remarkable conglomeration of contraptions – some big boxes with heavy lids, some on wheels, and one with a "His Master's Voice" trumpet. Some had to be carried by two men ... I put my monster beside Pete's and explained to the German who regarded me with some suspicion that the next instalment still had to come.

At that very moment, all the lights clicked off and we were engulfed in a silent gloom, only lightened by the moonlight from outside. All the fuses had blown when one of the radios was being tested. New fuses were brought, the light flipped on again, and I pushed my way to the door.

Soon, red from exhaustion, I returned with the second box. Now the gym was illuminated with some candles. Pete whispered that the fuses had blown twice more, and now the Germans were out of fuses. They were in a vile mood, and they gave out receipts to everyone and put the owner's name on the radios. I arrived home just in time for the Radio Orange broadcast behind the chimney in the attic.

Madzy's own radio, brought back with them from America, was hidden in an awkward little hole upstairs behind a cupboard and the chimney.

After the war, according to the semi-fictionalized account, the narrator and her husband receive a notice to come to a barn and pick up their property: the confiscated radio.

During the last winter of the war, when there was no longer any electricity, many people's radios would have fallen silent, but some people had battery-operated sets – and batteries. In one passage in the diary Madzy reports bringing home a "cabinet" from a friend's house. In the taped narrative of 1976, she indicates that that "cabinet" was a radio. On another occasion, the diary refers to the radio as "the canary bird." There is evidence, therefore, that occasionally, even in that last winter, she and her friends were able to listen to a radio.

The story of the confiscation of the radios is told amusingly (and, of course, long after the event), and the episode was indeed one of the lighter moments of a grim time. And after all, there *was* a working radio hidden behind the chimney.

LYING IN BED after Gerard's birth, her mood alternating between anguished grief and the desperate need to keep home and family going, Madzy was already organizing the work that needed to be done. Wim's paperwork had to be returned to Mr Stratenus: Wendela delivered it.

Madzy's bed had to be lowered off the blocks. Income tax had to be paid: Wim's stepmother, Jet, who was good at finances, came to do it. Wendela took photos of Madzy and the children to send to Wim.

But for nearly six weeks there was no information concerning his whereabouts, no word from him, nothing.

> Sunday, May 24. Whitsunday. No, it is impossible, impossible, impossible. They've taken him to Germany, my Dicks,[20] my own Dicks! They can't do that, they can't take away my own Dicks! They *can't*!
>
> I've screamed these words, though while giving birth four days earlier, I didn't make a sound. I screamed so loud, so loud ...
>
> A week ago.
>
> It seems longer than a month ...
>
> Oh God, how much longer?

In the narrative photo album there are two photos of Madzy sitting in a garden chair. In the first I am standing beside her; in the second I am perched on a corner of the chair. Beside the first one, which shows her attempting a smile, Madzy wrote: "The first day downstairs – 20 May 1942. How sad, but Marianke's joy was a comfort." In the other, clearly taken a minute or so later, we both look a good deal sadder; Madzy is gaunt and grim. "All the same, we're not looking cheerful." No, indeed.

Haggard and grim as she was, this was the moment at which she really took up her new life, determined to do what had to be done. Photos on the same page of the album show her hugging the new baby and looking a bit better. Certainly she is smiling, and the smile was – to judge by the diary – genuine delight in the baby.

One thing demanding immediate attention was the garden. Wim had planted vegetables that spring, and the garden was important because of the increasingly stringent rationing of food. Already there were no potatoes to be had in the store, even with rationing coupons. Maintaining and weeding the garden, therefore – producing as much food as she could – was essential. She had gardened a little during her stay in England, but since her marriage Wim had done it. Now she had to pick up where he had left off. She received some advice from other people, read books, tried this and that.

Now that she was on her feet, she was busy all day long. Probably it was partly nervous tension and the need to distract herself from her fears and worries, but it also gave her a sense of accomplishment. One evening she reported what she had done that day.

Madzy in May 1942, out of bed for the first time after giving birth to Gerard, with Marianne

Evening: For a person who gave birth 11 days ago (last time I was still in the hospital) I have done quite a bit. This morning I tidied up the house and packed the silver because that will be stored at Tante Betsy's. I don't like the idea that we [Juus was with her], as women living alone in such an isolated house, should have so many nice things in the house. Then came Tante Gusta and Tante Ida[21] ... This afternoon we did some hoeing and raking in the flower garden. Then came Dientje, and afterwards we walked to de Boerderij [VaVa Hoogewegen's house]. This evening we sowed flower seeds. The garden is growing like mad. Several beds where I thought plants were not germinating are now displaying young plants – beets, carrots, beans, and cabbage, according to Dientje. The day after tomorrow Gijs [an employee of Dientje's] will hoe the potatoes. Tomorrow I will hoe the gravel paths, which look like a lawn. Well, and then I did a very brave thing – grabbing Kraaloogje [the vagrant hen], who still prefers to live in the orchard, and putting her inside the pen. I will do that from now on. The hens also got potato peelings again, which they devoured. I really feel again that I am the boss in my own house. I discovered that the shutters in front of the windows had not been locked since May 15. Wendela did not know that they should be. There is a lot to do. I also want to go to the loft of the barn to get the mattress down, otherwise the mice will eat it.[22] I cannot find your army swords.[23] The air gun I keep: a good weapon to have in this isolated place.

I read in the paper that we have to supply 15 eggs per chicken per year.[24] Fortunately I just put 32 eggs in preservative.

I put a little sign "Pull" on the garden gate, which had been mistreated by all the visitors.

I sent all your papers [relating to a part-time job of Wim's] to the Forestry service and wrote a couple of letters.

All the work – although I can do little, otherwise my back hurts too much – gives me a push to tackle life again and to hope for a happier time. No thinking, just work hard and drop into bed in the evening fagged-out. That is the best.

I gave Pankie her own flower garden where she may do the seeding herself. She is so excited about it that today, when I put her on the potty, she asked if there are already any plants coming up. She is constantly saying to me, "You are so nice!" The darling girl.

We don't read now in the evening, but instead we work in the garden. The corn is coming up and in a few places with four blades.

When will I have to transplant them? I don't think I'll have your advice in time.

I am also going to learn to milk the goat. And I'll clean its pen, wearing your coverall. Also the chicken pen, which is very dirty. The barn is a terrible mess.

Gerard was in the bath today for the first time and found it quite amusing.

On other days, in addition to the kind of work listed here, she collected firewood in the woods beside the cottage and chopped or broke it up. She mowed the lawn.

June 1, afternoon. As soon as Gerard had had his bath and was nursed and outside in the pram, I went to the garden. First I weeded the carrots and beets. Then I dug up the bed where the *koolmoes* had been,[25] and raked it, and sowed more carrots. Then I put in a row of lettuce where radishes and cress had been. Then it was 12:30. A bit later, after my rest, I'll weed the potatoes and tonight I might just do the beans. Soon the spinach bed will also be dug over but we are still cutting from it, and because in all of Holland there are no vegetables for sale we have to use the spinach up to the last bit.

The next day she reports where the country's agricultural produce is going:

Fifty per cent goes to Germany, 30% to the German army here, 10% to the Germans living in Holland, and 10% for the Dutch population, and most of that to the big cities in order to prevent unrest, and because in the country people are likely to have something. But no one has anything. For potatoes we have to wait until late July. (Where is that big basket that you had?) We still have 5 kg left over. We got nothing on any of our coupons last week, and those coupons have expired.

More immediate worries sometimes helped to form a screen against the bigger ones, but not always. The anguish was lying in wait for her when she was alone. On 21 May she writes: "There is one thing which I find absolutely unbearable. That is lying in bed and listening to the trains passing. Then I have the same feelings as on that unhappiest evening of my life: Friday 15 May, when I lay listening and waiting for you, not knowing that you were already no longer in Holland."

Elsewhere she writes:

I wait for the train which brings you to me: mid-September, you said. And again my heart beats and my throat chokes me and it is again as when we were recently married and I would walk towards the station in the dark and hang over the railing of the bridge and look at the commuter trains coming from New York. Which one would bring you home? And I wait and wait with beating heart, holding my breath and praying to God: "Oh bring him, bring him ... in this train, in this train."

On Sunday, 7 June:

Evening: And still it is so hard to rest in my trust in God. When, as happened this evening, I had busily watered the garden [with a watering can filled at the hand-pump] and hoed, and made the goat's stall clean and the barn tidy (everything done for you), and I think: "If Dicks came here now and said 'Matje, how neatly you've done that'" – and I'm suddenly convinced that you'll definitely be back today, and that I can't survive another day or night without you – then it is as if I break inside and don't know where I can find the strength to say goodnight to Pankie with a cheerful face and to whisper to her, as I do every evening, "Pappa will soon be coming back." Then I feel how much I love you, how poorly I have expressed that recently and how unhappy that makes me. Oh, Dicks, I love you more than anybody ever loved a man after nearly 6 years of married life. I love you so intensely that I would do anything to have you back in my arms. Let the British come and destroy the house and chase us out of this country in order to fight here; let suffering and difficulties come over us, if only you return very soon to your Matje, who can't live without you, not one day, not one night, not one hour. At this moment I am not a normal person any longer, my soul has gone with you to the camp and only my body walks around here and does my daily tasks: cares for the children, cares for house and garden, laughs and "keeps a stiff upper lip," as everybody remarks with amazement. But you've taken my soul with you. Do you feel that? Do you feel that I am with you, day and night, awake or asleep?

My Dicks, if and when you return, take me close in your arms and hold me tight, tight, tight to you and try to heal the hurt which has stricken me so deeply.

THE WAR WAS a constant presence. On 31 May, the day after the Allied bombing of Cologne, she had written: "Last night an unbelievable uproar from het Noordhout [the German anti-aircraft battery in the woods near de Hoogt], with shrieking shells above our heads, bombs that made the house rumble, and everywhere in the distance sirens." On 2 June: "Last night there was again a more-than-hellish racket: the flying went on for hours over our heads and het Noordhout fired so ferociously that the house shook and the glasses and bottles on the washbasin rattled. I fell asleep only at 2:30, and at 3:00 Gerard started crying, until 4:30. Can you imagine that I had trouble waking up at 7:15?" On 8 June: "Darling, it is already after 11:30, and if they start flying again in a few minutes there won't be much time for sleeping, with Gerard crying and Pankie frequently getting me out of bed with a bad dream. Therefore only a short talk."

Some things she never even mentioned. There were searchlights raking the sky, but it is not until she is in northern Canada, fifteen years later, that she writes about them because the northern lights remind her of them.[26]

In the 1976 taped narrative, reviewing the daily accounts in the diary itself and adding things not recorded there, she comments:

> During all those three years we were so much in danger of being bombed ... Airplanes were shot down several times; they fell in big fiery balls. Luckily no plane fell too near us, but I know that one must have fallen about half a mile away from us in the middle of the night – which, with bombs or ammunition in it, made a lot of noise. Big scares always happened when concentrated groups of Germans came and put up tents in the neighbourhood because those were the places where the Allies dropped bombs, and of course they knew soon enough by underground ways where these concentrations of either Germans or ammunition were. So when you go over this diary you see constantly how noisy it was during the nights and how little sleep we got. And of course by day we had to do our work and find food, so the days were very, very busy and very tiring.

For several weeks she received no news of where Wim was, or how he was. Then the long-awaited first word came.

> June 9, afternoon. This morning came your first "sign of life" from Nüremberg! But what was it! – in German, printed, and only the address in your handwriting, and the only personal thing was the date. And then your number, which affected me horribly.

And it arrived – after all that waiting – at a very strange moment. I stood with Pankie and Gerard on the platform at the railway station, waiting for Moeder Hans, who came walking towards us – and then Marietje came waving that card. What a deep disappointment, that nasty bit of paper. Yes, my boy, now I have to be thankful that you are alive, and healthy, and I know that on 29 May you were in Nüremberg. But I'm terribly unhappy. I had imagined your first card: "Dearest Matje," etc., etc. I had already, in imagination, received so many cards, but not this, not this ...

The disappointment and grief and anger bring on heart palpitations, and from then on she often mentions her health, not in self-pity but because so much depends on her ability to keep going. She had had heart trouble in the United States – she says it was caused by the heat, but one wonders whether the loneliness might have been sufficiently stressful to affect her health. Certainly now, in 1942, the stress makes her heart race and causes her to feel weak. It was to get worse, aggravated by the need to go out and scrounge for food (some of those journeys were an appalling physical strain), by the hunger she suffered in the last terrible winter of the war, by all the other stresses.

Throughout the three years of Wim's absence, she was surrounded by people – sometimes too many of them, especially in the last winter of the war when (with the addition of evacuees from the bombed-out city of Arnhem) the cottage accommodated about a dozen. In the earlier years too there were always local visits to be paid and visitors to be received, dealings with people who helped her in the house and the garden, and friends and relatives from further away. Because Madzy had no phone, anyone wondering how she was or whether there was any word from Wim came to the house.

She was almost never alone with the children, and she treasured the rare afternoon or evening when she was. Wendela stayed for several weeks, and then Wim's sister Lies came with her little daughter, Monica, apparently for a couple of weeks. Juus came early on and stayed until the end of the war. She was in her late fifties now, and she and Madzy were deeply attached to each other. But the situation was strained because Juus had well-defined ideas about bringing up children. She and Madzy often gave me different instructions, which made me fractious. Juus was possessive of children; besides, she no doubt regarded Madzy as still half a child herself. However, because of Juus's presence Madzy could go out visiting family and friends, including her brother Joost who lived in the care of three elderly ladies in

Driebergen, about eight kilometres away. She went shopping in the village and (especially in the last winter) made expeditions in search of food.

Besides Juus, Madzy often had part-time help. Marietje, the neighbour, assisted with housework, and Willem, the son of the estate gardener, did the heaviest garden work.

Her most difficult personal relations were still with her mother. Iete had come to live in Maarn after being evacuated from The Hague because her house was in an area that the Germans cleared to make room for artillery installations. She had to pack up in a hurry and put much of her furniture in storage, but she gave away many things. Madzy later recalled, "It's rather sad to think that most of our beautiful books – beautiful editions Father had collected, the old editions of Charles Dickens' books with the original paintings or drawings ... were sold for very little money. However, at that time we didn't care much about personal belongings. If we only were able to keep alive and see each other again at the end of the war, that was all we were aiming at."

In Maarn, Iete lived first in the house of the mayor and his wife, whom she knew, and then, along with quite a number of other evacuees, at de Hoogt. She visited Madzy almost daily, and her interfering ways (perhaps well-meant, but intensely tactless) were a trial. However, she helped Madzy financially, both with direct gifts of money and by buying black-market food.

Madzy also provided emotional support and reassurance to Wim's mother, Hans Hoogewerff, who lived in The Hague and, when the trains were still running, sometimes came to visit.

Other contacts were more sustaining. Christie van Notten and Dientje Blijdenstein lived less than a kilometre away. VaVa Hoogewegen was even closer. The local doctor, Ad van Kekem, and his wife, Dick, were good friends to us. Wim's Tante Betsy de Beaufort, at de Hoogt, had become very close to Madzy. Charlotte and Dick Kolff lived in Amersfoort, ten kilometres away. Madzy regularly made the trip by bicycle or on foot, and they were a source of support. Especially in the last winter of the war, they gave Madzy food grown in the greenhouses on their estate. Annetje Nahuys was manager of a small hotel located a few kilometres from Maarn. Near the end of the war, when the hotel was requisitioned as a residence for German army officers, she visited Madzy regularly with news she picked up and bits of food she was able to purloin.

These contacts in no way diminished Madzy's anguish and longing for Wim, but for the most part they were a help and support. The friendships they formed at this time continued for the rest of their lives.

FOLLOWING THAT first postcard from Wim, there was again a silence. It was not until 1 July that Madzy received the first real letter – the fifth that Wim had written (he numbered them). As soon as she had his address, she sent long letters herself. Before that, the frustration of not being able to communicate with him must, for such a "writing" person, have been a large component in her worry and loneliness.

Prisoners and their families were at first allowed to correspond in Dutch, but all the letters were censored. For this, Dutch-reading censors were needed, and by the end of the year the German authorities found themselves unable to handle the volume. To curtail the length of the letters, they began issuing prisoners with printed forms (letter-length and postcard-length) with ruled lines and instructions that nothing was to be written except on the lines. Half of the form was for the prisoner to write on and a half was for the recipient's reply. Wim was able to write in very small script (I had to use a magnifying glass to read the two surviving postcards), but even so the space was severely limited. The postcards had seven ruled lines; the letter-length forms were (as I recall) perhaps twice as long.

The cards and letters arrived irregularly. Madzy recorded the number of each one that arrived. The failure of some of the letters to reach her meant that communication was fragmented: some things that Wim wrote in those precious few words were mysterious or even alarming. To pass censorship, she and Wim wrote partly in a code that they invented as they went along. Mostly this code was clear to both of them, but once or twice she writes in the diary about being in an agony of confusion.

The overall lack of reliable information, and therefore the uncertainty, led to an incalculable amount of stress. There were rumours in Holland about where the POWs were, and about whether they were treated properly and had enough to eat, and about their being punished for disobeying the rules. No one knew where the rumours came from – Dientje Blijdenstein, in the diary written later in the war, was sure that they were deliberately circulated by the Germans. On 23 May, Madzy records a whole batch:

> They say that the 65 officers who went into POW camp 2 years ago have been added to your camp in Austria, that you waited in Bentheim until your suitcases arrived. They say that you are in Linz, Heiligenblut, Graz, Innsbruck. They say that you can get 3 parcels per month from us, and 2 parcels from the Red Cross, and that we can use your coupons for this, and that we ourselves can also send parcels (of 5 kg) containing books and clothing. They say that you can send a postcard 4 times per month and 2 letters, and we as many

Madzy with Marianne and Gerard in March 1943. Madzy sent this to Wim in
the POW camp: it is stamped as having been passed by the censors.

as we like (everything in Dutch). They say that it's a nice idea that you can wear your uniforms, and that you will be comfortable. And they say much more – that you have to do without collar and tie, and that you've had all your hair shaved off – so I'd better not write any more because it makes me wretched.

Some reliable information did filter back from the camps because, in the months following the imprisonment, specific groups such as medical doctors, and prisoners who were ill, were sent home. On 15 June Madzy visited a woman who had spoken with a doctor recently returned from the camp at Nüremberg on account of his health. When Madzy got home she typed a letter – careful, detailed – on onionskin, with several carbons, and sent the copies to her mother, to Wim's father and stepmother, and no doubt to Wim's mother. She reports that the prisoners are all right but that they lack occupation and that the food is barely adequate. Wim's suitcases arrived about two weeks after being sent, having been carefully searched by the Germans. Washing and sanitary arrangements are primitive. The prisoners have bedding but no sheets; those are still expected. Adjacent to the camp containing the Dutch POWs is a camp of Serbian prisoners, who are better supplied and frequently throw some of their rations and cigarettes over the fence to the Dutch.

There were rumours about what was going on in Holland itself, and also real and terrible news. On 22 August 1942 she mentions executions of the kind that became increasingly common.

> Boy Ruys[27] has been executed. We're all appalled. Poor May, poor Tante Anna. Five hostages also executed, all young men. The husband of Kathy Telders and two brothers-in-law of Flos Telders. It's as though we're all shattered – that's how it feels. Then I ask myself whether it would be safe here for you all. But over there in Poland[28] it is also not so wonderful. I worry about you every day, and will also do it when you are back here, so long as the war continues. It makes no difference. Life is gradually reaching its saddest point. And with each passing train, I think, "Dicks maybe?" I'm getting so tired, so tired.
>
> And then still the [Allied] invasion!

The only more-or-less reliable source of public news was the radio broadcasts from England, though sometimes the authorities there were out of touch with actual conditions in the Netherlands. All Dutch newspapers were controlled by the Germans, and Madzy never refers to them. There was a fragmentary underground press; I imagine that she saw those publications, but she doesn't say so. In the last winter of the war, with no electricity and most radios silenced, she makes few references to the larger picture of the war. She apparently knew little more than what she herself could hear or see: planes flying over, bombs falling, artillery fire, a sudden burst of activity among the German troops in the neighbourhood, more *razzias* to collect men for work in German labour camps, more executions or other punishment for local people who had contravened some regulation or irritated the authorities.

One of the most dangerous elements in all this was that there were Nazi sympathizers in Holland – no one knew how many, or who might turn out to be one. That a neighbour might be spying on you, reporting everything you did, added to the tension.[29] Again this is something about which Madzy was nearly silent.

IN THE FALL of 1942, Madzy enrolled me in a kindergarten in Doorn. I was apparently a loner, mentally older than my years, and Madzy felt that it would be good for me to play with other children. She talks to me about this on one of the tapes she made late in life: "I had to go in the morning with you on the bicycle and bring you there, over that hill and past 't Huis te Maarn ... After three days you started to cough and I kept you home, and then you started on whooping cough and pneumonia and that was the end of that *kleuter klasje*. I don't think you were ever unhappy about that at all, and actually I was happy too ... You hated it, and once you hated something, that was it."

Gerard caught whooping cough and pneumonia. At the same time (October to December 1942) Madzy was sick with jaundice, and she again got the terrible skin rash she had when she was pregnant with me.

One effect of the occupation was that schooling became irregular and soon stopped; the Germans would not allocate fuel to heat the schools. Madzy organized a class to be held in our barn. In the diary she barely alludes to it – self-censorship again, because in a memoir written after the war she says that it included "Jewish children that had to be hidden away and a Jewish woman, a very beautiful and intelligent woman, who took that in hand and made music and sang and gave little lessons and so on." It did not last long; after it failed, Madzy set up another little class. "I could only get three boys and you [Marianne] together, and the wife of the principal was a teacher and she gave lessons. But that wasn't too much of a success. And then those two girls came whose grandfather protected you when bombs were falling nearby ... *that* was not too much of a success. And then after those bombs fell, you were so afraid that you didn't want to leave the house anymore. And I can understand that, and at that time I had to give in."

From November 1942 to February 1943 there is a gap in the diary; when it resumes, the terrible aching longing for Wim's return has been partly replaced by a tone that is sometimes more calm and balanced but sometimes very grim. "10 February 1943. What a long time it's been since I last wrote! But we all have been sick – whooping cough and jaundice – and this book has not been touched. Besides, I did not have the need because I was able to write quite a lot to you, my darling. But now that we have to use those horrible forms and write telegram style I again need an outlet in this book."

With spring the outdoor work resumes.

> March 1. The following conversation took place this afternoon between Pank [Marianne], who in her warm winter clothes was sitting playing in the sandbox, and Mamma.
>
> Mamma comes out and asks: "Pank, what did Pappie do last year about the apple tree? Do you remember? How did he clean it?"[30]
>
> "With those brushes, you know, Mammie, those steel brushes."
>
> "Do you know where they are?"
>
> "Have a look in Pappie's tool cupboard."
>
> Pank carries on making a pie of sand.
>
> "Come along," Mamma says, "and then you can show me."
>
> We nose around in the cupboard.
>
> "They're black, and hard," says Pank.
>
> But we don't find them.
>
> Mamma looks round and sees them on high shelf in the barn.
>
> "Good for you," says Pank. "Yes, yes, that's them."
>
> "And how did Pappa cut off the dead branches?"
>
> "Oh, golly," says Pank, "with those scissors which you send back to Tante Lotje."
>
> "Well, then I'll have to do it with a knife. Do you happen to know how Tante Dientje's gardeners do it?"
>
> "Oh, yes, Mammie, with a saw."
>
> What do you say to such a helper?

This is a remarkable passage, showing her as the artist, detached enough from the incident so that she sees it from outside as well as inside.

In May she marks the first anniversary of Wim's being imprisoned with an account of how she spent the day.

Saturday, 15 May 1943.

It was a year ago ...

And the pain again tears through my soul, through my lonely heart ...

A year has passed, the blackest year of my life so far.

My thoughts today went back to that Friday, a year ago, and again I saw before me that little cradle with that rosy baby, a little world in himself in the middle of a sea of misery.

"They took my Dicks away from me!" – one cry of the many many cries from many hundreds of women, all those women who had to stay behind alone, bereft in their empty houses, their abandoned bedrooms, their lonely beds.

The day before yesterday our son was one year old. In my heart I was deeply thankful that this most dangerous year of his life had passed safely, but I wasn't actually happy. Real happiness doesn't penetrate through to my shrouded spirit. It is still as though I'm living in a cage and my soul is muffled up, numbed.

Maybe, later on, you'd be interested to hear how I spent this day. Up at 7:00 and quickly pull on a dress and open the shutters. Nowadays Pank does this with me, after she has got into her slippers and dressing gown. We go to the bathroom, and then Pank begs me for a slice of bread. Geert sits enthroned on his potty for the first time of the day. Juus makes tea and warms up Geert's porridge. When the shutters are open and we have assessed the weather, pulled up the weight of the clock, finished the slice of bread, we take our tea upstairs. I give Geert his porridge, we finish dressing ourselves while Geert is doing his "big duty" on the potty.

We had breakfast at 7:45 already, because the new food ration coupons became valid today and the food provider (me) had to be on her way.[31] Quickly discuss the menu and at 8:15 on the bike and away. De Greef fortunately had 3 heads of lettuce and (surprise) a bunch of carrots! At Steenbeek only coffee substitute, but also 1 kg of sugar and 2 jars of jam. Mailed my letter to you and went on to Driebergen. At Kraal got labels for the 7 jars of spinach I canned yesterday; at Haagedoorn calcium peppermints for you and pectin for canning fruit, also macaroni, barley, oatmeal, children's flour. Rusks at the grocer, but no sugar. Dropped off something at Joost's and then quickly back home and found Moeder Iete there, who was staying at Hotel Stameren but has now returned home. Sorted and put away all the purchases, then accompanied Moeder on part of her way back, then replied to the mail for Geert's birthday, and wrote another letter. Then lunch and children to bed. Made a parcel for you, changed my clothes, and on the bike to Suus de Boer to remember this day together[32] – taking her 3 turnips (which she can't get) and flowers. On the way home to the farmer for milk for Geert. Came home, had dinner and washed up, kids to bed. Read to Pank. Watered the lettuce in the garden and mowed the lawn. At 9:00 listened [to the radio] and then had a shower and washed my hair (I get so dirty from that garden work).

And, see – now I'm sitting in my dressing gown writing to you, and all the Saturday evenings with you pass before me, especially those in Leeuwarden with the portable bathtub in front of the living-room stove, and raisin bread afterwards. Do you remember, my boy?

After the brisk, rather hectic cheeriness, the passage ends on a darker note:

A year is frightfully long ... and there is no end in sight despite all the optimism.
But oh God, how long still do we have to endure?
And how?
And what then?
My heart is heavy with suffering and with the fear for the future.[33]

MEANWHILE MADZY and her friends continued some of the ways of peacetime. Visits were paid: though the tea and coffee were usually imitation, occasionally, for a very special event, someone would obtain the real thing on the black market. Milk, if there was any, was mostly skim; sugar and butter were rarities. But contact between friends and neighbours was essential for morale and for the exchange of information.

Hester Laman Trip, the friend who had soaked the labels off the suitcase to be sent to Wim, was to be married in spring 1943. Her family asked Madzy for some memories of their time in Leiden. Writing a poem for such occasions was a Dutch tradition; Madzy could find what it took to write one. But in it she says that what is *really* engraved in her memory is Hester's having come to keep her company when she heard of Wim's being taken prisoner. "Never shall I forget the image of you, with flowers in your hand, standing by Gerard's cradle – true to our bond of friendship."

There were other vestiges of normality. From time to time in these earlier years, Madzy mentions having a lesson in piano or in French conversation. Once she gives a talk on Homer, apparently to a French-conversation group. She takes bookkeeping lessons. Only the bookkeeping is mentioned more than once or twice, however, and even it soon petered out.

There are even touches of humour, because when she was her normal self, Madzy was often able to see the funny side of things. "I went to look after the goat, and then I saw that a wild rabbit had been at the cabbage. The gates don't close properly. I went to work like a born-and-bred carpenter and gave it my best effort, and hope that you won't ridicule my poor attempts when you come home. Better a funny-looking gate and cabbage, than a rabbit and no cabbage!"

In March 1943 Madzy went by bicycle to her Tante To, who had a birthday, taking me along. It was a major trip, thirty kilometres each way. On 30 July 1943, we made a day trip to The Hague. Madzy records wartime conditions: people sunbathing on bomb shelters, buses infrequent and hopelessly overcrowded. There was an air raid in progress when our train arrived; since the railway might be a target, we hurried away from the station and pressed ourselves against the walls of houses.

We visited Iete, apparently temporarily back in her house, did some shopping, and had a watery ice cream. Then we went home again on a very crowded train.

But the attempts at maintaining normality were "whistling in the graveyard," a small shelter for the spirit in the midst of a life of worry, stress, and deprivation – not least of personal liberty.

OF ALL THE letters that Madzy and Wim wrote to each other during his absence in the POW camp, the only ones that survive are two postcards from Wim. Because of the need to pass official censorship, however, and because of Madzy's decision to tell Wim only the good news so as not to worry him, it is likely that the letters she wrote would have added little to the abundant information in the diary.

So he didn't know much about her actual life, and she knew little about his. The effect of censorship is evident in the card that he wrote on 18 November 1943:

> Dear Mammie, Pankie and Geert. I wish you a happy and prosperous New Year and hope very much that your wishes in the new year will be granted. In the coming year Pankie has to be a good, obedient little girl, and Geert

must grow big. I hope we all stay healthy. I also send good wishes for 1944 to Grandmother [Hans], Oma Iete, Grandfather, Oma Jet, Tante Hansje, Tante Lies, Monica, Juus and Marietje. I had hoped to send them all together one of the 3 Christmas postcards which we had printed here in Stanislau, but they are not ready. When we look back on 1943, we have to be grateful that we all are doing so well in comparison with so many other people and we can look forward to 1944 with good spirits and hope. Many warm greetings to everyone from your Willem.

The card is stamped by the censors, so clearly there was nothing in it to which they could take exception. Whether there was any comfort in it for Madzy is another matter. The only meaning which I can find in it is that he hopes to be coming home in the new year, but surely that cannot have been considered reliable information.

Much later, however, he wrote about his three years in the POW camp.[34] He begins his story with the moment when he left the house in Maarn.

Madzy was still in bed with the baby on that nice spring day, and I said that I would be back on the train of 6:00 P.M. I took a scribbler with notes to study for an agriculture exam, but not a raincoat.

On the platform in Maarn I met the family de Beaufort who were seeing off their son-in-law, also a career cavalry officer, who carried a small suitcase. He told me that the night before he had been informed along the grapevine that we all would be sent to a prisoner-of-war camp.

[When we got to the German garrison in Ede] the Germans separated a small number of whom they had a record and who were later executed. We received a printed card to be filled out with our addresses, without any other words allowed, stating that our uniforms had to be delivered somewhere for sending to the camp. I wore a belt [with my suit trousers] but would need suspenders for my army breeches. Being afraid that the suspenders would not be packed, I included the word "suspenders" in the address.

By the end of the day they were on a heavily guarded train headed to Nüremberg.

Wim's memoir is factual and unemotional, giving no indication of the shock of being suddenly separated from home and family and sent to a prison camp in Germany. In the circumstances, however, it was a comparatively safe place to be. As the war continued, Wim writes, "More and more underground resistance developed and many men and women took part. As an officer I would not have been able to stay out of it. Many were caught and either shot or sent to a concentration camp." Many Dutch men, whether or not actively involved in the underground, went into hiding. The Dutch word for such men is *onderduiker*, diver: they dove out of sight. The reason for "disappearing" was to avoid being taken as a hostage to force the rest of the population to obey the occupying forces' decrees, or being drafted for work in German factories.[35] On 7 October 1942 Madzy reported that "half the village" had been conscripted for work in Germany: some of the workers were to leave the following day, and the rest the next week. Even when they went underground, men were not certain of being safe: if they were spotted by a German soldier, a Nazi sympathizer, or a neighbour with an old grudge, they might be reported.

In the POW camp Wim was comparatively safe. Unlike concentration camps, prisoner-of-war camps were governed by the regulations of the Geneva Conventions, set up to regulate conditions under which war wounded and prisoners lived.[36] Wim writes:

> In general we stayed healthy. We had our own military doctors and a dentist but few medicines. A few of us died from poor surgery in local hospitals, but otherwise we all survived. My eyesight when reading was not good and with several others and a German guard we went to the eye-specialist in the town and got glasses. It was an outing to be outside the camp.
>
> Life in the camp required adaptation. The first months were by far the most difficult, with the lack of any privacy, poor sanitation, etc. We were never badly treated by the Germans, but it was essential to keep busy. Gradually books arrived from home; also food parcels but they took a long time to reach us and food spoiled. Many of us received black ryebread which was steamed at home, not baked, and was always mouldy in and out with a yellow mould. We crumbled it and washed the grains. Later Red Cross parcels arrived, but we received far fewer than prisoners from other countries. They were not gifts but ordered and paid for by the Dutch government-in-exile in London.
>
> The parcels contained milk powder, canned meat and fish, instant coffee, margarine, and other basic food. They also contained cigarettes, which the non-smokers could trade for food.
>
> The camp food was poor, potato or cabbage soup, mostly water. One loaf of hard bread weekly containing sawdust and camphor against sexual urges.
>
> After four months we were moved to Stanislau, in the Ukraine, a week-long trip in crowded freight cars not knowing where we were going. A stop inside the fence of the concentration camp in Auschwitz gave us a scare, but

we moved on. The food was better there as the poor farmers were forced to deliver. We got musical instruments, requisitioned from the civilian population, for a 40-instrument orchestra, which gave concerts as we had good musicians and a conductor. Study groups were formed on countless subjects. I led an agriculture group, for which having books was helpful. Fourteen languages were taught, including those from Asia. We had a theatre group giving regular performances. There was a Protestant and a Catholic chaplain, who held Sunday services, and catechism classes and Bible studies. I was confirmed and when asked if I had been baptized I did not know, so I was baptized anyway.

In general there were two groups: those who studied every day and all day, even for exam credits in Holland, or were occupied in various jobs, for instance in the kitchen, sick bay, or working for escape. They were cheerful, clean, shaven; they darned socks and repaired their clothing; for them the time passed much faster than for those who played bridge all day, were grumpy, complaining about lack of cigarettes, were dirty and shabby ... I was fortunate with my interest in all that pertained to farming, having already hopeful plans of emigrating and living with Madzy and the children on a little farm. We could request study books, not by title but by subject, from the Red Cross, which were sent from the U.S.A. via Geneva, reaching us months later. This gave me books on farming in America which I wanted. In the last two years we were well up-to-date on the war news. There were several homemade radios. Some parts came from German guards, obtained in exchange for cigarettes. We had a secret group listening to the BBC. Nobody knew who or where, as there were always a few who would tell the Germans for personal favours. Each afternoon one reliable man from each barrack went to a meeting at a different place where the news was dictated, then during the evening meal, with our guard outside the door, the news was read aloud, then destroyed.

In January 1944 ... after the battle of Stalingrad ... we were moved to Neubrandenburg, between Berlin and the Baltic Sea. This was again an eight-day train trip. Accommodation there, in old wooden barracks, was far and far worse than in the big stone building in the Ukraine and so was the food, and there was no fuel. The Germans had no resources anymore, and farm production was much reduced for lack of manpower, equipment, fertilizer, etc. In the Ukraine they just took it from the population, which was not allowed in their own country.

I have quoted this at length because it provides a counterpoise to Madzy's story of the conditions under which she was living, and it is the reality behind the rumours that circulated in Holland in the early days of Wim's imprisonment.

MADZY, IN THE earlier part of her diary, writes longingly about the prospect of an Allied invasion that would liberate western Europe. That invasion came when the Allies landed in Normandy in June 1944, but it did not lead to speedy liberation. In fact, after that Madzy's life became even harder. It meant that there was actual fighting on the ground, spreading inland from the coast. The fighting caused interruptions in transportation, many more overflying aircraft, more bombing and shelling, more danger to civilians. Allied bombing increased, especially of concentrations of German troops or munitions, defence installations, and transportation corridors. Maarn was regularly bombed. Fighter planes chased trains and truck convoys. On 6 January 1945 Madzy records that several bombs had fallen in Maarn. This left a lot of broken windows in houses there – a serious matter in that bitterly cold winter as the glass could not be replaced.

Madzy's diary contains more and more references to rationing and the need to obtain food on the black market, either for money or by bartering belongings. Clothing and shoes had for a long time been unavailable in stores; by that last winter, her ski-boots, the cleats removed from the soles, were her only outdoor footwear. She unravelled her ski sweaters – relics, like the boots, of a more luxurious and leisurely life – and used the yarn to knit clothes for the children. The unravelled wool was kinky and impossible to reuse until it had been soaked and stretched: I remember wet yarn wrapped around boards and other sturdy objects, where it would dry with some (not all) of the crinkliness straightened out.

In the autumn of 1944 the electricity supply failed. The winter of 1944–45 was very cold, making the shortage of fuel and food even more of a hardship and for many a life-threatening danger. That winter, known in Holland as the "Hunger Winter," saw much suffering and a great many deaths. Starving people from the cities trekked into the countryside looking for food. People burned their furniture for heat and bartered whatever meagre belongings they still had.

Apart from there being almost no food anywhere in the country, the distribution network was no longer functioning. Railways and port installations had been destroyed. The labour drafts and other deportations had sent many Dutch men to work in German factories and driven others underground. Bakers, milkmen, workers from all parts of the food production and distribution network, were gone. Fuel shortages affected the food supply. Cars, trucks, and many bicycles had been confiscated. Most canal barges had been taken over by the Wehrmacht.[37]

No electricity meant no running water and no light. The long, cold northern nights had to be lived through. On a cloudy day it got dark at 4:00 P.M. Madzy and Juus would prepare supper (such as there was) and we would eat, and we children would be prepared for bed, all in the deepening darkness. What light they had was saved for later in the evening, for sewing by, or to allow Madzy to write. When oil was available, lights were made by pouring a thin layer of oil into a jar of water, then making a wick by inserting cotton thread through a piece of cork that would float on top. When they could, they worked by moonlight or the flickering light from the little wood heater fed with fallen branches.[38] I remember going into the woods on expeditions to gather kindling and anything that could be dragged home (and also mushrooms and beech nuts for food). I would sit close to the heater, feeding twigs through its open door to make the fire burn brightly enough for my mother to read aloud by. When there was no light, she told stories that she invented as she went along.

ON SUNDAY, 17 September 1944, the Battle of Arnhem began. Arnhem was only about fifty kilometres east of us, and the Allied airlift delivering paratroopers, guns, tanks, and other supplies flew over our heads. The aircraft included bombers, transports (many of them towing gliders), and fighters to provide protective cover.

In church that morning, Madzy heard the beginning of the operation. That evening she wrote about the events of the day:

> Sept. 17. They're here! They're coming! It's Sunday, and yesterday we were still in the mood of saying it might still take a while. This morning to church ... During the service hundreds of planes roared over us, actually irritating because although I told myself, "God, into your hands I entrust my children," still I wasn't at peace. When I got home they were in fact in a state of open-mouthed astonishment; they had counted 600 planes and then given up. Lunch at 12:30, Gerard to bed. And then I wanted to surprise Chris and Dien, because their little cabinet[39] is broken. So I went with mine through the woods. But I had barely set off when heavy shooting and much flying began. I arrived safely. At 2:30, though, there was more uproar – so bad I decided that I'd rather go home. I was, with the cabinet and the bicycle, just in the woods when planes came so close that I dropped

to the ground, bicycle and cabinet and all. Actually I lay there shaking with laughter because of my ridiculous situation, but still I got up and hurried on. I arrived home safely, but with my heart pounding.

There had been damage in the neighbourhood: a train at a nearby railway station "shot to pieces," a camp of conscripted workers set on fire:

> In the meantime, German trucks and cars came roaring and racing by on our little gravel road ... At 5:30 someone came by: "There's an army landed south of the rivers Lek and Maas! They're near Nijmegen! Arnhem is full of Americans!" She went off again. Then came Moeder Iete with the same news. We quickly ate supper and then I nipped over to tell Chris and Dien. They were in a state! Home again. They say that we aren't allowed to leave the house. Moeder left. Dien came at 7:00 with pencil and paper.[40] And now at 8:00 we've shut up the house because heavily laden cars are flying past, and we'd be fired on if we didn't do the black-out carefully. Now it's quiet for the moment. Sometimes the house trembles. Clothes and shoes lie ready in case we have to flee. Also the knapsack on the little wagon, and the bicycle with baby-seats. If I become too anxious I'll go to Dien, or ask Willem to sleep here. Now I'll read for a bit.

> 10:00: Not much news, for security reasons.[41] The British 2nd army is two miles over our border. Just now another enormous number of heavy trucks passed the house. Juus and I watched on our knees from an upstairs window. The soldiers were swearing, and sometimes they turned lights on, and they moved very slowly. Luckily there was nothing in the sky just then [no Allied planes], otherwise we'd have been fired on. Now the planes are flying continuously.
> Bedtime. I'm worried about the fact that I sleep so solidly nowadays that I hear nothing.

The battle continued until the Allied defeat and withdrawal from Arnhem on the night of 25 September – a setback that left Madzy discouraged and apprehensive.

FOR THE SAKE of morale, for the children, for pure defiance, the women occasionally organized parties. There was one on 24 September 1944, just before the Allied defeat at Arnhem.

Now I have to write quietly and in detail. It's Sunday evening after many emotions. This morning at 8, little news from the war front and we had breakfast in bed and made a nice little party of it because the weather was bad and I was not going to church. So we weren't ready and downstairs until 9:30. Then we had our little Bible lesson, and then we went collecting mushrooms despite rain. Up to then a usual Sunday, just as in peacetime. Already while we were still in bed, we had seen British planes fly over, but the weather was "wicked," according to the radio. After lunch it cleared up. I read to Pankie while Gerard slept, and we made a ragout of the mushrooms. Juus went out at 3:30 to pay a visit. I dressed the children and myself to go to de Hoogt for the second birthday of Nando.[42] We were late and on the road near Chris's house when my bicycle tire burst with a tremendous explosion. We walked to Chris and borrowed Dien's bike, and so onward, until we were safely at de Hoogt at about 4:30. After the congratulations and greetings we had just sat down with tea and cake when a fighter sheered over the house and immediately after that came an indescribable bang, and then another, and another. We saw the fighters circling in the direction of Maarn and our house. I thought they were aiming for the German trucks parked near here. Seven bombs fell, one right after the other; two of them I saw as they fell, and then we saw the clouds of smoke. I thought that our little house was going up in flames. Then there was silence.

We finished our cake and put on our coats, and then the telephone rang. At 't Stort [a house, occupied by relatives, close to the railroad] the ceilings had all come down and the furniture was covered, so could they all come and stay at de Hoogt? The police phoned to inquire whether bombs had hit the German gasoline depot nearby. I went carefully home with the little ones, who had had a bad scare. Rijnsoever's store windows were shattered, and people said that the house of the priest had been hit and that there was one person still under the rubble. Further on I heard that the post office and some houses were hit. At Steenbeek a couple of windows had been broken, at de Greef too, and the roof. Farther on it was less. At Chris's there was no damage, and we walked home with my bike with the flat tire. At home there was also no damage.

Everyone said that the bombs had been aimed at two locations where lots of Germans were living and where many German cars and trucks were always parked. "Unfortunately they missed by a few metres," Madzy wrote. "I'm a good deal upset by it – it was such a narrow escape for us all, and you ask yourself, 'Today you, tomorrow me'?"[43]

ANOTHER PARTY, on my birthday, fared only slightly better:

Oct. 5. It has been such a strange, strange day, my Dicks, this 6th birthday of our little darling. In the night there was constant flying and bombing in the distance. It was nice weather, and the entire day there was flying and we heard uninterrupted anti-aircraft artillery fire, which seemed to get nearer. In between all that we had to celebrate the birthday. Meanwhile the refugees from Arnhem streamed into the village. Everwijn Lange has 6 refugees, Tante Betsy 9 in outbuildings.[44] Christie has 6, plus 8 in Soria Moria [a cottage on the estate]. Someone – bombed out – came to me to borrow a bed. We also are waiting for refugees to be billeted here. Refugees passed by on bicycles, and one whole group came past with a loaded cart. Can you imagine how we could be in festive mood? With all that sadness around us? When at every cannon shot we think, "More people dead, and wounded, and homeless"? When the sky is a hard blue and the Tommies roar past overhead in groups of 100?

But it went off all right; Pank said it was a wonderful day, and that is the main thing. The slippers of rabbit fur[45] were beautiful, and the doll's clothes for Miemie still nicer, but when we sang "Long May She Live!" and the school desk[46] was delivered, everything was fine. All day she played in the desk, and she ate her meal at the desk. The visitors talked about nothing but the war and in the meantime we had to play games. Finally, singing – each carrying a chair, plate, and spoon – we paraded to the candlelit kitchen, where the big pan with pea soup simmered on the stove, and two cakes made of stacked pancakes stood on the table, each with three flickering candles. How I did miss you at that moment, my Dicks. You should have seen Pank's shining little face, and Gerard happily tucking in, with his hands neatly on the table, although there was hardly enough room.

The picture of the queen hung decorated above us, and all around us there is unbelievable suffering and destruction. The harbours of Rotterdam and Amsterdam are completely destroyed, all the wharves and warehouses. The building of De Haagsche Courant [an important newspaper] and the Planetarium blown up. All of [the island of] Walcheren inundated ... Yes, Dicks, our country is in ruins and it will take a lot to stick the debris back together again. And the people: broken, homeless, in rags. Soon we'll have to eat from soup-kitchens because there is nothing to be had on our ration coupons. The electricity will soon be cut off – at first we will have some from 7 to 10 and 6 to 8:30, and then half-current from 8:30 to 7, and that also will stop after two weeks. We live in a mood of emergency, in case we have to flee, with packed knapsack and bicycle and little wagon ready in the kitchen. Also for you I'll pack a small suitcase with clothes. I have to admit that inwardly I'm nervous, with all the uncertainty about you, the responsibility for the children, the lack of contact with you, the knowledge that this month there may be *the* final decision, the awareness that this winter will be full of deprivations – yes, one needs a deep faith in God, but fortunately I have that and I *will* and *shall* continue to stand firmly in my shoes on behalf of our dear children. "The final great battle of Holland is on."[47] May God save us.

The next day, two families evacuated from the almost demolished city of Arnhem were billeted with us.

6 October. Darling, such a day as today I've never had in my life. Yesterday, in spite of everything, we were having a nice party, and today we've got 8 refugees with us! I can't tell you how hard we slogged to get everything in order. It's a butcher and a cigar-dealer, each with a wife and two children. Juus is now sleeping in our bedroom, and her room is occupied by one family (named Molhuizen), and the other family (named West) is in the small room. The children all sleep on mattresses or little beds or on the floor, and even one in our crib. One couple sleeps in our guest bed, and the sofa bed from Dick [Dr van Kekem's wife] is divided into a bed and a mattress, for the other couple. It takes all our sheets and blankets (but they have some themselves), pillow-slips, towels. They are sitting in the kitchen by the stove, very happily – because last night they slept in a drafty hayloft with a ladder (one of the women is expecting a baby) and they were icy cold and sick. What a situation! And while we tidied, lugged things, and rearranged the house, there was a heavy roar of artillery fire, and planes constantly flying over our heads; the children were so scared that they followed me everywhere like chicks after the mother hen, too frightened to go outdoors. Now and then the house shook so much that I thought the windows would break.

I'm now sleeping with the children in the sitting room (Pank on the sofa) in a bed that Willem and I lugged downstairs. He packed all the glassware in a chest and many suitcases, and chairs and little tables are stored at his house. Any clothes that we can at all spare are put away because we have only one clothes closet for the four of us. And how long will we stay here ourselves? When might we have to flee? Again the piles of clothes are lying ready to be quickly packed.

... I can't tell you how exhausting it is to hear the roar of artillery and bombing all the time. Yet it's fairly far off, south of the Rhine and the Lek. They advance step by step. The Germans don't with-draw a foot without a fight, and however terrible it is we have to accept that this time the battle will be fought on our soil.[48] Because if Germany itself is attacked it will probably collapse. At least that's what I hope. They [the Allies?] are near Tilburg and moving in the direction of Breda, and we'll have to wait quietly and trust in God.

11:00 P.M. "Mamma," says Pank (who woke up and was so hungry – which ended up in a meal of two thick slices of bread with honey and a thick slice of ryebread), "Mamma, there's a car parked nearby blowing its horn."

"No, darling, that's one of the evacuees, who is lying above our heads snoring, like this!" And then I demonstrated – because she's never heard anyone snoring before.

Good night, Dicksy!

Before long, one of the refugee families left and was replaced by a third child and the elderly parents of the remaining couple. In the taped narra-tive of 1976, Madzy described the arrangements as they were for the rest of the winter:

Upstairs in our [her and Wim's] bedroom slept the West family, father and mother and three girls. In the little room under the roof slept the grandfather and grandmother of this family; they were in their eighties and had their golden wedding anniversary that winter. And in the other room next to our bedroom Juus slept with Joost [Madzy's brother, who joined us later that winter], and I slept down-stairs with Gerard and Marianne. And the only room we [Madzy's family and Juus] had to sit in was what we called at that time the dining room. The evacuees had the kitchen [an old-fashioned farm-house kitchen] as their living room.[49]

Madzy vividly illustrated one of the effects of the overcrowding:

[Oct. 25] Yesterday so many people used our toilet that the septic tank overflowed and the toilet was unusable. Now you have to imagine our "cigar-dealer" refugee, who in his ordinary life also worked as a mourner at an undertaker's – and who, at the moment of fleeing Arnhem, was wearing his mourner's clothes: a sort of dinner jacket with striped trousers, striped waistcoat, a shirt with a soft collar, and worn-out pumps – and who, on account of kidney stones, is exempted from digging[50] – he has today, in that outfit, with turned-up trouser-legs and rolled-up sleeves, been partly emptying the septic tank. I had to turn away on account of the stench and to conceal my amusement. So there are funny moments in these sad times.

A constant element is the tyranny and terror of the occupation:

31 Oct. This morning I had tidied the rooms and was just tidying myself when, up our driveway, came a fat guy in German uniform, followed by our local policeman. He stopped in front of my window (I had quickly put up my hair with combs) and said: "How many men do you have in the house?" It was our rascal Bos [the local police constable], but at that moment I didn't know that.[51]

I thought hard and, to gain time, said, "My husband isn't here, he is a prisoner of war, he's in Neubrandenburg."

"Yes, but how many evacuees – or are they seniors?"

Now I've never been quick in finding words and never will be, and so I admitted that I had two, but when he asked where they were I said that they were at de Halm [a neighbouring farm], though I knew that one was sawing wood for me and one was pumping water for me.

"What are they doing at de Halm?"

"I don't know," I said, and so they went on to de Halm, and I to the garden, and Molhuizen disappeared into the woods and West went to the doctor! *Enfin*, I finished dressing and went off with my milk can. And, coming back from the milkman, wobbling on the bike [wobbling because of the can of milk she was carrying in one hand], I met Bos, and he turned around and rode along behind me and shouted, "Missus, if your refugees don't report tomorrow morning at 7:30 at the Woudenberg-Scherpenzeel railway station, your house and furniture will be set on fire, and also that of Mrs van Notten, and 't Huis te Maarn."

"Very well, Mr Bos," I said calmly, and I went weaving home.

Well, by that time he had also warned people here, and I went to tell Chris, and we agreed that we would take our chance rather than letting ourselves be bullied by such a scoundrel.

Madzy and Christie agreed that if they had to leave their houses, they would go and live in a chicken house on a farm on the van Notten family's estate.

There were days when everything seemed impossible:

> Today a dark, sad day, the kind of day when all the misery, short-ages, cold, hunger overwhelms you, so that you can't get above it. In the first place there are all the primitive conditions in the house. The endless toil to get food and drink while outside it is either pouring rain and stormy, or there are planes flying over your head, which means a constant threat of danger and shooting. No news from Dicks any more; the last was of 11 Sept., which is 2 months ago. Marianke, who is difficult and, according to the schoolteacher, has to be treated firmly. *Enfin*, a thousand and one things which get a person down. And then all the worries and caring for other people which fall on your shoulders. I hear from my evacuees that at de Halm next door 19 people are living a dog's life in a muddy shed. One of my evacuees is expecting a baby in 2 to 3 months and has literally nothing. When I was out for food I met the funeral of the stationmaster and his wife, and Suus de Boer was walking tearfully in the procession. It gave me a pang in the heart to see the children walking, crying, behind the coffin. And tonight again an evacuee came talking about all her worries and grief. What can I do? Then I say that by Christmas it will all be finished, although I don't believe it myself at all. You listen patiently and sink a little farther in the bottomless depth.

The crowding caused by the presence of the evacuees, and later Joost, added considerably to the almost intolerable stress of the "Hunger Winter." Madzy was irritated by the dirtiness of our two rooms; they were intensive-ly used and could not be properly cleaned because in the terrible weather there was no chance to put the furniture outdoors and really scrub, no soap,[52] no hot water except what could be heated in a kettle on a stove with inadequate fuel. On 5 December she records that she stopped using sheets on the bed: it was no longer possible to wash and dry them. Later she bartered them for food.

Juus got on her nerves because (among other things) she felt that Juus ate a larger share of the food than she was entitled to – though Madzy readily admits that without Juus she would not have been able to go on the food-scrounging expeditions that kept us alive, though always hungry.

The diary entries for late 1944 dart back and forth between the war news and immediate local conditions. The personal and the global are closely connected in Madzy's mind; living conditions will only improve when the war is over:

> 6 Nov. If I get prematurely old then you know that these years have counted double, just as in the tropics, my dear Dicks.[53] The scare of last Saturday is still in my bones. It was a narrow escape, because two bombs fell on the bicycle path along which I had ridden a few minutes earlier. That they fell close to me I knew, but that they fell on the path itself I learned only today. As a result I'm scared. I've lost my nerve. Today there's bombing and shooting everywhere nearby (the smoke drifts over the garden).

> [7 Nov.] If you miss two pair of long kneesocks out of your wardrobe, Dicks, then I have to tell you that we drank them up. No, actually your son. Because I bartered them with the milkman for buttermilk (for a good long time to come, I think maybe to the end of the war) 3 times per week 3 litres! Because all our clothes are already gone, either given to the evacuees or bartered for butter or rye or wheat.

On 23 November she wrote: "I came home with a little can of milk, a little loaf of ryebread, and 2 bottles of buttermilk, with Pank on the back of the bike, all in pouring rain with soaking wet feet, hair, gloves, etc. It was so hilarious that Pank and I made a song about it, which we sang cheerfully." But that evening she was in a grimmer mood:

> Today it was already at 4:00 too dark to see anything clearly. Because it pours and pours. I've never seen so much rain at a stretch as yesterday and today. All the coats hang dripping, and my precious ski-boots are soaking wet inside. It will take them a week to dry because they mustn't stand by the stove [heat would make the leather stiff]. Such massive problems: where to hang things to dry, and how to dry them. I don't know how long we can muddle along with inadequate light. Today I bathed the children in the dusk and then could just manage to slice the bread. Until 6:00 we lived in the half-dark; I invented the most fantastic story about dwarves for the children,

6 Nov.: Als ik vroeg oud ben, dan weet je, dat deze jaren dubbelgeteld hebben, evenals Indische jaren (Dicks-lief)
De schrik van Zaterdag zit me nog in de botten; en het was een narrow escape, want er zijn 2 brisantbommen op het fietspad gevallen eenige minuten, nadat ik daar over gereden had! Dat ze vlak bij me gevallen waren, wist ik, maar dat ze op 't pad zelf waren gevallen, heb ik pas vandaag gehoord. Het gevolg is, dat ik bang ben. I have lost my nerve!
Vandaag is er overal vlakbij (de rookwolken hingen over de moestuin) gebombardeerd en geschoten (bij Maarsbergen zijn de Stationchef + vrouw + 2 kinderen gedood) Vanmiddag was ik net op Hoofdstraat om in Doorn mijn ... te laten maken, en toen begonnen ze weer de duiken en vanuit het bosch te saluten. Ik ben omgekeerd en naar huis gevlogen! Vrouwtje Jennas Toos heeft juist nog luiken gesloten om de ruiten te sparen, alles kreunde zoo. Enfin toen 't weer stil was, zei Juus: "nu kun je weer gaan" en ik won niet laf zijn en ik ging, maar oh Dicks, ik was zoo bang, zoo bang –

Het neurologisch ziekenhuis in Utrecht schijnt geraakt te zijn in plaats van de Ellett. Centrale
Ze gaan er helaas nog al eens naast. –
Piet Muidenberg is gevallen en behalve ...

A page from the war diary

while they ate their bread. They each had 3 slices, and we [she and Juus] therefore 2, but we also had brown-bean soup, and Juus cabbage and potatoes with rye porridge and buttermilk.

Such bread as we received on the ration coupons was far from appetizing: it had sawdust in it, and as a result Madzy suffered from a swollen abdomen.

The evacuees looked after their own food, but Madzy often fed others besides her own family. To a hungry *onderduiker* she gave the leftovers intended for our supper. On another day she records: "I made the rounds to a number of known sources in order to get 1 kg potatoes from each. Altogether I must have collected 10 kg and so I could bring some good cheer to friends who had nothing."

Rye was one of the grains most regularly available, the only cereal crop that could be grown on the area's sandy soil. Madzy used it for porridge and bread. In the taped narrative, she describes how they made the bread: "We put the rye kernels in the coffee grinder to make them fine and then I formed the flour into loaves with a bit of water and a bit of salt, and then we steamed that by putting a brick in an old pan and then putting water as high as the brick and on that brick we put the loaf (it sort of held together because it was very sticky stuff anyway by that time) and then it had to steam for about four or five hours."

ON 5 DECEMBER – Sinterklaas – there was a party at 't Huis te Maarn. Madzy mentions this party, and so does Dientje in her diary. Dientje gives the complete text of a poem Madzy wrote; the writing of humorous poems was a Sinterklaas tradition. This stanza conveys the mood: "We look anxiously at the sky while furiously pedalling our bikes – with no tires or brakes because that way the Germans won't take them. A plane? I'm not happy ... Over there, in that den of enemy soldiers ... shooting! Bombing! Oh ... oh ... We're still alive!"

The traditional jokiness of the Sinterklaas poem here becomes the grim humour of the survivor. Each of the nine stanzas lists problems they are all facing – read aloud at the party, it must have raised much rueful laughter – and each ends with the declaration, "We're still alive!" It is an assertion of physical survival but also of the survival of the spirit, of morale, of obstinate determination to keep going.

The entries of that winter are dominated by food: rationing, what we eat at each meal, what she obtains on coupons, by barter and by just plain begging from friends. The rations, and what she obtained on the black market or received as gifts, were not nearly enough for adequate nutrition or even to keep the family from being hungry. She talks about going "*op het zwarte pad*": "*op pad*" is a lighthearted Dutch expression for being on the road, out and about, but "*zwart*" is black – the black path, the black market.

Five days after Sinterklaas, a Sunday evening, she has time for a lengthy diary entry. More than half of it is about the struggle to find food:

My dearest Dicks, now I'm going to have a quiet talk with you; in this way I have at least some contact with you. Ever since Sinterklaas I have been constantly on the go to get food because it's in such short supply and I'm getting so thin that I'm afraid to get so short myself that I cannot be for the children what I should be. From Vlastuin I got 1 bottle of milk (the dairy plant has been bombed and we got nothing from the milkman) and I got 2 kg old green peas. From van Beuningen I got 1 bottle of skim milk and 5 lbs of ground wheat! Somebody was able to barter 3 bedsheets and 3 pillowslips for me, in exchange for 35 lbs of wheat. At de Rumelaar and de Haar I got nothing now, but from Wolfswinkel and de Rumelaar I'll get something in January.

Then I decided to go to Rika[54] yesterday. It had suddenly snowed heavily but that's better than nice weather [good weather was utilized by both sides for bombing], and on your bike I slogged through the snow. It was an indescribable trip: 1½ hours going and 2 hours coming back. I left at 9:00 and was back at 1:30 because that afternoon I still had to go out for milk and bread. I came home with 7 lbs of rye, and that nice Rika gave me a large piece of head cheese and a bag of green peas and all the requirements for real pea soup: sausage, meat-bone, 2 pigs' feet, and onions. Also 5 lbs of rye flour. I gave her my red woollen dress. Later I will get some more rye.

That soup! Oh, my boy, how we did enjoy it! It was, of course, our entire meal; we had only 1 slice of bread besides, without butter, so it was a saving in bread and butter. That makes a lot of difference for the whole week. Rika also gave me some milk, and we could have an extra cup of coffee.[55] How important food is, particularly for the children to get enough.

But about yesterday: that trip was actually too much for me, especially because of the deep snow and the mud, because I sometimes sank in over the pedals and had to walk for quite a stretch. And really, Dicks, in the end, because of my hunger, I could hardly push on – although for breakfast I had a bowl of porridge made with water, and one thick slice of bread with butter. Rika gave me a glass of milk, and offered me a slice of bread – notice that, Dicks, my former maidservant, who understood that I was hungry (I had after all come to beg food of her) offered me bread! I didn't accept it.

But when I was in the middle of a deserted stretch of the road, I thought: "I can't go any further, because of the hunger. But if I stop to rest here, then I'll never get home at all."

Enfin, I reached home, exhausted and with heart palpitations, but I did have this and that in the house again. I had an hour's rest and ate something, then just went out to fetch the milk and our loaf of bread (made from our wheat). Then the children had their bath, then I myself. What a day! The bath is just in a little tub with a kettle-full of warm water, but we got clean.

I have to have quite a bit of food in the house, Dicks, because everyone who drops in is hungry. Friday morning first Moeder Iete, who got a bowl of porridge; she is so thin and walks so much. Then came, all of a sudden, on the bicycle, Tante Lot Roest van Limburg[56] and Tante Lotje Suermondt.[57] Tante Lotje looked ashen because she had been overcome by cold and hunger in Doorn. Both got a reviving cup of coffee made with our last milk. (We adults get no milk any more on coupons. Marian 1 litre skim milk per week and Ger still 5¼ litre of milk per week.) In the afternoon came Miss Gleichman [Madzy's former music teacher was billeted at de Hoogt], cold and wet, because there is no heat in her room yet – and hungry: therefore again 2 cups of tea[58] and 2 slices of home-steamed rye bread with a little scraping of butter. (We don't get any butter any more, only Gerard gets ¼ pound every 14 days).

On the new coupons we get only 1 kg of bread per week, 1 ounce of cheese per 14 days, and Gerard a package of children's drink powder and, this time, 600 grams of bread (last week it was 200 grams). That's all: no sugar, jam, oatmeal, legumes, etc. – nothing, nothing, nothing.

And so we come to today. The weather was good, and I hardly dared to go to church. Last week I turned around and came home, and 2 weeks ago there was much shooting and bombing in Maarn. But this week the service was being held at Tante Betsy's again.[59] So I went on your bike, but just then the planes started to fly, and one Tommy[60] came over very low because a German car passed me at that moment. Then I was so scared again that I jumped off the bike. I intended to go back but had to give my heart a rest, but then Dientje came up with the boys [the two sons of her sister Christie] and so

I went on with them. Fortunately there was no flying during the service. It was a very simple and a very good service, and I enjoyed it very much. The preacher spoke on the theme of "hope: a quiet, calm hope – not an impatient hope." I went back safely with Dien.

So the days go by; we rush through the daylight hours to catch up on all the things postponed from the previous long dark hours. A little more than 7 hours of daylight against 17 hours of dusk and darkness. Luckily only 11 days and then we will have had the shortest, darkest day. The nights are long, but the children wake me up often, sometimes 10 or 12 times a night, and then I always have to look for a match, light a candle – oh, Dicks, with children everything is still more primitive and difficult. If you only consider how many times the chamberpot has to be emptied because the children may not go on the toilet because they get a rash that the evacuees are suffering from. It is impossible to describe all the primitive details of our life these days, but I will bless the day when we have electricity again. No, there is only one day to which I look forward, and that is the day on which we are with the four of us together and alone again.

She begins this passage by saying that she is going to have a calm talk, and indeed it is calmer than some other entries are, with their moods of wild longing, or feverish irritation, or despair. I have quoted it almost in its entirety because – vivid and well-written – it is almost like a short essay on women's lives in wartime.

A week later, after covering much the same domestic ground with some agitation, she then reports on other people's situations:

My evacuee came back from Arnhem today (we had already given him up, to my great anxiety). He reported that there was nothing left any more in their house. The Germans stand with horse and wagon in front of the doors of the houses and take *everything* away, absolutely *everything*, dishes, children's clothing, even a violin without strings. He's lost everything. And it's the same with many thousands of others. I was yesterday at Vlastuin, who said, "Madam, before the Germans are gone they will have plundered us empty too." This poor country that will be left for us!

And so the days pass in sad darkness – and still we have to see the light of Christmas shining ahead of us. Yes, I do see it, but it's often dimmed by the darkness on earth.

If they are going to plunder us here, what will we do? I don't know.

And then I'm worried about something else: that my health might break down before you are home to take over the leadership. I have so much trouble with my heart.

THE TERRIBLE conditions continued for the rest of the winter. Madzy consulted the doctor about her heart palpitations and was told to stay home and take it very easy for a week or two and then slowly resume her usual work. Seeing herself naked in the mirror, she was shocked by how emaciated she was.

On 7 January Juus had her birthday, and Madzy wrote about her great fondness for her in spite of the strain brought on by the war, the rationing, the crowded living conditions. A few random cards arrived from Wim (three at one time, all together, and later another one) but all were weeks or months out of date.

The increased flying, bombing, and shooting meant that liberation was coming nearer – or so everyone hoped. But in the meantime they intensified the danger and the tension. On one of her outings, Madzy wrote, six fighters flew low over her head and attacked a target very near her, and a VI (a flying bomb) fell nearby. Her acquaintance Mrs Bentinck and her daughter-in-law and a lady visitor were arrested because munitions had been found in the shed. (Dientje Blijdenstein also mentions this incident in her diary, writing that the munitions had been dropped by the Allies for the use of the underground.) In the next entry Madzy reports that Mrs Bentinck (evidently released) has gone into hiding and that her house is going to be blown up.

On 25 February Madzy writes that munitions were found near our cottage and that she has reported them to the authorities. She comments that she feels safer with evacuees in the house, "because in these times there are roaming men who are in hiding, hungry people, *razzias*, Germans, so-called Dutch police, etc." She would not like to be alone at night with only Juus and the children.

Dientje, in passages she added to her diary in postwar revision, writes that in February 1945 one underground group in the area was found. Three leaders were arrested; others, who escaped, destroyed papers. An underground newspaper stopped publication, depriving the local people of more or less reliable news. There was also increased danger from the Dutch Nazis.

One morning I refused to go to the little informal school because the previous day a large bomb had fallen close to me on my way to school.

On 25 January Madzy slogged through the snow for three hours to get one pound of rye. She gave Wim's corduroy trousers to Dick Kolff in the hope that he would be able to barter them for food for her. She bartered more of her own clothes for food. Later she traded one of Wim's uniform coats for butter.

On Sunday evening, 28 January, she used her last drops of oil to make some light. She was sitting huddled in a blanket beside the little stove, with an infected breast, feeling sick and miserable. That afternoon while she was feverish and in bed, twenty-five or thirty bombs had dropped in the neighbourhood; the house shook and the children came screaming, crawling into her bed for shelter.

IT WAS in March of 1945 that Madzy's brother Joost came to live with us. Two of the three elderly ladies who had been caring for him had died that winter, and the third was unable to carry on by herself. Moving him to Maarn was a problem: he was unable to walk the eight kilometres, so Madzy found someone who had a horse and an ancient carriage. Joost remained with us until after the end of the war, when other accommodation was found for him.

MADZY frequently expresses in the diary her faith in God, and writes of praying for divine support and help. This piety never appeared in her ordinary conversation and, since there are no surviving diaries for other periods, we have no idea whether it was typical of her inner life. A fragment written in 1954 reveals a belief in a much more remote deity. But it is clear – and entirely understandable – that in those years of almost intolerable strain, anxiety, and danger, she found support in religion. Not only was going to church a social activity, and very important for maintaining morale and a sense of community, but faith in God helped her to endure and carry on.

In February 1947 she would write a letter to her brother Paul, then back from the Dutch East Indies where he had been in a Japanese prison camp. They had just spent some time together, and she had been struck by what she called the "unhappiness" in his eyes, "as though your soul is in a dungeon." In her letter she gives heartening advice to him to forget himself, lose himself in his work and his family, and trust to Christ. She writes that she has complete trust in God, even though life will sometimes push her down. "But I will always come out on top, because I always see Christ standing beside me, and when I can no longer deal with life I say, 'Here, Jesus, you must carry my cross for me. After all, you said that you would do it, so here it is!' and then I will overcome it. Don't tell me that Christ doesn't exist, because that is the stupidest thing you can say. Open your heart to him, and focus your thoughts on other people."

It may be the best articulation of the faith that helped to keep her going. To her God was a father looking after his children, a trusted source of help and support. She attributed the family's survival to his care. It is a simple piety: there are no complicating ruminations about the German soldiers being also God's children. The voice articulating it is that of a child – a desperately fearful, overstrained child.

The circumstances of those last eight months of the war had placed her in a very difficult position. She was the authority ruling the lives of her own children, Juus, and the evacuees, and for a few months, her brother Joost. When the father of the evacuee family refused to turn up for a labour draft, it was to Madzy that the authorities came, she who was threatened with eviction from the house if the man did not report.

By now she was becoming accustomed to that position, but still it felt wrong – as well as, in the circumstances, extremely dangerous – to be so placed. There were almost no other trusted men to look to for help. At one point, after another *razzia* to round up adult males for work on the rebuilding of German military installations in Holland, she remarks that it was becoming very much a world of women and children. Such men as there were in the neighbourhood were German soldiers, a few farmers, or men in hiding or working in the underground. No wonder she found some comfort in the thought of a fatherly, benevolent God who would look after her.

THE TURNING point from the depths of the war to liberation is hard to pinpoint precisely. On 26 March 1945, four local people were executed by the Germans. Madzy still writes in the depths-of-war manner:

> This afternoon I bicycled to Charlotte [Kolff] and came home out of breath because for the last part of the trip I was followed by 6 fighters circling low, looking for something. In the end they fiercely attacked [a nearby railway cutting] just when I had to cross the railway. Finally one came over low while I had to pass two carts with horses (also a favourite target for mortar fire) and someone with a gun began to fire on the fighter. Fortunately I was soon home ... I brought spinach and potatoes.

Maarn was now in the front line of battle. In that same entry she writes: "This past night there was such ferocious fighting close by us that the house sometimes swayed back and forth." In 1976 she would recall:

The end was pretty grim because the front came nearer and nearer and it was getting more and more dangerous for us ... And the shells were flying, zooming over our roof, and all these things were very unpleasant and very scary. I must say that I am surprised that I don't show my fear more in my book. Maybe I was so dulled by all the noises – and the noises were terrifying; we were surrounded by cannon thunder so that the little house was shaking on its foundations. And this was such a regular situation that I suppose a person just gets used to it and doesn't think too much of it. And then when there was a rainy day, I managed to go out and get food, because in that weather you were fairly sure that there wouldn't be any bombings. And then I managed to get back before the sun peered out from behind the clouds because then you knew that the Allies would come with their bombers again.

The Germans were slowly being pushed back, and their desperation led to even more arbitrary behaviour. There were constant raids as they tried harder than ever to locate and destroy underground activities in Maarn and the woods around it.

But then, in the course of a few days, things begin to change.

Thursday, 29 March '45: All organized resistance of the Germans has ceased. The English themselves will determine the moment of ceasefire. Delivery is close by.

How it appears to our hearts – our poor battered hearts that have been turned to stone – is impossible to describe. The pulse beats in our throats, our stomachs feel woozy (and not only from hunger), we wait ...

Yesterday and today it was incredibly quiet. One off-course VI came over in the distance, and one airplane. The tension hangs in the air. No bombs, no shooting, no uproar, no squadrons of overflying aircraft, nothing, nothing, only silence ...

Tuesday after Easter, 3 April: Too many things are happening to write about them all. Besides, I'm overcome by a paralyzing exhaustion; it's as though I can't handle the last straws ... The front is approaching from all sides. And what is still facing us? However, there are some amusing things happening. The Germans are streaming past and each group leaves something behind that can't be taken along.[61] Annetje came yesterday with half a pail of pea soup (with meat!), a loaf of bread of 14 March[62] (but valuable to us, especially in soup) and – 3 soles. One went to the evacuees, the other two were gobbled up (not by me – I can't stand fish) because we haven't seen any fish since 1942. Then Bob Hudig brought "something that we hadn't seen for a long time," as he put it – 5 soles! Two for the refugees, three again fried and relished by my four hungry mouths. Moreover we received, for Easter, a total of 37 eggs! An ample number went to the evacuees (as did portions of the pea soup and bread and milk).

All the same, the war was not over. On 20 April, a German soldier came to requisition two of the three downstairs rooms in the house. In great haste the house was rearranged. Twelve people had to be crammed into the remaining four rooms – but by then Madzy had made so many emergency arrangements that this further one did not seem to cause her much of a problem. Everything was just ready when another soldier came to say that the rooms would not be needed after all. The Germans, it appeared, had planned to set up a big artillery piece next to the house and another five at de Halm, the neighbouring farm. "Well! we just escaped a grim death!" Madzy comments.

That night she slept in her clothes because there was lots of flying and shooting: anything could happen and she wanted to be ready. The following night it was fairly quiet, but on 22 April she reports: "We had not yet put out the light before a terrible uproar began. There was fierce fighting in Maarn. Grenades shrieked over our heads and the little house shook. The children were terrified and both huddled with me in bed. This continued until four o'clock; nobody closed an eye. Then we dozed a bit." The next day she heard that several houses in Maarn had been hit.

And she still had to scrounge for food: a coverall of mine was bartered for butter. She made a hasty trip to Amersfoort – very dangerous, lots of Germans around, great risk of her bicycle being requisitioned – and came back with turnip tops, radishes, and potatoes.

On Sunday, 29 April, she writes:

> And now there is nothing to do but wait: endless and impatient waiting for the latest news, unconditional capitulation. And oh! the last waiting, after five years of endless patient waiting, is so extremely hard. A day like today is just a matter of counting the hours and longing for someone to bring news. The curfew is still in effect: no church, therefore, and only from 5 to 6 P.M. a chance just to get out – because what can you do on the street from 8 to 9 on a Sunday morning? It was, moreover, filthy weather: wet snow and fierce gusts of icy wind. I calmly held an extensive children's church service, and

knitted the last wool (from unravelled socks). Everything is the last: the last wheat and rye, the last gravy cubes and rice and soup-paste and leftover bits of butter and fat and jam and sugar (all presents during the past days from people who now feel that they can give away some of what they have been hoarding) ... From time to time a German soldier uses his last ammunition to kill a rabbit or a hare in the woods.

Just before noon the English began to drop food parcels over the starving cities. Compared to them, we are still well off for food, though I'm suffering from either hunger or a stomach-ache, possibly an ailment brought on by the rye. We ate the last eggs out of the *kalk* [preservative], although they were slightly spoiled.

On Wednesday, 2 May, she reports that the port of Rotterdam has been opened to admit food shipments, and one highway is open to the Allies. Air drops of food are taking place: the cities have priority. Some food will, she hopes, eventually reach villages like Maarn through the rudimentary distribution system being set up, and something is expected from the Swedish Red Cross. But "we will have to stay hungry for a little while longer."

At bedtime that day she writes:

This evening we had a tremendous sensation, actually a foreshadowing of the big liberation experience which we hope to have. We heard for the first time in days the droning of an airplane; the children were frightened again, but I said, "That's the Tommies with the food parcels" – upon which everyone ran into the garden. We saw in the distance a huge airplane flying low, and then it was gone. An hour later, more droning, and then four planes came over the *Knorrebuurt* [a nearby cluster of houses]; they shaved over the treetops, huge white birds with red crosses! The cheering in the *Knorrebuurt* was deafening. How can anyone describe our emotion when, just a little later, five of these enormous birds came right over our small house? We yelled, we jumped, we cried – what didn't we all do? The emotion is indescribable; it is as if a small window suddenly went open and we could see into a peaceful future. My heart beat like a crazy thing, the children clamped themselves against me – in short, it was an almost frightening, choking sensation, a foretaste of the emotions that will overcome us when we are at last free again.

There were six more planes the next morning. The news on the grapevine was that peace was imminent, but the population was warned to observe the curfew and be very careful because the situation was still volatile. There was particular danger from the Dutch ss who, on 3 May, shot down a Red Cross plane.

Many years later, in a short story about these days, Madzy wrote (in English): "Last night, an odd sound woke me. When I dared to peek over the windowsill of the bedroom, my eyes met a weird scene. Rows after rows of heavy war equipment – tanks, trucks, guns, armoured cars, all pulled by teams of sturdy Belgian Percherons filed past our cottage. No human voice, no orders, no talking – just silent robots leading the horses. The only sound, the rattling of chains and creaks of the harnesses, the marching feet, the heavy thumps of the hoofs, like a silent film with added imitation sound. A beaten army in retreat."

On 4 May she heard that on the following morning at 8:00 the German army would surrender unconditionally to the Allies. However, on 5 May a woman in Doorn was shot dead for being on the street during curfew. It was said that there was jubilation elsewhere; but in the area around Maarn, where the Dutch ss was still in action, things were tense and dangerous. Armed German soldiers cycled past the house.

On Sunday, 6 May, Madzy went to church, taking me with her, although she did not know whether the curfew was still in effect. It was lifted that afternoon.

> Because many people were observing the hours of curfew, the church wasn't full. It was an improvised service, and therefore all the more spontaneous. The reader could not continue because his glasses misted over with the emotion, the organist had to be revived half-way through by the district nurse, the minister (Dr Koolhaas) could sometimes go no further because of the tears. But it was powerful, and after a thundering sermon and many suitable psalms and hymns we ended with the Wilhelmus [the national anthem]. No one's eyes were dry, and people often couldn't continue singing because of the tears. Even I was overcome. For little Panksk it was an unforgettable experience. "For the first time we really sang the Wilhelmus, Mam!"

But it was still not safe: "This evening two bicycles were requisitioned right in front of my door and we couldn't do a thing about it." Unexploded munitions were found under the viaduct in the middle of the village, and elsewhere, and were detonated – making a noise very much like war itself.

The next day, however, Maarn was finally able to celebrate with flags. Allied troops were in the neighbourhood. Madzy talked to a young English soldier.

On 9 May an incident occurred that was to attain almost mythic proportions for her. She mentions it briefly in the diary, but it appears in a much more detailed form in *Land for Our Sons*, and she wrote a short story about it in her old age.

In the diary, she records that she went to Charlotte Kolff to ask for food. She found the house and greenhouses bombed and totally demolished; Charlotte, who was there among the ruins, gave her some spinach, but nothing to eat or drink on the spot. Having had a meagre breakfast of rye porridge made with water, and a single slice of bread, she was very hungry.

> At 11:30 I had, therefore, to turn around and start walking back [her bicycle tire was flat]. I couldn't take the inner roads so took the main road along the moors. No car gave me a lift. I was half fainting from hunger, so that when I saw on the moor an Allied canteen surrounded by tents, I begged for food. At first nothing, then they relented and gave me delicious biscuits and a dessert of custard with apricots, and real tea with sugar, and I was given 4 tins of fish and sausage to take along. Unbelievably revived, I danced home.

In *Land for Our Sons*, about twelve years later, she deals with it this way:

> It was a hot day ... The sun beat steadily on my skinny body, the trails were sandy and heavy-going. Pretty soon I met obstacles, long coils of barbed wires, deep bomb-holes, trees felled over the path. I had to carry my bicycle over the trees, carefully easing my way past barbed wire, and soon I got a flat tyre.
>
> I plodded along until I reached the road which led to the Kolffs' place after a sharp curve. Before coming on to the road I had to crawl through a barbed-wire fence, and pull my bicycle up from under it.
>
> Out of breath, I leaned for a moment against a white post. It looked new: I gazed and saw a large white sign with a drawing of a skull and two crossed bones underneath. In large, black letters was painted: DANGER! DANGER! LAND MINES!
>
> God must have been with me on this trip.
>
> I took the bicycle and walked towards my friends' house. Turning the sharp corner I strained my eyes for the welcome sight of their rows of greenhouses, and then I had to sit down. For what I saw were rows and rows of skeletons, broken windows, blackness; a tall blackened chimney stood lonesome in the centre.

In this account there is no reference to meeting Charlotte or getting spinach; she says that an old man pottering about among the ruins told her that the Kolffs had survived the bombing and fire but were now living in the town three miles away.

I turned round empty-handed. The sooner I reached home, the better. Passing the danger sign I hesitated; the trail would be much shorter, but should I stretch my luck that far? Shrugging my shoulders wearily I turned away from it and followed the road; I had managed to keep alive that long, I might as well begin to be careful.

And so I came to the stretch of the moorland. It went as far as the eye could reach, and was completely deserted. There was no trace of shade. I put one foot in front of the other, and passed the time in my usual way: day-dreaming. I dreamed of the day that Bill would come home, of the day that we could start living again.

I smelt something. Looking up I saw at the side of the road on the edge of the moor some army trucks. For a moment I was scared, but I could not turn back, so I went on putting one foot in front of the other. The smell got stronger; I had not smelt it for years. They must be Allied soldiers!

When I reached the trucks they had just finished their meal and were packing up. One soldier was scraping the plates, dropping the left-overs on the moor. My eyes followed the falling food; I looked at the man, and before I knew it, I had said: "Is there some more left? Can I have it?"

For a moment he looked surprised to hear his own language spoken here in this foreign country, then he shook his head regretfully.

"Sorry, miss," he said with a Canadian accent, "but our orders are ..." He stopped; an officer had come from behind the truck and asked him something.

The officer looked at me with an apologetic air. "Sorry, miss," he said, "our orders are not to give food to civilians; there are so many hungry people, you know."

"I'm so very hungry," I murmured ...

The officer shook his head again, and as I turned around, I must have fainted for I don't remember that I went and [seated] myself against the wheels of the truck, yet that was where I found myself, warming my thin hands around a large mug of hot tea, with sugar and milk!

Five Canadian soldiers are standing around her. They give her a plate of food as well as the tea, but after a few mouthfuls she cannot eat any more. They ask about her and tell her about their cousins and brothers who have died in the fighting. When she is able to get to her feet and leave, she finds that the basket of her bicycle is filled with packages of hard biscuits and bars of chocolate. The soldiers leave first: she watches them jump into their trucks and drive off. "Leaning on my bicycle I looked after them for a long moment. 'I'll never forget it,' I said aloud, like a vow: 'I'll do what I can to repay my debt.'" ... "'We'll go to Canada,' I said. 'I still have to pay a debt there. We'll raise our children like good Canadians, to replace the ones who have fallen for us.'"[63]

MADZY'S CENTRAL concerns were now Wim's return home (she did not even know if he was alive) and persuading the evacuees to leave. They had been told by the authorities that they would not be able to return to Arnhem for two months, but finally, on 16 May, they left, apparently to stay with relatives elsewhere. Madzy was determined also to find a place for Juus and Joost. She wanted to have the house ready for Wim, whenever he came: there would be only the three of us waiting for him.

IN MARCH of 2001, Bill wrote his account of this time.

> Neubrandenburg, where the POW camp was located, is in eastern Germany ... On April 27, 1945, we knew that the Russian army was very near and could hear tanks firing.
>
> Our German guards and their officers were in a panic, and they wanted all the POWs to walk westward to an unknown destination. Our Dutch commander refused: it was much safer to be in a POW camp than in a column on the road in greenish-grey uniforms similar to the German uniform. Our commander had to sign a document saying that we were staying on our own risk. [The Germans left.] We got shovels and dug trenches, and we painted "POW" in large letters on the roofs of the army huts. At our gate, several of our officers who were fluent in Russian stood ready to explain to the Russian troops that we were POWs.
>
> In the night, the first Russian tanks arrived. All went well. These were "crack" troops, very disciplined. They took axes and chopped the gate posts down as a sign of liberation. Then they went on. Next day, disorganized Russian soldiers and their women came walking along the road, with little wagons with poor horses and some supplies. A Russian officer stayed as their commander for our camp. Our Dutch commander asked about food

supplies. The Russian commander said that they did not have any but told us to go into the countryside and get it.

In April, in starved Germany, there was nothing except cows to slaughter, so we had meat. No bread, potatoes, or anything else. The Germans had partly demolished the power plant in the small city, so we had no water, no light. We had to use water from a shallow pool where the Russian horses waded to drink and the women did the washing. We boiled the brown water, of course. Then our Dutch army engineers repaired the power plant; there was only a little fuel, but we got water for very short moments.

There were a lot of patients with stomach ulcers among us who needed milk, so a "milking crew" was organized. I was one of them, and we went with a little cart and a poor horse to a nearby valley where the cows had not been milked for days. All the Germans [the local population] were hiding in the woods, and some of my friends found a barn where a great many of the population had hanged themselves from the joists. I roamed around and came upon a shoe-cobbler shop, where Russian POWs had repaired German army boots and were now fixing their own. They taught me how to resole shoes, and I took some leather to do the shoes of Madzy and the children. I also took a small hammer which I still regularly use, a cutting knife, and an awl.

Our Dutch kitchen staff had cooked all our food during all those three years. Now they needed transportation to get whatever food they could find in the country, and firewood. For this they needed some horses. The only ones available were the ones which the Russian army abandoned because of poor hooves. In our camp were two sergeant farriers of my original pre-war regiment, so I knew them well. Our camp was on ... an estate, with large stables and their own blacksmith shop. So our two farriers went to work, and I went there to learn blacksmithing from them – having emigration very much on my mind.

So the weeks of waiting passed. I forgot to tell that about six weeks before liberation an order from the Allied Commander, General Eisenhower, had been delivered by the underground to our Dutch camp commander. It said that no POW was allowed to go home on his own (on foot or a stolen bike or by whatever other means). Hence we waited for orderly transport.

Madzy had had no word at all from Wim (so far as the surviving records show) since receiving three postcards on 29 December 1944. On 20 April, his birthday, we sang *Lang zal hij leven* ("Long May He Live," the Dutch equivalent of "Happy Birthday"), not knowing whether he *was* alive.

After the evacuees left, Madzy and her helpers worked hard to clean the house as well as possible without adequate soap. "Now the house is ready to receive you and we will be together again," she writes.

Though she still had to go out for food, she stayed home as much as possible so that she would be there when he came. On 19 May she writes about him in the third person – "Where is he and why do we have no news?" – as though she feels him to be suddenly much farther away.

On 20 May came the first news about Wim's camp: a newspaper reported that Neubrandenburg had been liberated by the Russians and that all the prisoners were in good condition.

On 30 May, Piet van Notten, the husband of her friend Christie, came home from Neubrandenburg and said that Wim would be home in two or three days. On Thursday evening, 31 May, she writes:

> Today it has been one awful tension, so that my heart hurt constantly and Juus got some valerian from Ad [van Kekem, the doctor]. I'm not leaving the place until he, my very dearest, has returned. This evening I nearly collapsed, but then Piet van Notten came. That gave me a push, and by way of distraction I washed my hair – taking the chance that you would not come while I was doing it because Piet said that you could not come before six o'clock tomorrow evening. Oh, God, what a heavy disappointment! – not so much psychologically as physically, because that pain in my heart is so gnawing and irritating. I'd better go and lie down and read a bit in order to get through the night (perhaps the last one I spend alone?).

"Today is hell," she wrote on Saturday, 2 June. The second large notebook was also full by now, and these entries were written on sheets torn from a scribbler. On 3 June she was told that it might be another two weeks, and she thought she was going to snap. Meanwhile, many friends, expecting Wim to be back, came to call. Each visit must have caused her more grinding pain.

BACK TO Bill's narrative of 2001:

> One afternoon there was great excitement as some fifty Russian trucks drove into the camp (all American-made). Immediately orders were issued which trucks were assigned to the men from specific huts. We gathered up our belongings. I had made, long before, a real knapsack with straps, from my suitcase.

Our group was slow and when we came to our assigned truck it was full, taken by others who officially should have had to wait for the next transport. They said it would be coming the next day. There were not enough trucks for all of us, probably only for a little more than half the total POWs in the camp. They drove off and we stayed behind.

Next day the Russians said, "No trucks," as later the railroad would be repaired. So we walked to the station in the little city. No train. We slept and waited all night on the platform. Then a freight train with empty open coal cars came and we stood up during the trip which was about five hours, going very slowly. The bombed railroad yards were unbelievable. Then we were stranded again until finally some trucks came which brought us to the Elbe River demarcation line. After a short wait, a convoy of British trucks came which brought us to a huge army complex in Lünenburg, just south of Hamburg. We each got a puff of DDT blown under our clothing against lice and fleas, which we did not have. Then we had a shower, a good meal, a night's sleep in good cots, and English breakfast – all cared for by many German women.

Then we were off in trucks again, to a very small dirty army barracks close to the Dutch border. There was no furniture at all; we slept like sardines on the floor. There was no food at all either, as the Belgian cook had run off with all supplies. Next day we were off in trucks again to Holland – but only as far as the border, where we were supposed to be cleared. But the Dutch authorities, though knowing that we were expected, got tired of . waiting and had gone home because it was a Sunday. (A nice day.) We sat in the grass, and somebody from the Dutch border office gave each of us a cigar.

After all the delays we had become very impatient. But later that day we were brought to Oldenzaal [the Netherlands] with the announcement that next day we would have to stay and wait a day. I was billeted at the house of the owner or editor of the local newspaper, where I was very nicely treated. I gave them a cake of soap I had saved for home. (I had saved also, from American food parcels, Nescafé, Prem, chocolate, and other things – all packed in the homemade knapsack, which served the purpose very well.)

We walked around in the city, but it was again a day lost. We were fed up by the endless delays and waiting. We were told that next day we were not going to Weert in southeast Brabant – where the first convoy had gone, and from where it was hard to get home as all the bridges over the large rivers (the Meuse, Rhine, and Waal) had been demolished. Instead we were going to a conference centre called Woudschoten near Austerlitz, very close to home (about forty minutes by bike at the most). I knew the location well, having passed by there many times. So I asked my host for a large yellow envelope. I wrote a message to Madzy, and on the envelope I wrote that it was a message of a POW to his wife, with address and directions and a request to deliver it. In the envelope I put some pebbles for weight.

Next day was a triumphant trip through Holland. We cheered at every living soul on the road. Taking the route from Amersfoort over the moors, we would come to the junction with the road from Woudenberg to Zeist, where we would turn right to Austerlitz. When the trucks were making the sharp turn, a man jumped off his bike in response to our cheering. I flung the envelope in between the trees towards him standing on the bicycle path. The envelope dropped literally at his feet. I saw him pick it up and read the address (with my request to deliver it) and get on his bike.

Madzy tells what happened next, though it was not until four weeks later that she wrote it down, the final diary entry. On Monday 4 June, she was sitting drinking a cup of coffee at 11:00 in the morning.

Suddenly Dick Kolff's game warden stood at the window with a note from – Wim! From him himself! In which was written, that he was at the border (on Sunday afternoon) and hoped to be home on Wednesday or Thursday after registering in the camp at Austerlitz! My first reaction was, "Oh, *another* long wait!" but then I was so happy and so thankful. In the afternoon I got on the bicycle and went to the camp to find out what was going on. I was welcomed in very friendly fashion but was informed that the officers were not expected before Wednesday. I left behind a letter and a chocolate bar.[64]

The next day (feeling much refreshed after a restful night without constant waiting and listening) I phoned the camp. There I learned that the officers were tired of waiting and could come home at any moment. I was in a state again ... and the waiting resumed.

At quarter after one Willem and Cornelia van Tuyll came to visit and stayed talking until 3:30 when suddenly a strange man stood in front of the window with a note from – Dicks! He had passed the Viersprong [the intersection where Wim had flung the message from the truck] and would (he wrote) try to get quickly through the registration and walk home.

Now I've forgotten to tell that Vader and Jet had also on that morning (this was all on Tuesday, 5 June) come by car, assuming that Wim had already come home a long time ago. Desolately they went to have lunch at de Hoogt. When, therefore, I got that note,

I sent Willem van Tuyll to de Hoogt, and I myself jumped on the bicycle. Vader and Jet in the car, and I on the bicycle, arrived at the same moment at the entrance to the camp. (I nearly ran down a little boy who crossed carelessly in front of me.) We were, however, not allowed into the camp. But then came a tall officer who had already been registered and was looking for transportation to Den Haag. I sent him on my bicycle to seek out Wim. He came back alone to report that everyone was looking for Wim, and then he went back. A few minutes later (Jet and I peering up the driveway) I saw the officer came riding towards us again with someone else – and only when they were nearby did I recognize my dearest one.

The diary ends there, at the moment when she and Wim saw each other – it does not even describe their meeting. It had been intended as a record for him of the lives she and the children led while he was away, and it stopped once he was home again. But both, separately, completed the story later. Wim did so in his 2001 narrative:

We were soon at the conference centre and jostled in line to get registered as quickly as possible. Then, while I was still waiting, a cavalry friend, Chris Henny, came and said, "Your wife is at the gate." So I went and met Madzy, and was surprised that Father and Jet with the small truck[65] were there also; they would take Chris Henny back to Wassenaar, near their house.

It was of course a delightful moment for which we all had waited all those years. I was so overcome that later I realized that my first embrace was not as passionate as it should have been. I said good-bye to Father and Jet, who went home, and I took Madzy inside with the two bikes. (Willem de Bruyn, Madzy's faithful helper, had brought my bike. In Holland every man can wheel an empty bike with one hand while riding his own.) I pushed my way to the desk and asked if I could come back next day for the formalities, which was OK.

So Madzy and I bicycled home through the beautiful woods on the little picturesque bicycle path I had ridden so often. When we neared home, we saw Juus, Marianne, and Gerard standing on the Maarnse Grintweg in front of the house, looking out for us. It was a wonderful homecoming, but Gerard was afraid as I was in uniform and looked very much like a German.

I think that I arrived home 5 or 6 days after Piet van Notten had come home. Madzy had waited all those days in frantic uncertainty, and I in endless frustrations because of all those delays. Anyhow we were both so thankful that I was home and that Madzy and the children (and other relatives) had survived the dangers and hardships of the war. Strangely I don't remember at all what I did in the following days, while remembering this story in the smallest details.

In the 1976 taped narrative, Madzy finally told her version of what happened after the diary ends.

It was a strange feeling to see him back. He had begun to get slightly grey when he left, not very much; when he came back he was completely grey, not as white as now, but certainly grey. He was trim, clean, well-dressed; his uniform was in good shape. He had kept himself in good shape altogether. He looked healthy, well-nourished and happy – a little bit puzzled and confused, of course (you can imagine) but everything was fine.

He went back to the main building and took me along. Grandfather took the other officer, and so Grandfather and Oma Jet left, but at least Grandfather had seen Dad and he went home very happily ...

Finally we were left alone; we could go home. And here we were, bicycling home along the very well-known lanes through the woods, towards our little house where we knew that two little children were just simply staring their eyes out of their heads to see when Dad would come. Well, it was quite a trip for Dad; he hadn't bicycled for three years, and after some time he began to feel it rather in his feet and his legs, I think, but he managed it.

Finally, when we came driving up near the house, all of a sudden there came a little girl running, running, running, calling, "Pappa, Pappa, Pappa!" And a little boy who wanted to follow his sister in the same way – but of course in those three years he had made a sort of an image of a father, and he hadn't made an image of a father in a uniform. A man in a uniform, for him, was a German. So as soon as he saw Dad jump off the bicycle and open his arms for Marianne, Gerald stood still, turned around, ran into the house and hid under the bed upstairs – because he thought that the Daddy about whom we had talked to him and told him stories, that Daddy was a German. And it took a little while until we had been able to explain to him that he wasn't a *German* soldier but that he was a *Dutch* soldier. But only when Daddy changed his clothing (I had put his summer suit ready – a very easy suit, I suppose, grey slacks, a sports jacket) and when Dad had taken his uniform off, so that he looked like an ordinary man, then Gerald slowly crawled out from under the bed and peered at this man and very, very slowly came towards him and put his hand on Dad's knee and looked with his big blue eyes. And Dad looked down at his son whom he had seen as a baby of not quite forty-eight hours old and now it was a little sturdy chap of three and a half years old,[66] and now they had to make acquaintance with each other.

FOUR WEEKS after Wim's return, and in the middle of much activity, Madzy remembered that she had not quite completed the story and took the time to do so. Clearly she regarded it as having a beginning and definite ending – in other words, as having a literary shape. This is a writer's diary: we have seen that even in her most desperate moments she was not only reporting on events but recording her feelings and doing so with a writer's self-awareness.

In the course of writing this chapter, I have been reading the diary again and again, selecting passages to quote, searching for things, mulling over particular bits. It is a harrowing story, but one of compelling interest because, apart from everything else, it traces the development of a human being, the growth and strengthening of the spirit. There is a progression from the helplessness of the early days to the self-reliance and resourceful-ness of the bad winter of 1944–45. There is always despair and longing, but there is also an obstinate and sometimes fierce determination to cope, to endure and survive and make sure that the children survive. Everything is aimed at keeping going until Wim returns. Several times she says, "I can't go on" – and then does. As she must.

The diary records the inner life and the outer in about equal portions; the shifting back and forth, the interweaving, contributes immensely to the power of the story and the insight it gives into her life. Almost every part of her life and her being is there.

We see her becoming traumatized – and observing the process in such painful and yet absorbing detail gives new depth and meaning to the over-used word. Madzy knew little about psychology, but she recorded with extraordinary vividness the process of traumatic suffering endured and sur-vived.

Although she was intensely happy to have Wim back again, the damage remained, even though she pushed it out of sight. She became again, at once, intensely dependent on Wim, and from then on her worst times occurred when he was away from her. When we were in Canada, he went alone to Holland four times. On at least two of those occasions she was distraught, a helpless victim of the revived demons that neither she nor we understood, terrified that this time he would not return.

Her self-reliance did not desert her completely, but from 1945 on she was self-reliant within a safe context – doing her share of what needed doing, making decisions and contributing to the shaping of the family's life, but never again doing it without the companionship and support of Wim. In some significant ways she was a leader in the family, but there was little of the postwar feminist in her. As we have seen, she vowed to submit her life and needs to those of her family.

During the period covered by the diary, she had been surrounded by other women who were strong and resourceful and assertive, but she regarded their and her own achievements as a matter of coping in exceptional circumstances, second-best in the absence of husbands and other men. In one of her later short stories she writes about a man who returned from an absence during the war: the wife tells her small daughter that Daddy is the boss now, and there is no hint of irony.

At the moment when the diary ends, the door closes on her inner life, and it never again opens as widely and for as long. Some letters reveal bits about her inner life, though most of the surviving ones are cheerful and informative rather than reflective. There are glimpses in miscellaneous jottings, and passages in short stories and a novel fragment that, though fictionalized, seem to suggest something of her inner life. Once again I as biographer have to piece together fragments.

THERE IS AN epilogue to the story of those wartime years in Maarn. In May 2001 I was there on a trip that was part holiday and part research for this book. I was sixty-two. I stayed with my Tante Greet Blijdenstein, ninety years old at the time, daughter of Tante Betsy, cousin of Wim, sister-in-law of the Christie and Dientje mentioned so often in the diary. Greet and her husband had spent the war in Florida, at what until then had been their winter home. She was, therefore, not part of the world of Maarn when I was a child there, though I had met her on some of the postwar trips I made back to Holland.

On the 4th of May, Tante Greet and I had dinner in a restaurant in Maarn. Every year on that evening there is a two-minute silence to remember all those who died in the Second World War, both soldiers and civilians. (I had not known this and had not planned my trip so as to be there on that date.) As the moment approached, one of the restaurant staff came round and reminded people about the two minutes of silence. Sitting there with my hand curled loosely around the stem of my wine glass, I *did* remember the war dead, but I also found myself deeply moved at being in Maarn taking part in that brief ceremony – being back where I had been fifty-six years earlier.

During those few days, Tante Greet drove me around the area. I saw streets in Maarn named after people mentioned in my mother's diary. We looked at de Hoogt from the outside (it is no longer in the family). We had lunch with Jim van Notten, one of Christie's sons, and his wife, in 't Huis te Maarn. I read the diary that his aunt Dientje Blijdenstein had written during the last winter of the war. I saw (from the outside only) the cottage where we had lived.

On our outings, Tante Greet and I drove back and forth through the woods. There were no anti-aircraft guns, no planes, no bombs. Even though this was not my first visit back to Maarn, it took *this* trip, and perhaps the two minutes of silence, to convince me that the war was over. It led me to reflect that perhaps Madzy never quite realized it, and that in her heart of hearts she never again felt completely safe in the world.

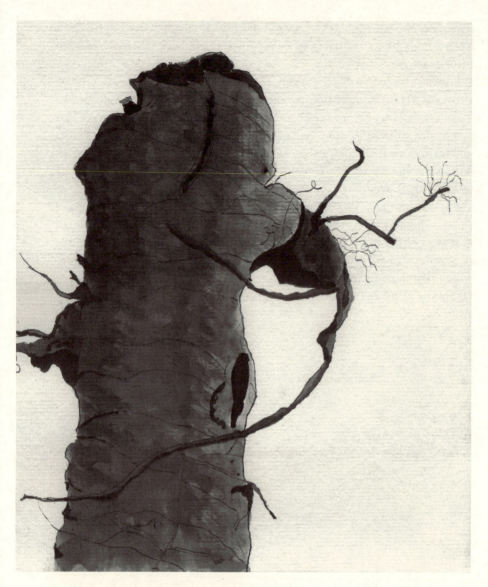

Beech trunk, painted by Madzy in late middle age

CHAPTER SIX

Holland after the War, 1945–1947

AS THEY BEGAN to pick up their interrupted lives in the summer of 1945, Madzy and Wim were part of a whole country that had to be rebuilt. Geert Mak, in a memoir and social history of the Netherlands in the twentieth century, writes that immediately after the war the country was "almost everywhere a total pile of ruins."[1] All types and levels of administration were in chaos. One family in eight was without a home and had to find accommodation with others. Ten per cent of the population owned only the clothes on their backs. In many of the poorer parts of the cities, more than half the children went barefoot. One-quarter of the industries and communication infrastructure had been destroyed or severely damaged. The roads and larger railway stations were full of discharged soldiers returning home and people returning from compulsory labour in Germany, from imprisonment, from hiding.[2] Dikes had to be repaired, flooded parts of the country drained, bridges rebuilt.[3]

Everything – clothing, shoes, food, building materials, fuel, natural resources – was scarce or unavailable. Because there were scarcities in other countries as well,[4] it was not simply a matter of importing what was needed. North America was really the only source, and goods from there, because they had to be paid for in the war-devalued Dutch currency, were extremely expensive.[5] It was not until the end of 1947 that the Marshall Plan was established.[6]

In the Dutch East Indies (which became Indonesia in these years), the war for independence was being waged – a severe drain on Dutch manpower, money, and fuel that would otherwise have been available for rebuilding Holland itself.

The supply of currency had increased during the war, and the scarcity of goods was causing prices to rise. To prevent severe inflation, the Dutch government reformed and stabilized the currency.[7]

Recovery would, as it turned out, happen quite quickly. By 1958, when we visited Holland, everything seemed to be in order again. But in 1945, massive rebuilding was needed in the country as a whole and in people's lives.

MADZY, as we know, had intended to give her war diary to Wim when he returned from the camp, so that he could share at least some of our experiences of those three years. For unknown reasons, she changed her mind. Perhaps she wanted to put that time behind her and face forwards. Possibly she was reluctant to reveal the neediness – she would have considered it weakness – that appears in those pages. She may not have realized that it is also a record of astounding strength and courage and resourcefulness – or, if she did, she may have been uncomfortable at the thought of seeming to boast.

Suppressing some of the realities of her experience, however, did nothing to minimize the gap between her and Wim created by three years' separation. They reconnected, but he never understood what she had really been through until he read the diary after her death. Her dependency on him after that time may have been an attempt to obliterate the gap, but a real sharing of her experience might have served the purpose better.

She painted the picture of those three years for him in much less dark colours than the reality; Wim did not realize until he read the diary just how much bombing and danger there had been in Maarn, how Madzy had exhausted herself scrounging for food. During my work on this book, he said that he wished he had read the diary soon after his return from the camp, if only so that he could have thanked all the people who helped Madzy with food and moral support. Her minimizing of the hardships meant minimizing the help she had needed, received, and given.

AN IMPORTANT source for this period is Madzy's correspondence with Virginia Donaldson and her daughter Rosalie Worthington in the United States.

During the war Virginia had tried to locate us through the Red Cross and the National Refugee Service.[8] She had written to us early in the war and received no reply: postal service was completely disrupted. It was not until September 1945 that she and Madzy resumed contact; but what had till then been a matter of polite letters was transformed into much more vital communication. Virginia and Rosalie immediately began sending us parcels. They asked Madzy what the family needed; her detailed letters of thanks are a catalogue of what was sent.

In her first letter, written on 14 September 1945, Madzy wrote that shoes and clothes were still nearly unobtainable, especially winter clothes for the approaching cold weather. (Central heating was rare in Holland at that time and our house had none.) She was wearing "five-year-old stockings, mended and remended." Underwear was a problem: she had altered some of her own and Wim's so that we children had two sets, one on and one in the laundry. Each of us had one pair of shoes for Sunday and wore wooden shoes in the garden. Madzy herself had no winter coat and only one warm sweater, covered in patches; her other sweaters had been unravelled and converted into socks and sweaters and underwear for us. She asked for a cake of toilet soap because what was available in Holland on coupons was very harsh on the skin. Wim asked for a pair of rubber boots. The scarcity and need is shown by the fact that when Madzy, in one of these parcels, received a sweater that did not fit her, she unravelled and reknitted it in less than a week.

"Food is adequate now," she reports, though "meat, fats, butter or margarine, sugar are scarce. Milk is adequate tho' not overmuch." She reported happily that she and Wim had one good tire each on their bicycles: "It is a luxury, you know, to have good tires, and we have had times that we went along on bare wheels, or had to walk."

The correspondence gives insight into other aspects of their lives. In that first letter, Madzy wrote:

> William is in the army again now after having enjoyed a leave of three months. You can imagine that these were heavenly months and we talked by the hour to tell everything we had done and passed through in the three years of his absence. Fortunately he did not suffer much damage in camp, although I think his nerves are still not as they used to be; moreover he has chronic colitis for which he has to keep a strict diet; of course that is difficult in an officer's mess ... He was rejected for tropical service [in the war in Indonesia], for which I am truly thankful, for that will mean that he is not obliged to leave us again for three years as many of the other officers have to do now. Although he is not very much interested in military work, he has to do his duty to his country, but as soon as he is able to secure his leave from military work, he will take it; we plan to immigrate to Canada. These plans will keep us cheerful through the difficult months ahead.

The optimistic tone conceals some hard realities. Wim was still a cavalry officer and, as Madzy said, after three months' leave he had had to return to active service. The cavalry was converted to a tank regiment, and Wim was sent to be retrained. Quite apart from the fact that by now he and Madzy both loathed the military life, Wim – the lover of horses, plants, earth – hated the work with tanks, hated being in those metal boxes, hated working with munitions. But he could not resign because the Netherlands was still fighting in Indonesia, and it was unthinkable that an officer should resign under those circumstances.

In September 1945, then, he was sent to a training school in Bergen op Zoom, in the south of Holland, to be retrained for work in tanks. He spent no more than a week there and then, because of the colitis, was medically discharged.

He returned to Maarn by a roundabout route because the bridges over the big rivers dividing the country had not yet been rebuilt. Madzy, notified of his coming, was at the railway station at eight o'clock in the evening. There was only one usable railway track, and the signal lights had not yet been repaired. The station master was waving a red lantern at the oncoming train, but when the telegraph machine began ticking, he handed the lantern to Madzy and told her to swing it. When Wim got off the train and he and Madzy embraced, she said, "Home for keeps."

He obtained a low-paying job for a couple of months in an apple orchard, doing some pruning but mainly sorting the apples that had just been picked. He had hoped to learn something about fruit farming, but it was not a useful experience. He was, however, allowed to take the damaged apples home.

Then Willem de Beaufort, the brother of Wim's Oom Ferd of de Hoogt, offered him a position in the office where the extensive estates belonging to the de Beaufort family and other landowners were managed. By this time Wim had earned the diploma that qualified him as an estate manager (*rentmeester*), and he accepted.

He writes in his memoirs that the atmosphere of the office, and the work, were entirely those of the "landed gentry" of a bygone time. "At the funeral of the owner of one of the largest estates all the tenant farmers with old top hats, the game wardens, the foresters, the bookkeeper, myself as *rentmeester*, also with top hat, lined the path leading to the village church." He was uncomfortable with these old-fashioned ways; furthermore, his interest in the practical aspects of farming led him often to take the side of the farmers against that of the landowners.

It was during his eighteen months there that he and Madzy made plans to emigrate to Canada.

BESIDES WHAT is indicated in the letter of 14 September 1945 to Virginia Donaldson, we know very little about how it was for Madzy and Wim to fit together again and resume their marital and family life. Undoubtedly they both suffered from the traumatic effects of war, danger, separation, uncertainty, and captivity. Wim had been literally a prisoner for three years; Madzy, living under enemy occupation, endured captivity of a different sort and had suffered much more danger, terror, and hunger than he.

Wim, recalling that time of reunion, reported that everything was wonderful, that he and Madzy were intensely happy to be together again. That was undoubtedly true so far as it went, but it cannot have been the complete picture. Madzy's almost constant cheerfulness then and during the rest of her life was no doubt often genuine but also, perhaps frequently, a way of reassuring herself as well as the rest of us that everything was (or would be) fine. Trauma survivors are good at dissociating themselves from what hurts. We remember that, in the war diary, she wrote that her letters to Wim in the camp would give only the good news; she would record the bad parts in the diary. Not only was she skilled at achieving that kind of separation; she considered it the right thing to do. What we needed after the end of the war, she evidently decided, was the speediest possible rebuilding of our lives, individually and as a family.

Her remark in the letter to Virginia about Wim's nerves is no doubt an understatement. He had returned abruptly to family life, and to a country in disorder and collapse, where almost everything was rationed or unavailable, where everyone suffered some psychological damage. At home he needed to resume his position as head of the family – tactfully aided by Madzy – but his unawareness of the dynamics that had developed among his wife and children during his absence no doubt blinded him to signals, innuendoes, implications. Just as Madzy decided not to show him the diary or tell him how awful wartime conditions had been, so she probably did not fill in many details about the family situation, hoping that everything would now be all right.

We children were, of course, strangers to him. He had never known Gerard at all, and I had changed from an essentially happy and secure child of three-and-a-half into a moody, difficult, and undoubtedly bothersome girl of six-and-a-half. Madzy herself would have been in some ways a stranger, no matter how hard she tried to be the cheerful, supportive, tactful person he needed, no matter how she tried to protect him from knowing the ways in which she had changed and been damaged.

His presence demanded readjustment. Gerard and I were used to regarding Madzy as the authority in the family. For the previous three years, the men in the household – the refugees and Joost – had been subservient to her; they were certainly not authoritative and trusted leaders. No doubt we continued to regard Madzy as the head of the household – and Madzy,

Madzy, Wim, Gerard, and Marianne, January 1946

making every effort to reintegrate the family, probably had to remind us that Pappa now filled that position. While it was a relief to her to hand over the reins – or at least share the responsibility – surely there was adjustment needed in day-to-day life.

When Wim returned from the camp, Gerard had curly blond hair – not very long by modern standards, but long enough to be distinctly curly. At that time, however, longish hair was unacceptable for boys. Wim, upon his return home, said that it made Gerard look like a girl and insisted that it be cut short. The issue of Gerard's hair reflected Wim's and Madzy's different priorities. Very likely she regarded Gerard's blond curls as being part of his whole gentle and lovable personality. She was more inclined than Wim to see the individual. She was also more permissive, especially with Gerard whom she regarded as a sacred trust, the baby who was born just before Wim had been taken prisoner and whom she had to protect until he returned. Now, as regards Gerard's hair, she gave in to Wim.

Madzy was the pivotal figure in this readjustment, and for the rest of her life she monitored and mediated, explaining us all to each other. Her remark in the diary about "counting herself out" misrepresented the reality; she was central to the family. The dependence on Wim that she often showed obscured his dependence on her. Their relief at being together again, and Madzy's readiness to be submissive but also supportive, made it work. But it may have been at considerable cost to herself – cost that, perhaps, she did not measure, or want to measure.

A hint of how she felt comes from a forty-three-page fragment of a novel entitled *Never Too Late*, probably written ten or twelve years after this time. It is narrated by Atti,[9] a Dutch woman who had spent the war in circumstances much like ours. (Madzy gives a precise description of our cottage in Maarn.) Atti's husband, Marius, a ship's doctor who has been away for the whole war, asks for a divorce when he returns. After the divorce, Atti marries a Canadian, Ken Vandyke, and moves to Canada. The "present time" of the story shows her, now middle-aged and a grandmother, trying to decide whether to return to university.

In one scene, Leonard, Ken's son by his first marriage, challenges Atti on her deference to his father:

> "Marmie, it is your decision, not his. Don't always hang around his neck. Since when did you take a decision, a real serious one, without Dad backing it up?"
>
> I thought for a while. I had to confess, I did depend largely on Ken's judgment, and when I knew he approved, I felt safe. Had I always been like that? Not when I was young; I used to make my

own plans, shape my own future, feel responsible for my decisions. Also, when I was married to Marius, he was away so often, I just couldn't wait to talk things over with him until he would be back for a few days in between his long trips with the ship to America.

No, it had started probably when I was so numb and hurt after the war by the war experiences, by Marius; and when Kenneth took over and led me by the hand, I was only too glad to leave everything to him. It had become a habit with him and me.

The passage surely gives a reliable glimpse into Madzy's state of mind following the war. So does another scene in which she is talking with Ken about her first pregnancy after she married him. Ken asks, "Were you unhappy in those days, Atti?" She replies:

Unhappy? I really don't know. It may be odd, but I feel that unhappiness is really a state of mind, which we bring upon ourselves. I feel within myself that whenever I am unhappy, it is somehow due to a mood, an attitude towards life and the events which come to me. If I feel healthy and strong-minded, only real calamities can make me unhappy. If I feel tired or lost, the tiniest occurrence can down me to a depth of misery. But there are moments in life though which I live without much reaction. I go through them with a numbness of mind which borders on callousness. During the time I expected Johnnie, I was still so overwhelmed by memories of war and terror, hunger, longing and fear, that I had not realized whether I was happy or not. I just lived or vegetated, whatever you would call it.[10]

Ken, hurt, remarks that he thought she was happy, and she consoles him by saying that in that case she must have been: "How could I otherwise have made that impression?" But it is an evasion, a bit of marital tactfulness. That numbness was not happiness, and the description could have come straight out of a textbook on post-traumatic stress disorder.

My conjecture about her state of mind after the war is corroborated by a remark in *Land for Our Sons*. When dealing with our family's move away from the farm in Terrace, B.C., in 1956, she writes, "The time was past that I needed a place of retreat, a spot in which to bury myself."[11] Among her and Wim's reasons for going to the north of B.C. in 1947 was the need for safety, a natural reaction to the fears and dangers of the war, but she is also talking about her own emotional and psychological needs during the preceding years.

Significantly, in both passages from *Never Too Late*, the real information is conveyed in the narrator's unspoken words. Atti's mind moves on two separate tracks, public and private. The remark to Ken that she must have been happy is – as the reader knows – a lie. Thinking about this, I begin to understand why Madzy wrote so much autobiography and semi-autobiography: the complex, subtle, often dark realities of her inner experience, for which there was little permissible outlet in her life with family and friends, had to be expressed somehow, even if they never saw the light of publication – perhaps *because* they were unlikely ever to be published. She could leave the question open: write it and see what it looked like, then decide whether to aim for publication.

What comes through vividly is the difference between her outer and inner lives, and the fact that she felt the need, in her relations with other people, to be silent about so much of who and what she was.

I myself was one of those who enforced that silence on her. Our expectations – and her magnanimous and self-denying willingness to be what we wanted her to be, as well as her sense of duty and her own very human need for approval – led her to separate her inner and outer lives. I wish I had been aware of this at the time, had been able to find a way to rectify it. As it is, by writing this book I can allow her at last to speak, and I can listen to what she wanted to say. I can let all of us listen to what she might have told us had we been listening *then*.

But it was she herself who chose self-denial and, therefore, doubleness.

THE LAST pages of the narrative photo album contain only photos, no captions. Among them are three pictures taken just after Wim's return during a visit from Wim's mother: one shows her with Wim and the children, and one with Madzy and the children. There is a separate one of Juus.

The two pictures of the family are taken against the wall of the house – it is easy to imagine Wim and Madzy changing places and handing over the camera. We are standing in a stiff row, and my teddy-bear and three dolls are sitting against the wall. Our few hens are pecking about in the foreground. All of us wear grim faces. My grandmother's arm is tucked through Wim's in one picture and Madzy's in the other, and she is apparently holding my hand, but there is no sense of anything warm or comfortable. Wim is wearing extremely shabby clothes;[12] Madzy is watching the hens and gives the impression of not being present at all.

These photos do not necessarily reflect how things always were during those years, and it is likely that my grandmother, with her difficult temperament, cast a pall over our spirits. All the same, it is a record of how things were at that moment. Especially it is the look on Madzy's face, spiritlessly staring at the pecking hens, that stays with me. It is a perfect visual representation of the numb, hurt state which she describes in the two passages from the unfinished novel, of the disconnectedness of the trauma survivor. The fact that, more than ten years later, it was still there needing articulation in *Never Too Late* shows that it was much more than a passing mood.

IN THE SUMMER of 1946 Madzy and Gerard and I spent a week or two at the seaside in Bergen-aan-Zee, in a cottage belonging to Christie and Dientje. Wim was working; he remembers coming with Jan Blijdenstein, the brother of Christie and Dientje, in his car to fetch us home. His recollection is that Madzy did not enjoy the holiday. I remember only the horrible jellyfish; I don't think I had much fun either.

Writing to Virginia Donaldson on 30 August 1946, Madzy reported that she was expecting another baby. Like Gerard, this one would be born at home, as "you must be near dying to be taken into the care of the hospitals, in which is a great lack of nurses and material." Joost was born on 1 November 1946.

Six weeks later, in another letter, she gave a word-picture of the family, writing in the cheery tone she used for such public communications:

> The children are all right; Marian is going to the village school (this is her third year) and likes it very much; Gerald being four years old is still at home and enjoys playing in the garden. He is full of interest in his little baby brother and helps me every day when the baby goes into its bath. The little one, Joost (a very old family name), is all right too ... I feed him entirely myself. I feel very well, have some help in the mornings and do the rest myself. William is away by day, but when at home he helps too, carries wood for the stove and repairs everything in the house when broken.

The winter of 1946–47 was very cold. On 9 March 1947, she wrote, "With only two small spells of thaw we had ice from the middle of December, and there is still no outlook of spring. The winter crops are spoiled already, and as the farmers have not yet been able to do any ploughing, the summer crops will be very late too. So food will be scarce again. Fuel is nowhere to be had, even if one still has a precious coupon for it." No doubt we were again gathering fallen branches in the woods next door.

She reported that the baby slept in an unheated room but that the hot-water bottles kept him warm even though his hands were often red with cold. "The older children have no school due to coal-shortage. It is very bad for them all, for education practically stopped during the last war-winter, and now again this stagnation in learning; they will become so backward and will have to work so much harder later on, without Easter vacation or the summer vacation much shortened."

These letters are full of elaborate thanks for the parcels. After receiving the first one, Madzy writes:

> We shall never be cold anymore mentally nor bodily, for your sweet cares have warmed our hearts so much that we shall always feel warm and happy. The gloves are so practical and warm! And the pair of little knickers for me, just what I was in need of! I had only one rather good pair and the rest is in lamentable condition! The woollen scarves are so nice. Little Gerald put on the red woollen cap and would not be separated with it anymore till bedtime. And then that lovely cake of soap! You do not know what a luxury it is to wash with real soap. We washed ourselves for quite a time with a kind of "soap" made of clay, but one could as well not wash oneself.

It was in Madzy's nature to thank people extravagantly, to make much of anything they did for her, and to belittle what she did for them. In this case, there was also the reaction after the desperate hardships and shortages of the war: wearing a new pair of stockings or a sweater without patches, washing oneself with real soap, must have been heavenly. Certainly there was also genuine gratitude, and the need to express it in what was after all her second language. And no doubt there was a good deal of embarrassment; Madzy hated having to ask for help.

IN THE EARLIER letter to Virginia of 14 September 1945, Madzy said that she had not yet received any news about Paul and Mita and their four daughters, who had been in the Dutch East Indies at the outbreak of the war. As it turned out, they were alive but had spent the years following the Japanese occupation of the region in Japanese prison camps, Paul in one and Mita and the girls in another.

In March 1946 they returned to Holland. Madzy, in the memoirs she recorded in her old age, wrote:

> Their war started later than ours and ended later too, and during all those years we didn't know anything about them. We couldn't get any contact via the Red Cross. We didn't know whether they were

alive, what condition they were in. But I am not going to tell you about all those gruesome things. If you ever want to know them, I can tell them to you.

[When they returned] they had only tropical clothes. Here and there they had been able to get a sweater and a pair of shoes, but it was a bedraggled little group of people that arrived finally at Moeder Iete's house in The Hague. We gave them everything we could spare and we borrowed things.

Mita and the girls stayed in The Hague till the middle of December, except for the third daughter, also named Madzy, then fourteen. She lived with us in Maarn from about April to September 1946 to be tutored by my mother to bring her up to the required level of education. The children, after having had no schooling for those years in the camp, had to fit back into the Dutch school system. Young Madzy was also in bad health and needed country air. The youngest, Janneke, who was about two years older than I, also stayed with us at some time. In 2001, when I visited her in Holland, she told me that she kept trying to persuade me to come and play outside, but that I always wanted to be indoors – a clear reaction to the experiences of the war.

The Adama van Scheltema family were also badly scarred by war. In a letter my cousin Madzy wrote to me in 1998, she said that during that summer in Maarn she was shut up inside herself, unaware of what was going on around her. She wrote too that both of our mothers were *"op een laag pitje,"* a Dutch expression meaning that they were operating on "a low flame," and that we children were, as a result, living in an emotional vacuum.

MADZY AND WIM had begun thinking of emigration during the war. Their plans are mentioned in the letter to Virginia of 14 September 1945: "William had this Canada-plan in camp already and read quite a number of books about the country and the fruit-farming over there, in which he is specially interested; he wants to buy a fruit-farm, build his own little house and start life all over again. For us Europe is too full and narrow, and William expects another war before we shall die!"

In *Land for Our Sons*, she gave more details:

The last letter-form I received [from Wim in the camp], seven months before he returned home, contained an obscure sentence, meant to escape the censor's sharp eye: *When Dolly has gone, Bill will take Max and the kids to visit Frank.*

Dolly was our secret name for Adolf Hitler; Frank was short for Franklin D. Roosevelt ... The sentence meant that when the war ended, we would all go back to America. And it so happened that in my last letter to Bill, sent the day before, I had written: *I wouldn't mind taking the kids to Frank some time in the future.*

One of the first things Bill did after his return from the camp was to inquire about the possibilities of emigration [to the United States]. It would not be as easy as he had thought. America's quota for immigrants was small.[13]

So they considered Canada. As we have seen, they had been to Canada in 1938 and Madzy's image of the country, based on Quebec City and the Eastern Townships, was one of French cafés and shops, of a long-settled countryside.

Their plans for emigrating crystallized when, in 1946, Wim and Madzy had lunch with Peter van Stolk, a cousin of Wim's. Peter had moved to Canada in the mid-1930s, and in 1946 he and his Canadian wife, Enid, were living on a farm in Terrace, in the north of B.C. They and their small daughter, Betty Lee, came to Holland in the summer of 1946 to visit Peter's mother and sister.

Madzy and Wim visited them there:[14]

After lunch we sat in a large, very impressive-looking library and while Peter talked with Wim, I sat on the couch with Enid, Betty Lee between us, and listened to enthralling stories of the small town in which they lived, right in the middle of the forests, with brooks and streams full of trout, with apple trees and wild berries, and much sunshine. Life was simple: for meat the men hunted moose, deer, bear, goose, duck. For fruits the women went berry-picking in the woods. Every cottage had its vegetable patch, and a pasture for a cow; most had chickens and a pig. In short, one went to town only for groceries and the mail – there was no delivery of mail there yet – and to have a nice chat with everybody, for everybody knew everybody!

This Edenic vision turned out to be almost pure fiction. It was what Madzy and Wim wanted to hear, and so – whatever Peter and Enid actually told them – it was what they heard. By the time Madzy wrote this passage, she had lived in Terrace for seven or eight years; she does not comment on the differences between expectation and reality, though there is a touch of irony in her tone.

During that visit in 1946, Peter told Wim that there was a train between Terrace and Prince Rupert, a larger town. When they reached home, Madzy and Wim looked up British Columbia in their atlas. There, indeed, was Terrace, and there was Prince Rupert, and there was the red railway line connecting them. Wim measured and found that the distance was about a hundred miles. In Holland, with its good railway system (by then returning to pre-war standards), that was not a major trip; they would be able to go to Prince Rupert for the day, perhaps see the dentist, have lunch or tea, and be home in the evening.

That too was mostly fiction. When they got to Terrace, they discovered that there was one train per day (eastbound one day, westbound the next, both passing through Terrace in the middle of the night). The trip to Prince Rupert took up to six hours, depending on how many moose were on the tracks and how many parcels had to be delivered to isolated houses along the way.

Other images of Canada came from the Jalna books by Mazo de la Roche that Madzy read. But they depicted a prosperous colonial aristocracy living in southern Ontario.

Besides these unrealistic images there were, however, more substantial reasons for leaving the Netherlands. Wim, in 2002, wrote about his fear of the Russians and of another war.

> I had been liberated by the Russian army and for some eight weeks had witnessed their occupation of Germany, which was simply terrible. Mom and I had two young sons who maybe would have had to serve in World War III ... The Russians were [in 1947] at the Elbe River, which is only a few hundred kilometres from the Dutch border, which it would have taken their tanks less than a day to reach.
>
> During the war I often realized that if we had stayed in the U.S., Mom and you two would not have been in dangerous Maarn and starvation. Neither of us wanted to live through another war. The Cold War fortunately did not turn into a hot one, but it was close. During [World War II] we both were wishing for life together in a safe place. We did not emigrate for better living conditions materially; we knew that we would have less prosperity in Canada.

Alluding to postwar East Germany, he wrote: "We could have been in that situation, and then we would have said, 'Why did we not get out when it was still possible?' I even thought that if we settled in Canada, some relatives could come to us for safety when severely threatened." Moreover, if another war broke out and he was still living in the Netherlands, he would have to go into active military service again. Madzy had an additional reason for wanting to emigrate: she needed to free herself from her and Wim's parents who criticized her hair style, her clothes, her way of bringing up the children.

After the talk with Peter and Enid van Stolk, it did not take them long to reach a decision. Peter sent Wim a letter agreeing to sponsor us. On 2 January 1947 a Canadian consulate opened in The Hague, the first one on the European continent. On the morning when it opened, Wim was there with Peter's letter:

> A long line of people stretched along the sidewalk and a Canadian commissioner handed forms out but nobody was allowed in. I showed the letter and was the first one admitted. The immigration officer and secretaries sat idle amidst brand new furniture waiting for the first applicant and that was me. I had a pleasant talk with the man, who had an artificial leg, obviously a veteran. I had also proof of my $6000 in New York.[15] Everything was OK and my name was entered as the first Dutchman accepted for immigration. This was quite a record considering the huge numbers that followed.

On 9 March 1947 Madzy reported to Virginia, "We hope to start on the *Delftdijk* of the Holland-America Line, which goes from Rotterdam via the Panama Canal to Vancouver; from there we shall take a boat to Prince Rupert and then go by rail to Terrace, B.C., which is ninety miles from Prince Rupert."

One of my few memories of this time is of my father painting our future address onto the steamer trunks and crates. For each letter he used a metal stencil over which he brushed white paint. I remember being astonished to think that those crates and trunks would find their way to the other side of the world with just those few letters on each. The trunks would be used over and over again for our many future moves. I remember seeing the last of them in the 1990s, and I wish I had kept one as a souvenir.

Just before we left, someone took pictures of us. They are "public" pictures, the family neatly dressed and having a good time. Gerard and I hold hens in our arms, smiling happily; Madzy and Wim each piggy-back a child. Several show us sitting decorously but cheerfully on the bench in front of the house.

Expecting to set off in early July but in fact not leaving until the second of August, we ended up having to stay with relatives. We spent some time with Hansje, Madzy's sister, still unmarried, and then with Wim's father

On the eve of departure for Canada: Madzy holding Joost, Gerard
standing on the bench, Marianne, and Wim

and stepmother. It was from there that, on the morning of 2 August, we went by taxi to the Rotterdam docks. The farewells had taken place already, and no one came to see us off. I can still see the widening gap of dirty water as the ship pulled away from the wharf.

AT THAT MOMENT Madzy picks up the story again: we have her diary-letter of twenty-five single-spaced typed pages written on board ship. She made three copies, one for her mother, one for Paul and Mita, and one for us to keep. Wim attended to the correspondence with his family. Whenever the ship reached a port, they posted their letters and picked up the mail that had been addressed to the Holland-America Line offices in those cities. Madzy's diary-letter is a continuous account of the time from leaving Wim's father's house to our arrival in Terrace. It is a public account, with almost none of the inwardness that is so remarkable in the war diary.

Nevertheless, like the newspaper columns she wrote from America, it reveals a good deal about Madzy. She is observant, interested in details, painting vivid word-pictures in a bright style with an occasional slangy or pithy phrase that – to me, reading it now – brings her voice and manner clearly to mind. She gives detailed information about foreign places most of her readers would not have been able to picture.

The trip from Rotterdam to Terrace took nearly seven weeks. It would have been possible to travel by ship to the east coast of Canada and then cross the country by train, but there were restrictions on the amount of money that emigrants could convert into other currencies and take out of the country. We were allowed to take only $90 for our whole family – even then, a miniscule amount. The journey on a Dutch ship could be paid for in Dutch guilders; Wim and Madzy could use their scarce Canadian dollars for the trip from Vancouver to Terrace and the expenses of settling there.

The *Delftdijk* was a freighter that carried a few passengers. For the main part of the trip, until several families got off in Los Angeles and San Francisco, there were twenty-six adults on board, eight children aged four to ten years old, and three babies. The *Delftdijk* had served as a troop ship during the war and was now on its last voyage before being completely overhauled. When both of its engines gave out in the middle of the Atlantic and it lay bobbing in silence on the waves, Madzy referred to it as "our old carcass of a boat." Freight had priority, and at each port of call there was unloading and loading. Madzy writes that, because of the noise and the smells, it was always an advantage when the portholes of our cabin faced away from the quay rather than overlooking it.

The ship became one of our many temporary dwellings. Our cabin contained two sets of berths, and there was a private bathroom. Joost, not yet a year old, slept in the bathroom: the large basket that was his travelling crib fitted neatly into the tub. By way of a salon for the passengers, there was a library not far from our cabin. Madzy did our personal laundry by hand and hung it on a clothesline on the rear deck of the ship.

The meals at first overwhelmed her. It was by now more than two years since the end of the war, but in Holland rationing was still stringent. She described the first lunch on board: "The white bread, the chunks of butter with it, the meat and other delicious things, filled us with wonder and a certain feeling of guilt that we would get this fare every day now, whereas those at home never have it." In one day on board ship, she wrote, we consumed the equivalent of two weeks' meat ration in Holland, and in two days a two weeks' butter ration. When she had trouble with a tooth and had to have it pulled by the ship's doctor, she conjectured that the problem arose from suddenly having so much more meat to chew. She was also impressed with the four pieces of good soap at our two washbasins.

The crew members, she learned, received one-third of their salary in dollars; when they reached American harbours, they spent it thriftily on household supplies (dishes, linen, underwear, tinned food) to take to their families in Holland. The abundance of merchandise in the stores in the port cities astonished her; she wished she too could buy things to send home.

She described the vast expanse of ocean on which it seemed that the ship made no headway at all. The only assurance that we were moving came from the map in the upstairs hall on which the ship's progress was traced; the ship was in fact travelling about 350 miles per day. There was also a clock showing when we passed from one time zone to the next.

The voyage took us through the tropics in August. There was no air conditioning, though there were fans. The heat meant more frequent changes of clothing, so Madzy had more washing to do. Nights were hot. During the worst of the heat, she found herself able to accomplish little beyond reading. The only relief came from a swimming pool, which the crew built of lumber, lined with a tarpaulin, and filled with ocean water.

In Curaçao Madzy and Wim were given a short tour by an army officer who had been with Wim in the POW camp and was now in military service. He picked them up at ten o'clock in the evening in his Dodge convertible, drove them around for two hours, then took them to a club.

We drove along a beautiful asphalt road for about ten minutes and then approached the city. The houses on both sides were all very small, single-storey, stuccoed, and all painted in soft pastel colours. In front of the houses were ornate fences; larger houses with two storeys had balconies with ornamental railings, as if at any minute a Spanish woman in a mantilla, like Carmen, might come out to listen to the love song being sung from below her ... There were lots of cars ... parking is such a problem that people going shopping sometimes have to park 2 km from the store. We approached the centre of the city: more of those little houses, each with a piece of land, all with closed louvred shutters. Here and there a black woman in a colourful dress and headscarf, here and there a lit veranda where people were sitting.

She saw houses dating from the seventeenth century, and the inner harbour with its sailing ships, which brought fruit from Venezuela. She reports on vegetation, climate, currency, and language spoken, with an absorbed interest in everything she saw and was told.

From Curaçao we headed to the Panama Canal. At the Atlantic end of the canal, Gerard, looking at the coast, burst into tears. Madzy wondered if he had hurt himself, but he said, "I wish it was Holland, that it was Maarn." It is one of the few references in the letter to homesickness: this is not a document that deals with much that is negative.

In Cristobàl Madzy and Wim found mail from Holland – the first communication, and a great pleasure. From there we went through the canal, described in detail, together with historical information about its construction. The ship docked in Balboa, and one morning we took a bus to Panama City where we ate ice-cream cones and Wim and Gerard had their hair cut by a barber "right there on the street." Madzy bought a cheap summer dress, her first new one since before the war.

In addition to brief bouts of seasickness, the family had a few illnesses – occasional children's ailments, heat rash in the tropics. Madzy slipped and fell on a wet floor and was in bed for two days with what the ship's doctor diagnosed as a slight concussion.

The weather was good for the most part – no real storms, only two spells of rough seas in the Pacific which seem not to have been severe – but Madzy was sensitive even to lesser movements of the ship and several times had to lie down while others were still on their feet.

This journey was, for her, a kind of holiday. She had no meals to cook, no cleaning or major laundry to do. She wrote the diary-letter and no doubt letters to other family members and friends, knitted an outfit for Joost, did the washing. She gave us children English lessons. She began reading

Alice's Adventures in Wonderland to me, but we found its particular kind of fantasy frightening, no doubt because during the war we had had contact with horrors that made Alice's adventures seem too real to us. The voyage was not a complete holiday but an interlude between the past years of wartime and postwar Holland, including the months of hectic preparation to emigrate, and the future which at that time she could hardly imagine. We were between two lives, travelling from the known to the unknown.

By the end of the trip, Madzy was becoming restless. She wanted her own house again, wanted to get on with her life.

Vase of flowers, painted by Madzy in late middle age. Gerard's comment:
"It shows the sense of force inside her."

Terrace from the air

CHAPTER SEVEN

Terrace, British Columbia, 1947–1956

We sailed into the Strait of Juan de Fuca ... and from the beginning of this strait to Vancouver is still seven hours' travelling. On both sides are higher and lower mountains; occasionally rocky islands, very thickly forested, and we smelled the fresh piney scent. It was all so gorgeous and so different from all those other harbours that we've entered up to now! We delighted in it, and the Canadians among us were excited and wanted to show and explain everything.

The view is spectacular; the city [of Vancouver] lies against the mountains. On the left the forested mountains, some with snow on the tops, rise from the water; on the right is the city, with many trees, a beautiful park (Stanley Park, where strangers stood waving Dutch flags) among high buildings but also buildings of more ordinary height. A beautiful big bridge under which we sailed, and then turned right and docked. This brought us immediately in the city – five minutes' walk – and not one of those dirty harbour areas as in Los Angeles and San Francisco. On the dock walked some people who came to meet their arriving relatives; for us that was a miserable moment, because there was no one for us; it is so much a part of it, that when you arrive somewhere there is someone to meet you![1]

When the gangplank was lowered, one of the people boarding *did* come up to Madzy – a young man who turned out to be a newspaper reporter. He asked pertinent and impertinent questions, and the story that appeared in the paper was as superficial and misleading as a 2½-inch item might be expected to be.

The *Delftdijk* arrived in Vancouver on Saturday afternoon, 13 September 1947, and the coastal steamer to Prince Rupert would not be leaving until Monday evening. Bill had arranged lodgings for us for those two nights, but the *Delftdijk* captain said we could remain on board until Monday.

On Sunday we went by bus to White Rock, south of Vancouver, to visit Mr and Mrs McKim. Mrs McKim was an Englishwoman who had been a governess at 't Stort in Maarn. Madzy describes the bus, the trip, the scenery. There were stretches of newly cleared land where, she writes, "you could tell by the stumps how big the trees had been." She remarks on the fact that the houses were small, built of wood, and surrounded by gardens. "There isn't one house that is attached to another; they are all separate bungalows."

On Monday we again went to White Rock. In *Land for Our Sons* she explains that in Los Angeles she and Bill had received a letter from Peter van Stolk containing information about a possible job. In a short memoir written in 1959 she gives details:

> A wealthy lumbermill-owner in Vancouver had bought a farm out in the country and was looking for a Dutch farmer with family who would look after it. The farmer was to take care of the farm, which had some livestock on it, and to start planting bulbs, for the soil was good for bulb-growing there, and moreover the owner's wife was fond of gardening and wanted to grow quite an amount of bulbs. The farmer's wife was to look after the country home, and when the owner's family would come down for the weekend, she was supposed to do some odd jobs around the house.

In *Land for Our Sons*, Madzy writes that she and Bill had been thinking of this all during the journey from Los Angeles to Vancouver.

> [This proposal] had some very great advantages; we would find a home the moment we stepped ashore, and we need not spend our few precious dollars at all. We would have the chance of learning the ways of the new country. A serious-minded, careful person would have jumped at this marvellous piece of luck.
>
> But adventure had gripped us. Now that we had burnt our boats behind us, now that we had taken the jump, we wanted to go the whole way. Bill had had enough of being bossed by a superior who would regulate every step of his.
>
> We must have been slightly giddy in the head, for we threw every caution to the wind and said that now at last we were going to do what we really wanted to do, and that was going to that wonderful country up north, where everybody lived as he wanted to live.

However, before we would say a definite no, we were first going to have a look at the farm ...

It was a nice little farm – really a suburban place. There were two houses on it, one for the family, complete with interior decoration, chintzes, and an open fireplace; the other a very comfortable clapboard house with running water, bathroom facilities, but without trimmings.

We said no. Thank you very much, but no. And I still think we did the very best thing. Our life would have been easier, but not nearly so colourful. We would have missed a lot of experiences, fun and heartbreak, if we had stayed put there. I might not have written a book, and I have wished to do that now for several years.[2]

The wealthy man and his daughter who had picked us up in their car had from the start irritated Madzy with their air of superiority: "I felt like the maid who is taken out for a Sunday ride with her three little brats, poor soul!"[3] Being made to feel like a servant – the servant she would literally have been, had she and Bill accepted the offered jobs – decided the matter for her.

So they continued on to Terrace. Clearly Madzy was feeling adventurous – as she had done when she made plans to practise law in the Dutch East Indies. But she was also looking for "a place of retreat, a spot in which to bury myself."[4] The spirit of adventure and the need for freedom were real; but now she also needed safety. The frontier was expected to provide a sanctuary. Clearly, it was possible to venture into the unknown *with* Bill and the family, and the decision to continue with the plan they had made seemed the best way to give substance to their vision of their and their children's future.

What Madzy writes in *Land for Our Sons* about our arrival shows an interesting difference in mood from the diary-letter. Written on the spot and intended for the family in Holland, the letter is infused with the enthusiasm of travelling and the undeclared intention of showing what a good decision it had been to emigrate. *Land for Our Sons*, written about eight years later, was also intended for other people, and it is also mostly cheerful, filled with amusing stories and with accounts of pleasure and achievement. But the woman who wrote it had *lived* the reality of pioneering. The two versions are like parentheses, the first depicting how things appeared at the beginning and the second how they looked when, at the end of the time in Terrace, she assessed the experience.

Land for Our Sons begins:

On the wings of the land wind a scent of evergreens wafted over the deck of the ocean steamer. After the salty air of the Atlantic and Pacific, the nauseating oil smells of Curaçao and Los Angeles, and the tropical odours of Cristobal and Balboa, this fresh piney scent from the evergreens of Vancouver Harbour was like a glass of wine to the weary traveller. It went straight to my head.

The ss *Delftdijk* of the Holland-America Line was sailing into the harbour very deliberately. It had sailed into European, tropical, Pacific harbours, but now it was different. This was the final harbour for us. Here we would disembark, and when we set foot ashore we would know it to be the point of no return.

I was leaning against the railing of the passengers' deck, watching the freighter's slow progress, and a dismal feeling of loneliness came over me. Other passengers were leaning over the railing, craning their necks in happy anticipation, shouting, waving; in short behaving like fools. And here was I, with my family, and no one awaiting us!

I stared down at the eager group of people on the quay without the slightest enthusiasm. Why should I feel eager: Because the long, long voyage was over, because now we could stretch our cramped legs and feel solid ground under our feet once more? No, the truth was that I was scared – scared of this bewildering new country, with the many dark forests making a backdrop to the city. At last I knew I was scared, and was ready to confess it to myself. I knew, too, that Bill hadn't felt so sure of himself, because after one long glance at the coast and the city, he had muttered something about going to have a look at the baby, and had left me holding on to the braces of the other two children, so that they would not fall overboard.

"If only there was one person, one little person only, who would come on board to welcome us," I thought, and I scanned for a moment the upturned faces of the people ashore. But how could there be? I did not have a single friend in Vancouver. In fact, the only people I knew in the whole vastness of Canada were Peter and Enid, our cousins, and their little girl, Betty Lee; and they were waiting for us way up in Terrace, five hundred miles north of Vancouver. They did not expect us until the middle of next week.

I realized then how spoilt I had been all my life. Whenever I had returned from a trip abroad, there had been someone to await me eagerly, someone to listen to excited stories of my adventures and my conquests. But things were different now; I had to grow up. I was not a luxury-traveller any more, but an immigrant, just an immigrant, one of very, very many.[5]

In her youth she had indeed been a luxury traveller, a young lady from a privileged family travelling to Switzerland for the "wintersport," to England to attend finishing school and hike in Cornwall, to the coast of Norway, to New York by passenger liner to marry Wim. There was no shortage of clothes or money, and any discomforts were deliberately chosen as part of the fun, the adventure. And, as she says, all the trips ended with her returning to Holland. She set out from – and would return to – a place where she had family and friends and a recognized niche in a familiar social structure.

This time was different, and it is only eight years later that she can describe what it meant to be an immigrant, to be travelling into the unknown with no prospect of returning to where she had started from. We had few possessions, very little money. She owned one good summer dress. She had written, "At last I knew I was scared, and was ready to confess it to myself": The words "at last" can only refer to the previous months of decision-making and preparation and travelling, to the reality underlying the cheery travelogue written during the journey. It is not surprising that she was now scared; but admitting it was, for her, a considerable achievement.

FROM THE *Delftdijk* we transferred to the coastal steamer that took us to Prince Rupert – Madzy gives a delightful description of a brief stop in Ocean Falls – and then we journeyed inland the ninety-odd miles to Terrace.

The train left Prince Rupert at eight o'clock in the evening. This is the diary-letter again:

> So we travelled through the pitch darkness, unable to see a thing, to Terrace, along the Skeena River. The train frequently stood still: now at a farm, then for no reason (nothing visible in the darkness). It's a region which is so lonely and wild that it's impossible to imagine ... Terrace was the first larger place where the train stopped. We were delayed by a horse that walked along the track, which they could apparently not chase off.
>
> At nearly 2:00, someone announced "Terrace!" We saw nothing – everything totally dark. The train stopped at a station, but in the darkness I saw nothing of it. We were put off with luggage and all,

and suddenly someone looked at me searchingly: Peter van Stolk. What a meeting! We were all delighted, Peter not the least. He looked like a real *coureur de bois* in his leather vest and leather jacket, high boots and broad-brimmed hat. We were all loaded into his car (it was cold, it felt like frost) and we rode to his house. We didn't see much in the darkness – some stores and a wide road ...

Outside town we abruptly turned into a steep lane and suddenly the car's headlights showed a log cabin. From it jumped Enid and also small Betty Lee in her nightclothes. We quickly went indoors, where a large fireplace and burning wood fire awaited us and, on a shining wooden table, a delicious supper. What a warm welcome! We immediately felt at home. It was past 3:00 when we walked, lit by a flashlight, to our own cabin, where there was also a fire in a stove, and beds that welcomed us with open arms. How we slept! But I have no words to describe how beautiful the mountains were when we woke up in the morning and walked outdoors – mountains all around, lit up by the rising sun, snow on the highest tops, while Terrace itself lies sheltered against cold winds, sunning itself.

There she ends, saying that from now on she will write shorter letters to be sent by air-mail.

WE LIVED FOR two months in the cabin on the van Stolks' place. It was a simple house: kitchen, small sitting room, two bedrooms. There was no bathroom, only an outhouse.[6]

The next day Peter drove us into town; in *Land for Our Sons*, Madzy describes what she saw:

> The road I had seen vaguely last night was the same this afternoon, wide, deserted, with only a few houses on one side. It was a gravel road with here and there a nasty hole in it, but it was the main highway ... and in real good state of repair, Peter assured me. On the south side ran the tracks of the Canadian National Railway, half hidden behind some bushes. At a crossroad stood a building built of boards, two storeys high, with a flagpole in the front. The school! We all looked at it full of interest, except Marianne, who looked the other way. Still, she too would have to face it one of these days.
>
> Terrace's town consists of two main streets, which cross each other at right angles, with several side streets and roads. Just north of the river is the Canadian National Railway station. I had not been able

to see anything the night before, but I had not missed much. [Both main streets, Kalum Street and Lakelse Avenue] are lined with stores and little shops; there are the buildings like the post office and the Royal Canadian Mounted Police station, the Municipal Hall, and several churches and community halls.

During the war the army had built a training camp in Terrace, and there were groups of army barracks still on the outskirts of the town. Their Recreation Hall was taken over by the town, and called the Civic Centre. The army was in the process of selling some of the huts and army material. When we entered the town, therefore, I gasped, for here in front of us was a house moving in our direction: in fact it hobbled over the road like a snail, and I thought that it must be a common occurrence for the townspeople to take their houses along wherever they went.[7]

Having painted the larger picture, she comes back to her first impressions:

That first afternoon with Peter was pretty bewildering. As soon as we had turned a sharp s-curve, Peter said with certain pride, "And here is town."

We looked eagerly; we were too polite to say, "Where?" so we said "Oh," instead. We saw some trees, a small church, some shacks, some open spaces ... Nice leafy trees in a row now, and here and there a wooden building, a small store.[8]

Terrace was then a town of about fourteen hundred inhabitants. Enid told Madzy there was "no phone,"[9] but she may have meant she had no phone. A telephone system had been installed the year before,[10] but even in 1950 there were fewer than five hundred subscribers. In 1945, only forty-nine households had electricity, and by 1950 there were only 413.[11] There was no hospital, no dentist, no library, no bookstore; there were no radio broadcasts to be heard except an occasional signal from somewhere in the United States. The weekly newspaper contained only local news and advertising.

But Madzy seemed to enjoy it all.[12] Enid van Stolk wrote to me in 1998 in response to my request for any memories she might have,

I remember so well her arrival in Terrace with her little family. Such enthusiasm and expectations! She always had original and incisive and often humorous comments about life as she found it in Terrace ... The wood cookstove and outdoor plumbing must have been hard for her. She never complained.

I remember one day we were all harvesting apples. There were boxes and boxes of them. Your mom made it seem like a party and had all the children involved.

Madzy was thirty-seven at this time, Bill a few months younger. I would have my ninth birthday three weeks after we arrived. Gerard was five, Joost not quite a year old.

Madzy had already had a varied and eventful life, but nothing prepared her for Terrace.

BUYING A FARM was a priority. The real estate agent, after showing Bill and Madzy several places, took them to one to the north of town. It was near the end of the Eby Road, close under the "Bench," a steeply rising slope that was in fact where the bank of the Skeena River had been aeons earlier.

We stopped at a little gate beside two tall hawthorn trees. Entering through the gate we walked up a narrow path, which led to a small cabin with a partly closed-in front porch.

"The owner was a captain in the army; he worked here during the war," [the agent] told us.

In front of the little cabin stood a tall maple tree. It had a lopsided look. One side was partially dead, or dying, the bark gone.

"This is an old place," he explained further.[13] "It belonged to a Mr Eby, who was one of the first settlers here. He built a large house, very large according to our standards. The house had a porch all around it. He sold the place before the war, and it went from hand to hand. The owner who lived here during the war took boarders in; one afternoon the house burnt down to the ground."

"So that's what happened to the maple," said Bill.

Inside there was nothing but one room, partly divided by two partitions. On the north and west sides were two built-on lean-tos with tiny windows. But it was clean and practically new.[14]

There was also a good-sized chicken-house and a smaller barn, and twenty acres of land, of which only three or four were cleared. There were a few apple trees. The dense bush – tall trees and impenetrable, yards-deep underbrush – behind the cleared fields ran part-way up the steep slope of the Bench.

The original house, in the first winter (1947–48)

The next day Madzy and Bill bought the farm, and Bill began at once to prepare the cabin for the winter. It was late September; the snow creeping down the mountainsides was a warning of what was to come. While we remained in the van Stolks' second house, Bill went every day to the farm to work. The cabin had little insulation, no chimney, no electric wiring. Bill used sawdust (obtained free from the sawmills which were the town's main industry) for insulation, and bought some second-hand insulation from the army. He had a chimney built and wiring installed. "Bill came home around supper-time, and every day he reported some improvement to the farm. Some days he would pick apples and store them away for the winter ('Our first crop, how wonderful!'), then he would have dug a ditch from the well to the house, for I was to have a hand pump in the little kitchen. He went to his work with great gusto, and never had enough time. Instead of walking, he trotted."[15]

In the barn were small mangers with goat-sized openings. That gave Bill the idea of keeping goats instead of a cow for milk. He ordered two Saanen milk goats from Alberta; they were shipped by train and temporarily housed in Peter van Stolk's barn. Snooks and Lady Jones – a buck was added later – were the starting point for several generations of goats.

FOR THEIR FIRST Sinterklaas (December 5) in Canada, Madzy wrote one of the doggerel verses typical of such celebrations in Holland. Addressing Peter and Enid (in English), she wrote:

> A new life they'll build to forget the bad past,
> A new peace they will have; may this peace ever last!
> A new future they'll make for their girl and their boys,
> A life without horrors, with hard work and with joys.
>
> Thanks to you, my dear people, our life will be changed,
> Thanks to your hospitality could it be so arranged.
> Your warm welcome helped us in this difficult time,
> Your love urged me to toil o'er this wobbly rhime!

On 13 December we moved to the farm. About the first winter, Madzy writes:

> Often, when looking out of the small windows, I wondered how those desolate snow fields could turn into fertile stretches of soil, full

of wonderful crops. I was a girl from the city, with hardly any experience of growing things. I could not possibly understand how Bill, with the little help I could give him, was going to make a farm here.

Bill, however, was full of confidence; anyhow, that's the face he showed to the world. Whether he had his doubts, I did not know; he kept them very secret if he had them.[16]

The property was not a working farm, and there was little or no farming equipment. What was needed was bought, and every penny was turned twice before it was spent. The savings from the New York bank paid for the purchase of the property and also had to see us through the months until there was income from the farm.

Corners were cut. For years we gathered eggs in an enamel pan with a bucket handle that we had found on the town dump; it had a large hole in the bottom, but we covered that with hay, which also made a soft bed for the eggs. Because there was no money for furniture, Bill constructed a couch of lumber, with an old mattress for upholstery. (We used it until we left Terrace.) For seating at the dining table, he built backless benches. The table itself we had brought with us, a rectangular maple table he had made in the United States. He built bunks for Gerard and me; later there were army-surplus beds with lumpy mattresses. Peter and Enid donated an old double bed for him and Madzy. Joost continued, for the time being, to sleep in the big basket. All of us, for well over a year, slept in one tiny bedroom.

For transportation, Bill bought a pre-war Chevrolet, but that was a mistake. Within months he replaced it with Duke, a logging horse whom we used for farm work and also to haul logs out of our woodlot to be sold for ready money. For the next few years Duke was our only form of horsepower, pulling the farm equipment in the fields and the wagon or sleigh we used to go into town.

Immediately behind the house and farm buildings was a low-lying area alongside a creek; in the fall, when the creek was high, the land flooded. It was covered with a dense tangle of shrubby growth. The soil was excellent, however, so when Bill learned about a government plan to send land-clearing equipment around to farmers who requested it, he arranged to have this brush cleared. In one day the bulldozers did what would have taken years to do by hand; but the mess of saplings and undergrowth, roots and weeds and soil was left in five or six long parallel ridges, ten feet high or more, right across the land. Bill ploughed and planted the cleared spaces in between – amounting to perhaps two or three acres – but those brush piles had to be taken apart by hand, the burnable portions stacked and burned, restacked and burned again.[17] It went on for years.

Enlarging the house took second place to raising crops. In the fall of 1948, however, a year after we had moved in, work began on an extension. A cellar (for storing crops) was excavated and concrete poured that fall and covered with a temporary roof. In March the next stage of building was done. Madzy tells the story in *Land for Our Sons*:

> As soon as the weather turned somewhat milder Bill started. The snow was still high, but the sun was shining, as it shines only in spring; bright, sharply penetrating.
>
> We had made the plans in winter; three bedrooms on top of the basement; the present tiny bedroom was to be ripped out, and the gap between the old and the new building would become the dining-room; the kitchen stove should come there. The bathroom would be enlarged. The living-room would be heated by a bulky wood heater.
>
> A friend helped us for a few days, and the rest we did together. All other work was put aside: no laundry, no baking, I had done all that beforehand. My daily household chores took me less than an hour, and after that I was at the building, hammering, measuring, cutting tar-paper, holding two-by-fours.
>
> When I was young, a house was something found ready-made; how it was made never bothered me. Now, every board went through our hands, every crack was filled in, every measurement discussed. We knew by now, after two cold winters, how important a house is for the comfort of the family; the more care we spent on the insulation, the less fuel we would need during the long winters. And it took many hours of labour to cut firewood out of our woodlot.[18]

Photographs show the house with the old bedroom gone, the new addition still covered in tar-paper. "During the days [when] the old bedroom was ripped down, we slept, lived, ate and cooked in the one living-room. I began to feel like Robinson Crusoe, and realized that now I had survived these situations I was ready for anything. One night, still in March, we had to sleep practically in the open, with the old room ripped away, and we had no door to shut out the dark, cold spring night."[19]

The dining-room was quickly built because the two parts of the house had to be connected, but it was not until the following spring that the outside of the bedroom addition received a coat of wooden siding. It was also

The house being enlarged, early spring 1949. The original house is to the right, the addition to the left.

more than a year before there were bedroom partitions; until then, only the odd spare sheet or blanket hung where the walls would one day be.

The house was improved in other ways too. The original high, small windows in the living room were replaced by larger war-surplus windows with a multitude of small panes. Plumbing and a telephone (party line) were installed, and in our last few years a two-burner electric range with oven – but the wood-stove remained because it was needed for overflow cooking and for heat.

The chicken house, too large for our requirements, was sold to Ed and Anne Shaw, who bought the land across the road from us. It was a sturdy building and they planned to convert it into a house for themselves; they had it put on skids and dragged across the road. While the caterpillar tractor was available, Bill had our original small goat barn moved further back; there he built a machinery shed behind it and a hay-loft over the entire structure. Immediately behind the house in the fall of 1951 he erected a combination workshop-greenhouse, again with a cellar for storing the harvest. The greenhouse part would allow him to start seeds early to compensate for the short northern growing season.

Also in 1951, Duke was replaced by a small Austin pickup truck and, a bit later, a tractor.

The cleared area of the farm was never more than about seven acres. On it we raised potatoes, cabbage, celery, lettuce, cauliflower, and carrots, which were sold locally and, later, to Kitimat and Prince Rupert. We had apples for ourselves, and our own eggs. We had milk from our goats and occasionally sold some to people who could not digest cows' milk. The hay for our livestock came from a field on the van Stolks' place.

Like most farm women, Madzy did her share of the outdoor work. She and Bill had no regular employment off the farm; the kind of farming we did, and the nature of housekeeping at the time, kept them more than busy.

The household was much closer to those of the early pioneers than to modern ones. The house was heated by the cooking stove and, later, a heater, both of which had to be continually stoked with wood; it was our job as children to keep the woodbox filled, chop kindling, and also to stack wood in the woodshed after it had been cut in the woodlot, sawed into stove lengths (Bill did not have a chain saw), and split. We had brought a second-hand wringer washer from Holland; laundry was hung outdoors, though frequently the final drying had to be done indoors. There was a ceiling rack in front of the bedroom doors on which it could be hung, and in bad weather we ducked through wet laundry to reach our rooms. I remember frequently in winter bringing in laundry that was frozen stiff and, when thawed, would drip on the floor. There were no non-ironing fabrics, so ironing was a regular task.

At first, water for the laundry, housework, and personal washing had to be heated on the stove in a large, oblong boiler. Even when we eventually got an electric water heater, it provided only enough hot water per day for the laundry or a bath for one person. Our bathroom had no shower, only a tub and a toilet and basin.

In the cold winters and with the high humidity indoors, ice formed on the insides of the panes, in spite of storm windows, freezing and thawing. Towels laid on the window sills soaked up the water, and from time to time someone had to make the rounds, wringing them out into a bucket. They regularly froze against the window and then all you could do was stare at them helplessly and reflect that they might not thaw loose until the spring.

The floors were swept with broom and dustpan; our one tiny carpet was cleaned with snow or wet tea leaves to pick up the dust. Clothes were mended over and over; outgrown clothes were altered to fit someone else. Bill's pockets needed frequent mending because he carried tools in them; I remember doing it, grumbling. Madzy and I knitted socks, scarves, tuques. In the beginning we still received parcels of clothing from American friends.

Bed linen was also mended. Madzy bought sheeting by the yard from the mail-order catalogue and made sheets on her pre-war sewing machine. When they wore out in the middle, they were often turned sides-to-middle.

A cupboard with a screened opening in the north wall of the kitchen served in winter as a refrigerator. The cellar served as a cool store year round. Madzy baked all our bread as well as cakes, cookies, and pies. In the summer she did preserving, in cans or jars, and made jam. Almost everything was cooked from scratch.

She was not a particularly good cook; what she had done repeatedly, she did well, but she was not interested in food and seldom had much appetite herself. In a column written in 1963 for a Dutch-Canadian newspaper, she appealed to her readers:

> I need your help. I've been asked to include some recipes in this column. As a matter of fact, they could hardly have found a worse door to knock on than mine, because I'm the worst cook you could find in this country. It came about in this way.

Before I arrived in this country there was, as it happened, always someone who did the cooking.[20] When I arrived here, we first went to live in a small village in northern B.C. There all of a sudden I had to do my own cooking, and to do it on a wood-stove. You'll understand that in the beginning that wasn't much more than a substantial soup – it would stand there simmering even when the fire died down a bit or suddenly burned much too hard.[21]

She describes how Enid[22] "taught" her to bake bread. Two days after our arrival in Terrace, Madzy writes, the one local baker moved away. Week-old bread brought up from Vancouver did not appeal to her. She went to Enid for help, and Enid said, "You'll bake your own, of course. Come, I'll show you."

Well, she showed me precisely: you take a handful of this and a cup (without ear) of that and a dash of that and a pinch of this ... so it went on, and all of it done at a run, and all of a sudden there stood four loaves of bread rising in the warming-closet of her huge wood-burning kitchen stove, and she poured me a cup of coffee.

"Now that the oven is warm anyhow, I'll just make a couple of pies."

And with a cigarette in the corner of her mouth she went at it again, a handful of this, etc. (see above).

After another couple of cups of coffee and some delicious cookies (freshly baked), there stood on the kitchen counter four golden blond loaves of bread, three pies, and about a hundred cookies, and I was no wiser.

So then I bought a cookbook, and after a while out of my oven also came fairly edible bread, at least if the firewood wasn't too wet. And eventually I also baked regularly according to Enid's system (you know, a handful of this and a pinch of that) and therefore I can't at all give you directions for baking bread.

That column concluded with a recipe for beef stew – I can't help thinking that her tongue was firmly in her cheek – and so far as I know she never gave another.

Baking bread was, in fact, something she came to do well. She did it with pleasure, no doubt recognizing it as a basic and ancient human function rich with symbolism.

Her lack of interest in food and cooking has to be put into perspective. In the first place, for economy's sake we lived as much as possible on what we grew on the farm. That meant eating what was in season and what-ever could be kept in the cellar or preserved, and it certainly restricted her scope. What we did buy was frugally chosen: she used inexpensive meat, and we drank apple juice because it was the cheapest.

Another important but incalculable factor was the influence of those last war years of near-starvation, when obtaining food was an exhausting and dangerous undertaking. What might that have done to her relationship to food? Surely it would have produced complex feelings: gratitude at the abundance of food on the farm (even though the variety was limited) but also painful associations, and perhaps even some guilt at having so much.

Her housekeeping was eccentric and resourceful, sophisticated in some ways and primitive in others. Gerard recalls:

> Because Mam had grown up with servants in the house, she was not well trained in the many skills of housekeeping and child-rearing that women in less affluent circumstances might have been. One thing that she had learned about somehow was glycerine. The little house in Terrace had frightfully cold floors, and we children got chilblains on our feet – painful, then itchy as they healed. Mam would rub glycerine onto our feet and then put socks on them before putting us to bed. She liked to do this after the last dish-washing so that her hands, which were awfully chapped and cracked, could benefit from the emollient action of the glycerine. She had also learned that glycerine mixed with a bit of epsom salts would help to draw infection out of small wounds and would even draw a small splinter of wood or metal out of a hand or finger.

Madzy must, in her mind, have compared the life she had now with that of the war and postwar years. In Terrace we were better off in mate-rial terms. And the war had taught her what was really essential and what could be regarded more lightly.

Although some of the housekeeping was more complex than it is in modern houses, in other ways it was simpler. The house was small and our belongings few. There were almost no electrical appliances: a toaster, the washing machine, the iron, later the water heater and the small electric range.

All of us were always busy. We children, besides going to school and doing our homework, helped on the farm. During the school year we had chores after school – the work with the firewood, gathering eggs, helping to feed the livestock, sometimes doing the milking, assisting Madzy in the house. In the summer we took part in the planting, weeding, harvesting,

Marianne is riding Duke for this stage of the haying. A big clamp lifted the hay from the wagon into the loft of the barn; Duke had to walk back and forth to operate the rope-and-pulley mechanism. About 1953

haying, building. I spent much of one summer removing the broken putty from the outsides of all those small-paned war-surplus windows, reputtying, and repainting them all, and part of another summer applying stain and varnish to a set of dining-room chairs which we had bought unfinished. When Bill had to hill the potatoes or do other work requiring Duke to walk carefully between rows of plants, I rode the horse so as to guide him, and I rode him when he was needed to operate a pulley device for lifting hay from the wagon into the hay-loft.

We were allowed to say no: I was once assigned the job of plucking a newly slaughtered chicken but found it so horrible that I was given something else to do. When the barn was being built, I was enlisted to carry armloads of cedar shakes up the ladder to the scaffold where Bill was working, but I was terrified of climbing the unsteady ladder with only one free hand.

Bill introduced to Terrace the selling of carrots in plastic bags, and packing them became a regular family occupation. After dinner three or four of us would sit at the dining table with baskets of carrots, washed and with their tops removed, ready for packing. Bill would weigh them out on an old-fashioned scale with an arm along which a weight was moved. When the correct amount was reached, he passed it to the person beside him for putting into a plastic bag, and the bag would be passed to the next person to apply the twist-tie with a label identifying it as coming from our farm.

Madzy helped with outdoor work. After about 1951, she contracted rheumatoid arthritis and was able to do less, but she could still drive the tractor, and in *Land for Our Sons* she describes transplanting seedlings.

OUR SOCIAL LIFE during the first few years was restricted by the demands of farm work and building. But after the selling of the car, and before the purchase of the truck, our socializing was restricted by the fact that to visit someone beyond walking distance, we had to harness Duke. Neither the wagon nor the sleigh were covered, so in bad weather we sat in the open. At our destination, Duke would have to be hitched up and, in winter, covered by a horse-rug.

There was not much visiting, and there were no concerts or similar events in town. Terrace had little to offer besides the stores, the post office, and the church. We joined the United Church, and Madzy sang in the choir and organized a children's choir. She was briefly one of the leaders of the Girl Guide group to which I belonged, and she went to parent-teacher meetings. Bill was active in the Farmers' Institute and helped would-be immigrants and new arrivals.

The family on the wagon: Marianne, Gerard, Madzy, Jock, Bill. The chicken house has not yet crossed the road; the barn is under construction.

When we arrived in Terrace, we were the first postwar immigrants from Europe (there were some from before the war, like Peter van Stolk), and we were an anomaly in that we had not been farmers "back home." Shortly after us, other Dutch immigrants came, including Pem van Heek and his wife, Mien, and two small children. Mien recalls:

> My first contact with Madzy was in 1949 [by correspondence] when we were preparing to emigrate from Holland to Terrace, B.C. She certainly encouraged us, but advised us: "Take everything you cherish with you, everything you think you may need for daily living, also bring medication, bandages, etc., for you can't get anything here!" To this day I'm thankful for this advice when I look at my precious Dutch antique and modern furniture. But what to do with all those bandages that never got used? Ah well, maybe I'll give them to the Red Cross one day.
>
> Once we arrived in Canada, Madzy's advice and encouragement were invaluable for a young mother with a one-year-old and a brand-new baby. Our friendship in those early Canadian days went a long way toward filling the emptiness felt by the leaving behind of family and friends. Our similar background and youth in Holland meant that we had a close rapport.
>
> Madzy to me was consultant, friend, and mother.

There was also Teun van Burken, who had worked in the same office as Bill before we emigrated. A Dutch nurse, Mary van Maurik, came when the small Red Cross hospital was set up in Terrace. Rein (Ray) Doorman bought a farm and was joined by his brother Jan and sister-in-law Sacha, but they left after a few years. While he was still living alone, Rein liked to talk to Madzy; he told me recently that she was a great resource and a good friend.

Just and Hanneke Havelaar came with their four children in 1951, bought an acre and a half of our farm, and built a house. Because they were only a couple of minutes' walk away, we had regular contact. Just gave Gerard and me a few recorder lessons, and when their oldest son was ill in the first winter, Madzy went daily for several months to teach him English.[23] We were also on very good terms with Ed and Anne Shaw across the road. Ed was British, Anne Canadian. They were bookish people, and Madzy enjoyed their company.

Mien writes in a matter-of-fact way about "the emptiness felt by the leaving behind of family and friends." Undoubtedly Madzy had felt the same when we arrived. In her newspaper columns and articles written later, she paid special attention to the problems of immigrant women, often isolated on a farm, having little contact with either Canadian women or other Dutch women.

IN 1950 THE committee planning the Fall Fair asked Madzy to organize a display of Dutch items. She and Susie Adams – herself Dutch but married to a Scots-Canadian – set it up.

> We divided the table into two divisions: the one on the right was for "old Holland." We draped a dark blue velvet cloth over some boxes, and on top of that we arranged all the beautiful antiques the immigrants had taken along. There were silver spoons, silver snuff-boxes, brass bowls, and many more; there was an old-fashioned coffee grinder, and every visitor wanted to know how that worked. There was also a little square tea-light, to keep the teapot warm, instead of the tea-cosy of more modern times.
>
> On the left side we put "New Holland" – all articles Holland had been able to manufacture after World War II. People were astonished to see how much Holland had been able to do in such a short time (it was only five years after the war). There were beautiful woollen blankets, strong white linen sheets, sturdy corduroy work-pants. There was a variety of pots and pans, and other household goods. It was certainly a sight to make you proud.[24]

The intention was to give Canadians some insight into the Dutch, and to give the Dutch some pride in their heritage. This cross-cultural illumination was something Madzy had begun in her writings in the United States, and it was to run as a strong thread through the rest of her work.

I imagine that she was also thinking of her children's sense of identity, and her own. From the beginning, we spoke only English at home. Learning good English was, she felt, important for becoming Canadian as quickly as possible. At the same time, she did what she could to provide us with some of the culture and the mental stimulation she had been accustomed to in Holland. We had been able to take only very few belongings with us, including a harmonium, which is a small pedal-pumped reed organ, a few paintings, and books (almost none in Dutch). We brought a radio that turned out to be nearly useless in Terrace, either because it had the wrong frequencies for North America or because the mountains blocked reception. It was one of those radios with names of cities printed on the dial, and I read them with fascination: Berlin, Paris, Frankfurt, Oslo, Stuttgart, London. In about 1953, Terrace got a low-power relay transmitter; our radio brought from Holland still did not work, but with the very cheapest radio from the mail-order catalogue, we were able to receive CBC-AM. That contributed enormously to the cultural life in our house. The Saturday opera broadcasts were a fixture. I remember working with Madzy while listening to classical-music programs; if we missed the opening announcement naming a piece, we would try to identify it, discussing which composer it sounded like, or which historical period. Then we listened closely at the end to learn if our guess had been correct.

When finances permitted, we bought our first gramophone (78 RPM), later replacing it with a three-speed one. Madzy subscribed to a record-of-the-month plan offering classical music, and people in Holland occasionally sent us recordings.

The almost complete absence of good music in the early years in Terrace must have been a serious deprivation for Madzy. Sometimes on Sunday mornings, she would wake us by playing the harmonium and singing. The only two pieces I can now identify by name were the "Ave Verum" by Mozart, and César Franck's "Panis Angelicus." Gerard recalls that when Madzy heard a Strauss waltz on the radio, her body moved in time to the music, and she would say what a pity it was that Bill didn't dance:

> Mam truly loved music ... She told me that she had liked going to the French Huguenot church with Juusje because there was beautiful music. There was music in their house. Oom Willy played the piano. Tante Rietie sang, and Mam sang in the student choir in Leiden. She loved Verdi's *Requiem* for the rest of her life because the choir had performed it with hired soloists and an orchestra. She went to concerts. She played the harmonium that we brought with us on the ship from Holland – it was a heavy piece of furniture, and remarkable in that we brought few other pieces of furniture. She sang in the choir in Terrace. Her singing was brought to a sudden end by the damage to her vocal chords during the tonsil operation that was supposed to help her rheumatoid arthritis. She was very angry and upset at her loss of voice.

When we arrived in Terrace there was no library in either the school or the town, but Madzy learned that the Victoria Public Library sent out books by mail. We could borrow six books per family member and keep them for six weeks. We were sent a booklet of perhaps sixteen pages listing titles. If the requested book was not available, another would be sent. I remember sitting with Madzy at the dining table making up the list, and then eagerly greeting the next shipment.

In the beginning, she had little time for reading:

> People at home tried to keep us interested in home politics, in literature, in art. If I had had plenty of spare time, I would have loved to keep up with their magazines and books. Usually we got a whole bundle of papers from the post office, which clogged up our small post-box, and I always started to look through them right away, but to serious reading I never seemed to come. I stacked them neatly on a shelf, promised myself that in winter I would have oodles of time for reading, and ended up by using them to light the fire in the kitchen stove. Bill had always more than enough to study in the agricultural reading material, which was of more direct importance to him. I was interested in Canadian literature, Marianne had forgotten how to read Dutch [not true] and the boys had never learned it.[25]

Meanwhile she read when and what she could. Books were important to her. Her vocabulary, her quotations and foreign phrases, and the range of her interests all reflected her reading and knowledge. But quite apart from her interest in the contents, books were always a safe place for her, a small private space where she could for a moment forget the difficulties of her life and, later, the physical pain.

Friends in Holland and elsewhere sent books: Mita, her sister-in-law, regularly went to a bookstore and ordered books to be mailed to us. Virginia Donaldson and her daughter Rosalie sent magazines. We received copies of the *Ladies' Home Journal* from someone, and I remember Madzy loving the columns about country life written by Gladys Taber.

After we came to Canada she very seldom read Dutch by choice. She preferred English and French. She knew German too, but the war had changed her feelings towards all things German.

She always enjoyed some light reading, such as Georgette Heyer's Regency novels and other historical fiction. She liked the books of Pearl Buck. I don't know when she encountered the *Jalna* books by Mazo de la Roche; *Jalna*, the first of the series, was a big commercial success in 1927,[26] and we know that during the war she loaned some to a downed Canadian airman in hiding at the house of one of her friends. We brought to Canada as many of the series as she owned at that time (ten of them were in print by 1947, but I don't believe we had them all), and friends in Holland sent later ones as they appeared, so that eventually we had all or nearly all of them. Unquestionably they were escapist reading, but the fact that they were set in Canada gave them a special appeal for Madzy.

She read more serious material as well, including history, philosophy, and biography. For her birthday in August 1954 (no doubt by her own request) she received from Iete a copy of Bertrand Russell's *A History of Western Philosophy*. To judge by her markings in it, she was most interested in the chapter about Spinoza. In the margins of the passage dealing with Socrates and Greek philosophy, she wrote short notes using the Greek alphabet she had learned in school.

MADZY'S INTEREST in the past was not a matter only of reading books or owning old paintings. Her collecting of stones was later to develop into an interest in fossils (and, in a different direction, a hobby of polishing intriguing pebbles). She liked knowing that there had once been a blacksmith shop on our property: "While weeding I would very often hurt my hand on sharp pieces of iron. Our elderly friend, Joe Nelson, told us that on the place had been a blacksmith shop, also burnt down in the big fire [that destroyed the large Eby house]. The tons of scrap iron we dug up could have filled the hold of an Atlantic liner. And if every rusted horseshoe we found would bring us luck, it should last us to the end of our days!"[27]

She also reflected on the aboriginal people who occupied the land not so long before she had her hands in its soil. "In Europe we have to go back centuries and centuries to imagine such things, but here I only had to step a few steps and the past was there for the taking!"[28]

A part of the culture of our family in a broader sense was the correspondence with family and friends in Holland. Madzy's relations with her mother and mother-in-law, once difficult, improved when geography created a buffer. Or perhaps, as she said thirty years later, when she emigrated she left behind things that were more important than she had ever understood. Both she and Bill were good letter-writers: I remember them regularly at the end of a busy day, or on a Sunday afternoon, writing long letters "home." They wrote mostly by hand. I can picture the fountain pen that Madzy owned, as much a part of her as a watch or glasses. In her papers I have come across things written with that pen, and as I look at the bold round script, I see her in the act of writing.

Letters from Holland were intensely important. Bill would drive to town in the morning to deliver produce to the stores and go to the post office; when he returned he drank a cup of coffee with Madzy and they read the mail.

An incident that took place in the early years epitomized the link. As I have said, we joined the Knox United Church in Terrace. On the morning of Sunday, 9 January 1949, the church burned down. The congregation bought a war-surplus building, hauled it to the site, placed it on the foundation, and set about turning it into a place of worship.

Madzy described the events that followed:[29]

> A couple of days after the church had burned down, I went to see the minister, for I could imagine how he felt. Indeed, I saw him sitting in the dining room with his head in his hands, completely beaten. I sat down and said: "Don't worry, John,[30] the church will be rebuilt, that's for sure. And I will see if I can get a church bell for the new belfry. I have come from Europe and I always heard bells ringing on Sundays. That is one of the things I miss here."
>
> He looked at me. "How are you going to do that? We can't afford it!"
>
> I answered: "You leave it up to me. I am sure that somehow I will find help in Holland."
>
> I wrote a letter to our minister in Amersfoort, which is a town in the heart of Holland where we lived before we left for Canada. We had belonged to a church there. I explained it all in a letter to our former "dominee": "Do you think that somehow we can get a small bell for our church here? I can help with some money in Holland. We haven't any money here to give to the new church."
>
> I sent the letter and wondered if I would ever get an answer. These letters still went by train and boat. But two months afterwards there came an answer: "Just a Sunday ago, after my sermon, I read your letter from the pulpit to the congregation and after the service an old gentleman came to me. He said, 'I have a bell for that church in Canada.'"

The gentleman who came forward was General W.H.E. Vrijdag,[31] and he owned the estate which, as it happened, was located across the street from the house in the Bisschopsweg where Madzy and Wim had lived in 1938–39. The bell, hanging in a belfy on an outbuilding on the estate, was used to signal the workmen when it was time to start work or have lunch. Bill can recall hearing it from our house.

General Vrijdag said that he would donate it to the church in Terrace "in gratitude to all the Canadians who had liberated Holland."

The bronze bell, in its wrought-iron frame, was crated and sent to Terrace, where it arrived on 9 July 1949. The new church was not yet ready to receive it, and in any case the frame had to be altered slightly to make it fit the yet-to-be-built belfry. Madzy and Bill took it to the blacksmith:

"When he [saw] the bell, he said, 'Back in the old country, when I was still a lad learning the trade, Dad taught me to recognize the age of the various bells and also of the wrought-iron gates.' He guessed that this bell was at least three centuries old because the framework was of a softer iron than the hard iron used later."

The bell rang for the first time on Easter Sunday, 23 April 1950, for the dedication of the new church.

There are several epilogues to this story. One appeared in an article written by Vi Keenleyside and published in the 16 June 1985 issue of the *Islander*. In 1966, she wrote, the then-incumbent of the church received a letter from W.G.D. Vrijdag, the son of the gentleman who had donated the bell. Randenbroek, the estate from which it had come, was his parental home, and now he and his wife and daughter wished to come to Terrace to "greet the bell there and meet the people who listen to its voice now in Canada."[32] Mr Vrijdag, when he arrived in Terrace, told how – back in Amersfoort – the gardener on the estate had taken the bell down during the German occupation, presumably to save it from being confiscated and melted down. Mr Vrijdag and his wife photographed the bell where it hung in the belfry in Terrace, and on their return to Holland they gave a copy of the photograph to the gardener.

In a letter of 20 January 1982, the Reverend David Martyn, the incumbent at that time, wrote to Bill: "The bell is presently stored in the Church (it was removed from the roof to prevent vandalism) and will be reinstalled as a permanent feature when we build a new addition this coming spring. Your [wife's] work in the donation of the bell will be mentioned at the rededication."

Yet another epilogue comes from the *Terrace Review* of 16 May 1990. In the late 1960s, the church had been once again rebuilt. "The bell remained in place. But when the church was re-roofed at the end of the decade, the tower was taken down and not returned. [In 1989] five members of Knox United decided to build a tower for the bell." Remounted, it "once again rang out over the Skeena Valley on Easter Sunday 1990, 40 years after it originally rang."[33]

IN THE SUMMER of 1952, Iete came to visit us. Madzy had received her mother's cablegram proposing the visit with "mixed feelings."

> This does not sound very nice, but it is frank. There was more to the visit than meets the eye. Up till now we had been quite satisfied with our life and conditions here. Building the farm up from bushland

and a small army cabin, as we had, we had seen every change for the better as an improvement. I used to enjoy every new addition to our house, every shelf, painted room, or extra door for a long while after it was installed. Naturally we boasted about it in our letters home. By mutual consent we did not write to them about the more miserable conditions, about small illnesses and the like, so as not to worry people over there. The result is that we created a rather rosy picture of our life here, and of the comforts of the house. We did not see any need to tell every detail to those who were used to European standards, or I should say city standards. We had not said that our life here in the North was now and then a little rough around the edges.

But what would Mother say when she had to live this life with us? Could I make her comfortable enough, she who was used to a bus stop right in front of her home, a street with all sorts of stores right around the corner?

Would Mother have enough sense of humour to skip over the few small discomforts, and enjoy the beauty of nature, and the company of her children and grandchildren?

Then, too, I was afraid that if her eye might be critical, I would start looking at my life through her eyes, and learn to see the imperfections of it. Would her visit make me discontented with my life?

I needn't have worried.[34]

Madzy briefly recounts her mother's history, and then writes: "When you have lived through such adventures, and have known and successfully overcome hardships and primitive conditions, you are always capable of coping with them again. As soon as Mother had made up her mind to come, she had also made up her mind to accept whatever was coming to her." Madzy, incidentally, could almost be writing about herself here, drawing a parallel between her own adventurousness and her mother's.

Iete was nearly seventy-four, and at that time the journey from Holland to Terrace was arduous. It meant flying from Amsterdam to Montreal (a flight of eighteen hours) and changing planes there to fly to Vancouver. Then she would change planes again to fly to Terrace.

The first and second legs of the trip went well, but Iete became very tired. In Vancouver she was met by Mary van Maurik, the Dutch nurse who had been in Terrace but had by then moved south. Mary put Iete on the small plane that ought to have flown to Terrace but, because of bad weather, landed in Prince Rupert – a rough landing, which frightened her. Madzy, kept informed by means of teletype reports, telephoned a friend in

Prince Rupert to ask her to meet the plane and take Iete back to her house. Meanwhile, she and Bill drove to Prince Rupert – a four-hour trip because of the state of the highway.

The visit went well. Photos in the album record it. Because of the hot weather, the armchairs from indoors were grouped in the shade of the maple tree on the front lawn. Iete sat there with her book and her glasses and her knitting – when she wasn't going to town with Madzy or Bill in the truck, and being made much of by everyone.

One of the photos shows Madzy sitting on the edge of the porch; the caption, in her own writing, reads "Mom rests between clean-ups." Yes, indeed. The misgivings about how her mother would view our life in Terrace must have led her to work extremely hard at the cleaning and cooking and cheeriness. For part of the time I was not there to help because I had gone to a Girl Guide Jamboree in Ottawa.

Before leaving, as Madzy reports it, Iete told her, "I shall never forget this. I shall always see you all here in this beautiful spot, a happy, safe spot if ever there is one on earth."[35] But Madzy's sister, Hansje, told me much later that Iete, on her return to Holland, spoke with dismay about seeing her daughter living in "a hut." However, Madzy probably never knew that.

Madzy writes how she felt seeing Iete off: "When the small plane, dwarfed by the rough mountain walls on either side, floated like a spirit over the Skeena River, I was grateful for Mother's visit, for instead of creating havoc in my heart, she had given it new confidence."[36]

MADZY'S OBSERVATION about not putting into the letters to Holland all the less rosy details about life in Terrace indicates the difference between her public story and the private reality. Self-censorship continues – as even the limited time for writing letters, and the cost of postage, would have dictated. In *Land for Our Sons*, a public document, she readily admits to this self-censorship. My guess is that her private diaries written at that time would have given another picture.

To try to recapture more of her inner life, we have to piece together hints from here and there. Of the hundreds of letters she wrote during this period, only five survive, written to Virginia Donaldson and Rosalie Worthington, and except for providing a few dates they are not very helpful.

But there are other glimpses in *Land for Our Sons*. She describes how, when Bill removed the original small windows in the cabin's main room in order to install larger ones, Madzy was startled by the large hole that suddenly appeared: "A gulf of sunlight enveloped me. I was overcome with a strange fear. It was as if the whole outside world came charging in on me,

Iete, Madzy, and Marianne

as if all our privacy was gone."[37] What comes through here is not just the loss of privacy but a sense of sudden exposure and danger. Had she – for a second – relived a fear about how the house in Maarn would collapse if a bomb struck it, leaving her even more exposed and vulnerable than she already was?

Reflecting that her children, as they grew up, were helping with more of the farm work, she wrote: "When I realized, with quite a shock of surprise, that our toughest years might be over, I suddenly knew how tense I had been. It was really hard to be able to relax, and to let the children take over some jobs."[38]

MADZY HAD A strong maternal instinct, which had shown itself early on in her caring for her brother Joost. She was an affectionate mother, centring herself in others' lives and needs. I now realize that she had not only a desire to fulfil her maternal role and create a happy, safe family atmosphere; there was also that undefined guilt, the compulsion to atone, hinted at in the first entry of the war diary. Moreover, by creating a family life for us, she was finding her own emotional nourishment – satisfaction, justification, and safety. This skill of hers made the family more self-contained than was perhaps a good thing but, by providing all of us with a portable "home," saw us through the many moves that we had made and were soon to make again.

She delighted in creating little celebrations to mark some achievement like bringing in a crop before the rain, or completing a stage in the current building project, or our receiving good report cards from school. She could turn a chore into an adventure, infusing it with her ability to be happy in the moment.

She was not quite so well able to deal with our unhappiness. She would listen and sympathize and provide counsel, and then expect that the mood would be over: that was enough of that. When I returned home from an unsuccessful and profoundly upsetting attempt to begin PH.D. studies, she gave me three days to recover and then suggested I go to Toronto – a totally strange city – to find a job. Her writings suggest that in fact she reflected more about such things than appeared; in a story entitled "Alma Mater," she indicates that the fictionalized character representing me was the family member who had had the most trouble adapting to life in Canada, a remark that shows that she was observing her children and drawing conclusions about their inner well-being. At the time, however, we were mostly unaware of this. Perhaps she was afraid of fussing, or of inducing self-pity in us. She certainly wanted to leave us as independent as possible, free to find our own solutions and shape our lives (remembering that she herself had not been free enough). In the course of writing this book I have come to realize that putting things behind her – her way of dealing with difficulties – was more a public position than something she was always able to achieve. If she paid less attention to her own or other people's inner lives than is now the practice, it was not out of indifference but because in her time that was the acceptable stance. And her creation of a happy family life was a way of trying to *prevent* unhappiness.

Several of Gerard's memories of the time in Terrace throw light on Madzy's ways of relating to us. During the war Gerard had (like me) been terrified of airplanes. In an attempt to win him over to the idea of coming to Canada, Madzy promised him that there would be no airplanes there. "Somewhat like a year later – we were on the farm, and I believe that it was summer – a very small bush plane flew over," he recalls. "I rushed to the house in a panic of fears, yelling that there was an airplane. Mam tried to calm me by explaining that it was small and harmless, but I was adamant. 'You promised me!' I kept saying. And this was very serious, because one of the absolute tenets that Mam instilled in us was that promises must, under no circumstances, be broken."

Another of his memories from about this time showed that Madzy could be firm as well as understanding and indulgent. "I remember once being in town with her. I cannot remember what caused it, but I was in tears over something and would not stop crying. Mam announced that she was not going to be seen in town with a crying baby, turned on her heel and walked away. I was always terrified of being separated from her, so I had to run to catch up. Then she said that I might only walk beside her if I stopped crying and that she would only take me to town again if I absolutely promised not to cry. I believe that I kept my promise."

Our family life in those years consisted mostly in the work and the meals we shared, but there were some holidays – necessarily brief because of the demands of the livestock. Madzy and Bill and the boys made a one-night camping trip to Smithers, up-river from Terrace, and we sometimes went to the van Stolks' cottage at Lake Lakelse. There were a few picnics to Kalum Lake. We visited the ghost town of Remo, across the Skeena River, where there was the remnant of a hand-operated ferry that had formerly crossed the river to Terrace. I remember a walk to a ghost town on the Bench that captured my imagination sufficiently that later I tried to write about it.

There were no shared recreational activities except the swimming at Lake Lakelse. Bill once tried to teach us to play tennis, but I did not take to it, though I did play badminton in high school, and I roller-skated during the one year when my school was in a building close to the Civic Centre. The long walks to school provided lots of physical exercise, as did farm work. Sharing activities necessary for survival is not a bad way to create family solidarity and a storehouse of common experiences.

THE DECISION to go to Canada had not put to rest all the questions about the wisdom of emigrating – far from it. New issues would keep emerging. In April 1947, even before leaving Holland, Madzy had written to her niece Mill, Paul's daughter: "We thought a great deal about our parents when we were making these plans, but we are very sure that this emigration to Canada is on our way,[39] thinking of the future of our children; it was a choice between our parents (the past) and our children (the future), and after much weighing we have chosen the future. Whether this was a good choice remains to be seen." Evidently she believed that we children would adjust easily and quickly. In some reflections on immigration written to Bill in October 1959, she says of our later move to Ontario: "Here, after some trouble of adjusting, the children have found back what we took away from them by leaving Vancouver. Here, in another few years, they will feel completely at home."

If that was how she expected it to work when we were in our teens after three major and several minor moves, probably she had expected the adjustment in 1947, when we were so much younger, to be easier. She probably also felt that, after the bad conditions during the war, we would be happier living in a safer place. No doubt we were, but it was not an easy time, especially for Gerard and me. She seriously underestimated the enormous stress that immigration itself caused – the uprooting from a familiar place, the change to a different language and culture, the loss of friends and family – and overestimated our ability or desire to adapt. In focusing on the constrictions of living in the midst of an extended family, she seems to have ignored the support, nourishment, and sense of identity that such a context provided. She did not anticipate that Gerard and I would, all our lives, yearn for the family connections we would have had in Holland, the cultural stimulation, the atmosphere and resources of Europe, the look of European houses, cities, countryside. As it was, we were dealing with all the stress of growing up, as well as learning how to be Canadian (or not) in our individual ways. Each member of the family was finding his or her own way into the new life, from an individual angle, equipped with an individual set of fears and desires and images, and there was (as I now realize) far too little sharing of these experiences. It was Madzy who chiefly determined what could be discussed and what not; only after her death did Gerard and I realize how many of these suppressed problems and longings we shared. In Terrace we didn't talk about the past (except what qualified as "history"), so in spite of our closeness, we remained in some respects a cluster of five solitudes.

Once the first few years on the farm were behind her, Madzy apparently began to see things in a more complex way, though this complexity – being expressed in her writing and not her conversation – came to light only when I read her papers for this book. In a group of fragmentary writings from 1954, and *Land for Our Sons*, begun about a year later, she began examining the costs as well as the gains of immigration. The purpose of these 1954 fragments was to inform her children about their heritage – pushed much too far aside, as she was beginning to realize.

IN 1951, MADZY was sick with a bad flu, accompanied by a cold, a sore throat, and pain in all her joints. She told Teun van Burken, who was a gentle person and easy to talk to, that she was in *so* much pain. When she was first on her feet again, she leaned on a kitchen chair, shuffling along, pushing it ahead of her.

The only doctor in town, fresh out of university, diagnosed rheumatoid arthritis. "Nothing to be done about it," he told her. "Learn to live with it." She was forty-one at the time, and for the remaining thirty-three years of her life she did indeed live with it.

The doctor told her to have her tonsils out and she did, losing her singing voice at the same time. She took over-the-counter pain medications. She wore large men's shoes on her painful feet.

She and Bill discussed whether she should go to Vancouver to see a specialist, but she decided not to. She said she did not want to leave the family: the family was a safe place, Vancouver was a big and strange city. Trauma breeds fear: the prospect must have been too frightening to consider, and the sudden onset of the illness, and the way it handicapped her, would have undermined her confidence.

Her brother Paul advised her to come to Holland to see what could be done for her there, but she rejected that idea too. It would also have meant being away from the immediate family, and perhaps she feared that her mother and parents-in-law would once again decide things for her. She may also have been afraid that, once there, she would not want to return to Canada. Paul did, however, put her into contact with a friend of his, a specialist in rheumatic diseases, who wrote her a letter about the condition.

In January 1956 she wrote to Virginia Donaldson that the arthritis had been brought under control by cortisone and was much better. She kept doing housework, or as much of it as she could, but henceforth some activities were difficult or impossible for her.

For Madzy, who believed that her worth was based largely on what she did for others, it must have been very hard to accept these restrictions. Furthermore, they forced her to pay attention to her body – which, as we saw in the war diary, she regarded as a workhorse that had better not let her down. Now it often *did* let her down. The sudden awareness that she was no longer quite who she had been must have been deeply unsettling.

From then until her death in 1984, the arthritis was a major factor in her life and our family's. One of the reasons for our moving from Terrace to Vancouver was to find better medical care for her. The medical profession's understanding and treatment of the condition were still in early stages; she submitted to treatments that were experimental, and some made things distinctly worse. The arthritis, and the treatments, affected other aspects of her physical condition, including her vision and finally her hearing. Towards the end of her life she was in a wheelchair, and for the last two years she was completely bedridden.

ONE OF THE MAJOR effects of her illness was that, having more time to herself, she resumed writing. During these years she had been writing letters and diary entries, but in March 1954 she ventured into other genres, initially for her family but with an occasional glance at a larger public. A group of prose fragments in English, written close together, reflect a significant burst of writing activity, even though they are tentative, exploratory, incomplete. They are handwritten and most of them are dated, suggesting that Madzy saw them as an extension of the diary. She could have typed them, but typing was noisy, and she had at that time no place of her own to work. All she could do was make a bubble of privacy with pen and paper, probably when she was alone in the house.

One sequence was written on pages torn from a school scribbler. (At the time of writing, they may still have been in the scribbler.) What was perhaps the first entry (it is undated) gives important insights into her inner life and explains what she intends to do.

> My personality does not fit into this particular moment. There is nothing in this special space of time that attracts me. Most of the time I float blissfully through the days without realizing that one's personality has to fit into them as pieces of a jigsaw puzzle. They do, miraculously, until one becomes aware of a halt, a misfit; and that

is when life hurts. Sorrow, death, frustration, they all can hurt in their own ways but not as fiercely as when one feels an odd piece of a jigsaw puzzle.

I plan to write a book. I have got to do something with myself now that I have to stop doing other things I like better. I don't want to write. I even don't know how to write. I can read, of course, [to fill my time], but I get tired of reading and I want to protest and argue with the author the same as when I want to stand up and argue with the minister during a sermon. I have that feeling so very often, and it can grow so strong in me that I have to hold onto the pew so as not to shame myself and those who are with me.

My dear children, there may come a day in your life on which you will look back and ask: "Why do I act like that?" or "Why is my character built this way?" And you will look back not only into your own past but you will try to look into the past of your parents, your grandparents, what they were and what they achieved.

On your own past you will have a clear view, but further down the line?

Once upon a time we tore up our roots and sailed for new lands. We took you away from the comfortable houses of your grand-parents, and with the eyes of all immigrants we stared and kept staring at the future, partly out of fascination, partly out of fear. Certainly, we were fascinated by what lay ahead of us, and we plunged into it like all possessed, scarcely leaving time to breathe. But there was an underlying fear that if once we dared to look over our shoulders we should change into a salt pillar like Lot's wife! A look over the shoulder might bring homesickness, regrets, reminders of what we were missing.

So we briskly plunged ahead and forgot about our past. And we omitted to tell you anything about it. That was a mistake, for now you lack the sense of a background that may come in handy at any moment, be it only a bedtime story to one of your grandchildren.

Well, my dears, here I go. I shall try to build up your past and mine, I shall try to paint it in the same vivid colours it had when it was not past but present. I shall try to arouse in you the same snug feeling of belonging to a certain world that is gone but will never die. For all who were your ancestors have together built you up to the person you are. You might see something of one grandfather in yourself, you might even recognize one of your great-aunts in your daughter.

She went no further along that track, at least not then. The following entry, for Sunday, 28 March, is quite different:

Two mornings ago the house started its habitual turmoil somewhat earlier than usual. It happened like this:

I have a habit of waking up at 6 A.M. sharp, without any reason at all. Then I doze off again until 7, our time of starting the day. This morning I had dozed away again when a sound alerted me. But my consciousness was so far gone that it took me some time to come to the surface and in those seconds I lived eternity. I heard the sound, I registered it as familiar and very pleasant, but I just could not make the infinitesimal contact to realize what the sound was. "This," I thought, "is how a person must feel who had a stroke. He registers sounds, smells, visions, but he is just unable to make the contact. How very unnerving and frustrating."

Again came the sound and this time it pierced like a flash of lightning through my mind. "The honk of geese!"

Spring has come! The honk of the first returning geese stirs up the blood, laggard from winter cold, stirs up the spirit cobwebby from too much indoors, with such vigour that it hurts physically. But it is a pleasant hurt, like a nasty medicine from which you know will come health and new strength.

I was not the only one who had heard the glad tidings. From the boys' room came a surprising racket, imitation-honking.

The next item, headed "First thought," deals with modern education, and how impossible it is for parents to create happiness for their children. The children have to create it for themselves, and happiness is not in achieving the goal but in the process of working towards it. She quotes Hegel. On the same day she writes:

Second thought:
"When I was young ..."
"You always bring in the past, Mom, something that is over and done with and outmoded."
"Yes, but how else can I explain myself? I have to explain by using my experience, and my experience was born through the facts in my life upon which I look in retrospect. By looking over the good and bad happenings, over the mistakes and successes, over the encounters with different people, I come to a resulting opinion, and that is what

makes up my experience. The sum total. No, not entirely total. I am still adding to the row of numbers. The older one grows, the more numbers, the longer the addition, the greater the hazard of making a mistake. Thus the older one grows, the more careful one has to be in counting. Better to recount and again recount than to come out with a wrong total."

Third thought:

"Why do you look on your foreign past as a disgrace?[40] Instead you should look at it in a different way, for it will always be something special to you, an additional flavour, that Canadian-born children haven't got. There will always be a special door for you, to open and to investigate, with a number of great surprises and delightful memories. Be openly proud of being Canadian citizens, but never forget to be privately proud of your Dutch descent."[41]

An entry dated 31 March 1954 talks about altruism and its relationship to religious faith:

In some of us there is a strong urge to help others. But very often this urge to help originates in a desire to assert ourselves, to put ourselves on a higher plane instead of just helping the other fellow. For it gives us great satisfaction to help, it bolsters our ego very pleasantly. And now I wonder: should we stop helping other people because it only bolsters our egos and so is purely egotistic? Because we only want to get something out of it for ourselves?

So it is with religion. What other reason have we in serving God than making ourselves feel good and secure: gaining for ourselves a spiritual safety, a future security?

Having explored and defined her image of God as a spirit who "is in and around me" – a quite different image from the one she had held a few years earlier – she returns to the idea of service to others.

But for a God like that I can not do anything. I can not even, to please Him, help others.

So helping others is brought to a very low plane again.

But now I realize that by helping others purely for their own sake I might build up my own spirit and thus gain. Still it brings an egotistical smell with it.

Does a man help others purely altruistically? Does a preacher, a priest, a pope?

All better people than I am. Why do I bother then? Let me take out of life what it offers me. If it offers me a chance to help others and at the same time benefit by it myself, and feel pleasantly satisfied with my own efforts, why not take it? Life is not meant to be taken too seriously. Life is to be lived as it comes your way. As long as you do not want to force it, life is a pleasant business.

Not taking life too seriously might be an ideal – clearly understandable in view of how difficult it sometimes was for her – and her normal cheerful manner might be a sign that she was working towards that goal. But whenever we catch sight of her inner life, there is an element of profound seriousness and sometimes of worry, unhappiness, pessimism, or a raging struggle against limitations. The item for 2 April begins: "I can only be happy when my mind is free. Freedom of mind is a most precious possession ... Now that I am physically bound by narrow borders I can only survive decently if I can make and keep my mind free."

Both in that entry and in one three days later, she reflects on the relationship between religion and philosophy. Immediately after that, in an undated entry, she is more whimsical (but certainly also serious), in commenting on the fact that housewives, while doing the dishwashing and other chores, could exercise their minds by doing some serious thinking instead of "useless worrying and fretting."

She clearly had an urge to write, and wrote whatever came into her mind – just to *write*. It is the experimenting of the essayist, who considers almost any thought worth recording, perhaps to be developed later. It certainly suggests the professional writer's tendency to jot down ideas as they occur, and to do finger exercises when there is no time or concentration available for more sustained work.

Then there is a piece entitled "Your Heritage and Mine," fifteen single-spaced pages with chapter headings suggesting that she visualized a book-length work. In it she returns to the subject of why she and Bill emigrated. After dealing with their fears of another war and their desire for a better future for their children, she says that both of these were only "part of the truth":

You see, if you take part of the truth, of any truth, you often spoil the effect to such extent that it becomes a lie! Which is what you did not intend at all and what surprises myself most of all. Now imagine that you set out to tell the truth and end up by telling a fib! Of course you continue arguing that the fib is the truth, although in your heart you know better, and at last you are so muddled up by your own arguments that you shrug your shoulders and say: "Well, I meant the truth." Of course you meant the truth, but you told only part of it. In my life I have told a lot of such fibs and have been so startled by them that at last I found out the truth about truth: only if you carefully go to the root of a thing and if you tell all that is truly known about it to you, will you be telling the story such as you meant to do.

And that is what I mean to do now.

I want to show you the true reason for your being Canadian.

But there is more: I want to give you a picture of your background so that it will help you to make a true picture of yourself. If you are in your native country, surrounded by your relations, people of your own kind, in circumstances in which you and your parents and grandparents and ancestors have grown up, it is easy to know what is expected of you, how you fit in the picture. In fact, you don't realize it but subconsciously you know what you must do under certain circumstances, because it was done before your time by others whom you know or knew or have known through family stories told by some old aunt or granny. For instance I was brought up in such a way that I knew what was expected of me: I was to marry a respectable man, preferably one from a well-known, prominent family with some money, I was to have a few children, give them a good education, and live happily ever after. Daddy was supposed to work doggedly in an office, climb the ladder gradually, marry a girl of good family, provide for her and his children, and behave in every way within the restricted borderlines.

By uprooting our own lives and transplanting ourselves into entirely different soil, without any ties whatsoever except for the ties of common decency and our own common sense, we put you children in a position where you have to find your own way. If you want to look back, you will only see your parents right behind you, and behind their backs only an empty space filled with vague recollections of stories – about "when Mam was a little girl" or "when Dad was very young."

But you might want to know more. Or your children might want to know. And this may happen at a moment when we are not there anymore to tell.

There might be a moment that you want to see yourself in a clear light, to give yourself a sound account of your actions. You may ask yourself: "How did it come about that I showed talent in this or a morbid inclination to act such?"

And then you want to turn back the pages of our family album. Well, how about it, let's do it together now.

The passage is interesting both for what it says and what it omits. Madzy writes that she is going to get to the roots of the truth, the "true reason for being Canadian," but she never does. In what we have of this memoir, she does not even try. Clearly the reasons for immigration that she gives at the beginning are only part of the truth, are in fact a kind of "fib ... although in your heart you know better."

Perhaps, she found herself unable really to find or to articulate "the roots of the truth," or even face them. She was, after all, setting herself an extremely difficult assignment. Roots lie out of sight and have to be dug for, traced painstakingly. Reasons for immigration? The obvious ones had been often repeated, and she gives them once again. The "true reasons" may be buried, enmeshed in fear and desire and the images that we use to shape our lives. For all her interest in cause-and-effect patterns, Madzy frequently evaded painful and embarrassing probing: "We won't talk about that," or a similar expression, appears several times in her written memoirs.

In the next decades she would write a great deal of autobiography – in memoirs, journalism, history, and semi-autobiographical fiction. But she kept stopping or being distracted, as though she could not come to grips with it. She was probably telling the truth – or part of it – when she said that she did not know how to write, or at least not then. She had no one to discuss writing with; she chose not to talk to us, and in any case we wouldn't have been able to help with technical problems. Her isolation was self-imposed and perhaps essential if she wished to achieve anything.

Her difficulties were with both form and content. Autobiography and biography pose problems of structure, voice, subject matter, tone and style and pace, focus and proportion, privacy and publicity. I have faced them myself in writing this book: where does the story begin and end? What is the actual story? – assuming that it is more than a narrative of outer events. How do I handle the passage of time? How much information about ancestry can I fill in without boring the reader? What other material do I include or exclude – how do I even begin to decide what to include or exclude – and what do I make more prominent and what less so? What do I do about names and terms of address (is my father "Dad" or "Bill"?) How do I reconcile my role as biographer with those of daughter and sister? How do I write about myself as a minor character in someone else's story? How can I combine detachment and involvement?

Content posed equally intractable problems for Madzy. She clearly wanted to give a voice to her inner life, silenced by her self-adopted role of being mostly self-denying and cheerful. The need for privacy and the urge to write autobiography appear incompatible, but in fact they were, in her, inextricably linked. She was a born writer and saw her own life and the history of her immediate and extended family as her main subject matter.

In writing *Land for Our Sons* about a year later, she by-passed most of the technical problems by writing in a lighter, more casual style, not unlike the one she had developed for the newspaper columns written in the United States and the one she seems to have used for most of her letters. She permitted herself some revelation of her inner life; but there is a difference between the main account and the underlayer of hard truths that shows through only in brief, illuminating moments, tantalizingly allusive and incomplete.

When she came back to a sustained project of autobiography – in the memoirs which, in her last years, she spoke onto tape and had transcribed – she solved some of the problems of form and content by producing what is really oral history, a cluster of narratives, comparatively simple in form and mostly factual in content, in which she allows herself digressions and discontinuities. She solved the problem of revealing/concealing things about herself by writing mainly about her ancestors and other relatives. Of her own life, she covers only her early years, up to the age of about seventeen.

Not only autobiography but most of her other work is fragmentary and unfinished. She would write a first draft and go through it making some small revisions, but she seldom entirely restructured a piece of writing. She did revise and complete the newspaper columns and a number of short stories, as well as *Land for Our Sons*. As for the rest – clearly she was dissatisfied, put the once-revised draft aside, and started something else. All the same, she kept writing, and the sheer amount of uncompleted work attests to her persistence as well as her difficulties.

WHAT FOLLOWS the passage quoted from "Your Heritage and Mine" is headed "Chapter 11: Mom's pedigree" – but there is no pedigree. The chapter consists of two family stories, one about an early twentieth-century relative of hers who was ambitious, pompous, and a bit of a family joke, and who married a Spanish (Bourbon) princess. The other concerns a double-strand necklace of pearls that Madzy inherited. This story deserves more attention. She told it in different forms at different times. Besides that early version, there is one that may have been written a year later for a creative writing course; she revised it in 1959 to send to *Reader's Digest*, where it was rejected.

The pearls – a double strand, in graduated sizes, with a gold clasp – were an heirloom; they had been given to the first known bearer of the name Mattha Cornelia (1794–1820) by her husband, and they appear in a portrait of her that hangs in my dining room. They were intended to go to Madzy, another Mattha Cornelia. But in the generation before Madzy's, there had been no one bearing the name, so an aunt, Tante Lotje, had been the pearls' custodian.

Madzy was not very fond of Tante Lotje, whom she described as plump, kind-hearted, and not very clever. Madzy was supposed to receive the pearls on her eighteenth birthday, and she gives a lively description of the event, which consisted of a tea-party attended, apparently, only by elderly aunts and uncles. Tante Lotje arrived wearing the pearls and gave Madzy a bottle of perfume as a gift. Madzy, not at all looking forward to receiving the pearls, was secretly pleased.

Tante Lotje continued to wear the pearls (regularly, because it seems that pearls will die if not worn). During the war she had them on day and night, not wanting to leave them behind if she had to go to an air-raid shelter.

Then just before emigrating to Canada, Madzy and Wim were summoned to visit her.

> Our conversation was strained, and all the time I felt like jumping up and shouting "Goodbye, Auntie, please keep those pearls until you die." But in the back of my mind I felt that this was silly, that my other aunts never would forgive me, that a Mattha Cornelia had her duty, etc. etc. And then after a short, rather painful silence Tante Lotje lifted up her hands, unclasped the pearls from around her neck, stood up and said solemnly: "You probably have understood why I asked you to come tonight. I want to give the pearl necklace that once belonged to your great-grandmother,[42] and I hope that you, Madzy, and you, William, will look after it well." Then she walked around the table, stopped behind my chair, and for the first time in my life the famous pearls were around my neck. They felt heavy as rocks, and I felt like a cat that is about to be drowned.

When Madzy went once more to say goodbye before departing, she saw in the old lady's eyes "peace and joy in her own act." So the pearls came with us to Canada.

> The pearls were more of a burden to me than ever I had anticipated. Whenever I wore them I had to feel constantly if they were there. When I put them away in some secret spot, I forgot about them for a few days, but then in the middle of the night I would wake up and start to hunt for them feverishly. Sometimes I hid them in the linen closet, sometimes under my pillow, sometimes in an empty box in the grocery cupboard. The result was that I did not know clearly where they were hidden last, and I had to upset the whole house until I hit on them.

She wore them digging potatoes. She wore them at night "to keep them alive." But then she decided to sell them, because the money would be more important to the family than the pearls.

> One day a doctor's wife went to New York from here. I asked her to take the pearls along to have them estimated at a good jeweller's.
> When I brought them to her the day before she left, it was as if a load fell from my shoulders, as if a balloon took me up into the air.
> After several weeks we got an answer: the pearls were of little value. Many of them were dead, many of them discoloured by the sweat of the skin. The whole necklace was worth fifty dollars, a hundred at the most!
> And for that I had suffered such anxieties ...
> I asked a cousin who lived in New York to take the pearls to my mother on her first trip to Holland. Two years after we left for Canada, the pearls were back in Holland. A few months later my mother sold them for fifteen hundred guilders, and we bought some very necessary farm equipment and had it sent from Holland to us.

In all its forms she presents the story as an amusing anecdote with a twist in its tail. But there is more, and she saw it herself. The pearls represented the heavy hand of her ancestors: a Mattha Cornelia has her duty. It was one of the things from which she escaped by emigrating. More important, the pearls did not fit with her own image of herself. And yet, when she first wrote the story in 1954, she felt that she and Bill had rejected too much of their heritage. The pearls themselves were by then gone, but the story, with all its resonances, was worth writing down.

IF THE RHEUMATOID arthritis was one factor contributing to Madzy's resumption of writing, another one was the setting up of the Marketing Board.

In about 1954, under the auspices of the Farmers' Institute, "the farmers in the district were realizing that it would benefit their business if there were an organization which would take over the selling of their produce co-operatively. This was how the Terrace Marketing Board was born."[43] It needed a manager, and Bill took on the work, but he told Madzy he could not do it unless she would do the administration.

Our farm became the depot for all the produce; our house was the office. "The telephone rang all day, the [door]knocker had never been in use so much. Trucks with farm produce drove up and down the driveway. It was a daily race during the summer to get the bills-of-lading ready in time for the large transfer truck, which came and collected all the produce from the various farmers at our gate. But with all this the house grew too small."[44]

So Bill built an office onto his and Madzy's bedroom, with a door to the back yard so that the farmers could come directly into the office. Its two sets of windows overlooked a large stretch of the farm: "It was pure joy to sit there on a summer evening and see the sun, orange-glowing, sink behind the mountain tops."[45]

The room (see p.xx) became the nearest thing Madzy had to a place of her own. It was not quite a private room all to herself, but it must have given her a sense of being removed from the housework, with a desk on which the typewriter could be left open, ready for use. I remember standing in the doorway between their bedroom and the office, watching her type, her back to me, absorbed in what she was doing. And when the sound of typing came from the office, no one could tell whether it was bills-of-lading that were being turned out, or short stories.

MADZY SAID that she did not know how to write; being Madzy, she set about learning. In the spring or summer of 1954 she began taking a correspondence course in creative writing. Three or four short stories, some exercises she wrote for the course, and a revised version of one story have survived. One story is set during the war.

"Four Hours to Spare" deals with Beth, a woman living in an isolated house much like ours in Maarn. It is night and Beth is in bed. Her husband is "a spy" operating with the Dutch free forces in England, coming secretly to Holland to investigate and report back to the Allies. He has, on a couple of previous occasions, found a chance to visit her. On this night, she again hears the soft rustle of gravel – and there he is, with "four hours to spare." They have a bite to eat and some ersatz coffee and then make love, and at four o'clock in the morning he leaves again.

In the coming months Beth turns out to be pregnant and is tormented with worry: how will she be able to prove that the child is legitimate without endangering her husband?

And then the war ends and the baby is born – and has a birthmark under his left eye just like his father.[46]

Attached to the manuscript is a page of notes by the teacher of the course, who suggests ways of increasing the action and suspense. The manuscript is liberally marked up with her inked-in revisions; a subsequent version, "Curfew," has a proper title page and may have been submitted to a magazine. She has not, however, followed most of the suggestions for making it more suspenseful.

"Porker's Corner" does not take place during the war, but the setting is recognizably Maarn. It is a probably fictional tale of romance and obscure parentage.

The story based on the pearls is entitled "It's Odd How Pearls Can Roll." Rather effectively, it sets the pearls' early history, so European and old-fashioned, in the pioneer context of Terrace.

The final one in this group is "The Girl Briseïs." In it Madzy goes back to her education in the classics. Briseïs "fell into the hands of Achilles, but was seized by Agamemnon. Hence arose the dire feud between the two heroes, which is the subject of the *Iliad* of Homer."[47] Madzy recreates a few scenes from the Trojan War. At the beginning of the story, Briseïs is Achilles's captive and she loves him, but in the course of negotiations she is handed over to Agamemnon. When things go badly, she is returned to Achilles. Patroclus, Achilles's best friend and like a father to Briseïs, is killed.

It is a haunting story, and although it has a "happy" ending, the effect is of tragedy. Briseïs is a pawn not only of the gods but also of men and their warring factions.

All the stories except "Pearls" are dark in tone in spite of their "happy" endings. Even the jokey tone of the two family stories in "Your Memories and Mine" seems to me to be concealing something, though it is hard to make out what. Perhaps Madzy felt that telling the family stories in a light-hearted way would make them more readable, or perhaps she was embarrassed by their content. *Land for Our Sons*, begun shortly after, is by contrast mostly cheery and amusing; no need for apology or embarrassment there.

Land for Our Sons was probably begun in 1955 and was originally intended, apparently,[48] as a gift for Paul. But this plan likely expanded as she worked on the book. When it was completed in 1957, a copy of the typescript was indeed sent to him. He was so impressed that, via an agent in London, England, he arranged for it to be published. Knowing that it would therefore be read by other immigrants and aspiring immigrants, Madzy then revised it. Reaching this larger audience would certainly be, to her, both a responsibility and an opportunity. The book was released in 1958.

It is memoir, non-fiction, and most of the names have been only slightly changed. There are occasional difficulties with English idiom, but it must be remembered that when she began to write it, Madzy had been "living in English" for less than ten years. Much of it is a light-hearted account of immigration and the making of a farm – anecdotes about children, livestock, building, farm work. She writes with energy and humour, in the "public" voice of her journalism.

One passage concerns preparations for the Fall Fair of 1949 – not the one for which Madzy arranged the "Holland" exhibit. We were going to be exhibitors, and we assembled whatever we could enter in the categories laid out in the fair's program: "a Rhode Island rooster-and-hen, a White Leghorn rooster-and-hen, Daisy, our milkgoat, and Blossom, her yearling kid ... The boys had rabbits, Gerard could surely enter his dear Cottontail."[49] And we would enter Duke in the "farmhorse" category. The winner of the largest number of prizes in the livestock group would receive a silver platter donated by the Royal Bank of Canada.

All the animals were groomed the day before, and it was hoped that they would keep themselves as clean as possible. Duke was put into his pasture and the gate firmly closed.

> Next morning I got up bright and early; there were many things to do before Bill would be off to the Fair. I jumped into my jeans and sweater, started the fire in the kitchen stove, and then turned around to see what kind of weather it was. Someone was looking at me through the window. I blinked my eyes, looked again: someone was staring at me!
>
> "Ger, get up!" I yelled. "Cottontail is loose!"
>
> Instantly there was a great noise; the three children rolled out of their beds and grabbed their clothes.

"You goof!" shouted Marianne. "You didn't put her in her box last night."

"I did so," protested Gerard.

There was no point arguing: Cottontail was out and, after being chased around the garden in a vain attempt to catch her, she dove under the house. The attempt to shoo her out produced an offended skunk, whom we apprehensively watched stalk away; when no one was watching, the rabbit also emerged and was caught.

Then, while serving breakfast, Madzy noticed that Duke seemed not to be in the pasture. However, the other livestock had to be delivered to the fairgrounds, so Bill borrowed a horse, Dot, from a neighbour and hitched her to the loaded wagon.

> The whole thing by now queerly resembled Noah's Ark. Before Bill had time, however, to settle himself comfortably on the front seat, Dot thought it time to depart. Dot had something on her mind, and that was her breakfast, from which Bill had so cruelly torn her away. Instead of trotting off to the right, in the direction of town, she galloped off to the left, barely missing a gatepost, and headed for her stall. Bill rallied to the situation in true ex-soldier-like fashion. Standing with his legs wide apart on the wagon, the reins held tightly in his hands, he gave in to Dot's whim until he had reached her driveway. There, with a wide curve, he manoeuvred her back to the road and in the direction of town. The wagon, swaying and swinging, creaky in the joints on the two left wheels in the curve, followed with the noisy cargo of cackling fowl and mackering goats and yelling kids.[50]

Madzy, who would go to the fair later in the day, had been watching the departure with a neighbour. They drank a cup of coffee to calm down after all the excitement, and then the neighbour went home.

> I accompanied her as far as the gate. The sun did its very best to pierce through the autumn fog; it was quiet as only an autumn morning can be. The busy summer is over, the long winter is ahead, the world lies hushed as if waiting. Dew dripped in steady rhythm from the branches on the leaves of the alders along the road. A bee zoomed from nasturtium to marigold. Leaning against the gate, I savoured the spicy aroma in the air, when I heard a rustle; it was faint

and came from the other side of the road, somewhere in the bushes. Peering to the left I saw the branches of a bush move. A dark object peeked very carefully out of the dense growth.

"Oh, Duke," I said softly, "how do you come there?"

He looked at me with a question in his alert eyes; his ears were pricked up.

"Duke!" I called. "Come on, Duke, come on!"

Slowly, looking straight at me, he came up out of the bush. His coat, that beautiful shiny coat of yesterday, was caked with mud from head to tail. His mane was entangled with brambles and leaves and little sticks. He must have had a wonderful time, I thought, looking him over. He ambled over the road, and came up to me; with his nose he rubbed over my shoulder, nuzzled my neck.

For a fleeting moment I considered trying to clean him, and ride him uptown. But that was sheer nonsense; even Bill would have a hard time to get that coat clean.

"So you don't want to be an exhibit, eh?" I said. His eyes were on the same level as mine. I really thought, he knows what I'm thinking. I opened the gate and he came into the driveway. I took him by the halter and led him into his pasture.

We never learned how he had escaped. He turned and hung his heavy head over the fence; I felt in my hip pocket and found a sugar lump. Duke kissed me. That was all I wanted; I did not mind the silver platter of the Royal Bank any more.[51]

The book's epigraph is a quotation from Gerard de Nerval: "Homme, libre penseur! te crois-tu seul pensant/Dans ce monde où la vie éclate en toute chose?" (Man, the free thinker! Do you believe that you alone think,/ In this world where life bursts out in all things?[52]) I'm not sure what she meant in choosing this passage; if I were, it would perhaps give another glimpse of her inner life. She had read French poetry in her youth – the names of poets and the odd quotation would appear in her conversation. It is a compelling thought that one day – putting the laundry through the wringer or making out a bill-of-lading for crates of celery – that quotation came to her and she decided to use it.

Land for Our Sons is the first important work in which she deals with issues of immigration. In the journalism and unpublished stories written in the United States, she had written about exile, roots, the feeling of being a stranger; but she and the other Dutch people she knew there had been temporary expatriates, certain to return to Holland before long. Being an immigrant was very different, as she realized when the *Delftdijk* steamed into Vancouver harbour. This was for keeps.

In several passages in the book she talks directly about immigration. She stresses that she is not speaking for other immigrants but is talking about *her* views and *her* experience:

> We hoped to find a life of freedom in Canada; a life free of traditions which tie down one's personality too much, traditions which drown the individuality ... We hoped to hold onto the positive qualities of tradition, and thus give our children the valuable influence of their background, without hampering them with it. We had made up our minds to conform to Canadian standards as much as we possibly could, to assimilate everything as soon as possible, and to show the children the wonderful advantages the future held in store for them.[53]

And again:

> Did I miss city life, I, who had spent most of my life in the city? Did I miss a tea-room, a beauty parlour, a museum, a concert hall? Or did the beauty of the country, the freedom of life here, weigh up against the lack of those? I did not know. I had not been long enough in this country. I had been too busy to come to such conclusions. Daily life had been too engrossing, the days had been too full to feel any lack. I could read books, and though there was no bookstore, I could order, could subscribe to book-clubs.[54]

One thing about which she was clear was the matter of schooling. "The education the children received at school was quite adequate, although many a Dutch immigrant grumbled about it. It was much easier than the Dutch equivalent, and superficial in some respects, but the subjects which concerned the practical side of life made up for the lack of theory. Marianne did not have to cram rows and rows of foreign words, dates, or theorems into her head, but what she learned about social conditions, behaviour, contact with others was far more to the point, considering the life she was going to lead."[55]

But, Madzy admitted, she had problems with the informal kind of education – the bringing up of children. The children she saw in Terrace went to bed whenever they wanted, were allowed to eat after they had brushed

The main road and railway from Prince Rupert to Terrace, running along the bank of the Skeena River. On the back of the photo, Madzy wrote: "The overwhelming lonesomeness and isolation of Terrace, B.C."

their teeth at night, seemed to stay away from school when they wanted to. The manners and ways of my brothers' friends and mine were so different from what Madzy had been used to when she was a child that she was constantly disoriented. The first day after our arrival, she heard a little girl address Enid van Stolk by her first name, and then do the same to Madzy herself.

> When I asked Enid if Betty Lee called her mother's friends by their Christian names, Enid looked very surprised. "But yes, of course. Why not?"
> "Well, it sounds rather funny, don't you think?"
> "But I see this girl almost every day; you can't expect her to say Mrs to me all the time?"
> "In our country she would at least say 'aunt'."
> "But, my dear, I am not her aunt, why should she call me that?"
> I had to confess that I saw reason in this explanation, and soon I got used to the custom.[56]

We have no direct evidence from this time as to whether she longed for Holland, but later she wrote that she had been suppressing homesickness "since 1947." Bill says that his homesickness began in Terrace. He was glad to leave Holland, he says, but he missed the historical background that is everywhere present in Europe.

IN MARCH 1955 we made a new acquaintance, Bob van der Hoop. He was working for the Aluminum Company of Canada in Kitimat, forty miles south of Terrace, and had heard of us probably through mutual acquaintances in Holland. He came to visit, and on 14 March 1955 he wrote to his mother about us:[57]

> I decided to go to Terrace last Thursday to visit the Brandis family, and hope to get some advice from Bill about landscape possibilities in Kitimat, where I was placed in charge of the contractor working for Alcan. I arrived by train and was met by Bill and daughter Mary Anne. After doing some shopping I met Madzy, Bill's wife, and their two sons Gerard and Joost. Daughter 17, sons 12 and 7,[58] lovely children, brought up in "limited freedom" (as we were at home) in a typical family atmosphere, which is Dutch, although a Canadian influence is mixed in as much as possible.
> We all got along famously, played the card game "Banks" and other games. They showed me around, are proud of their banty-hens, look after

the chickens, the firewood, their own rooms, etc. Mary Anne helps in the household and in summer they all help when Pa is too busy.

Bill works very hard and has lots of energy and initiative without which he would not have gotten where he is now. From a cabin with two and a half rooms it has now become a small house with 3 bedrooms, dining room, living room and kitchen, lovely.

At the moment 2 more bedrooms and a veranda are planned. His sheds and barns are also self-built as well as a cool room for his vegetables.

Grounds are 8 to 10 hectare which are productive and worked with a small tractor. Products are lettuce, endive, cauliflower, cabbage, and potatoes mainly.

Admirable, especially when you hear how it was when they arrived, how primitive the contacts with the outside world, no doctor's help, etc.

This lack of doctors for instance has been a great set-back for Madzy. She suffered severely from arthritis and was bedridden for weeks or months at the time, would then have to be fed and helped by Bill or the children and started to get a "round back" and swelling in arms and hands and fingers. But at present she gets better slowly, with the help of better medicines, and thanks to a very strong will power. The change in her over the last two years must have been very noticeable. I saw photographs of two years ago where she appears a pretty, lively young woman. Now she shows her age.

But they both seem to be happy and content, and you notice that in many little ways.

In fact, I believe they form the nucleus more or less and the pillar of the Dutch community and many others.

Madzy's arthritis was one reason for the decision in the late fall of 1955 to sell the farm and move to Vancouver. As well, I would be ready to begin university in the fall of 1956, and my interests and abilities suggested that my future would not lie in Terrace. Gerard's interest in art and music would also certainly take him elsewhere; in the last pages of *Land for Our Sons* Bill is quoted as saying that Gerard was "going to be a professor, like his grandfather and great-grandfather."[59] Jock, aged nine in the fall of 1955, was determined to be a farmer, but Bill hoped that he would "cut his own farm out of the wilderness."[60] If Madzy and Bill stayed in Terrace, the family would be separated, perhaps by very long distances, and at that time, before easy air travel, that was a serious consideration.

There were other reasons too. For Bill, now that the farm was a going concern, the challenge was gone. For Madzy the years had acquired a too-predictable routine. They were ready for a move. Pem van Heek was taking

The house as it was when we left

a correspondence course that would lead to a university degree in forestry. Bill inquired and learned that the University of British Columbia would give him a provisional standing of two years on his qualifications in agriculture and estate management, and that if he did well he would be able to earn a B.Sc. in agriculture in two years. Madzy's law studies in Leiden, and the fact that high school in Holland had provided her with some of the requirements for a B.A. in Canada, would earn her enough standing so that in two years she too would be able to acquire a degree. Her intellectual life had been on hold, but now that she was forty-five years old, and physically handicapped, and with the children growing up, it was becoming important to her again.

In a short prose piece written "To Dicksy" on 20 October 1959, she adds a further reason: "The children needed, too, a pair of parents to be proud of. Not just simple small farmers."

It did not break their hearts to sell the farm: they wanted something new, wanted to see more of Canada.

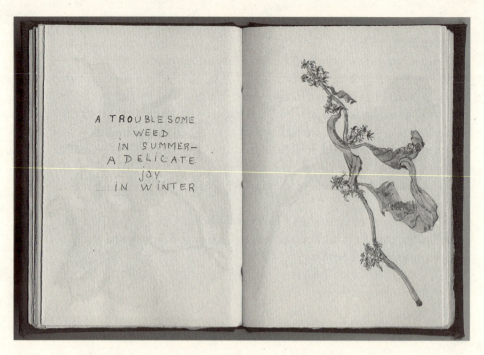

A TROUBLESOME
WEED
IN SUMMER—
A DELICATE
JOY
IN WINTER

From *The Whatman 1873 Book*, which Madzy created in 1977

CHAPTER EIGHT

Vancouver, British Columbia, 1956–1958

THE TWO YEARS we spent in the Vancouver area reconnected Madzy with the university life she had loved so much at Leiden. They revived and nourished the intellectual in her, sidelined by marriage, the war, and the farm. Now, twenty years after leaving Leiden, she picked up some of the dropped threads.

We did not go directly from Terrace to Vancouver. The farm was sold early in 1956; the winter of 1955–56 Bill worked in a furniture store, and after the farm changed hands he went to Abbotsford, just east of Vancouver, to take a summer job with the B.C. Department of Agriculture.

The rest of us remained behind in Terrace, living in a motel. The plan was that we would stay there until the end of the school year. But Madzy could not bear to be separated from Bill for that long – or perhaps could not wait to start the new life – so we went south sooner, and we finished our school year in Abbotsford. Bill rented a motel unit there as temporary quarters for us all.

I sat beside Madzy for part of the flight to Vancouver. As we looked out over the tangle of mountains, Madzy said that if we had *flown* into Terrace eight and a half years earlier and seen all this she might not have found the courage to stay.

We had just had an imaginative experience of that wilderness. The previous summer a small plane had been lost in the mountains in poor weather. The search operations, based in Terrace, involved twelve aircraft. Madzy wrote in *Land for Our Sons*, "At every clear moment the planes went up, and the droning of the machines overhead, circling, searching, reminded me of the war."[1] The search was given up after two weeks, the lost plane never (so far as I know) found. Madzy continued:

This incident showed me how isolated we lived, closed in by forests and forests and still more forests, with mountain range after mountain range. Instead of giving me a feeling of security, it began to smother me. I found myself longing for the horizon of an ocean ... The time was past that I needed a place of retreat, a spot in which to bury myself. I felt like travelling again, I wanted to know more about the country ...

When I talked to friends like that, some of them looked with a strange expression at me. They were happy here. But then, we all own an individual soul, none is like the other.[2]

THE MOTEL UNIT in Abbotsford was cramped space for five people: to find the quiet I needed for studying for my final exams, I sat in the car. After the end of the school year we lived in a new and unattractive triplex in Burnaby for about five months.

That transitional period between leaving Terrace and starting classes at UBC must have felt to Madzy like a major change. Bill was away all day; so were Gerard and Jock and I until the end of the school year. Very likely it was now that she finished *Land for Our Sons*. Paul's birthday was at the end of August, and I imagine the manuscript was sent off to reach him in time. He apparently replied with a telegram saying that he would like to find a publisher for it in England and, via a literary agent, he did. It was apparently this publisher who, objecting to the name "Madzy," advised her to call herself "Maxine."

She may have done other writing too. One strange story, entitled "Anna's Stamp Album," is obviously from comparatively early in her writing career because the very rough first draft that we have is typed single spaced and on both sides of the paper. Writers soon learn to leave room for revision, and this was especially important before computers. The story – shapeless, hard to read because it is dense with insertions, cut-and-paste alterations of order, and other revisions – appears to contain nothing autobiographical. The first-person narrator is a man named Arnold; the setting is not much like our surroundings at the time, though it resembles the Fraser Valley more than the Skeena Valley.

With what else did she fill her days? She may have written stories that did not survive. She had the use of the car, an Austin sedan. Perhaps she went to the library. We joined the United Church there. Gerard remembers that we picnicked at the house of one of the people Bill worked with. We went at least once to Bellingham, Washington.

IN BURNABY we unpacked our furniture, because the intention was to stay there for the two years of Madzy's and Bill's university studies. Madzy would have had things to do like finding a doctor and a dentist and enrolling the boys (Gerard was fourteen and Jock nine) in school. For outings we went to the White Spot restaurant in New Westminster to eat blueberry pie. Madzy's knack for making little things special helped us through a summer that, with all the newness, all the moves, felt to me unfocused and depressing. Both Madzy and I were writing; it may be at that time that we bought a second typewriter.

Then in the fall after classes had begun, an incident happened that led to our moving house again. Gerard had a run-in with our landlord about the ducks and bantams he and Jock had been keeping in the long, narrow garden, and we were given very short notice to leave. Madzy applied to the university for an apartment in one of the residential camps. There was a unit available. Gerard wrote: "She and I went to look at the apartment and it was filthy – smelled of dirty diapers. But Mam was cheerful and optimistic and said that we could make it into a nice home in no time. She was right."

She was not sorry to leave Burnaby. It was a considerable distance from the campus, and Marine Drive, our route to the university, was plagued by thick fogs. Gerard's school "was run by teenage gangs," which worried her.

She and Bill were both now attending classes full time at the university. Having been told that if he proved himself, he would be able to take his B.SC. in agriculture in two years, Bill in fact obtained it in one year; after demonstrating his ability by earning a first in organic chemistry, he graduated at the end of the year. He spent the second year doing graduate courses but never wrote his thesis. Madzy had hoped that if he got a Master's degree he would be able to teach at university, which would have kept them connected to the academic life. However, he felt that his inadequate schooling in Holland had not given him the solid foundation that he needed for teaching.

Madzy's university transcript shows that she enrolled in the College of Education. On the basis of high marks in the very demanding "state" exams at the end of the Dutch equivalent of high school and the near-completion of her law studies in Leiden, one year of courses at UBC would earn her a Bachelor of Education. She enrolled in courses in practice teaching, introduction to teaching, a survey of education, classroom administration, educational psychology, teaching methods (French), teaching methods (Latin), and Virgil.

The decision to study for an education degree is easily explained: teaching would bring in money. But her heart was not in it, although I remember that she was interested in the ideas of William James. Moreover, her arthritis was a continuing handicap, and it was probably becoming clear that the physical demands of teaching would be too great. Her marks in most of her education courses were mediocre, except for a first in the survey course which, being a form of history, would have interested her. She also received a first in the course on Virgil. At the end of the academic year, she withdrew from the program. In the summer she took a course in "Roman Writing," and that fall she enrolled in the Faculty of Arts and Science, taking courses in ancient history, classical architecture, Horace, Latin composition, and medieval Latin, and two courses in Canadian history. At the end of the year she received firsts in ancient history, Horace, and medieval Latin.

In April 1958 she began correspondence courses in history and psychology but withdrew in July to take, instead, a "directed reading" course in Ovid. By then we were living in Antigonish, Nova Scotia. When she wrote her exam at the end of the summer, she received a first. That summer she also took two English courses at St Francis Xavier University in Antigonish; with that she completed the requirements for her B.A., which she received from UBC in October 1958. She did not return to attend the graduation ceremonies, but we have a photo of her wearing an academic gown and hood.

To complete the account of her academic work: in 1960–61 she took two courses at McMaster University – Old French, and French poetry from Baudelaire to 1950 – receiving seconds in both. In summer 1961 she earned a first in elementary Russian. In 1964–65 she started "Beginners' Greek" but withdrew. However, in 1966–67 she took a correspondence course in Greek from Queen's University and earned a final mark of 87 per cent.

I have put this material together, even though it moves beyond the boundaries of this chapter, because it indicates something about her academic life and interests during these eleven years. She focused on classics and history as well as modern languages; she even talked once or twice about wanting to learn Chinese.

FROM NOVEMBER 1956 to May 1958 we lived on the UBC campus. Acadia Camp had been built for war veterans and their families and was very simple accommodation – the units were of army-barrack design joined in loose clusters. The floors were covered with battleship linoleum. We had a two-bedroom unit; for the first five or six weeks I lodged with a family nearby and ate my meals at home, but then space was made for me in the apartment. The boys had one small bedroom, I had the other bedroom, and Madzy and Bill slept on a fold-out couch in the living room. There was a

Madzy in gown and hood, October 1958

bathroom and a minute kitchen. Laundry was done in the wringer washer, using the bath for rinsing and an outdoor line for drying. The kitchen was so small that there was little room for storing food, and the refrigerator was a tiny under-the-counter one. I remember Madzy doing the housework hurriedly before or after classes, before or after the studying and essay-writing that now filled almost all her spare time. Gerard recalls: "On Tuesdays she had a class until five or six o'clock and I was given the assignment to cook the supper that day. On the way home from class she would stop in at the grocery store to ask the Chinese owners what I had bought for supper. 'Number one son, he buy ...' she would be told, and then sometimes would buy something extra. I think that I often made Kraft dinner."

For the first time since we had known her, I think, Madzy was really in her element. She had enjoyed many aspects of the farm, but the academic life was her spiritual and intellectual home.

Going back to university in middle age was less common then than it became later, and was rarer in Holland than in Canada. Aware of this, she wrote about it several times, describing the life, explaining her reasons. In her novel fragment *Never Too Late*, the central issue is whether a woman of forty-four will return to university to become qualified as a teacher. At the beginning of the story the narrator, Atti, is feeling restless and lacking in purpose; she hates the role of "grandmother" that her daughter, by having a baby, has just imposed on her. Her stepson, Leonard, a medical student, suggests that she return to university. She discusses the matter with her husband, Kenneth (this is her second husband, Leonard's father), but he calls it a "ridiculous plan." (This, incidentally, did not reflect Bill's views: he encouraged Madzy.)

The narrator's fearfulness at even thinking about attending university, her sense that she will be out of place among all the young students, comes through clearly. She is regarded as an oddity by both the students in the registration line-up and by the registrar and his staff. She is dismayed to find that her Dutch degree in classics is not considered of equal value with a Canadian one; she has to take courses in Latin and Greek to demonstrate her knowledge of those subjects, and an English course to show that she is competent in that language. She is afraid that she will not be able to do it, reminding herself and the registrar that it has been more than twenty years since she was in university. The registrar is encouraging:

"So you think that I can do it?"

"I don't think that, I know that," he said with an encouraging smile.

"All right, I'll take on the challenge," I said.

He got up. "Fine," he said, "we need people like you in this country."

I walked home ... When I passed by the Arts Building I walked inside, and peered in one of the lecture rooms. Would I really dare to sit on one of those desk-like chairs which have one arm broadened for support of a scribbler? Would I really like to sit there for hours and listen to a professor? Do you think I could keep that up? Don't let me think too much about it now.

When I entered the house I saw my rooms in a different light. There was purpose in life again, and for a moment I had that feeling of self confidence I had had when I was young. I felt strong and capable of doing things, that feeling which I had had before I was crippled with arthritis.[3]

When the fragment ends, however, she has still not resolved to undertake the venture. There is a page of general observations on the lives of married women and the reassessment they have to make as they grow older and are no longer so much needed by their children. Having considered the women who settle into contented middle age, busy with bazaars,[4] she deals with the kind of woman who is not satisfied with that:

It is the woman who had an interesting job, or was studying an interesting subject before marriage, and drops this completely at her marriage, who will feel lost. Many of these women suddenly grow haggard, nagging, unhappy, even physically ill. Even if it comes into their mind that they would like to do some work in the line they used to know before, it often happens that they lack the courage, for they are under the impression that after a certain age the brain has deteriorated and is unable to concentrate as in youth.

The trouble is that these phases run into each other unnoticed, and the woman notices only a certain unhappiness which she can't explain.

That woman is me, Kenneth. I just cannot believe that I could ever really learn something by heart. I sit here this evening, alone, while Dereck [their youngest son] has gone to bed, and Leonard has gone to the University for a meeting of his medical society, and Kenneth is so far up north. I am frightened. I have seen the university today, and I would love to be a part of it, even if it is only for a short while. I would like to walk around over the paths between the flowers, and feel that those flowers are growing also for me. I would love to sit down in one of the classrooms, and feel a new meaning in my life.

Why then am I so hesitant?

On that poignant note, the fragment ends. If it was written before she actually enrolled, the breaking off may be explained by the fact that she was still uncertain whether it would work out. The description of campus is that of an outsider: later, she was to write about campus life as one who is part of it, understands its rhythms and pressures. Whenever it was written, what she says about the vague unhappiness, the fears, the lack of purpose has the ring of real life.

Another short story, entitled "Alma Mater" – never polished or published – describes a typical morning in the life of a woman who is both a mother and a student. The opening depicts the university as a huge vacuum cleaner inhaling students in the morning. Then the story switches to the other "mater," Meg, getting her children off to school and her husband to his classes before she herself also goes to class. After the family has departed, Meg is briefly alone.

> A sudden silence hit the little suite, one third part of Hut 13 of Acadia Camp on the campus of the U.B.C. With a deep sigh Meg poured her first cup of coffee, and settled herself behind her toast-and-egg. Through the kitchen window she watched the girls leave the dormitory for the first lecture hour. Their colourful umbrellas brightened the dullness of the bleak autumn morning with bright dancing splashes. It made her think of a painting by Matisse, and this brought her thoughts abruptly to her lectures of this morning.
>
> "French, and philosophy, and philosophy, this morning," she counted in a soft murmur. "In the afternoon Latin, an hour free, and Guidance at the end." It was one of her heavier days.
>
> At nine sharp, the dishes washed, floors swept with the long corn broom ... the little two-bedroom apartment was tidy. Meg put on lipstick, combed her short dark brown hair, with a grey spot here and there. With a quick grab she tucked her textbooks and clipboard with notebook under her arm, and banged the front door behind her. The whole family had left for school.

Though less successful as a piece of writing than *Never Too Late*, this story gives an even stronger sense of being autobiographical. The "vacuum cleaner" passage at the beginning includes a vivid picture of car-pool loads of students with lunchbags inside the rear window heading for the campus (something we had seen when driving in from Burnaby), the university parking lots filling up, the students slamming car doors and hurrying to their first classes. This is indeed an insider's description of campus life. It was probably written during the one summer we spent in Acadia Camp; surely she had little time for writing during the academic year.

Recalling that summer, Gerard wrote: "She took us to the beach often, and enrolled us in swimming lessons at the big pool on campus ... Mam sat in the bleachers with her books. She also took her books to the beach, leaning against the logs and reading as we dug for abalones."

That summer, Bill again worked for the B.C. Department of Agriculture. One of his jobs took him to Vancouver Island for ten days or two weeks. We joined him for the weekend and went to Butchart's Gardens.

THIS WHOLE period is described in the memoir Madzy wrote a few years later for the *Nitor*, the VVSL publication in Leiden.

> Soon after the war we moved to the west coast of Canada. The distance of six thousand miles between Holland and our small wooden bungalow in the still-rough north was large, but larger still was the difference between the very different ways of life. During the following years it seemed as though everything that we left behind in Holland grew vague in the overwhelming effect of new and strange impressions. Language, food, dwelling, views on life, everything was different, frighteningly strange, and yet it all had to be assimilated in one way or another. The result was that for a time we turned ourselves away from what lay behind us. But after some years there came moments for quiet, inward thoughts; moments in which you ask yourself: "Are we heading in the right direction? What have we attained, and what has this done for us in a spiritual way?"[5]
>
> On a winter mid-morning I sat in the deep windowsill staring out over our snowed-in valley, with the Rocky Mountains in the background, when Bill returned from his trip to town in the truck. He called out, "Put on the coffee pot; there are several letters from home."
>
> In the pile of letters was included an invitation to take part in the upcoming V.V.S.L. reunion. Bill smiled: "Well, what's stopping you? Pack your suitcase. The eastbound train is tonight at two." Again I stared eastward in the direction of the Rockies: beyond that lay three thousand miles of Canada and three thousand miles of Atlantic

Ocean. But it was as if suddenly the v.v.s.l. atmosphere, complete with friends, came into our bungalow like a wind. A thought shot into me: "There lie all those beautiful, dear memories, lying behind you, just for the grasping. Don't despise them but use them in your present-day life. They will bring you the stability and the depth that you need in order to make this new life worthwhile."

It was probably this feeling of background that gave me the courage to become a student again after all those years. A Canadian degree was for Bill as well as for me a way of doing more for this country ...

As "mature student" I belonged to that group that devotes itself totally to studying, although I had my housekeeping to do along with it, and observed the life of the younger students from the side-lines.

Going on to describe Canadian student life for her Dutch readers, she concentrates on the younger students. Since she is writing for the publication of a women-student organization, she touches briefly on sororities but explains that most women students at UBC belong instead to drama clubs, sport clubs, and other organizations.

SHE KEPT three essays written for her courses. "On Bertrand Russell," written for one of her education courses, deals with Russell's philosophy of education, and earned her an A and the note "This is a very fine paper." She quotes a passage from Russell's *The History of Western Philosophy* (the book she had received for her birthday a few years earlier): "To teach how to live without certainty, and yet without being paralysed by hesitation, is perhaps the chief thing that philosophy, in our age, can still do for those who study it."[6] She finds this idea in his philosophy of education and works out the ways in which it appears there. The essay resonates with her own approach to life, or at least the ideals she set for herself; she may be talking about Russell, but her tone suggests that in most respects she agrees with him:

> Whereas he strongly believes in growth, change, progress, all which create uncertainty, he advocates an inner courage which will sustain a life without hesitation. His concept of courage is based on self-respect, for humility leads to self-abasement, which in turn creates a desire for the respect of others or a reward in the life hereafter. Courage will also be gained by an impersonal outlook on life, for if a person can forget himself while applying to a definite goal in life, he

will be less haunted by fear of death, and consequently he will face death with an inner courage.

She reports having written a letter to Lord Russell asking him whether his views on education had changed since 1926, when he wrote the book *On Education*. He replied: "As for the book On Education that you write about, there are two opposite respects in which I no longer quite agree with it: I think that in that book I exaggerated the amount of discipline to which an infant should be subjected during his or her first year; *per contra*, I did not allow quite enough for the need of discipline in instruction in later years."[7]

Madzy's comments are those of a mother: "In this respect I disagree with him; experience has taught me that harmless discipline in early life will establish habits which lead to self control, and which consequently save much time in the following school years. Russell advocates an early infant school, which in my opinion is a sound project in these times when the Old Nanny is obsolete and the mothers are harrassed by too many details of daily life."

For her classical archaeology course she wrote a paper on "The Athenian Agora," illustrating it with diagrams carefully drawn by hand. The professor remarked that she had relied too heavily on two out-of-date sources but gave the paper a B, commenting on the amount of work she had done.

The third, written for the ancient history course, is entitled "The Characteristics of Italian Agriculture"; it received a grade of 12 out of 15. The essay ends with a sentence that must surely refer (obliquely, whimsically, perhaps a touch rosily) to Bill: "Through the ages, through the ups and downs of the agricultural tides, the farmer has remained the same: a hard worker, an early riser, a lover of the soil, and notwithstanding all hardship, the most contented man of the world."

A NOTE written on a double sheet torn from a notebook deserves quoting in its entirety because it so clearly shows how Madzy's mind worked.

April 23 [1957]. I am sitting here in one of the education classrooms waiting for the bank to open. Hardly anyone is around. I have just told Prof. Boyes that I withdrew myself from the teaching program. It was rather a deflating moment, deflating for my ego. For I had braced myself for a long talk, explanations and all that. Instead, when I was called into his office he had another woman with him sitting there. Both were sitting, I standing. (I am not used to such treatment.) So he asked me what I wanted to say. I told him. "Well," he said, "I am sorry to hear that. But I think you are wise." I tried a sort of explanation, but no use, he was already quite resigned to my decision, stood up half-way and shook my hand to say goodbye! I was completely bewildered. I ask myself: what is it? He was nice, he was charming, he was cheerful to the boys when I introduced them to him yesterday on the campus. And now, he discards me as a piece of Kleenex. Is it my fault? What do I do wrong? I love people, I love him for he is a nice kind soul. I liked to talk to him, but usually, when I went to him, it was he who talked. I listened. He liked that. All the time I was here I tried not to be a bother. I tried to be as pleasant as possible. Still, I fear they thought I was a bother. No, it is not that. But they pretended interest, and they have not got it. It makes me feel lonely and terribly disappointed in mankind. – Do I expect too much? Do I do these things myself? I may. Now that I think it over, I might have hurt many of the people around me in the same way. But wait! All of a sudden a happy free feeling surges through my soul. If it is so, then I am not bound by people, not bound by ties that will eventually suffocate me.

The only thing I'd like to know is, what my position is now. For I might like to work for a M.A. if possible. I'll talk to Prof. Logan.

Too many ties in life is not good. It fragmentizes you. It may bolster up your ego, but it fragmentizes your soul. I am glad for this quiet moment here in this classroom where many cross-currents are blending into an atmosphere of its own.

On the rest of the sheet is a shopping list: "bread, sliced meat, milk, potatoes, vegs (carrots, grapefruits), M.A. skirt, G. shirt, bank, photo Moeder, large envelope, coffeepot stand." Madzy's life went on – the combination of inner and outer on this single piece of paper is like that in the wartime diary.

Meanwhile *Land for Our Sons* was heading towards publication. The contract is dated 30 May 1957. I recorded on 23 February 1958 that I was reading proofs, and the book came out that August, a few months after we left Vancouver.

SOME EXCERPTS from the journal I began keeping in the summer of 1957 give further glimpses into Madzy's life. In September she and I went downtown to buy a raincoat for me. Trips into the centre of Vancouver were rare: our daily needs were satisfied by a grocery store, bank, and post office on campus and other stores just outside the university gates.

I mention that Madzy received 92 per cent in the course on Roman writing she had taken that summer.

On 11 November I report: "There is a family movement to stay in Vancouver and for Mom and Dad to work here. Then I could stay at home and go to UBC from there. I love the idea."

At New Year's, there is this:

> Last night we had a party here with Ben, Kees who is a Dutch friend of Ben's, and Blanche MacIvor, a Scots friend of Mom's. The whole thing worked well. Gerald was off to a party at a friend's so Jock and I played games with Ben and Kees while Mom and Dad talked to Blanche. There was lots of food and music ... Then ... consternation. Gerald was home and asleep by 3:00 when his guppy had babies. Mom and I saw one, which was almost immediately eaten by the angel fish. This morning there were two, both of which Gerald saved. They have young every ten days or so: the angel fish won't starve.

An entry written several months later gives more detail on our lives at that time.

> Sun. 30 May: It has just occurred to me that this diary by no means gives a comprehensive picture of my average daily life. It only hits the high or the low spots. It makes no mention of quiet Sundays at home and the regular Sunday TV supper [watching programs like *Father Knows Best*, and George Burns and Gracie Allen], the regular round of lectures and the people I meet daily ... It makes no mention of the lovely moment when Mom and Dad and I have stopped studying for the night and collect in the kitchen for a snack of toast, apples, peanuts, or yogurt, and a chat, when I sprawl comfortably with my feet propped against the stove and I feel very close to everyone. It makes no mention of the times when we are all studying, with one or two typewriters going, when I am sitting at my desk, the desk top flooded with light, the rest of the room hollow and dark, with drifting wreaths of cigarette smoke; of the noisy delightful dinners we have in our much-too-small apartment and our often repeated longings for a real normal house of good size, with a garden; of the sun which wakes me by shining through the gold curtains into my room or the cold street light

which stares in at night; of the traffic to and from the Camp which passes my window, cars, motorcycles, bikes, people walking; of the green spring haze of new leaves among the black trunks in the tiny woodlot across the road.

IN ONE OF her courses, Madzy met another older student, Beatrice, a teacher and social worker, who had raised six children before going back to university. She and Madzy met in a history course taught by Albert C. Cooke, whom Beatrice married in 1963 following the death of her first husband. After we left Vancouver, Madzy and Beatrice corresponded, and the Cookes came to visit Madzy in Ontario in the late 1960s.

Madzy also had contact with Mary van Maurik, the nurse who had spent a short time in Terrace while we were there and who now lived in North Vancouver. Peter and Enid van Stolk moved to Vancouver during this time, and we visited them. Jan Croockewitt, one of our visitors in Terrace, was now living in the Vancouver area and once took us sailing. Anne and Ed Shaw had left Terrace too and were now living just south of Sechelt, where we visited them. Bob van der Hoop was in the south; once he borrowed a car and took the boys and me out for a day.

A new friend was Freek Vrugtman, who was working as lab instructor in a course Bill was taking. He married after this time, and he and his wife, Ina, were to become close friends of our whole family.

CULTURALLY, Vancouver had more to offer than Terrace, though this was the 1950s, before the development in Canada's cultural life that was to take place in the following decades. I heard all the Beethoven piano sonatas played in a series of noon-hour concerts, and went to a student performance of *Twelfth Night*. Gerard saw *The Importance of Being Earnest*. He recalls that we "went *en famille* to an exhibition of Emily Carr's paintings at the Vancouver Art Gallery and to the Theatre under the Stars for a performance of *The Pyjama Game*; also to the Zoo and the Aquarium in Stanley Park." Radio reception was good, and we had a small TV set. At Christmas we all watched *The Nutcracker*, and there were weekly broadcasts of Leonard Bernstein conducting the NBC Orchestra. Except for specific programs like this and the Sunday-evening sit-coms, we rarely watched television; Madzy regarded it as more of a cultural resource than an entertainment medium.

A very tight budget and little income limited what we did, with a family of five to be got through the two years of Madzy and Bill's studies. Going to plays and concerts also takes time and energy, and Madzy was already as busy as she could manage. Her arthritis was draining her energy, sapping her will to go out after a very busy day. I have the feeling that for her even being on a university campus was a form of culture. With every pore she absorbed the atmosphere, and her courses were a heady dose of mental stimulation.

BOTH MADZY and Bill would finish their studies in the spring of 1958. The previous summer, after obtaining his Bachelor's degree, Bill had been offered a job in the B.C. Department of Agriculture, but he had already enrolled for another year's courses and turned the offer down. Next year, when he began applying for jobs, the provincial government was not hiring, so he had to go farther afield.

He heard of a position in Antigonish in Nova Scotia and went to see what the town and job looked like. He must have brought back favourable impressions, because on 9 March my journal records that we had a family conference and decided to move to Antigonish.

There were other factors in the decision besides the unavailability of jobs with the B.C. government. Bill found Vancouver too Americanized; the Maritimes had been settled earlier by Europeans, and Bill had liked what he saw. Besides, it was much closer to Europe: it might be possible to make a trip back to Holland one day.

JUST BEFORE WE left Vancouver, Madzy's doctor had advised her to have all her teeth pulled: this, it was believed, could relieve the arthritis in some way, and the fact that she agreed to such a drastic measure indicates that her condition during the previous years must have been bad. The operation was performed in a hospital, and Madzy was fitted with dentures immediately, before the gums had healed properly. So far as I remember, she shut up within herself most of the pain and misery and the further damage to the pride she had always taken in her physical appearance. It was in this condition, then, that she made preparations for the move.

We left Vancouver by train on 2 May, having already shipped all our belongings, including the car. Bill had arranged for us to travel in one of the coaches designed for immigrants: each coach had a kitchen where passengers could prepare their own food. We boarded the train carrying boxes of groceries and dishes. To take advantage of the fact that we were crossing Canada from coast to coast, we arranged overnight stops in Ottawa and Quebec City. With those delays, the trip would take us a week.

The rail cars became another "home," just as the cabin of the *Delftdijk* had been. We occupied two sets of seats – seats by day, berths by night. By day they housed a homey clutter of books and other belongings, and there we ate the meals Madzy and I cooked. I remember Madzy waking me in the morning by handing a mug of tea between the curtains into my upper berth. When the train stopped, we walked up and down the platform to stretch our legs, breathe some fresh air, and mail letters and postcards. In Ottawa we stayed in the Chateau Laurier and went to the Parliament buildings. In Quebec City we stayed at the Chateau Frontenac and walked around the French part of town. We ate restaurant meals, had baths, slept in a bed that wasn't moving.

The visit to Quebec City brought Madzy and Bill back to where they had begun in Canada – to the trip they had made from New Jersey in 1938. Madzy must have reflected on the distance – not only geographically – that she had travelled in those twenty years. And, having studied Canadian history, she now understood the significance of what she was seeing.

And then it was on to Antigonish, and another new start for us all.

Dried leaves, painted by Madzy in late middle age

CHAPTER NINE

Antigonish, Nova Scotia, 1958–1959

ANTIGONISH, in eastern Nova Scotia, is the site of St Francis Xavier University. Bill had been hired to work in the university's Extension Department as a horticulturist.

The Extension Department had been set up in 1928.[1] Under its head, Father Moses Coady, it gave birth to "an original community development program" – later to become the Antigonish Movement – designed to deal with poverty in the eastern counties of the province and further afield. The Movement's goal was "self-help, adult education, credit unions and cooperatives." After the Second World War, the Antigonish Movement spread to developing countries: the philosophy and practices that had worked in eastern Nova Scotia during the Depression were relevant to the Third World. Students from those areas came to "St FX" to study, and took what they learned back to their own countries.

Beginning in 1930, the Antigonish Movement "addressed many of the themes that would reappear later in liberation theology and in popular education ... the importance of self-confidence, self-reliance, critical consciousness and solidarity ... the connections between community development, economic co-operation and social justice, and the affirmation of the social mission of the Church expressed in an ethical commitment to the poor and the oppressed. The Antigonish Movement has influenced adult education and community development programs throughout the world."[2]

In 1958 the Extension Department was working with the local co-op store and the credit union to improve conditions of rural life in the six eastern counties of Nova Scotia. It provided information about crops that suited the soil and climate of the area and promoted vegetable production – which, Bill told me, was non-existent at that time. He travelled through the region visiting farms and addressing farmers' meetings.

THE POPULATION OF Antigonish – about five thousand in total – was 90 to 95 per cent Roman Catholic, but there were small Anglican and United Church congregations. We joined the United Church.

Following our arrival on 9 May we lived for a few weeks in a small, shabby apartment building that, on account of the smell, we christened "Codfish Palace." Bill and Madzy quickly bought a house, and at the end of the month we moved into it. It was at the edge of town, with residential streets on one side and open land and a creek at the back. The neighbourhood young people played baseball behind our house; soon Gerard, Jock, and I were playing with them, and I was interested to see that kids of all ages, from quite young ones to some in their early twenties, played comfortably together. I had never known a community life like it.

Once again we had to find our way into a new town. For us the baseball games quickly made superficial connections, though I missed the intellectual contact with my university friends in Vancouver. Des Connor, one of Bill's colleagues, and his wife, Etta, became my parents' friends. But my impression is that Madzy's emotional and social life again centred mainly on the family.

One of the highlights of the summer for her must have been the publication of *Land for Our Sons*. She probably received the first copies in July, because a letter survives dated 1 August from the associate editor of the *Atlantic Advocate*, a regional magazine, saying that they had been sent a review copy. They would be happy to review it, but would she please confirm that she now lived in Antigonish. The review appeared in the September issue and was favourable: "*Land for Our Sons* is a book of interesting experience, sincerely and effectively related. I hope there is to be a sequel some day with something of the author's life in Nova Scotia in its pages."[3]

Madzy's connection with the *Atlantic Advocate* was to flourish. Eventually the magazine published six of her short stories, and her relations with the editor were always very cordial.

THAT SUMMER, Madzy took a "directed reading" course in Ovid from UBC and also two summer courses at St FX, one on literary theory and one on the English novel. I took the same literary theory course and one in political science; we registered on 7 July and wrote exams in the second week of August. Madzy received her B.A. from UBC on 24 October.

ABOUT THE first of October, Madzy also began full-time work for the Extension Department, taking charge of its small library. This consisted

The house on Cedar Terrace in Antigonish

of one room: shelves bearing about eight thousand books,[4] a counter, a typewriter, a telephone. It was three years since there had been a full-time librarian, though one of the nuns had occasionally spent some time there.

It was the first employment Madzy had had other than homemaking, farming, and the occasional writing. She committed herself to the work with conviction and energy. One of the first things she did was to set up a books-by-mail program, seeing it as partly personal self-development for readers and partly a form of extension education. Not only did the philosophy of the Antigonish Movement favour such a project but her experience in Terrace must have come back to her as she imagined herself into the lives of the families in the isolated small towns and hamlets of eastern Nova Scotia.

We know she began this program immediately because on 15 October 1958 she wrote a circular letter describing the books-by-mail program. The letter was mailed to "several hundred" households:[5] "Books are sent out, free of charge, throughout the Maritimes. In one of the books you will find a sticker, to be used on the return parcel. In that way you can return the books without paying postage. Books may be kept for one month."[6] She lists the subjects on which the library has books, mostly practical things like farming, forestry, beekeeping, raising livestock, furniture-making, dressmaking, and knitting. There are books on religion, history, travel, and biography, and novels and children's books. People are invited to ask for a "family parcel."

The letter is also directed to people living in Antigonish itself, where there was at that time no public library. For their benefit, the letter states, the library is open from Mondays to Fridays 9:00 A.M. to 12:00 and 1:30 P.M. to 5:00, as well as on Saturday mornings and Tuesday and Friday evenings.

In a report submitted on 3 March 1959 to the director of the Extension Department, she writes that 125 people "answered the circulars, and have become more or less regular borrowers. During October 35 parcels went out. In November the amount had risen to 50." During part of December and January the library was closed (because the librarian was away – about which more hereafter) but even so "during December 50 parcels went out, and in the second half of January 52 parcels. During February ... 98 parcels; this is at the rate of four parcels a day average."

She reports that, since her taking the position, the library has acquired "thirty new books on farm management, farm machinery, and farm methods" as well as a subscription to a magazine entitled *Farm Mechanization*. She has also obtained (and now distributes) free material on "sheep raising, beekeeping, foresty and forest conservation, and woodlot management." She has contacted the departments of fisheries in Ottawa and Washington for free literature; she has also taken a subscription to the *World Fisheries Abstract.* To help meet the demand for children's books, she has obtained the loan of fifty books from the Catholic Women's League library. She reports on the numbers of books loaned to townspeople: 200 in October, increasing to 365 in February. "University students use the library frequently"; so do high-school students, all looking for material for essays. "The foreign students[7] spend much of their time in the library," and two reference books have been acquired to help them.

IN NOVEMBER 1958, Madzy began writing a column for *The Maritime Co-operator*, the Extension Department's bi-monthly newspaper. Her columns consisted mainly of book reviews, but there was usually a short introductory section. She wrote fourteen of them. The first two were called "Dusting the Book Shelves"; after that the title was shortened to "Dusting the Shelves." In the first column she explains the title by saying that it is the librarian's customers who, by using the books, keep them dusted.

The columns are chatty and colloquial. Sometimes the chattiness conflicts with the proselytizing intent and the serious subjects of the books described. Because the subscribers would be supporters of the Extension Department and the Antigonish Movement, she deals frequently with books about the cooperative movement, better farming practices, or self-education. The main purpose of the column was to inform readers about specific books – and categories of books – that they could borrow from the library.

The first column includes only one review and then lists six other books that might interest readers; later ones usually contain more reviews. The column of 15 February is entirely devoted to a book entitled *Hurt Not the Earth* by E. Newton-White, then just published. Madzy begins with personal experiences:

> When you go by boat along British Columbia's coast or by car through British Columbia's interior, you are struck by the poignant sight of so many deserted sawmills or farms. The sagging roofs, the pieces of derelict equipment tell of the busy activity that once went on there, of the hopes of the people who once laboured there.
>
> When you travel by train cross-country, hundreds of similar forlorn places hurt your feelings. In the prairies, in the Canadian Shield,

all through the Eastern Provinces, and finally in the Maritimes, the thought hammers perpetually at your brain: "What waste, what terrible waste of precious resources. Man seems to have picked a few choice bits from the earth, as we do from a platter full of dainties, and then he has left the place ... for what? To whom?

It is this fact of wanton waste, this thoughtless destruction of precious resources, that Mr. Newton-White puts as a terrible warning to us in his book.[8]

We see something here of Madzy's inner life. She had sat on the deck of the *Prince Rupert*, or at the window of a railway car, not merely as a sightseer but as an observer, intent on *seeing* Canada, assessing, understanding. She refers to other parts of the world where land, trees, and water are husbanded carefully, to "soil used intensively for centuries that still yields crops in abundance because of the rebuilding program."

She writes a long column on biographies, all of them with an uplifting element (this with an eye on the "self-help" philosophy of the Antigonish Movement): Florence Nightingale, Helen Keller, Abraham Lincoln, St Francis Xavier, Joan of Arc, and others.

She also writes with enthusiasm about a small book entitled *Housewives Build a New World*, by "Emily" [actually Emmy] Freundlich:

> She explains that each household is an economic unit in itself, and all our households together help to form the basis of the national economy. Now we housewives are really the persons who decide how much bread must be bought, how many groceries, how much money we can use for clothing, how we have to divide the space of our house among the members of the family. We do in a small way what the leaders of the nation do in a large way.
>
> Think of the responsibility a housewife has really, if through her daily task she influences in a tiny way the economy of the nation. It makes you feel proud of being a housewife, and our task, which sometimes looks like drudgery, takes on a new shine. In this little book Emily Freundlich tells how housewives in other countries influenced the economy of their nations, and how they bunched together cooperatively, by creating co-op stores and the like.[9]

Self-respect, self-help, cooperation: Madzy found these ideas congenial. Immigration itself had been a matter of self-help. One of the principal documents of the Antigonish Movement was Father Coady's book *Masters of Their Own Destiny*; Madzy and Bill, by coming to Canada, had firmly taken charge of our family's destiny.

She devoted one column to books about Nova Scotia history. In another, written in March, she observes that at this time of year a lot of people have colds, so she reviews books dealing with nutrition. She writes about books by women. She deals with books about gardening, travel, home decoration.

Some of the columns are uninspired; it's not surprising that she found no enthusiasm for writing about the *Concrete Handbook* ("how to use concrete") or *Operating Principles of the Larger Foundations*. Some chatty or humorous bits sound forced. But, inspired or not, the steady increase in library circulation figures indicates that they worked.

Madzy would be able to skim some of the books, but the reviews suggest that she read a number of them from cover to cover. No doubt much of the reading and writing was done during slack times in the library: how she must have loved having such a place in which to work and read and write!

Shortly after her first book column appeared in the *Maritime Co-operator* on 15 November, she also began writing regular columns for *The Casket*, Antigonish's local newspaper, under the heading of "Extension Speaks." She wrote fourteen of these over the next six months. Their purpose was to explain to general readers the work and philosophy of the Extension Department and to promote the ideals of the Antigonish Movement. She used a variety of devices; some of the columns describe and explain – and, not infrequently, exhort – while some are narratives, almost parables.

To describe the work done by the Extension Department, she uses what was no doubt a real-life situation: one of the staff takes a group of overseas students on a tour of the department. After urging the need for continuing education throughout one's life, the leader shows them the director's office, the store-room, the offices of the *Maritime Co-operator* and of secretaries and fieldworkers, and finally the library. Monsignor Coady, the Movement's founder, comes into the library and tells the group about the work that the department does, both in Atlantic Canada and overseas.[10]

She writes about the need for farmers to regard their farms and woodlots as living entities and as resources. As in the *Hurt Not the Earth* review, she is talking about sustainable development before that term was invented.

> Here in Eastern Nova Scotia we hope a new pulp mill is about to come; that will be good, it will give work, it will bring prosperity to many, it will improve the economic situation in our province. Many farmers possess woodlots: they will be able to make money with their

woodlots. But will they do this with their eyes on the future, or will they just grab, and think only of the present time?

A woodlot is an investment; used in the right way it will bring in a crop, just as a field brings in a crop, and so it will be a valuable asset for now and for the future. But the farmers must know how to make good use of their woodlots; and it is not hard to get the right information, the Extension Department can help out here. Therefore, it is not a question of "Do I know?" but a question of "Do I Care? Do I care enough for my farm, my children, the future generations of Nova Scotians, to exploit my woodlot in the right way?"[11]

In other columns she describes ways in which her readers can improve their lives: one column urges the advantages for fishermen's families of having a vegetable garden, another deals with the idea that work can be enjoyed and not just endured or even cursed. In a column about the pleasures and benefits of reading, she includes a plug for her books-by-mail program. She describes a group of farmers talking about whether to let their sons go to high school: one of the men declares: "If you wish to keep your boy on the farm, don't send him to high school."[12] Madzy – using the voice of the Extension Department fieldworker who is present – argues against this position.

One gives us a glimpse of her experience at UBC: "We have discovered that our brains do not get slower when we get older. To many a person who has started to study again as an adult, it comes as a pleasant surprise when he sees that learning is not so hard as he has expected it to be. In fact, it is easier in some aspects: when you grow older you see things in a different way, you look at them more critically, and learn to choose what is important and what not. Moreover, you possess the will to work, and work hard, in order to reach your goal sooner."[13] Recognizing, however, that actually attending university is impossible for most of her rural readers, she explains what is possible. They can take correspondence courses offered by the Department of Education and short courses from the Extension Department. They can learn from the agricultural representatives and fieldmen sent round by the department, and they can borrow books by mail from her library.

She knows that her readers grumble about the unsuitability of Nova Scotia's soil and climate for farming but suggests (in line with Extension Department policy) raising sheep, blueberries, or bees, and exploring the possibilities of tourism. If her readers are interested but do not know where to start, they can borrow books from her library.

She knows that her readers run into debt buying TV sets and bedroom suites, so she writes about how, during the war, people in Holland learned how little they really needed for survival.

To connect her readers with the larger world, she deals with the dangers of communism and the atom bomb. She understands how helpless many feel, and urges that the co-op movement – and informal cooperative efforts in general – are a way in which "small men" can help to create a better world. She talks about the importance of the Antigonish Movement to poor people in distant parts of the globe.

It is clear that, through Bill and other people in the department, she learned about the interests and problems of the people who read what she wrote. She imagined herself as well as possible into the minds and lives of her readers, knowing that they were mostly people with little education and a narrow and isolated existence, fearful of anything strange, most of them lacking the will and energy and money to change their lives. She writes earnestly and with dedication; she supported the ideals of the Antigonish Movement and had no hesitation in promoting them. In these columns she never talks down to readers; she does not pretend to be one of them, but as much as possible she talks their language. She challenges them to enlarge their lives, to be more enterprising and far-sighted, to undertake a process of self-renewal. What she writes, and how she writes, give us insight into her own adventures in self-renewal as well as into the world around her.

She was also writing some fiction. *The Maritime Co-operator* of 15 December 1958 printed "Marina Comes Home," a rather moralistic short story. The *Atlantic Advocate*, in its June 1959 issue, published the first of what were to be six short stories; this one would have been written during the spring of that year.

And she occasionally gave talks (as Bill did regularly) on the local radio station.

ALL THIS professional work – so new to Madzy, and probably so stimulating – was interrupted by a very important event: our first trip back to Holland, which took place in late December and January 1958–59. Because of our modest means, the expenses were covered by Bill's father and stepmother. We had been in Canada for just over eleven years; diligent correspondence had kept the ties strong and close. Now that we were geographically nearer to Europe than we had been, the trip was feasible.

Because the five of us could not all be accommodated by any one host, Madzy worked out a schedule by correspondence, in advance, of who would stay where and when. She and Bill of course wanted to see as many people as possible, to renew the connections for themselves and make links between us children and the relatives whom we knew hardly or not at all.

Inevitably she felt a certain anxiety: what would people think of her children, who had grown up without many of the social graces expected of young people from good families in Holland? She had done her best, but ... I imagine that she worried about our clothes, manners, fluency in Dutch. She had, in 1947, been glad to leave behind the older generation's criticism of her. She was no more likely now than she had been then to measure up to their expectations, and her children probably even less so.

Quite apart from all this, I imagine that she wondered how being in Holland would feel to *her*. Would she be so happy there that the return to Canada would be difficult? Would she hate Holland? Either way, would the trip be a mistake?

We left on Saturday, 20 December. The plan was that we would drive to Sydney, leave the car with an acquaintance of Bill's, and fly to Gander, Newfoundland, where KLM had arranged for one of its planes en route from New York to Amsterdam to make a special stop to pick us up.

On that Saturday morning, I was at the radio station where I had a half-time job writing commercials. Madzy phoned to say that there was a cold front coming which would turn the wet roads to ice, so we would be leaving earlier than planned. One of my colleagues drove me home, and after a quick sandwich, we left. It was snowing by then, but we moved faster than the cold front. We flew to Gander and slept that night in a hotel at the airport.

Our scheduled departure was for ten o'clock the following evening. We spent the day in the airport, turning one bench in the waiting room into a temporary home with books and bags and clutter. But the plane from New York was delayed and, after sort of sleeping in our bivouac, we finally left at six o'clock on the following morning (22 December). We flew all day (this was the era of propellor aircraft) and even then, instead of arriving in Amsterdam (fog covered the mainland), we landed at Prestwick, Scotland. After a night in a hotel there, finally, the next morning, we arrived in Holland, finding a whole crowd of relatives at the airport to meet us.

Because I spent much of the visit apart from Madzy and Bill and my brothers, my journal does not contain much about Madzy's activities, but I've collected information from other sources. Her Leiden year-club, Spuit Elf, with whom she had maintained contact by letter, arranged a dinner where they would all meet. She saw other friends such as Tini Sandberg, with whom she had made the walking tour in Cornwall and who had been a friend ever since. In the article she wrote for the *Nitor* a few months later, she says that she went to Leiden.[14]

The five of us were together on several occasions, including Christmas dinner in The Hague at Iete's house, and the traditional drinking of hot chocolate on New Year's morning at the large flat of Bill's father and stepmother in Zeist. We went to Maarn to see the people who had been our neighbours there, paying short visits at six different houses. We stayed with and near Paul and Mita, and had dinner with them at a wonderful restaurant in Amsterdam. In between, we saw elderly aunts and young cousins and every other sort of relative.

A revealing episode recorded in my journal was a phone call Madzy made to me while we were staying in different places. She was worried that, because I was having such a wonderful time, I might want to remain in Holland. Had she been wrong to bring me back, exposing me to temptation, unsettling me? There had apparently been some pressure from an aunt and uncle for me to stay. She said she was afraid she had lost me, and would I please reconsider.

I, for my part, was tempted to stay but had never seriously considered it nor, so far as I can remember, discussed it with anyone. I wrote in my journal that I hoped I had set her mind at rest. She may, in part, have been transferring her own feelings to me. Considering the incident now, I catch a whiff of the kind of conversation that the adults must have had, and perhaps something of the persuasive influence or even pressure that Madzy always found so hard to bear.

WE LEFT Holland at midnight on Wednesday, 14 January, and were back in Antigonish at six o'clock on the Thursday evening. Bill has told me that he and Madzy found the drive back from Sydney to Antigonish across Cape Breton Island dispiriting. The little unpainted houses on the empty hillsides looked so poor, the whole area so bleak. Bill remembers saying: "Is this what we came to Canada to live among?"

I had not wanted to leave Antigonish, but when we returned I was homesick for Holland. There must have been a good deal of talk in the family about the trip, and about our feelings about being back in Canada. My journal entry for 17 January reports that Madzy felt we had been right to emigrate, and the next day I wrote that whenever I spoke in favour of Holland, Madzy spoke up for Canada. The following day Bill expressed a strong longing to live in Holland again. On 19 January I had a serious talk with them about whether I would like to go back permanently.

But in a few weeks we slipped back into our Canadian lives, and whatever yearnings we felt went underground or were woven in among the enjoyable aspects of the lives we actually had. I took up skiing and Madzy gave me an elementary lesson on the slope behind our house. We gave a big impromptu party. One evening while Bill was away, Gerard and I laid linoleum tiles in one of the rooms. To celebrate, Madzy made a late-night supper of pancakes and syrup.

All the same, the trip had unsettled us. In my journal on 3 March I report that we were talking about leaving Antigonish.

One of the reasons was a change of direction in the Extension Department. While we were away, Father McKinnon, who had been the head of the Department and had hired Bill – a marvellous man, Bill said, enthusiastic, encouraging, with new ideas – was transferred by the bishop. The department was now headed by Father Gillis. When Bill went to present himself, Father Gillis said there was no future in vegetable growing in eastern Nova Scotia. Bill realized that the program would likely be discontinued and that he would then be out of work.

Bill had, in fact, been disappointed the previous summer by the farmers' lack of interest. Cape Breton had been settled by immigrants from the Scottish Highlands who had been evicted from their crofts because the landowners wanted the land for sheep. At the time Bill was working among them, some were still living a life that was a couple of centuries behind the times. The "farmers" were, in fact, primarily fishermen. Until June – the end of lobster season – they did no work on the land, and by that time it was too late to start most crops. Even when they put seed in the ground, as Bill saw on his visits, the carrot plants were tiny and the weeds high.

Bill was then close to forty-eight years of age – old for starting a new job. But he learned of a position at Niagara Brand Chemicals in Burlington, Ontario, just west of Toronto, and went for an interview. On 30 April he received a telegram saying that he had been accepted and would begin on 1 June. He would go ahead by himself; we would stay behind for a couple of weeks and follow by car. The house was sold, and we packed and shipped most of our belongings, so that by the time he departed on 30 May, we had only the barest necessities left.

It was in this state of spartan disarray that the Dutch vice consul from Montreal found us when he visited on 4 June. He had come to talk to Madzy about translating *Land for Our Sons* into Dutch. The Dutch government had set up a service to help people emigrate; having heard about *Land for Our Sons*, they asked Madzy for permission to have it translated and published in Holland.

Madzy asked whether she might translate it herself, so that she could add explanatory material that had not been necessary for English readers but would make the book more useful for Dutch would-be immigrants. The Dutch government agreed to this; *Land voor onze zonen* was published the following year under the auspices of the Intergovernmental Commission for European Migration in Geneva and the Dutch Emigration Service in Den Haag[15] and was widely read in Holland.

On the inside front cover the Emigration Service describes the book (one hopes that the ponderous style was not too discouraging for potential readers) as one from which "many aspiring emigrants can learn useful lessons ... By means of this book they will be prepared for a new life and encouraged in their doubtfulness; their unmotivated, unreasonable expectations will be tempered with moderation. Those who remain behind ... obtain a clear image of the lives of those who emigrate. Mrs Brandis's many years of experience as a writer give this book the easy, journalistic style which is indispensable for this kind of work."

SOME YEARS after leaving Antigonish, Madzy wrote about an experience she and Bill had during the early months of 1959. She describes a farmers' meeting in one of the isolated houses she had been trying to visualize as she wrote her columns, corresponded with borrowers, filled orders, and packed parcels.

It is winter; Madzy and Bill are driving through wind and sleet up a rutted driveway to a lonely house on a hill.

> We were on our way to a meeting of a group of farmers who had gathered around their battery-operated radio to listen to the weekly farm broadcasts, a government project. Some six to ten farmers would form a club, ask the government for information material that accompanied this broadcast including sheets on which they could write comments or questions. And enclosed were booklets with up-to-date farm news for everyone.
>
> In this way the government tried to help the farmers to improve their farm methods and get better crops. The group would choose a leader. They would first listen to the broadcast and then discuss among themselves the material they had heard. Finally, the leader would fill in the forms with remarks or questions, and the meeting was over.
>
> Bill, as extension worker, and I, as librarian of the extension department, had been asked to go to one of those meetings to give our opinion of the usefulness of this project.

When they arrive, they are taken to the kitchen.

The heat that met us was overwhelming. The old kitchen stove was on full blast. The smell of drying clothes, pipe smoke, sweat, and fish hit us like a wall. It was as if we had stepped into a scene of a hundred years ago. The small oil lamp in the centre of the table shed a feeble light so that a few people only could be vaguely seen. On one side of the radio sat an old man in a rocking chair, holding his right ear with his hand, as near to the instrument as possible. At the other side a younger man sat at a table with papers in front of him – obviously, the group's leader. Behind him against the wall sat three or four men – it was too dark for counting – on a sagging iron bed. Another sat on a straight wooden kitchen chair, but as soon as I entered he got up and disappeared somewhere in the background. I silently sat down. Bill found an upturned wooden box.

Near the stove stood a tall grey-haired woman of about seventy years old, her face stern and bony, full of wrinkles, her hands work-worn, her back as straight and stiff as a rod. She threw a short, disdainful glance at me and then turned her back to feed the flames of the stove with another big chunk of wood. On the stove stood the largest enamel teapot I had ever seen. In it she threw another handful of tea, for us, I suppose, and the boiling tea let off a cloud of steam.

When the broadcast ends, the radio is turned off. There is a long silence. The old woman serves tea and cookies.

The scalding, strong tea had loosened the tongues of the men a little. The leader asked if there were any questions or remarks that he could fill in on the form. Reluctantly, and after much hesitation, a man would say a few words which I could not understand. Bill tried to join into the conversation without much success.

... Finally the meeting seemed to peter out and we prepared to leave. Just before I got up, the woman came straight to us looking us in the eyes and said a few sentences. At our bewildered looks she turned back to the stove with a shrug of her shoulders. A man in the corner on the bed guffawed. The leader said to us, rather apologetically, "She only has the Gaelic." A man asked us, "Don't you have the Gaelic?" We shook our heads in shame.

When we drove off in the storm that seemed worse than before, a window behind us dimly glowed through the sleet and the snow. The wind howled around the lonely house on the bare hill. So it had stood a hundred years or longer. Driven out of their homeland, the people had built their lives over again exactly as they had left them behind. They had come as pioneers and had remained pioneers – strangers to this land where they had put their feet ashore with so many hopes in their hearts.

Written perhaps ten years after the event, it is one of her most effective stories, and also one of the most chilling, not only for the subject matter but as an oblique commentary on the work she had been doing, the ideals she endorsed. It was in no sense meant to be an adverse comment on the idealism of the people among whom she had worked: it was a reflection on the gap between the ideals and the reality. Unquestionably there were families, and areas, where the gap was much less.[16] But sadness permeates every line of that story: these were some of the people whom her efforts had not reached, could probably never have reached.

And behind the last paragraph resonates *our* experience of emigration. Only a month or two before this, we had been in Holland, reconnecting to *our* roots, to the life we had left behind.

Scene with bare trees, painted by Madzy in late middle age

CHAPTER TEN

Burlington, Ontario, 1959–1965

WE LEFT Antigonish to join Bill on the afternoon of Friday, 12 June. It had been decided that since Prince Edward Island was the only province in which none of us had yet set foot, we would drive to Burlington via P.E.I. That detour, and one or two other stops on the way, meant that the trip took a week. Madzy was in a light-hearted mood: this was travelling, a short holiday in which she could indulge her adventurousness – but safely, in the family capsule.

The car, the Austin sedan we had brought by train from Vancouver, was as full as it would go. Besides the four humans, there were some house-plants, a bowl of goldfish, and the cat. A box of kitty litter sat on the floor behind the front seats. We took equipment to make our own meals; we would look for motel cabins with housekeeping facilities but were prepared to cook on picnic tables. There was a mandolin, which one or another of us occasionally played during the drive. A roof rack held suitcases, and over that was a sheet of sturdy plastic. At the last moment we discovered that our winter coats, hanging behind a door, had not been packed in the "big" luggage, so they too were stuffed in.

With the heavy suitcases on the roof rack, the car careened a bit. The plastic loosened and flapped. On P.E.I., the flapping spooked an approach-ing horse pulling a buggy, and the horse swung in front of our car. Madzy slammed on the brakes and everything that was loose in the car lurched.

On the last evening of the trip, Madzy phoned Bill to indicate at about what time we would arrive, and he was waiting for us at a designated inter-section of the highway. He could see us coming from some distance away. By then the plastic covering the roof rack was so frayed at the corners that we could no longer tie it down properly. Gerard and I, therefore, sat in the back seat, each with an arm out the window to hold down the back corners. All the same, the plastic bellied and flapped. When this apparition hove into view Bill said to himself, "That's my family."

For our immediate accommodation, Bill had rented a furnished house from an elderly couple who were away for the summer. He and Madzy bought a house, and we moved into it on the first of August. It was a dignified but not luxurious two-storey building with a good-sized garden, located on a dead-end street.

We were again starting anew. Madzy and Bill were forty-eight, I was twenty, Gerard was seventeen, and Jock was twelve. It was not a good summer for any of us. I was unable to find a job, though I tried. The boys and I hung around the house. The weather was hot and humid – something we were not used to – and there were many thunderstorms, which Madzy and Gerard especially disliked. When they happened in the middle of the night, we gathered for a snack. Usually it was chop-suey loaf – an iced fruit bread, one of the staples of Madzy's housekeeping, bought at the local bakery.

Madzy, in addition to finding a doctor and a dentist, getting the boys ready to go to a new school, and driving me to McMaster to arrange for the upcoming academic year, was translating *Land for Our Sons* and doing other writing. She acquired a car of her own – another small Austin – and loved the freedom it gave her.

To compensate for the ways in which her worsening arthritis restricted her life, she expanded in other directions, fighting with the combination of hope and desperation typical in such situations and delighting in what she could still do and could invent, discover, undertake. The circumstances of our life in Burlington were, again, very different from those in other places, and she adapted to them while holding firmly to what was for her the core: the family, her writing, her correspondence.

In October 1959, four months after arriving in Burlington, she wrote the reflection on immigration from which I have already quoted. It was couched as a letter to Bill, though he was not away at the time. In it she assesses our situation, writing that it had been a mistake to leave Vancouver:

> As soon as we realized the mistake, we looked around, and the next best thing was Burlington. Here, after some trouble of adjusting, the children have found back what we took away from them by leaving Vancouver. Here, in another few years, they will feel completely at home.
>
> But we parents still have the frontier of Canada in our veins. We can't get rid of that. Burlington to us feels plush, and too settled, too wealthy and too confident of its own prosperity and solidity and permanence.

We have to stay here, for the children's sake. But when they have started their own lives, who knows?

It was by now a well-established conflict – the tug between, on the one hand, freedom and the simple life of "the frontier," and on the other the need for civilization and culture, for some part of what they had left behind in Europe.

In my journal I record that in December we discussed the possibility of moving west again – all of us – the following summer.

Besides thinking ahead to the time when we would be independent and she and Bill could shape the rest of their lives to suit themselves, Madzy was also thinking intensely about issues involving immigration. Our moves within Canada were in part the consequence of the original move from Holland, further attempts to find a place that suited us. Our futures, for Madzy, came to interweave with the larger picture of the lives of Dutch immigrants in Canada, and in these years she wrote about many facets of the subject. Besides preparing the translation of *Land for Our Sons*, which was published the following summer, she must have written the short story for the December issue of the *Atlantic Advocate*, an article that appeared in the winter 1959–60 issue of a magazine entitled *Emigratie*, and the article published in the *Nitor*, the VVSL magazine, probably in 1960.

THE SUMMER and fall of 1961 – two years after our arrival in Burlington – is again a period when we catch glimpses of Madzy moving through her days, see something of her outer and even her inner life, because a small group of letters survives. In early August 1961, both Gerard and I were travelling: he – getting a ride with friends – went to Antigonish, and I left for Holland.

The first of Madzy's letters to Gerard is dated 6 August and talks about their taking me to the airport the day before. She had not been well that summer, and that day was a marathon for her. Jock was also sick, but he insisted on coming along. At the last minute I did not want to go (I was very depressed) and had practically to be pushed onto the plane. On the way home from the airport, Madzy and Bill and Jock visited friends for dinner; Jock did not feel like eating. "When we drove off, after some time Jock lost his headache, became ravenous, so we pulled up at one of those places where they also have a golf range. So we sat eating hamburgers with coffee and pies, while looking at people hitting golf balls. It was midnight!"

When she wrote the letter the next morning, she was sick in bed, with both eyes inflamed. She was unable to study for the upcoming final exam in the summer course in Russian she was taking at McMaster. "But I do not care, really," she writes. "As long as you and Marianne are safe and happy, I am glad. The house is so empty."

Four days later she writes again, "just a note" – but the letter is a page and a half of single-spaced typing. She has been cramming Russian all day. She would like to take another course in it. But "I had three requests for tutoring again, new ones, and I feel, and so does Dad, that this source of income is very welcome to us in the coming years"; it would bring in more than a hundred dollars a month.

A week later one eye is still inflamed; it gives her a constant headache and makes her dizzy. She is going to see the optometrist and perhaps a specialist. The weather is hot and muggy, with violent thunderstorms and big hailstones, then cooler. Jock mows people's lawns, brings home a stray kitten; Bill is refinishing the top of the dining-room table. "I had *8* batches of laundry after you two left, and the machine lost its belt again! I washed your leopard-skin blanket; it washed beautifully, came out very fresh and clean, and ... several sizes smaller!!" She is feeding the neighbours' cat while they are away. Her friend Tini Sandberg is arriving, and they are going to drive to Upper Canada Village in Eastern Ontario. "Jock spends most of his time in the garage. He made a blow-torch, and now a jet-engine. He plans to try it out today, so may the gods help us!"

The inflammation in the eye is caused by the arthritis, and the doctor tells her to wear a shield over it to give it rest. She is forbidden to read. She does not ask him about writing, fearing to have that prohibited too. The eye continues to cause pain that over-the-counter medications do not cure, so she will have to consult a specialist. She wants to be able to drive when Tini comes.

"Pekoe [the cat] misses you, but is now chewing on a chicken bone and forgetting her sorrow."

She asks Gerard to buy three copies of the August *Atlantic Advocate* for her because there is a story of hers in it. "I am so happy, this is another 50 dollars, I think."

She *did* write the Russian exam that August. Gerard told me that she was very ill but she insisted on doing it and finished the course with a first-class grade of 77 per cent.

Tini Sandberg stayed for four weeks. She was the kind of woman friend Madzy had never managed to make in Canada. The contact between them had remained strong, and I can only imagine the talk and the sharing that must have taken place. In spite of the eye problems, that must have been a very good time for Madzy.

The eye problem was part of what proved to be a year-long bad spell in Madzy's physical condition. The cortisone that she had been taking for some years – probably since Terrace – had enabled her to be as physically active as she was. Her Burlington physician, Dr van Vierssen Trip, had increased the dosage because, with her body becoming accustomed to it, she required more to achieve the same results. By now the side effects were visible; for one thing, it caused her to have a "moon-face," which she hated. Also (and much more seriously) it made her skin paper-thin, so that even brushing against upholstered furniture could cause it to tear.

In the late summer or early fall of 1961, Dr Trip – realizing that her inner tissues must be equally fragile – instructed her to stop taking the cortisone. The effects of the abrupt cut-off were dreadful. She suffered from nausea and excruciating headaches, so that in September and October she had to lie for weeks in a darkened room. The weather was hot, and there was no air conditioning in the house; she lay in her dark room suffering, while Gerard and Bill tried to make appetizing bits of food for her.

In the second half of October, Bill's father and stepmother came to visit. When they returned to Holland, they told me how serious Madzy's condition was – the family's letters to me had made light of the matter – and said that I really must go home. Of course I did, arriving on 11 November.

Madzy improved only very gradually; by the beginning of the winter she was on her feet but still unable to read. In my journal, I record on 29 July 1962 that she had been unable to read for a year, and she herself, in a letter written in September 1962, says that she was blind for more than seven months but has regained vision in one eye.

She recovered somewhat, but from then on she was more sensitive to cold, tired easily, and was in constant pain.

THINKING OF how it must have felt to her to live with arthritis helps me to see her as a person, a woman.

I catch a glimpse of the woman in her attitude to clothes. She disliked shopping for clothes and let some newly bought garments hang unworn in her closet for as much as a year until she got used to the look of them. Once, when she needed a new winter coat, we went together to a store in Toronto that sold clothes for tall women. She bought the first or second coat she tried on. The shop assistant could not believe that such a choice could be made so quickly, but Madzy knew precisely what she wanted. It was a grey wool coat, very classic. I wore it for a time after she had no more use for it.

Madzy in the kitchen in Burlington

She was proud of her figure and her naturally wavy hair. She loved casual slacks and sweaters; she referred with distaste to the garters and stockings that she had had to wear in her youth, and to having been required to wear a girdle even though she was so slender. I don't recall her ever wearing shoes with high heels, even in the earlier years, because they would have made her taller than Bill. For "neat" occasions she wore tailored suits, or skirts and sweaters, or occasionally a dress.

She loved dogs, and we had dogs and cats whenever possible. She loved beauty in music, art, nature. She was intensely creative; when the effects of the arthritis blocked one form of creativity, she found another.

At one time during this period, she "ran away from home," as I put it in my journal. It was a Saturday evening, and she simply drove away in her car. We were at first not aware that she was gone; then we spent three-quarters of an hour looking for her before she returned. I have no idea what prompted it or where she went – perhaps just the few blocks down to Lake Ontario so that she could be alone. How often, I wonder, had she *not* given in to such an impulse?

She took her role as mother very seriously, perhaps because she was often unsure of herself. She was never confident of the standards to use in bringing up her children, and she felt her way as carefully as possible, taking from her own past what still seemed relevant, adopting whatever Canadian ways she could accept or felt to be appropriate. There must often have been conflicts between the two sets of standards; parenting was never easy for her. She blamed herself when things went wrong – which meant "wrong" by her high standards concerning the peace and harmony which were supposed to prevail in families. Discussions of problems were got through as quickly as possible; problems were things to be fixed rather than symptoms. My memory is that she did not delve extremely deeply into the real roots – though the material I have been using (and seeing for the first time) for this book indicates that she was or became aware of how deep those roots sometimes are and how intractable some difficulties can be.

Her writings about immigration connected at every point with our experiences as a family, and as five individual immigrants. One question, which became important by the time we reached Burlington, was whom we children would marry. For instance, would I marry a Canadian? A Dutchman? A hybrid like me? Madzy had a partiality for Englishmen, feeling perhaps that ethnically they offered the best choice.

She was pleased when we were popular with our contemporaries. A solitary young person worried her. She seems to have recognized that I needed time alone for studying and reading and writing, but if I was alone too much, she took it as a bad sign. She worried about my being lonely and introverted.

In March of 1965 she wrote about me to my friend Audrey, saying that she was intensely worried about me. "She is so lonely, so maladjusted, she starts overeating again, and dressing in sloppy clothes. Do you think she should see your psychiatrist? Or would it harm her? ... She has so few friends and you are one of them."

She and I had disagreements during these years. Part of my lifestyle in my McMaster years – coming home late from parties, drinking beer, having crushes on men – was an attempt to be like my contemporaries, part of it was trying out this and that to see what fitted. My sense of identity was sometimes very shaky. I had no old friends around me, let alone cousins and aunts and uncles – none of the family and social context that helps one to get one's bearings, to learn ways of relating to people and dealing with major issues in life. Madzy sometimes had to reprimand me, and then I always felt immensely guilty.

Believing that children ought to be on their own by their early twenties, she nudged me into leaving home. It was not done unkindly, but the nudges were unmistakable. Leaving home was very difficult for me. Home was a comparatively safe place; the as-yet unrecognized mood disorder I was suffering from made the rest of the world seem strange and dangerous. Furthermore, I liked being with my family. They were interesting people, almost the only ones I knew then who felt like "my kind of people." Madzy knew that, I think, and I sometimes felt that she grieved over the necessity of my leaving and tried at the same time to hold onto me. (Clinging to people and simultaneously pushing them away is something that trauma survivors do, and both of us were trauma survivors.) There was a conflict between what she felt to be her duty as a mother and the strong bond between us. Immigration was a factor in this: my leaving home might have been easier for both of us had the network of extended family and old friends been nearby to offer us other connections.

Another parenting issue involved Gerard's sexual orientation. Gerard believes that she was aware early on that he was gay; he recalls that her first indirect allusion to it occurred in Antigonish:

> Mam learned from someone that there was a man in town who was approaching teenage boys for sex. She explained it to me in a very calm way, so that I didn't see it as violent. She said that she thought that I would not like it, that I would be too fastidious. But she added, "If one of my children was homosexual, I would love that child just as much as the others." That

was the greatest present she ever gave me, the reassurance of her unconditional love. I realize in retrospect that she must have already recognized my sexual orientation, but she left me free to discover it and express it when I was ready.

When we lived in Burlington, Madzy's doctor said that he could give Gerard hormone injections "to cure the disease";[1] she and Gerard discussed it and decided not to accept the offer. Madzy later told Bill about Gerard's being gay; both of them were understanding and supportive.

Madzy also respected his wish to have a career as an artist. He had one or two part-time jobs during those years, but art was what he wanted to do. In 1963, the two of them began taking art lessons together.

IN BURLINGTON we were suddenly in much closer contact with Dutch people. We had Dutch friends, among whom Mien Heersink was one of the most important, and travelling to Holland was easier. I went to Holland for three months in the fall of 1961, Bill went in the fall of 1963, and Madzy went in December 1963. There was a Dutch store in Burlington, and Madzy had two Dutch doctors, working briefly as receptionist for one.

When there were Dutch visitors, the conversation always included talk about where everyone had lived in Holland and gone to school, and also to whom they were related. In a small country, there was a good chance of overlaps. I remember their voices caressing the place-names; when, recently, I was using maps to plan a trip to Holland I heard them again, naming towns and cities, streets, public buildings. They would describe the route they had taken as children from home to school or to visit a grandparent. I recognize how important a ritual that was, not only for each person reliving his or her past but for the group, defining who they were, searching for things they might have in common.

A consequence of the appearance of the translation of *Land for Our Sons* – which sold well in Holland – was that a Dutch women's magazine, *Prinses*, published an article about our family in the issue of 28 July 1962. The author was P.J. Risseeuw,[2] a Dutch writer who was travelling in Canada and who, apparently in October 1961, came to Burlington to visit us.[3] He had read *Land voor onze zonen* and writes, "I felt privileged to meet that plucky family, who had created a farm under difficult conditions. The farmer, and his hard-working wife with her university background, had not balked at getting their hands dirty; now they were working in other ways to recompense the country whose sons had fought for our liberation."

IN 1963, BOTH Madzy and Bill travelled to Holland, separately. She wrote to him while they were apart, and most of these letters survive. Bill went in October, his first trip by himself. His parents were elderly; charter flights were affordable.

The two sets of letters, again, suddenly, open a shutter and reveal her inner life. She wrote almost daily, sometimes twice a day. The first letter was written on Tuesday, 1 October, before Bill had even left Burlington. It was intended as a surprise: he would not be looking for a letter so soon after his arrival in Holland.

Naturally she did not have much to tell. She talks about their arrangement that she would not drive him to the Toronto airport because he worried about her driving home in rush-hour traffic, but she was "allowed" to meet him when he returned, "three weeks from tomorrow." She says, with more than a touch of bravado, "That (fortunately for me) doesn't sound so very long. I'm going to do a lot of painting." She reminds him to tell his father and stepmother about a painting course she is going to take at the local arena. She has to break off writing to help Jock with his French homework, and what with one thing and another it is not until the next day that she continues. She talks cheerfully about picking chrysanthemums in the garden ("the warm weather is bringing them into bloom – such a lovely scent!") and about Jock's stamp collection which she is looking after for him. She asks Bill to suggest what presents she can send to people in Holland for Christmas. She mentions Gerard going to McMaster with a friend who has a sports car – "delightful to see those two tall fellows folding themselves into that tiny car, waving as they shot around the corner. Wonderful, that student life!" This is Madzy's cheery tone, public, busy, optimistic.

On Friday she writes again. The first part of the letter is to Bill alone, and the second to him and his parents, for him to read aloud to them. She is writing at the moment when his plane is leaving Toronto. Apparently she had driven him to the airport after all and had broken down into tears at parting. She apologizes for her weakness: "I am so dreadfully ashamed of myself." She cried as she drove home, cried while she made herself a cup of tea. Then she sat down at her easel, still crying. But she felt she had to encourage him to go, for his own sake and also for his family in Holland. "You may blame me for not telling the truth [about the homesickness] but if I had told you how I felt about it, you would never have gone."

The part of the letter written to Bill and his parents as a group is cheery again. She refers proudly to having provided him with an outfit of new clothes. There is chat about the children, and then she returns to "living with" Bill during his flight.

The following morning she writes to him again; she had expected a phone call from her sister, Hansje, at four A.M. but when the phone rang there was no connection. She cried bitterly at the disappointment and then, out of sheer loneliness, phoned Bill who, she knew, would just have arrived at his parents' house. Shortly after that, she succeeded in connecting with Hansje.

The letter goes on to raise the question of their returning to Holland for good:

> What is the use of us staying here in Canada? I have always maintained that I will never go back to Holland, but now I waver.
>
> You know, I think the reason why I cried so much since you left is that all the homesickness comes tumbling out, which I have forcibly suppressed since 1947. Of course we are all homesick, but I had decided by myself in 1947 that since you had come back alive from the war, I was not going to spoil it again by becoming homesick (as in 1936–38 [in the U.S.]) and I was going to push it through. And I did. I really made the grade.
>
> But now I wonder whether I was right. For I *know* that you are homesick.
>
> You know, I love this land, the beauty, the wideness. But what good does this do me in my condition? On the other hand, I long for people *to belong to*. And I have absolutely *none* here except you and the kids. What will happen to me when the kids go their own way? Moreover, you then will be all alone in caring for me, which might be a terrible burden later.
>
> Dicks, I realize that I say all this in a very emotional mood, and maybe when you are back I will rally. But I have since long (ever since I really realized that I may have to end up in a wheelchair) worried about this terrible loneliness for both of us. You have no friends here, and excellent friends in Holland. Moreover, there are all sorts of people who will help you in your care for me. And if one of us will die, is the other going to stay *all* alone here?

Then she goes on to practical aspects of a possible move back to Holland: the children's lives, his work (she knows that he dislikes his job), the possibility that doctors in Holland "might do something for me to patch me up and keep that wheelchair horror away from me." Now that he is in Holland, he might make some discreet inquiries about a possible job. She again recognizes that she is being emotional, but says her loneliness "has crept up on me since my activities have been more and more curtailed, since we came to Burlington."

The next few letters are much the same. There are passages dealing with her loneliness and homesickness, and cheery "public" sections. That Saturday, 5 October, was my birthday; I had come home from my apartment in Hamilton, and all four of us were together. Madzy reports that she made a nice dinner and afterwards we sat by the fire. She says we talked about everything from *Beowulf* (which I was studying in my postgraduate course in Old English) to aesthetics.

She writes cheerfully that she thinks a lot about Bill and his parents, calculating what time it is in Holland and what they might be doing at that moment. Her Dutch idiom is casual and racy, her tone jaunty.

To Bill, in English, she writes that she had talked to her (Dutch) doctor and he had given her a sedative. She had talked also to Gerard and to me about the possibility of returning to Holland for good:

> Marianne was enthusiastic: "Then I will come and visit you every summer holiday!" she exclaimed, "Tremendous! I'd love that. And I would know you would be looked after well, for they are all simply frustrated by the fact they can't do anything for you, and they want you to get better medical care." But poor Gerry was unhappy: he did not want to go himself; he said he would look after me, etc. When I asked him whether he would not prefer to live in Europe where art was so much more developed and mature, he said he was afraid for the military service. I thought he might be exempt from service because of his back. I said we would have to come to Canada every year in order to get our old age pension. He was still doubtful. Then I dropped the matter.

Unquestionably our reactions had a lot to do with the family dynamics, with our awareness of Madzy's homesickness, with our own mood at that moment.

The next letter, written later the same day, reports that she has been to the oculist and received bad news about her eyesight: the arthritis has got into her eyes, and her vision will deteriorate – slowly or more quickly. She says that she will do as much reading and studying as she can while she can, and considers acquiring a small harp, which she will be able to play in spite of the lack of strength in her hands.

On Tuesday morning the cleaning lady is there. This help is very necessary because all the emotions have had their effect on Madzy; she has more pain and has to lie down more during the day. But she is painting her own Christmas cards, using Chinese brushes. In the course of the letter she changes from typing to handwriting because that is less painful. The previous evening she and Gerard sat in the garden with a cup of coffee at seven o'clock in the warm weather. The bats cheeped over their heads; the setting sun lit up the yellow leaves on the trees.

In the next letter she is calm, starting to assimilate the bad news about her eyesight. While she still has her vision, she will paint and paint, because that will help imprint the beauty of the world in her memory. She has bought two of the largest prepared canvases that she can get at the local stationery store; during the upcoming long weekend, both she and Gerard are going to paint. Gerard is "a real strength these days, and so is Jock, they are both so sweet and feel with me."

On 12 October she writes to Moeder Hans, Bill's mother. The fact that Madzy felt able to write confidingly to her indicates that a great change had happened in their relations since the war. She expresses fears for Bill's safety: in Holland he is driving his father's car, although she has asked him not to because it is a strange car, on strange roads, with strange traffic regulations. Her entire life depends on him, she writes; if anything happens to him, after the children leave home she will be entirely alone in Canada, and increasingly helpless. (In part this is true; in part it is the fearfulness of trauma.) But if they return to Holland, she reflects, they will lose some of their freedom – and she knows from her former experiences how irritating she will sometimes find the family. She wonders whether Bill would be better off if she were no longer there so that he could marry a younger, fitter woman and live in the country. (She had written in her letter of 5 October that in Canada the loneliness of life in the country scared her, whereas in Holland she would love to live in the country.) She feels that with her illness she may not live very long, and she also says that the severity of the pain leads to this despair.

She addresses her mother-in-law as "little Mother," and the tone is that of a younger woman writing to an older one, asking for advice – and, even more, for understanding, comforting, empathy, protectiveness. It is an aching, anguished reaching out, and its tone reveals how lonely Madzy was and how much in need of contact with someone from the older generation and from a family and tradition like her own.

She ended up, however, not sending the letter. She encloses it in one to Bill, explaining why she is doing so. She fears it may upset Moeder Hans: "so I send it to you, and you can think and talk it over; that will be easier for you."

This letter to Bill begins: "Darling, as usual when you are away I am completely lost unless I am writing to you; I did that when we were engaged, tried to do it when you were in camp (then I wrote everything in a large book we still have – and even now Jock urged me during supper to write a book about my experiences during the war), and at various other moments. So now."

An article in *Maclean's* classifying marriages led her to consider how theirs was working. With the children growing up, she and Bill could perhaps do more together: they might read history books aloud to each other and discuss them. She admits that she does not tell him everything: "For instance, I do keep away my pain and worries from you to shield you, and so do you vice versa. I wonder if this is right. At least we can easily mend this lack." She also writes: "I always try to be independent; this is my pride. I must get rid of my pride. I am afraid I still have to resign myself to this. But I want to learn."

In this letter she again raises the issue of Bill's driving his father's car. Referring to Bill's father, she conjectures:

> He does not realize that with you my life stands or falls. If you were not to come back to me, I should have to go into a home, for I do not want to be a burden to any of the children. I can still care for myself now, but God knows how long this will be.[4] I thought that Father being somewhat of an invalid himself would have understood, but I do realize that it is impossible for them to understand how much it costs me to let you go so far away, with the risks involved. Life is pretty grim sometimes, don't you think? But all this makes me realize that I do not want to move back to Holland for again I would clash with the ideas of those whom I love so much and who love me, but who still have different ideas about things than I have ...
>
> However, my precious darling, this can't be helped, and is beyond our control. If Father says you can take the car, and how silly if you don't, how can you get away from it without looking silly in the eyes of your father? That is why I love it here; here I am free, though lonely, here I can do what I feel is the thing I should do, and who cares what others think of it. I begin to see things more clearly now, I think.

In the days since Bill's departure, she has worked her way through a whole range of emotions and reasoning. The issue of driving the car crystallizes this, and the outcome is that she feels that (at least at this moment) the perilously unstable scales come down on the side of remaining in Canada. The letter moves on to the miscellany of daily life:

> Well, I have done my good deed for today, I saved the life of a sparrow; and while I was doing this, Pekoe was almost run over. So I sit here slightly breathless, and am going to put clean sheets on my bed, put a laundry in, and do my Friday shopping ... We have a long weekend to come, with lovely weather. The forecast is for warm weather, and they expect 63 people will die on the roads because of it.

That afternoon she sits down at the typewriter again. The autumnal garden looks beautiful. Gerard had been asked to act as consultant at a sale of original art to be held at the Simpsons-Sears store, and is talking about going to Europe next summer. "Jock has those spots again." The three of them were going to visit friends in Grimsby that evening.

The mail had brought a letter from Bill – apparently also writing almost daily. She replies:

> I suddenly was sorry for my disturbing letters, for they seem to upset you terribly. Of course since we both decide we should talk more freely to each other, it is better so, but sometimes it stirs up a lot of mud! I even get the impression that you are rather glad that I was homesick, for that you were even more homesick and now at least see a chance of perhaps going back? You seem very eager, or is this only because of me? I knew that you had often homesick feelings, which I counteracted by saying: no, I wouldn't think of going home, and so that was that. – However, I feel very doubtful that going back to Holland will bring the solution. Once there, after a tremendous lot of trouble and sadness, we may long to be back; the children may either stay here, or long to go back, etc. Is it not easier to stay where we are until the children have all settled down? Or to forget the whole thing and just remain homesick as before? I have a strong feeling that we are taking these feelings too seriously, and that first we should see if we can't make our lives a bit more exciting here, even with my health.

She touches on the possibility of his finding other work in Canada, since he is unhappy with what he has. But then she writes: "Darling, why not forget about it for the moment. Enjoy your stay, look around you, but don't see it all through a rosy viewer, and when you come back we will talk and talk. I feel better today ... and even with all the threats above me, I feel I can enjoy life, even here."

Another letter arrives, in which again he deals with these important issues; she advises calm and clear thinking and says again that they will talk when he returns. "For the children mean a lot to me, and so does this country, but I do feel that it is you who really intensely longs to go back and live in Holland; you have so often doubted the wisdom of our emigration, far more than I. This does not say that I have not been homesick, but that does not include that I want to go to Holland within the next years, unless my health really turns for the worst, and I can't look after myself. So, let's leave it at that."

In her letter of that Sunday she refers to a phone call between them that morning. He had sounded strange, and she writes: "I wish we would just stop thinking and writing past each other."

Her letter of Sunday, 14 October, is the last one we have. He returned ten days later, and she would certainly have kept writing as long as there was a chance of his still being there to receive mail. But those last letters have not survived. On this Sunday evening, she is going to put on her dressing gown and sit by the fire and read. "Ten days are soon over. And what joy it will be to see you again!!"

It is an extraordinary sequence of letters. It reveals a good deal about Madzy's inner life, and her awareness of the differences between her own and Bill's inner and outer lives. It shows her emotions at odds with her reason, and how she deals with the conflict. It shows her expressing and analyzing, and observing herself doing it. Like the war diary, it suggests something about the writer she might have been if her work had not been circumscribed by her physical handicaps, the literary genres she chose, and her move from Dutch to English.

The frantic mood immediately after Bill's departure is that of early parts of the war diary; his absence stirred up the old trauma and the fears for his safety, fears that something would prevent his returning. When he came back from Holland, she denied having written along those lines and then, upon being shown the letters, "regretted her weakness in revealing her secret."[5]

ON MONDAY, 2 December, barely six weeks after Bill's return, Iete, Madzy's mother, died suddenly. The phone call came as Madzy was washing the breakfast dishes. So as to be there for the funeral, she left that same day, flying from Toronto to Montreal and changing there to a KLM plane to

Amsterdam. She wrote to Bill while on the plane that she was not sure whether she would be able to manage the coming weeks. In Burlington she could, more or less, design her days to accommodate the pain and handicap and keep herself as comfortable as possible, but away from home it would be much more difficult.

Once in Holland, she again wrote almost every day. She talked about the people she saw, about funeral arrangements (she was asked to choose the music). "I find Holland quite disappointing somehow," she admitted, clearly surprised at herself. "I live in a dream, but long for Canada."

She wrote again on Wednesday, 4 December: "Darling, it is late but I shall just write to you for I am lonesome for you. People are nice here, but I don't feel at home. If I could have taken a plane next week I would do it." She found the houses very cold, even though Paul and Mita, with whom she first stayed, had put an electric heater in her room and provided a hot water bottle and three thick blankets.

She spent the night before the funeral in Iete's house in The Hague. Her mother's servant Dientje was there too. "It is a rather empty feeling to know that this is the end of a very important part of my life," she wrote. "I can't help looking around to imprint on my mind all these rooms in which I spent such a very large part of my teen-age years. I feel rather unreal, as if I am in a very bad dream and I cannot wake up. It is simply impossible for me to realize that Oma won't live here any more. Every time I walk around she seems to say: 'Here, you can hang your dress here,' and: 'Dientje, bring quickly a warm cup of tea for Mrs Madzy.'"

The funeral was on Friday, 6 December. She refers to it in a letter written the next morning; by then she was staying in Utrecht with her sister, Hansje, brother-in-law, Wiet, and their five young children. Wiet was a doctor, with his office in the house, and it was an extremely busy household. Downstairs the breakfast dishes were being washed; she was not allowed to help. Annie, the servant, was vacuuming. Madzy felt in the way. "I miss you all very, very much, and long for my own family, home, food, bed every moment of the day."

She was also exhausted. "Yesterday we were up at 7:30, then came the whole business with the funeral which lasted until almost 2 o'clock, then we went back to The Hague, where I had a bite to eat (I was too upset to eat at the reception in the funeral home) then we travelled (after some business talks with Giebel [her mother's "man of business"]) to Utrecht where we arrived at 5 or maybe 6, we had dinner at seven, we talked until ten."

There are no details of the funeral, but she recalled it years later in her memoirs:

Almost exactly forty years after my father's death, I came again to this place for the funeral of my mother. When we walked from the funeral home I was the first one behind the coffin, and I felt very lonely because, apart from the fact that I was alone, all the people behind me were fairly strange after all those years I had been away on the other side of the Atlantic.[6] Behind me, Hansje walked with Wiet, Muike, and Cathrien, and behind them Paul and Mita. Suddenly I felt an arm slipping under my arm and that was Wiet ... Again we climbed the very steep hill, up where you can hear the sea, the sounds of the waves on the beach and the wind blowing through the stunted evergreens. When I was standing there, I thought, "What a lonely place this would be if it wasn't inhabited by so many dear people. All around my mother would lie her dearest ones – father beside her, our Joost would come soon, Tante Johanna and Oom Willy right opposite on the other side of the path, Tante To and several more of our relatives, our dear relatives."

And that is why that place is not a lonely, sad place to me but almost a part of my past, a past full of colour, of joy, of sadness but above all of warmth and love.

On the day after the funeral, she reports that she still had many things to do: visits to relatives, business talks with Mr Giebel. She had to decide which pieces of furniture to take from her mother's house, not just sentimental choices but practical ones: what she could afford to have shipped, what could be accommodated in our house in Burlington. Then the packing and shipping had to be arranged for.

She found that life in Holland was lived at a hectic pace. People drove fast, moved fast, talked fast. She was very tired, and her body was becoming stiffer every day. (By "stiff" she often meant "painful.")

On Monday, 9 December, she writes that she is "homesick all the time" – and now, unlike two months earlier, she is in Holland feeling homesick for Canada. The coming days will be taken up with disposing of her mother's clothes and making further decisions about dividing belongings. In the letter she lists what she has chosen: her mother's desk, a big bookcase, the silver tea-set complete with tray, the copper hot-ash container, pail, coal shuttle, "and every copper thing that belongs to the hearth." There were also paintings. In the end (not mentioned on this list) the shipment would include one or two small oriental carpets and an ornate carved cabinet brought from the Dutch East Indies. She declined "the clock," probably the tall-case clock that stood in her mother's entrance hall.

Iete had, in her will, left something to each of us: for Bill, a large mahogany blanket chest, for me, an emerald and diamond ring, for Gerard a watercolour by our ancestor Charles Rochussen.[7] Iete had not known what to designate for Jock, so Madzy would choose something. Anxiously she asked Bill whether she had made the right choices, but of course she would not receive his reply in time. There would be more business in connection with the inheritance from the sale of the house, when that occurred: Bill could correspond with Mr Giebel.

Her trip home was fortunately easier than it might have been. It was faster because she flew by jet. She was supposed to change planes in Montreal, but the weather there was so bad that the KLM plane landed in Toronto. This was a godsend because in the end she had taken far too much cabin luggage with her, including the silver tea-service with its large tray, wrapped in a thin mattress rather like a quilt, which was supposed to be good for people with arthritis. She had said in her last letter that she would show the customs officials the newspaper clipping about her mother's death to prove that what she was bringing were things from her parental home, so the airline authorities must have taken pity on her. She was whisked through customs. The little airport bus delivered her to her own door because she was the only passenger.

The lift van containing the furniture and paintings arrived by ship the following summer in Hamilton. It was delivered to our house and unpacked there, and when the huge crate was empty, the men from the trucking firm offered to take it away. "No, no!" Madzy protested. "That's my crate. I paid for it." Bill took it apart, and the lumber was later used for building projects at the house in Carlisle, including wainscoating in the basement room.

On Iete's birthday in 1964, the first after her death, Madzy wrote a poem, in English. It is full of aching longing. To someone who knew only about the stresses between them during earlier years, this emotion comes as a surprise, but in fact there had been a great softening of relations since then. Distance had enabled Madzy to achieve her autonomy and had removed the irritations that had caused so much strain during her youth and the war.

Madzy recalls the day when she heard about her mother's death, and then, tracing the events after that, asks rhetorically where her mother's spirit is now. She recalls her own feelings in the plane going to Holland:

Surely you must be here, Mother,
Thousands of feet above the ocean
That kept us apart all those years,

You with your hands pressing the window
Through which I stare
Over the plane wing
Towards the horizon and the rising sun
I press my cheek against the coolness
Of the pane that separates us.
How I wish I could break it
And plunge into your arms, Mother,
But I've still so much to do
Down there, back on the earth ...

The poem follows the events of that time: the night she slept in her mother's house, the funeral. She ends in Burlington, sitting at Iete's desk:

The desk where you wrote me
Your many letters full of love and anxiety.
This desk with many
Tiny drawers. And when I open
Just that one, you will come out and
Embrace me with your love
Surely you must be here –
or – are – you –

HERE ABRUPTLY the shutter closes again. We have no surviving letters of hers for the next six years. But it is possible to guess something of her inner life.

Most importantly, the letters she wrote from Holland, while full of loving references to family there and appreciation for their efforts to make her comfortable, say nothing about wishing to move back permanently. After all her longing and anguish of two months earlier, her aching desire to live in Holland among her family and friends might well have been confirmed when she was actually there. Yet the letters contain none of this – only homesickness for Canada and for her own house and immediate family. Possibly her mother's death closed a chapter, and the furniture, paintings, and carpets she inherited may have transplanted enough of the Dutch atmosphere so that she felt more at home in Canada.

She went back to Holland three more times, with Bill. His trips by himself in those later years – there were three of them as well – were again agony for her. She focused on how she, with her steadily declining health, would manage "if something happened to him" and she were left alone, depending on her children for care. She believed that it was appropriate for spouses to be dependent on each other, but she did not want to be dependent on us.

WRITING WAS a very important part of Madzy's life in Burlington. But it was an almost completely private part; she did not share the work-in-progress with us. Perhaps we did not show enough interest; perhaps she preferred to keep it to herself.

As we have seen, she spent the first months in Burlington translating *Land for Our Sons* and, since the book was being published largely for use by immigrants, adding further information. For instance, she gives the distance from Vancouver to Terrace,[8] and describes how mountainous British Columbia is. In the English version, she simply mentions that the van Stolks' house was a log cabin; the Dutch version has a description of how a log cabin and a fieldstone fireplace were built and how the chinks between the logs were filled in pioneer times. When referring to the hospital in Terrace, she explains that in isolated communities in Canada the Red Cross will build a hospital which will later be taken over by the town.[9]

She keeps in mind not only what her Dutch readers do not know but also what they *do* know. When telling the story of meeting the Canadian soldiers on the heath near Maarn in 1945, she writes, "We still had barely half a loaf of bread, that awful dirty-smelling bread"[10] – knowing that most of her Dutch readers, fifteen years after the end of the war, will remember what she is talking about.

Also at this time she wrote the article for the *Nitor*, the VVSL magazine, reviewing her life in Canada

She wrote more stories for the *Atlantic Advocate*. "A Call in the Fog" had appeared in May 1959, just before we left Antigonish, and five more were published between December 1959 and November 1963. These stories all draw on her experience – in Holland, Terrace, and Antigonish – but two are especially interesting for the insights they give into her inner life.

In "Foreigner in the Family," the eighteen-year-old daughter in a Dutch-Canadian family becomes engaged to a Canadian. At first it appears as though it is the young man who is the "foreigner," but in fact it is the mother who, having trouble accepting the engagement, feels like an outsider. There is a resolution at the end: the young man, whose own mother abandoned him when he was young, "adopts" the narrator (his future mother-in-law) as mother. But the frightening sense of feeling a stranger in one's own family sticks in the reader's mind (at least it did in mine). It may indicate how Madzy contemplated her own children's future marital decisions.

"Adult Student" recounts a day in the life of a middle-aged university student named Kate, vividly portraying her sense of living in two worlds, those of the university and of her family. The first and largest part deals with her driving to the university and her dealings with the younger students. She is asked to help sell tickets at a play being put on by the French students that evening, and the phone call she makes to her husband startles us into an awareness of her other life which, until now, has been far in the background – and clearly also in the background of Kate's awareness. University is more than the socializing and courses: it represents the life of the mind and the escape from domesticity. Kate never forgets that she is older than her student friends; what she mostly *does* "forget" is that she is wife, housewife, mother. At lunchtime she saunters about campus in the autumn sun, drops into the bookstore, then goes to the cafeteria where she joins the line-up for food. A student from her French class joins her and they talk – typical student talk but, for the narrator, enriched with meaning because she cannot take all this for granted. She regards herself as having *won* this, wrested it from the clutches of whatever forces would have blocked her access to it.

Besides these glimpses into Madzy's student life, the story contains reflections on generations, on the future of the young people she talks to (including one from an unnamed African country). She makes a remark to Helen, a student friend, which she immediately regrets and frets over; when she sees Helen later in the day, there is no sign that the girl resented the remark:

> Kate felt relieved, for she hated to be considered a meddlesome woman. With her own two daughters she had always had close contact, but that was largely due to the fact that she had left them alone to make their own decisions, giving advice only when asked for it. Why had that remark to Helen escaped her? Was it that she became more and more convinced that the children of this present world, through no fault of their own, suffered more than the adults?[11]

Madzy had not completed many short stories before this and, so far as I can tell, had submitted only one or two for publication. Having a story accepted by the *Atlantic Advocate*, and then another, and another, must have assured her that her writing was worthwhile. She recognized that profundity and complexity would have been out of place in stories for this type of magazine. In any case, these seem not to have been her strong points. Her characters are not complex, but she sketches them deftly, so that by the conventions of the genre and the time they are recognizable human beings. The doubts and insecurities of the mothers in the stories are always convincing: she writes best when she is closest to autobiography. Dialogue sometimes sounds artificial; the characters' thoughts are more adroitly phrased. There is a predictable element in the plots, but that predictability comes largely from the form and the context. She mastered the craft of plotting well enough so that several of the stories have a real sense of suspense. We know that everything will turn out well but not *how* she will contrive this.

IN SEPTEMBER 1962, after the publication of the fifth of the six stories, she received a letter from L.S. Loomer, the magazine's managing editor. He explained that he was compiling the results of a readership survey and that there seemed to be a certain dissatisfaction with the fiction being published. "I am not sure whether we are being too erudite, whether we are dropping too far below the heads of our readers, or whether they really want the banging and shooting type of fiction." After admitting that there have indeed been some poor stories, he continues: "I am happy to say that I have, personally, nothing but praise for any of the Maxine Brandis stories we have used. Consequently I value your judgment very highly, and would be glad to consider your comments. I can tell by the way you write that you have keen critical faculties. If you did not, you would not obtain the high standard you do, which can only be reached through sitting in harsh judgment upon oneself."

Madzy's reply is dated 27 September. It shows she obviously enjoyed the question and the challenge. She has, she says, considered his question not only in the light of the magazine's editorial policy and standards but also as giving her guidance for stories that she would write for the magazine in future, and perhaps for her work in general. Her letter reveals much about her own ideas and guidelines in writing.

She guesses that the readers of the magazine are of above-average intelligence. The magazine dealt with topics important in the Maritimes. The issue in which "Adult Student" appeared contained articles on "The Cost of Our Universities" and "Bilingualism and English-Speaking Maritimers," and a tribute to poet E.J. Pratt. Earlier ones contain articles on an industrial exposition in the Maritimes, on Atlantic ports and shipping, on Canada geese in Newfoundland, on the pulp industry, and on the hardiness of garden plants.

When she was working in the library of the St Francis Xavier Extension Department, she says, she noticed that the magazine was read by the foreign students. After having read "a good amount of interesting articles on the problems of the Maritimes ... they settle down for a story that will take them out of themselves, that will hold their attention, that will make them relax, but it must also give them some food for thought." She feels that the kind of story that "will go over well" is one that deals with a problem relevant to people in the Maritimes and that ends with a resolution of the problem. She reports that the several radio talks she gave in Antigonish (she cites, as one of the topics, "my opinion on bringing up children") were of great interest to women, and that they came to the library to ask her advice.

She says that she has debated whether to set her stories in the Maritimes or whether to use different settings "so as to give the readers an insight into the problems of people in other parts of the country. I decided that it was 50–50; sometimes a story set in the Maritimes will thrill some persons, for the Maritimers feel that their country is not enough recognized elsewhere, and if it suddenly is used as the setting for a story it gives them an additional pleasure."

With the editor's request in mind, she has gone through back issues of the magazine, and sums up her conclusions. Some of the stories are entertaining but "they have no meaning, they don't give food for thought." Some are just sketches; some are remote from the lives of Maritimers. She puts her own stories under the same microscope and finds that they also do not measure up to the guidelines she has formulated, and resolves to do better. She advises the editor to look for stories that provide insight and information and a guide in the solving of problems. "The nucleus of the story should be real, but the people and the setting purely imaginary."

It is no surprise that she felt that the stories should provide help and information as well as entertainment. Much of her own work does this. All her newspaper columns have that as their principal aim, and in *Land for Our Sons* she gives insights into the realities of immigration and pioneering.

TWO OTHER pieces of short fiction dating from this time have a strong autobiographical element. One, entitled "It's Odd How Pearls Can Roll," I dealt with in the chapter about Terrace because it was apparently first written then. In 1959, she revised it. The other is a sketch in the form of a letter from a mother to a fictionalized fifteen-year-old son. It is entitled "Just Mom." The narrator, wakeful in the middle of the night, makes herself a cup of cocoa and tries to figure out what is worrying her. The first thing she is concerned about is what the world will do to her son as he grows up. She sees it as a violent world, but admits that this is only her image and that her son is of a different generation, with different experiences and perceptions.

> You are not worrying about the world which is waiting for you to grow up. If you ever should worry, but you don't, for you are fast asleep by night, and too busy by day to worry, but if you should worry, then you should worry about me, your Mom, who is so completely out of step with the world around her. She is still clinging to a world that has since long vanished while she was looking after the family ...
>
> Oh, darling I see it now: I have felt it. Because I felt the world around me was changing, it scared me, and I warned you, and criticized what was real to you and unreal to me.
>
> The world goes on while Mom stays put. Mom may give you a fleeting sense of security, but she gets on your nerves too. For you resent the fact that she gives you that sense of security, as this hurts your craving for independence. It is the moms who make beatniks of their children, and then blame them for what they are. We bring forth children, smother them in a cotton-woolly world of our own making. When the children escape because their smothered souls burst out of their cotton-wool shells, they are blamed for being ungrateful! Ungrateful? For what must they be grateful? Surely not because we wanted them in the first place?

She sketches a picture of the difference between generations and attitudes:

> ... those times when you came home shouting at the door: "Listen, Mom, teacher told us in science ..." or: "Say, Mom, look at this", and I answered: "Yes dear, but first I must put up the potatoes", or: "Not now, darling, don't you see I am in a hurry?" Those were the times when you were busy growing up, while I stayed behind.
>
> That is just it. When I was old enough to have children, I thought I had reached the peak of my growing process, the blessed state of adulthood.
>
> Sorry, darling, but I forgot to become adult.
>
> Sorry, darling, I even forgot to die in time ...
>
> There was an island off the coast of Greece, where in ancient times food was very scarce. Therefore, the inhabitants had made the rule that every person who had reached the age of sixty should drink a cup of hemlock; thus he would not needlessly use up precious food.

Of course I could swallow the contents of my bottle of sleeping pills right now. The thing, however, is that I have seen a glimpse of the world through your eyes, and I am intrigued. I am growing curious. I'd like some time to try to understand it better. I'd like to know what will come after the beatniks, the hydrogen bomb, the lunik, the monkey-in-space. I'd like to see how you youngsters will tackle the problem of undeveloped countries, African nationalism, Red China; how you will cope with the next economic depression.

Darling, I can't just pack up now, and leave this world of yours before I have tried to get a better grasp of it ...

This cocoa was good. My stomach feels warm and cosy within me, I'd better go to bed now.

Please, darling, give me some time to grow up with you. I can take those pills if I prove to be too rusty to learn after all. But you are fifteen now, and I may try to catch up with you somehow, sometime.

Reading this now, reflecting on it, I hear my mother's voice and catch so very clearly a whiff of her spirit. There is no reason to think that the dark thoughts of suicide were entirely fictional; death must sometimes have looked like a welcome release from her suffering, though so far as I know she never spoke of it, and her innate optimism and obstinacy fought vigorously for life. Writing, however, allowed her to express what could not be expressed in any other way.

My attention is also caught by her saying that she can always take the sleeping pills if she is "too rusty to learn" – as though the ability to learn is the only justification for living. For her it was certainly one of the main ones.

THE SUBJECT OF immigration was always in her mind. It had appeared in the unpublished fragments of 1954 and in *Land for Our Sons*. In Burlington, it was, however, the focus of almost everything she wrote. She dealt with many facets drawn from her and our experience: the longing for Holland, the delight in the freedom she felt in Canada, especially in the north; the ways and degrees of adapting; the nuances of shading in the balance of choice and advantage, ties and love, between Canada and Holland.

When we arrived in Burlington, our first trip back to Holland in 1958–59 was only six months behind her and the separate trips she and Bill made in 1963 caused an explosion of thought and feeling. In these years we had more visitors from Holland and contact with Dutch people in Burlington and Hamilton. Madzy had a Dutchwoman, Mrs Boersma, to clean the house.

Immigration was also an issue in her speculation about the future. What would she and Bill do when we children were independent and they were free to move if they wished? In the "Reflections" of October 1959 she talks about going north again; in the letters she wrote to Bill in 1963 she considers whether they might return to Holland for good.

And what about our futures? She knew that both Gerard and I had been finding it hard to fit back into Canada after the trip of 1958–59, although in my journal I report Gerard saying that he wanted to stay in Canada but make frequent trips to Europe. We longed sometimes for European culture and life. She knew that homosexuality was more accepted in Holland (at least in cities like Amsterdam, and in the Anthroposophical circles to which Bill's mother and sister belonged) than in Canada. Whatever the precise details of our maladjustment, she must, at least sometimes, have seen it through the lens of her own sense of not really belonging here. Would we be better off in Europe? My journal records that the family sometimes discussed it.

Unquestionably her thoughts were darker when she was ill. Lying with eyes closed in a darkened room, as she did in the fall of 1961, and being for a year nearly blind, so that vision in one eye was an improvement[12] – we can only guess at the anxiety and yearning that tormented her. When she felt better, able to drive her car, to read, to write, she felt less vulnerable, happier in Canada because she could take advantage of the relative freedom it offered.

The fact that immigration, which had earlier been regarded as a *fait accompli*, was reversible raised many issues.

In 1959 she wrote an article for the Dutch government magazine *Emigratie*.[13] In the accompanying biographical note she is identified as the author of *Land for Our Sons*, the Dutch translation of which would soon appear. Part of the article is an account of Madzy talking with a Dutch immigrant woman, probably an amalgamation of a number of such women whom Madzy had met. Though she has lived in Canada for years, the woman speaks virtually no English; she is aware that this is a problem and urges three of her children who are still in Holland to learn the language. In her home in Canada "naturally" they speak only Dutch. She attends a Dutch church. When she goes shopping, she takes along one of her children or grandchildren. Madzy urges her to join evening classes in English at the local school, but the woman protests that she is too old to sit in a school desk.

Then Madzy describes a young woman who had come into the St Francis Xavier Extension Department Library. Dutch by birth but married to an

Englishman, she longed very much for Holland but said she could never go back. She was losing her Dutch and was ashamed to write to her mother; at the same time, however, she did not feel at home in Canada and knew little about it. Madzy began sending her books about Canadian history and geography.

Both of these women are in a sense foreigners in their own families. Though concerned about their plight, Madzy must also have been impatient at their unwillingness to help themselves when the remedy was easy to find. Even this, however, she understands: some of us, she writes in the same article, have "a vague feeling of shame if we give ourselves too completely to this new country, because we feel guilty towards our own country, that shaped and schooled us and that we love so dearly. We are afraid to give ourselves totally to Canada because we feel the connections with Holland gradually slipping through our fingers."

Homesickness is a very unpleasant emotion: "It doesn't only cause us sadness but it gnaws at our health." A doctor told her once that among emigrant women he had a number who suffered from stomach ulcers and nervous ailments (and arthritis? she might have wondered).

The article ends with a personal anecdote. She recalls going with her family to Ottawa, to the tomb of the Unknown Soldier. Walking around the monument, she noticed a wreath that was not yet wilted, with a ribbon of red, white, and blue – the colours of the Dutch flag. Two days earlier, Prince Bernhard of the Netherlands, the consort of Queen Juliana, had placed the wreath there in memory of the Canadian soldiers who had given their lives to liberate Holland in 1944–45. She laid the end of the ribbon across her hand, feeling a bond as fine as a spider's web connecting her to Holland. "Before the heart overflow[ed]," she moved away. "While I went slowly down the steps I suddenly realized very clearly again that however completely we try to become part of this new and beautiful land we will never lose the bond with the soil from which we sprang." Madzy's feelings connected her to Holland even while her head talked common sense about "becoming Canadian" – though the division was no doubt more complicated than that.

THE CONVICTION that learning about Canadian history and geography would help immigrants to feel at home here led Madzy early in the Burlington years to write a history of Canada in Dutch. It was entitled *Zo was Canada* ("this was Canada"). We have what is most likely the first and only draft, originally 179 double-spaced pages, but the first twenty-eight are now missing. It was slightly revised by hand. We have no records to show what she had in mind about publication, though I remember that at this time she made contact with a Toronto publisher of textbooks and other non-fiction.

On the file folder containing the manuscript, she wrote: "To know Canada is to love Canada – *Canada kennen is Canada liefhebben*." Under the title appear the words "*verteld door Maxine Brandis*." "*Verteld*" means "told": this was intended as a story, not an academic work. At UBC she had taken courses in the French in North America and Canada since 1867, and she had reference books so the story is reliable history, reflecting the approaches and attitudes of the period in which she was writing.

As always, she keeps her readers constantly in mind, using phrases designed to connect immigrants to Canadian history. The style is serious but not solemn; she explains some of the implications of the events she is writing about, bearing in mind what her readers might or might not know. She indeed sees herself as a story-teller. "You must remember ..." she writes, and "As I told you about Frontenac ..." The Dutch immigrants for whom she is writing are (she points out) among the successors of the French, English, and other nationalities as Europeans "building" Canada. Having compared Simon Fraser reaching the mouth of the Fraser River in 1808 with John Cabot setting foot on Cape Breton Island 311 years earlier, she writes: "Somewhere in the twentieth century and somewhere in those 6,000 kilometres we new Canadians stand. We are doing our own exploration; we also bring something beautiful from our own homeland to this new country. We also build towards Canada's future and cast our eyes forwards. Explorers are we all, each in our own way."

In early 1960 she wrote an article about francophone-anglophone relations in Quebec entitled "Het Franse Element in Canada" ("the French element in Canada"). She was writing it, she tells us, as Paul Sauvé's funeral was taking place (he had died on 2 January 1960).[14] She deals with some of the history underlying the situation, and very likely she used the first section of her history book as the first draft for the article, greatly shortening and recasting it. If this was so, then she had at least the first part of that book written by the end of 1959, having begun it immediately after translating *Land for Our Sons*.

IN 1962–64 SHE wrote a series of columns for *De Nederlandse Courant in Canada* ("the Dutch newpaper in Canada"), by then a well-established weekly. Probably, having realized how difficult it would be to find a publisher for *Zo was Canada*, she felt that this was a better way of reaching Dutch immigrants.

The first article, "De plaats waarop gij staat ..." ("the place whereon you stand ...") was submitted in September 1962 and accepted. The editor, Dr Schippers, evidently asked for more articles, and she immediately wrote one; the accompanying letter says that her health is better and that she can see out of one eye; "the pen flows again." She suggests the title "Kof-fiepraatje" ("coffee chat"); clearly they were planning a series of columns designed mainly for women readers.

In the late summer of 1962 a woman writing columns for the paper under the name "Hyacinthe" had returned to Holland from where she had written a piece dealing with Dutch emigrants to Canada who, regretting their decision, had moved back to Holland. When Hyacinthe asked these people whether they were happy to be back in Holland, many said that they would be glad to return to Canada if they could.[15]

Madzy in her article reflects and elaborates on this, reminding the women who would have read Hyacinthe's column of all the good things in Canada. The tone is gentle, ruminative, quietly encouraging: on such a sensitive subject, striking the wrong note could be hurtful. This first article was published in the issue of 13 October 1962, and two weeks later Madzy's actual columns began to appear under the "Koffiepraatje" heading.

The twenty-two dated columns we have run from October 1962 to February 1964, but there are ten others for which the clippings or carbon copies are undated. One appeared after that time, to judge by the typewriter used, and the others probably along the way, where there are gaps in the dated series. For short stretches the column appeared every week, but there were also interruptions. After one such interruption, Madzy explains that one of her children has been sick; at least once she herself was sick; another break happened when she went to Holland for her mother's funeral. She received $5 per column of about one thousand words.

As would be appropriate for a chat over a mid-morning cup of coffee, the columns are colloquial and conversational. Many of them begin as though Madzy were welcoming a few friends to the house: "It's a perfect day for a friendly chat over a cup of coffee, with the dishwashing done and the beds made. It's half-and-half weather, can't make up its mind whether it's freezing or thawing," she wrote in a column on 16 February 1963. The approach, tone, and subject matter indicate the kind of readers Madzy was addressing: immigrant women who were accustomed to that very Dutch kind of social occasion and, no doubt, tried to organize such get-togethers themselves or, if they were living on farms or away from other Dutch women, longed nostalgically for them. In the early 1960s, few of these women would have worked outside the home and, like the woman Madzy describes in the article for *Emigratie*, it was they who were most homesick for Holland. They were also the ones who had the most difficulty in "becoming Canadian," and many of them allowed the language barrier to isolate them from Canadian housewives living nearby. As their Dutch husbands and children became more Canadian, the women might feel themselves "foreigners" even in their own families. Madzy understands them: hadn't she spent more than eight years on a farm herself? In her case there was no language barrier, but it was easy to imagine herself into their lives.

In the first article, then, she deals with the issue of whether to go "home" again. She does not delve deeply, and she never quite faces the fact that some immigrants ended up feeling at home nowhere, that this was the price that the immigrating parents had to pay for the better life they hoped to provide for their children. She does recognize that for most immigrants returning home is not a solution. Though this column was written before her own crisis of 1963, she has clearly already been thinking about it and perhaps discussing it with Dutch friends. Now, in 1962 – likely drawing on her experience during the trip of 1958–59 – she says she has "outgrown" Holland; it has changed and is in fact not really "home" any longer. The immigrants' nostalgia is for an idealized life and place, and the people they have left behind.

She refrains from following this train of thought too far, yet she does not whitewash very much. "In [Hyacinthe's] earlier letters sounded sometimes an undertone of this sort: Holland has improved a great deal; the people have acquired a larger outlook, they look past their borders. If I had known all that before we emigrated, maybe I myself would also have stayed home." Madzy concludes that, had Hyacinthe returned to Canada,[16] she would have written something like this:

> If we women sometimes find it hard to manage, let us think about the good things in Canada: the ties of friendship that you've made, the closer connections that often develop within an immigrant family, the appliances that make housekeeping easier, the cars which many of us now have and would never have had in Holland, the children who enjoy the freedom of this land and are able to adapt so quickly and who don't want to go back, the many bothersome restrictions which people have to live with in an overpopulated country like Holland.[17]

Madzy recalls a book she read entitled, like her column, *De plaats waarop gij staat*: "The place whereon you now stand is also sacred ground. Isn't it all God's earth? Live your life in this place and don't look back; try not to worry too much about the future. Look round you at what you have and hold it as a priceless possession in your grateful heart."

She knew that this often painful and intractable aspect of the immigrant's situation plagued many of her readers, distorting or even destroying their lives, just as it would later drive her to agony when Bill was away. "What have we done!" Most immigrants know that really it cannot be undone, that the only thing to do is keep moving on, building anew and, even harder, finding the courage to do so.

Some of the columns that follow this one are loosely constructed, jumping from one topic to another; others are more focused. All are thoughtful: informative or encouraging or admonishing or reassuring. At times she interprets Canada to new immigrants. Some readers might be recent arrivals; others might have been here longer but because of their shyness, language difficulties, and hardworking lives, might have learned little about the country. She encourages her readers to venture out and make contact with Canadian society and culture and educational opportunities. By writing about the contribution of the Dutch to Canada, she encourages them to feel better about themselves and be more confident. She writes about Canadian history and regional characteristics. She describes Upper Canada Village, a pioneer village in eastern Ontario, and writes about the artists Emily Carr and Tom Thomson. She discusses the relations between francophone and anglophone Canadians and explains the historical roots of the situation, using examples from the way a family works. In the column of 23 March 1963 she describes the books of Mazo de la Roche and says that from them she learned a good deal about Canada.

She knows that for many of her readers, coming from the farms and small towns of Holland, immigration meant not only a change of language and culture but a transplantation into a much more modern world – modern in ideas and attitudes as well as in material terms. Her cosmopolitan background set her apart from many of her readers, but she had enough acquaintance with other immigrant women to write understandingly about this gap.

She also deals with education. She stresses the importance of children finishing high school. Knowing that many immigrants consider Canadian schools inferior to Dutch ones, she explains that each country has its own educational system and priorities. Dutch education might be more focused on specific subjects, but Canadian education covers a wider area, concentrating on preparing children for life. You can't judge how your children are doing in the short run, she says; you have to wait for long-term results.

That provoked thoughts about how children in immigrant families live. Having talked about the fact that in the world of 1963 young people have to absorb far more information far faster than her generation did, she reflects that it is no wonder if teenagers are sometimes tense and impatient. But the adults have to keep up with the modern world too: if they don't, they lose contact with their children.

> For us, immigrant-mothers (and also fathers) it is doubly difficult to continue understanding our children. Some do it without too much problem or thought, they do it by instinct; but some of us really have to think about it. Because it is not only a new language that we have to learn, not only a new country with which we have to become acquainted; here in this country the people – like people everywhere – have their own ways which are different from the customs of the community we've left behind. When we leave our place of origin, we don't understand what a huge change we are going to have to deal with; we sometimes don't realize it even when we are *in* the new country, we sometimes think that we can pack our old customs in the suitcase and lay them neatly in the cupboard in our new country and bring them out when we want to.
>
> But our children don't accept this; and if we don't go along a bit with the new, we lose our children. Please read carefully what I said: "a bit." Because after all we remain ourselves – our conscience, intelligence, and experience are what we draw on for making decisions. But before anything else we have to try to understand our children and see their problems from their perspective. Only then are we able to make a mature decision, express a solidly based opinion.
>
> Oh, yes, I know, that's a row of fancy words, and when you're faced with it you're still groping around in the dark.[18]

She winds down on a casual note. "There, now, see what I've done. I was sitting here in the sun, quietly musing, and now I've got myself all worked up." The light ending does not belittle the seriousness of the subject.

She writes about fashions in clothes, the death of the Pope in 1963, space flight, the World Series, the conversion of the Dutch Princess Irene to Roman Catholicism. In one column, already quoted from (see chapter 7), she describes how she learned to bake bread.

From time to time I catch glimpses of our family. One column addresses readers who, like her, lived in Holland during the war:

Among us coffee-friends there may be some who also had a young child during that time and who also must sometimes have wondered anxiously what those terrible events must have done to them. Were they too young to have understood anything, or did their inner selves suffer without our being able to prevent it?

I know for certain that they were deprived of something that for children of that age is very important, and that is the sense of safety, of security. Young though they were, the events shook them, and many of them will spend their entire lives searching for something that will again give them the security they need to be able to live their lives.[19]

In a passage like this I feel my mother observing Gerard and me and reflecting more deeply than we were aware on our personalities and lives and futures.

In an undated column she writes about preparing to send a family member on a trip to Holland:

It has certainly happened to some of you that a family member went to Holland, on business, or to visit someone who was sick, or just for a vacation. No, I don't mean a trip by the whole family; that's an entirely different matter. Then we all pack our suitcases, we all live in enormous excitement. Everyone wants to take lots of things that can't go along, especially when you're travelling by plane. And we mothers tell the children, every moment, "Child, sit up straight, eat neatly, where are your manners? What will Grandmother think?" And when we're finally over there, and the child sits at table with a hand in the lap, like the Canadians, and you make a remark about it, then Grandmother says soothingly: "But he has very good manners, and he's really doing his best," and the child looks triumphant, and you sink back into thankful quiet.

No, it's a completely different thing when just one member of the family, usually the father, goes. Beforehand he is extra busy at work, and therefore the wife-and-mother has to look after everything. And she does that with the greatest care, because in her imagination she sees the whole trip happening and feels precisely what is needed.

She wants her husband to be neat so that they on the other side can't say: "How sloppily they dress there." She figures out presents for family members, and buys them carefully, and wraps them beautifully.

And then, when the last shirt is ironed, and the last tie pressed, when the neat suit has come back from the cleaners, when all the socks are mended, and when the last kiss is exchanged ... then a clenching sense of emptiness seizes the heart that remains behind.

And that is the moment when you ask yourself, "What have we begun? Why did we ever think up this ungodly plan to emigrate, and actually do it too?"

It would have been so much easier and nicer to remain home, in Holland, which is still "home" to us. If you as wife and mother are sick, there is always someone to care for the children and look after you. If you're in a tight spot, there's always some reliable person to talk it over with and to whom you can open your heart. If sorrow comes to the family there will be many trusted people to help you carry the grief and thereby lighten it a bit.

She encourages her readers to realize that they are probably stronger than they think. She ends the column with: "Look how I've suddenly turned preacher!" And then she advises her readers to eat yoghurt, very common in Holland and by the early 1960s also available in many supermarkets in Canada. "It's good for you. Sprinkle some brown sugar and corn flakes over it."

The column of 1 February 1964 deals with her own trip to Holland the previous December. She knows that going home for a funeral is a common experience in the lives of immigrants.

On 2 December I was busy washing the breakfast dishes when the phone rang. With one hand I held the dish that I was washing, while the suds dripped on the counter, and with the other I picked up the phone:

"Hallo?"

"This is Holland, one moment please ..."

When I laid the phone slowly down I knew that my mother had just died, suddenly and unexpectedly, and that on that same day I would be on the way to Holland ...

Indeed, at four o'clock I was in the air, and I saw Canada gliding away beneath me, not only in actual fact but also in my feelings. Canada suddenly had no reality for me, my whole being reached forwards to the small country where the parental house was suddenly disappearing, the house that I wanted once more to experience, together with Mother.

Describing how Iete lay at home in her own room, Madzy draws the distinction with the Canadian custom of having the deceased in a funeral home. She talks about the arrangements to be made, about the cold weather and chilly houses. The column, after the first few paragraphs, is superficial – probably because she was not yet ready to reflect more deeply, and in print, on the ways in which the events had affected her.

These columns are among the best of her published work. However good her English generally was, her writings in Dutch have a sinewy flexibility that adapts itself to every subject. They have some of the tone and quality of parts of the war diary, slipping easily from narrative to description to introspection, from information to analysis. Sometimes the chattiness and other devices are a bit forced, but she had a good sense of what was suitable for the medium, and of the needs and anxieties of her readers.

Yet for all its interactions with her outward life, writing was for her a private world. In it she could be alone, follow her own thinking and reflections and concerns. In "Just Mom" the narrator (awake in the middle of the night) had written: "How good it feels to say just what comes to my mind, without anyone interrupting the trend of my thoughts. It is just me with myself, just Mom with Mom."

It is difficult for most of us to imagine how physically painful it must have been for her to do all that typing: the impact needed to operate a typewriter must have hurt her arthritis-riddled hands cruelly. Sitting now at my computer – with its light touch, with my painless hands – I try to imagine the effort of every keystroke, the obstinate determination and absorption and sense of purpose that drove her through all the writing she did in these years. But it is no wonder that she revised and retyped only the work that she thought had a prospect of publication.

And how wise of her to try drawing and painting, so much easier on her hands.

GERARD TELLS the story of this new pursuit:

When I was studying Fine Arts at McMaster University I got into the habit of having my hair cut at a little barber shop in Westdale. Next door was the Westdale Gallery. The owner, Julius Lebow, carried art supplies and art books, did picture framing, and sold art in a small way ... He also gave exhibitions to local artists whom he wanted to encourage, Paul Fournier, Ann Suzuki, Don Nixon and Norma Waters among them. I began to buy my art supplies and an occasional book there, as well as handmade pottery by Helen Brink.

When I was in my second or third year I went in and saw a show of pen-and-ink drawings by Norma Waters, and I exclaimed to Julius that I wished that I could draw like that. Julius suggested that I should talk to the artist about private lessons, telling me that Norma lived in Kilbride and giving me her phone number. When I called her about it, she said that she didn't like giving classes to just one person and suggested that I bring a friend. When Mam heard about this, she said that she would like to take drawing lessons, and so we began going together. This event opened a new avenue in our lives, especially when later we lived in Carlisle ...

It was only now that art became a regular part of Madzy's life. Norma was an excellent natural teacher. She knew just when to leave us alone and when to interrupt and guide our efforts. She was particularly suited to Madzy's temperament; Madzy wished to be free in her use of line and colour and often ignored the distinction between representational and abstract images. Norma had studied with one of Canada's first abstract artists, J.W.G. McDonald (usually called "Jock"), and she too moved easily between the representational and the abstract.

Norma taught us contour drawing, which helped to form Madzy's style. Even the later drawings that were filled in with washes of colour showed a clear and well-studied contour. I also think that Madzy's mind grasped a linear pattern better than one based on areas of tone and colour. Her oil paintings, of which there were far fewer than her drawings, were developed in terms of separate brush strokes rather than masses of colour.

Gerard began his second year of university in the fall of 1962, and we know from Madzy's letters to Bill in October 1963 that by then she was already painting. So it was somewhere in there that the art lessons began, and they continued for about three years.

At first, Madzy painted mainly in oils, though it was for drawing that she and Gerard had gone to Norma Waters. The oil paintings were mostly of the Burlington garden in different seasons: the bare-twigged birch tree in the snow, the crab-apple tree in full spring bloom. There were also a lot of ink drawings and watercolours. Madzy liked drawing the white-pine roots that the stump fences in the countryside were made of, and she drew

Branch with fungi, painted by Madzy in late middle age

dried leaves, fungus growths from the trunks of trees, and other natural objects.

Early in 1964 she had an operation on her right hand, an attempt to repair some of the damage done by the arthritis; Gerard remembers her that spring doing several oil paintings with her left hand. "Mam never fancied herself as an artist," he writes, "always calling it a hobby, and only exhibited once, with me, when I had my very first exhibition in Burlington in a shop on Brant Street in the spring of 1965. But she recognized the therapeutic value of the activity and used it to distract herself from the pain and boredom imposed by her illness."

He writes about Madzy's attitude to art in general:

> Mam encouraged my decision to try a career as an artist by paying for our drawing lessons with Norma, by buying art materials at Julius Lebow's gallery, by nurturing the friendships with Norma Waters and Ann Suzuki and their circle, but mainly by her attitude that it was a perfectly acceptable thing for me to do. There had been artists in both her and Dad's families – that made it especially acceptable. Perhaps she had been able to discern talent in my early efforts. Perhaps she realized that the independent artist's life was more compatible with my homosexual nature than a career where I would have to hide my sexual orientation. Perhaps she enjoyed the idea of her children doing some of the things that she had not been able to pursue. She really seemed to enjoy contact with the creative people we began to meet after moving to Carlisle. She made regular trips to Julius Lebow, and to the farm where Elizabeth Hoey and her daughter Martha did fibre arts and ceramics. She bought work from all these people.

One unexpected effect of the art lessons was that Madzy acquired a dog. Norma and her partner, Ulo, a sculptor of Estonian origin, had a dog whom Madzy met during her visits to Norma's house. She writes:

> Ulo was a strange person but also very friendly. A man – tall, strong, mid-forties, I should say – an artist – a very good artist. He carved sculptures, mostly religious, ordered by churches. I had seen several of his Christs on the cross and Mary figures and other religious statues and they filled me with awe as centuries-old sculptures do. This doesn't happen often with sculpture, because it is not my favourite form of art. I suppose I liked them so much because I love wood.
>
> Ulo had a dog, a lovable dog. Now, I do love dogs, but this was the dog I really loved best of all the dogs I know.

Madzy painting in the garden in Burlington

Ulo shot himself – in real life his suicide attempt failed; but in the semi-fictional account that Madzy wrote more than ten years later, he died, and the dog was found "hidden under the kitchen table curled up in a little bundle." The dog's name was Riki; he was a mid-size dog with a rough grey coat and the gentlest of temperaments. He had always been shy of people, but had lost his fear of her and would come up to her wagging his tail.

The last pages of the story are missing but the end of the actual events survives in family memory. Riki was sent to the animal shelter; Madzy, hearing about it, went with Gerard and Bill to get him, and he lived out his life in our family. A year or so later he was joined by a puppy, Folly, and she too stayed with us until her death.

THE PROCESS of acquiring the land that was to become Brandstead, Madzy's last home, began during this time. When I returned to Burlington from Holland on 11 November 1961, I told the family about the country property that Madzy's sister, Hansje, and her husband owned. On a Sunday soon after, Bill and I went for a drive in the country near Carlisle, a tiny village about ten miles north of Burlington. We drove past a piece of wooded land with a clearing in it but with a screen of trees between it and the road, and with a "for sale" sign. We walked around and loved what we saw. The next week Bill phoned the real estate agent to ask the price but found that it was unaffordable.

During the year that followed, our whole family on our Sunday morning walks sometimes went there; no one was buying it. Bill again phoned the real estate agent and learned that it had finally been sold.

On Saturday, 26 September 1964, Bill drove past the property for the first time in two years. No one had built on it, and it was again for sale. When he and Madzy returned the next day, they noticed that in the interval a "for sale" sign from a different realtor had been nailed to a tree. This suggested to them that the owner was impatient to sell. On the Tuesday, Madzy and Bill bought the property, six and a quarter acres (two and a half hectares), for a lower amount than the asking price of two years earlier. Madzy put into it the money she had inherited from Iete. We named it Brandstead, the homestead of the Brandises in Canada.

Bill immediately built a wooden cabin about eight feet square; I helped him put on the roofing during a glorious Sunday towards the end of October. He installed a tiny wood-stove, and during the months that followed we often went there on a Sunday and lit a fire in the stove to make coffee.

Madzy loved these outings, but with her poor health she initially had some fears about living there. She would be alone by day while Bill was at work and Jock at university. They had bought the property because Bill liked living in the country; for herself, once again, she was not so sure. But the problem was solved by Gerard's deciding that he would like to live at Brandstead too. He had graduated from McMaster that spring with a degree in fine arts. He wanted to be an artist: at Brandstead he would be able to live inexpensively, helping with the work on the place by way of compensation to Madzy and Bill, and would earn actual cash by doing part-time teaching and by selling his work.

Gerard's presence removed the one objection that Madzy had had. It was decided that he would live there for a year to help Madzy and Bill get settled but, he says, he just stayed on. After that first year he made a small monetary contribution, and later he paid rent. He built a separate small studio, and when the separation of the two buildings proved impractical, the studio was taken down and rebuilt as a wing of the house, with part of the basement of the main house becoming his work-space. He lived there until after Madzy's death.

Bill designed the house himself, and construction began in March 1965. It was ready for the four of them (I was living in Toronto) to move into at the beginning of June 1965.

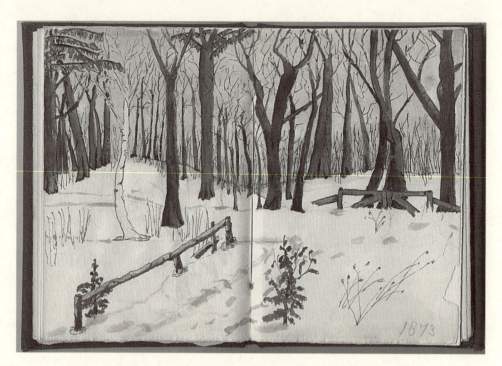

Brandstead in winter, from *The Whatman 1873 Book*

CHAPTER ELEVEN

Brandstead: The Last Home, 1965–1984

MADZY SPENT the last nineteen years of her life at Brandstead, the longest she had ever lived in one place. It was a period marked by worsening arthritis. There were several crises; after each one except the last, she regained some portion of what she had lost, but the graph declined overall.

Like a tree, however, which when threatened will produce an unusual abundance of blossom and seeds, she had in those years an outburst of creativity in many directions. It showed itself not only in her writing, painting, drawing, and close-up photography of flowers but in handicrafts and in a variety of intellectual explorations. These interests were miscellaneous, and a number of them were brief in duration: some were cut short by her being no longer able to manage them, others because she came to the end of a project, or because she had slaked her curiosity, or because something else caught her attention. But at every stage she used her remaining faculties and capacities as fully as possible.

The perpetual conflict between her inner and outer life must gradually have worsened. Increasingly unable to do the things she wanted to do, she also had to accept help and even ask for it. Her independent spirit raged at this. She *hated* being dependent; a crucial element of her self-image was being the one who helped others. Asking for and accepting help – doing it gracefully and with sensitivity towards the care-givers – was a triumph of character and will power and love. We can only guess at the effort it must sometimes have taken.

IN JUNE 1965, when the family moved to Brandstead, Madzy was fifty-four. Gerard was twenty-three. Jock was eighteen and beginning his first year at McMaster; he enrolled in economics but soon switched to anthropology. I was twenty-six and working at the CBC; I lived in Toronto and visited every few weeks.

Madzy at work with camera and tripod, 1970 (*above*) – and the results of her
work (*right*): a cosmos flower with bee, and a Mugho pine

Brandstead circa 1971, from the road

The house at Brandstead was a wooden rectangle. In its initial state before it was extended, it was described by an appraiser as "a winterized summer cottage." The driveway curved around a gigantic oak tree that was part of the screen of vegetation between house and road; Madzy had chosen the building site so that as few trees as possible would have to be cut. Because the bedrock was close to the surface, the house was raised above the lawn and garden behind. An outcrop of loose glacial debris separated the lawn from the vegetable garden. Beyond the garden, and to either side of the clearing, were more trees, mostly oak, beech, ash, and maple. The property was exceptionally hilly; in its two and a half hectares there were several sharp ups and downs. Because of this, none of it except a strip along one side had apparently ever been used for agriculture, though in the clearing were signs that there had once been beehives. These visible traces of history pleased us and were an important part of the character of the place.

At that time the area was rural. The road was gravel. Carlisle, about a mile away, was a crossroads hamlet with a post office, general store, church, gas station, and a bank open two days a week.

Bill continued to work in Burlington, a twenty-five-minute drive. Jock drove to McMaster, about forty-five minutes away. Madzy had a car of her own, a dark-green Austin which she called Paddy.

THE MOVE to Brandstead had brought Madzy and Gerard nearer to Norma Waters, living a couple of miles away in the village of Kilbride. Through Norma, Gerard recalls, they met a circle of other artists:

> Ann Suzuki and Lloyd Kinnee, who rented the house on the Cedar Springs Road after Ulo's unsuccessful suicide attempt, Cal Whitehead and Fay Dubois, who bought a tiny log cabin on the McNiven Road north of Kilbride, Dorothy and Lorne Looker, who lived south of Carlisle, and Aiko Suzuki and Alex Slavnics, who lived in Toronto but came to Kilbride quite often. We also got to know Don Nixon, then living in Hamilton with his mother and grandmother.[1] It was always clear to me that Mam preferred to talk with the men rather than with the women, although I never saw her being the least bit flirtatious. She found them more interesting, perhaps, or maybe it was just a habit established in childhood, when she adored her father and older half-brother, Paul, and even her mentally handicapped brother, Joost, but got along less well with her mother and sister.
>
> A few years after we had become friends with the artists' circle, Ann and Lloyd got married. In deference to Lloyd's parents, there was to be no alcohol served at the reception, which was afternoon tea. Several of the men

Madzy with her oil paintings in front of the small cabin, Riki at her feet. The paintings were stored in the cabin: the pail between her feet suggests that she has put the paintings outdoors so that she can do the spring cleaning.

had, however, equipped themselves with flat flasks of whiskey or brandy with which to lace the tea. Mr and Mrs Kinnee were apparently oblivious to this fact. Mam was having quite a jolly time, as she often did when she was with these friends. When she had had her teacup refilled, she went over with it to Alex Slavnics and asked, "Alex, is your heart still going glug-glug?" Alex reached into the interior pocket of his suit jacket and deftly poured a measure of liquor into Mam's tea.

There were very frequent parties in those years [1965 to 1975] – my memory suggests that almost every weekend there was one at someone's house ... There were many warm summer days when at least some of the group would meet to swim at the old mill dam that created the pond at Progreston, which was less than a mile from our house, and very often those present would be taken back to our place to sit on the lawn under the aspen trees for tea, and sometimes beer or sherry. Mam would go swimming with us, even though it was painful for her to get into and out of the water. But once she was weightless in the pond, she could move freely and easily, using the European breast stroke in a slow but graceful way. It was wonderful to see her moving so comfortably, even if it was for only a short time. These swimming afternoons had to be discontinued eventually because the creek became too polluted, but by that time Mam was virtually unable to get to the water. I can remember a few times when Dad and I brought her in the car and used the wheelchair to move her right into the water, but lifting and moving her became too painful for her, no matter how careful we tried to be.

Mam continued to draw and paint. She used watercolours and coloured inks, and Chinese brushes as well as pens. Whenever Norma came she would go to Mam's little study to see the latest efforts and give her encouragement.

Gerard and Madzy also went to Toronto to the opera:

Aiko Suzuki and Alex Slavnics used for a number of years to do the makeup for the Canadian Opera Company. Mam and I went for several years, even taking season tickets. We drove in the green Austin to the O'Keefe Centre in Toronto. (Dad didn't care to come with us.) When Alex heard that Mam was a great admirer of the baritone Louis Quilico, he offered to take Mam into the singer's dressing-room during intermission, although this was, strictly speaking, forbidden. As soon as the curtain had come down, I delivered Mam to a certain door where we met Alex, and I returned to our seats. About ten minutes later – and just before the lights went down – Mam came back walking more lightly than I had seen her do for years.

"*Such* a gentleman," she whispered to me, "and he kissed my hand when Alex introduced me."

We were really not fitted to belong to that somewhat bohemian world of the artists, and I am still amazed that we were accepted as completely as we were. Mam became someone quite different from her usual self in that milieu – more humorous, lively, and joyful. I'm sure that she recognized that I was far too strait-laced to ever become a "bohemian" myself, although she may have had some silent worries that I might fall into the habits of heavy drinking and smoking.

After the move to Brandstead, Madzy took a real interest in the "genteel" side of gardening, Gerard recalls, although by that time her illness prevented her from taking a very active part in it.

> But such was the wide range of her interests, her really multi-faceted personality, that she got involved just as much as she could. She and I established a small rock garden. She had a bit of money of her own and felt by then secure enough financially to spend some money on things like books and music and plants. We ordered bulbs every year from the Cruikshank catalogue (a novelty to us – all those different varieties of crocus, daffodil, tulip, and the "little" bulbs). We discovered that a couple near us, Mr and Mrs Bogle, sold perennial plants, and we went there several times per year to buy some. She was delighted by Dad's interest in rhododendrons – both of them remembered them from gardens in Holland. Mam joined the Flamborough Horticultural Society and very soon became its president. She put her considerable organizational skills into it, looked for better speakers, enlarged the annual flower show, etc. I was told later by one of the old members that the best years of the society were when Mam was its president.
>
> Even when she was confined to her wheelchair, she would join us in the annual ritual of putting the house plants out on the terrace in May, and then in the cutting back and repotting in September to keep them over for the winter. At that time she also had quite a number of plants in the little corner room with two bright windows, and she used them frequently as subjects for drawings and paintings in the winter.

Here we see Madzy in late middle age becoming again a different kind of person – evolving, expanding, as she had always done. Gerard wrote: "I think that she was remarkable in her ability to take pleasure in what she *could* do, instead of groaning about what she could not do." Her strong

Madzy with Riki – a photo that captures something of the athletic
young woman she had once been

spirit, and the delight she took in living and in the beautiful surroundings at Brandstead, motivated her to do what she could within her limitations, to be creative in life as well as art.

Gerard was an important part of making this lifestyle work. He was showing himself to be a very talented artist and was laying the foundation for his later career in wood engraving and making handmade books, published under the imprint of "The Brandstead Press." He and Madzy encouraged each other:

> When I became interested in printmaking and bought a printing press, Mam took a lively interest and participated to the full extent of her abilities. The first press, a heavy Chandler and Price platen press, needed two people to operate it – I would turn it by the fly-wheel and add ink from time to time, while she put in the blank paper and pulled out the printed sheets. Several of the early books from the Brandstead Press were printed that way, including the bilingual children's book, *Pekoo, the Cat Who Talks / Pikou, le chat qui parle*, which she wrote especially for me. For a good part of this time, Dad and I had to ease her down the stairs to the basement in her wheelchair, and again up the stairs when we were done, although I remember taking her down and up alone at certain times. One of these times was when the FLQ crisis was on, and Mam and I were printing late one night when Dad was away. We were listening to the news on the radio as we printed and, when midnight came and we were almost finished, Mam said, "We'd better be careful. Trudeau has invoked the War Measures Act. If someone looks through the window, we will be seen as operating a clandestine press and we will be put in jail for printing subversive pamphlets."

SHE DID LITTLE writing during those first years at Brandstead, other than letters, now written by hand. Painting and drawing were easier. For many years she painted cards to accompany gifts or mark special occasions. She also did some wood-burning; I have a tray with several images of leaves incised in a pleasing design. In Gerard's kitchen hangs a piece of board with three knots in the wood: Madzy saw that they made the pattern of an owl (two eyes and tummy) and around them she burned the outline of the owl and the tree-branch it sits on.

In Gerard's view Madzy was not a great artist, but her interest in and appreciation of art were genuine. He believed that, had she not been hampered by illness, "she would much rather have spent what little leisure time she had hiking or skiing or swimming."

Gerard

But she had the wonderful ability of being able to find pleasure in the very act of learning, even if the subject was not one in which she had previously taken any interest.

The first time that I realized how interested she was in art was when she took the family to the art gallery in Vancouver to see an exhibition of paintings by Emily Carr. I had read two of Carr's autobiographical books shortly before that and had told her something about this adventurous woman's life, and Carr's fearless, unconventional lifestyle appealed greatly to Madzy. I remember that she already knew something about Carr from Peter van Stolk, who had one or two of Carr's paintings.

In Antigonish, Madzy took apart a little paperback book on the Impressionists and mounted some of her favourite reproductions on pieces of coloured construction paper and put them up near her work table.

Most of her drawings and paintings show subjects drawn from nature, plants including roots, branches, fruit, and leaves. She was not particularly attracted to "pretty" subjects like roses or violets. This inclination was supported by Norma, who suggested subjects like dry leaves, gourds, corn stalks and even dried, smoked fish. Norma encouraged us to make drawings of our own hands, but this was not only technically difficult but psychologically so for Madzy, whose hands had once been slender and strong and beautiful but were deformed by arthritis.

Her pictures express so well the tension between a spirit longing for freedom and spontaneity coupled with a life devoted to conventional values of practicality and duty. She had in her a streak of the Bohemienne, but she could never commit herself to it without betraying her solidly middle-class background. So we find images of prim, straight-trunked trees surrounded by rather exuberant backgrounds. She loved to wet the paper and let coloured inks float on the wet surface, but these areas are always contained within firmly drawn outlines. Rarely were strong colours juxtaposed. There is one uncharacteristic watercolour of a deep ultramarine vase full of green, red and orange leaves and flowers.[2] It doesn't seem to have been more than an isolated departure from the sepia, grey, ochre and green palette that she used in most of her work. The Apollonian side of Madzy's character always held the Dionysian firmly in check.

The pictures she chose to frame were almost always the more conventional ones; a study of a geranium, a birch tree in the snow or a pine among rocks. The freer images, the more abstract, were mostly left in the sketchbooks. She often said of those, "It got away from me." I believe that she couldn't, even in her art, easily allow herself to "let go."

One of Madzy's most successful projects, in Gerard's opinion and probably also in hers, was a series of studies of small natural subjects done on folded sheets of Whatman paper – made in the 1870s, bought by mail from an auction in England – with which she and Gerard created a small book.

All the subjects were drawn from things observed on Brandstead. Many of the drawings were done in the winter, but, since Madzy surrounded herself with dried grasses, seed-pods, twigs, lichens, feathers and fossils, not to forget the potted plants, she was not short of inspiration. A couple of the centre-spreads of the book's signatures are landscapes; these were partly observed from the windows, partly taken from memory. She almost never worked from photographs. She called the book *The Whatman 1873 Book*.

Since I was to bind it for her when the images were complete, I was more involved in this project than in any others. She needed my help in deciding which pages would face which, and how many blank leaves were to be reserved at the beginning and the end. There is a hand-lettered caption facing each drawing, written in pen in the same ink as the outline of the drawing. The azalea, hibiscus, and African violet are quite strong in colour, while the milkweed pods and a number of studies of leaves are monochromes, many in a warm sepia, some in neutral tint or sap green. This book is a sort of climax of Madzy's work in this medium. She enjoyed the lovely paper, 105 years old when she used it. She completed it in time for Bill's birthday in 1977. The fact that the book keeps the drawings away from light means that the colours are as fresh now as when she painted them, unlike some of the framed works which have faded badly.

Each illustration has a few words of description and comment on the facing page, which she printed in block letters. Some of them are almost like tiny poems: "Even / a fungus / on a rotten stump / has beauty."

Madzy had no illusions about being a professional artist. Except for an exhibition we shared in Burlington in 1965, I don't think that she ever exhibited her work publicly. She worked for her own pleasure and shared the results with her family and close friends by painting individual cards for birthdays and other occasions. Her style was highly personal. She imitated no one but followed her inclinations and made art one of the threads in the tapestry of her life.[3]

THE ARTHRITIS and related problems were by now a serious disability, and there were episodes of acute illness. In January 1966, during the first winter at Brandstead, Madzy was in hospital with a stomach ulcer, and in

March she suffered with a five-inch-long gash in her leg – a result of her skin being made fragile by the cortisone – which healed very slowly. That October she was in a wheelchair for a time after breaking her hip. She had one foot operated on in January 1969 and the other the following October.

She was, however, still able to do quite a few physical things. She did a certain amount of her own housework; a neighbour, Irene Prine, came in once a week to clean, took the mending and ironing home with her, and sometimes helped with freezing and preserving. Freezing vegetables from Bill's garden was a regular seasonal activity, and in the early years Madzy also made jam, usually with Irene's help. For as long as she could, she did some baking and most of the cooking. After she and Bill joined St George's Anglican Church in Campbellville, Madzy took on the church's book-keeping. In 1966–67 she took a course in Greek by correspondence from Queen's University and earned a final grade of 87 per cent.

THE CHRONICLE of the Brandstead years is thickly sprinkled with the names of visitors. Madzy's old friend Tini Sandberg came several times, and so did Bill's sister, Lies. Madzy's sister, Hansje, came a year after the move to Brandstead, and later made three more trips. Three of Hansje's children came at various times: her oldest daughter, Muike, was there for nearly three months to improve her English, and Cathrien, a stewardess with KLM from about 1979 to 1981, regularly visited during stopovers in Toronto, taking a bus to Burlington and being picked up there. A cousin of Madzy's came with his wife, and so did a cousin of Bill's with her husband. The niece of Juus, Madzy's nanny and herself an old friend of Madzy's, came to stay. There were new friends, like the Salm family from Ottawa, distant relatives by marriage.

Friends from B.C., Hubert and Jill Bunce and their children, would camp in the small cabin that Bill had built immediately after buying the property. Pem and Mien van Heek came, and Beatrice and Albert Cooke.

Both Jock and I were part of the Brandstead world. Jock left home after finishing university but visited frequently. He brought his partner Barbara in the earlier years, then his wife, Suzanna, and eventually their son Darwin, born in 1980. Jock travelled a good deal but at that time was based in Toronto; he lived for a time in a reclaimed ocean-going tugboat he owned, the *Salvage Prince*, which he docked in Toronto harbour.

I worked at the CBC until December 1966; in January 1967 I joined the English Department at Ryerson Polytechnic Institute (now University). I was very busy during the academic year, but I settled into a routine of going

Madzy's sister, Hansje, and Jock

Marianne about 1980, with Madzy's dog Katie

to Brandstead for a Sunday-morning visit about every third weekend. In summer I usually visited more frequently and stayed longer, especially when there was a crisis or when Gerard was away. In the summer of 1970 I had mononucleosis and spent two months at Brandstead. Both Jock and I had rooms of our own that served as guest rooms when needed.

A significant addition to Brandstead was Gerard's partner, Don Bragg, who moved there in the summer of 1979 and was to remain until after Madzy's death. He was a thoroughly integrated part of the family, devoted to Madzy and she to him.

Hubert Bunce in 1998 wrote a short sketch of Madzy and Brandstead as he remembered them:

> Our image of Madzy is inextricably entwined in her so delightful surroundings of Brandstead. The garden, the forest, the bird song, the bees, the chickens and the goats. The cabin in the garden where we stayed so many times, it seems now. The ever-green enclosure of a forest shutting out the outside world. An enclosed world, special, recreated an image of another world to us, of far away Terrace, a world created by Pem and Mien van Heek, our other Dutch friends ... To us a Dutch world, though in no way comparable to the grand and gracious world of Holland ...
>
> Madzy, someone kind, generous, warm-hearted, brave in spirit, philosophical, sensible, loving to reminisce, to recall the golden days, struggling always to overcome the present pain, to keep moving around her enchanting home, around her lovely garden, around her world. Created so much by Bill, his skills and labour with love for Madzy. So many natural beauties of garden and home, so pleasant, so green, so relaxing to us in our visits, so gracious a welcome as though we were truly family or better still, family with no baggage, utterly free to come and go.

There were other visitors from nearer by, such as Yvonne and Gus van der Feltz, and some of the artist friends to whose houses Madzy was gradually less and less able to go herself. Mien Heersink, her Burlington friend, visited regularly, in the last few years frequently on Sunday mornings.

WE ALSO travelled. Gerard made two extensive trips to Europe, one of them to visit the locations where paper was still being made by hand. I went to England regularly and also to Holland. Bill went to Holland alone three times and he and Madzy made three trips there together, in 1967, 1972, and 1973. During the one of July–August 1967, Madzy attended a reunion of Spuit Elf.

The garden side of the house at Brandstead

The trips stretched her physical resources as far as they could go, and beyond. After the 1967 trip, she had to lie in bed for three months with a pinched nerve in her shoulder and spent three weeks in the hospital. In her Christmas letter to Beatrice Cooke that year, she wrote that she was doing physiotherapy twice a week.[4] After the trip in 1972, she was physically exhausted and emotionally drained.

WE CAN PICTURE something of life at Brandstead in the summer of 1969, four years after the move there, because Bill went to Holland and again saved Madzy's letters.

To set the scene: Madzy's niece Muike had been staying at Brandstead since May and would return to Holland a few days after Bill left. Jock had just spent a year in Jamaica with CUSO (the Canadian University Service Overseas). It had been an extremely difficult year for him; he had taught in a slum school in Trenchtown in Kingston, which he described as being at that time probably the worst slum in the western hemisphere. At the end of his time there, when he was making plans to go home, he was hired as navigator[5] on a private yacht going from Jamaica to Puerto Rico. Because of a hurricane, the yacht had to put ashore in Haiti (then under the dictatorship of "Papa Doc" Duvalier) and the crew was imprisoned in a military garrison. When they were visited by a priest and served a suspiciously luxurious meal, Jock decided that things looked serious. He used his knowledge of French, and his wits, to write a letter to the prison commandant, persuading him to release them. When Jock reached Miami he picked up the motorcycle that he had shipped from Jamaica and, drenched by a hurricane moving up the coast, drove to Brandstead. He had just enough money for gas but not for bed or food. He scrounged where he could, and at one point was given a dollar by a policeman who was worried about his ability to drive safely; the policeman also arranged for him to get a free meal and a box lunch at a diner. "I was a bit of a wreck," he recalls of the whole experience. "It was a fast way to grow up."[6] He returned a day or two before Bill left for Holland.

Madzy and Gerard drove Bill to the airport on the evening of 7 August 1969, and the next day she wrote to him. I had left early to go to Toronto, and she had driven with Muike to McMaster ("Perhaps after you are retired we'll take an evening course, each a different one but on the same evening at the same time! I was keen to start again!"). Then they went to Burlington to pick up some lumber for Gerard before returning home. "I lay down awhile, then tea, then cleaning of beans, then dinner, and finally freezing [blanching and packaging the beans for the freezer]."

She remarks that Jock's experiences have aged him:

> His skin is rough from the wind and weather, his hair is in bad shape and the beard makes him look older, but it is more the whole expression. The boyishness has gone out of it since Christmas [when we had last seen him] and he is older than his age. I hope he will have some fun in life again ... I feel that he is still living under a cloud. Gerald thinks also that he is still very tired. We leave him alone, and he enjoys that very much.

On 10 August she writes:

> It is teatime on Sunday, my dear, and I am all alone [on the lawn] under the aspen trees with the dogs. Mui is watching a beautiful movie on TV, and Jock and Ger went to watch a motorcycle race or something. A cricket in the rock wall chirps and another under the trees answers. It is wonderfully quiet, and I lap this restful moment up like a thirsty soul. I know I wouldn't like it quiet all the time, but this is wonderful. It is not very hot, just right. Pam[7] is coming home on Wednesday "to make up her own bed again" [after Muike's departure]. Now that Jock will be in and out again, it will be hard to figure out where to put guests. Both he and Pam *do* like their own rooms so much.
>
> The days are very busy, and go very fast, what with still more stories from Jock, and plans and preparing meals, and washing and mending. Jock is leaving on the train Tuesday [for Nova Scotia][8]: he has to be in Toronto at 9:20 A.M. so I suppose I'll bring him to an early train, perhaps to Oakville [where he could catch a commuter train]. We'll inquire tomorrow. Ger found an enormous anthill in the cabin, something terrifying. He sprayed it, and pretty soon he's going to sweep the dead ants up. He says there are tens of thousands. Pekoe came home with a small dove last night, which is quite lively, but has a big wound under its wing. Ger and Mui try to keep it alive, and bandage the wound regularly.
>
> Jock is becoming more and more himself again, notwithstanding the beard. The eyes look less unhappy. He has to send a dollar to a policeman in S. Carolina, who pressed this money on him, for fear that Jock would ride the bike without eating enough. A gesture like that restores your trust in man again a bit ... At present Jock is giving

Mui a ride on the back of Mango Tree [the name of the motorcycle]! So, I just made a snapshot of it, Mui beaming, and so is Jock. He is really looking much more cheerful. The trip from Miami to [here] was the hardest of all and he says he doubted whether he could make it, and was afraid he'd caught pneumonia.[9] But apart from a slight cold, all's well.

Her concern over Jock gives rise to an impulsive, ambitious plan the following day:

> With this condition of Jock's in mind I suddenly knew what kind of "holiday" I'm going to take; it'll take much of my savings but I think it will be worth it ... I'll take a plane to Halifax on Sunday, August 24, will arrive shortly after lunch there, and find Jock and a rented car at the airport. From there we will meander along the coast south-eastwards, look at all sorts of small places, sleep somewhere along the Atlantic coast on Sunday night, go on to Cape Sable where Jock knows a small hotel with charming people, go around the south coast and sleep near Cornwallis perhaps, and more coast on Wednesday. On Thursday, at about noon, we will take the train in Halifax [to return to Toronto]. He has a ticket (coach), I a roomette. When I have slept enough, he can sleep in the roomette. We'll share the meals that come with the ticket. He may hop off at Montreal and bum around a while there, learning more about film makers, etc. I arrive in Toronto on August 29, at about 2 P.M. and either Ger or Pam will pick me up and bring me home. I'll be showered and rested when you arrive home [from Holland] a couple of hours later. Isn't this a wonderful plan? Though I don't plan to talk or discuss future plans with Jock, perhaps in doing something he always wanted to do, and in having some familiar person around for whom he has to do things, of whom he has to take special care, he may find some meaning, some comfort, some aim in life.

The next day Madzy writes: "Tonight Ger and I will have to risk our lives again to bring Muike into the underground inferno of the charter flights departure" – referring to the experience of taking Bill to the airport a few days earlier. Meanwhile a friend of Jock's, with girlfriend, turned up and spent the night; Madzy cooked dinner for everyone before she and Ger and Mui set off for the airport. The weather was very hot and humid.

Two days later, in the continuing heat wave, she and Irene have cleaned the house and dealt with the mountain of laundry from all the guests. There are beans to put in the freezer and bookkeeping to do for the church. "We were too hot to cook, but had left-overs," she writes.

> I got through the laundry, washed Paddy [her car], and was ensnared in Ger's bookkeeping, which he can't make out anymore, so I promised to do it for him from now on. I carried the piggies [guinea-pigs] to bed and fed them. You see how independent and helpful I can be? It makes me feel good.
>
> The nicotiana is smelling lovely, the crickets are whispering their usual song. In two weeks you will be smelling and hearing all this again. Will you have changed? Will I have changed? When life has once been put into motion, its course can not be changed. But we must not be afraid of motion and change.

There is no indication anywhere to reveal what she was referring to in these last obscure sentences.

The final surviving letter in this series is full of the details of ordinary life: the weather is now so cool that she lit a fire in the fireplace, she and Gerard are freezing garden produce three times a week. A skunk visits daily, "much to the excitement of the dogs."

These letters contain no hint of the agonizing homesickness she felt when Bill was away in 1963. When she and Bill went together to Holland three years later, however, I wrote to a friend, Anne Eyolfson, that Gerard and I had misgivings about whether Madzy would be able to manage it, but that she was always so wretched when Bill left her behind that this time she was determined to go along. So we know that the cheeriness of the letters, though real, was only part of the reality; Gerard and I, on the spot at the time, understood something of what she was actually feeling. Her distress during Bill's absences in this period probably had less to do with homesickness than with her fear that, if disaster befell him, she would have to depend on us or go into a care facility.

THE BIG TRIP to Nova Scotia went as planned, except that Jock came all the way home with Madzy instead of stopping off in Montreal. They did indeed drive along the south shore and up to Truro. They wandered along beaches gathering seashells, and on one occasion Madzy fell asleep on the beach in the sun.

Madzy and the dogs (Riki, grey, and Folly, tan)

She wrote a card from Lunenberg to Bill's father and stepmother: "Jock and I are having a wonderful time; lovely weather, sun and some wind off the sea. We stop in all kinds of small places that you don't otherwise see, and nose around on abandoned wharves and docks."

Jock told me that they went into stores selling collectibles and junk and visited the boat yard in Meteghan where a sailing ship was being built in the traditional way. To Madzy's delight, they were allowed to go all over the yard.

TWO YEARS later, on the morning of 12 August 1971, Madzy had a sudden and extremely serious attack of peritonitis, a rupture of the intestine. Gerard was in Europe; close friends, Ina and Freek Vrugtman, were staying in his flat. Bill, at his office in Burlington, had just learned that he would have to fly to Ottawa at two o'clock for an afternoon business trip, and he phoned to tell Madzy this. Ina answered the phone and reported that Madzy was in terrible pain. It was then eleven o'clock; he decided that he could stop in at Brandstead on his way to the airport. By the time he arrived, an ambulance was on the way, Madzy's condition was grave, and Bill cancelled his trip. Ina had phoned me and I had come from Toronto, and Gerard was summoned back from Holland five days before the end of his two-month journey.

The operation was a long one. The surgeon reported to Bill that Madzy was in very bad shape. The intestine had ruptured in several places; the tissue of the intestine and colon was paper-thin and extremely difficult to stitch. They had done the best they could, but further ruptures could happen at any time.

She was in a coma for several days, and later said that she had seen many images from her childhood, and of her father. I remember one of those days, sitting by her bed, knowing that she was "not there" and might not pull through. The room overlooked Lake Ontario, but all I could see from where I sat was sky and monarch butterflies against the blue, setting off on their autumn crossing of the lake.

Her recovery was slow; she had almost no reserves. She was forbidden for the time being from taking the medications that had kept the arthritis somewhat under control, so that, apart from the after-effects of the surgery, she had intense and constant arthritic pain. She had no appetite, and Bill was the only person who could persuade her to eat even a tiny amount. For ten days in September, he himself was in the hopsital for a small operation and could visit her regularly during the day. I stayed at the house with Gerard until the beginning of September, but I was teaching only three hours per week at Ryerson that year and after classes started I still spent much time at Brandstead.

It was a month before I could report, in a letter to my friend Anne Eyolfson, that Madzy had said, "Well, I'm here again," and had begun to take a bit of interest in life. She was in the hospital for about two months, and when she came home spent almost all her time lying on her bed, though dressed.

Writing to Anne on 1 December, I reported Madzy saying to me that she was keeping a young spirit together with a ruined old body. But even the spirit was not always (was perhaps, at that time, rarely) young. In my journal, on 24 November, I wrote:

> Two days ago, on Monday evening, Gerald phoned to tell me that on Sunday they had had a very hard time with Mom, who couldn't stop crying and wishing she was dead and so on. It was so bad that Dad somehow got hold of a doctor to prescribe an anti-depressant, on which she is now living – maybe literally living. Gerald and Dad, as always, take the brunt of it, and I feel rather guilty and very confused. It's not Mom's illness so much as her state of mind which has made the change; she's been ill before, but as long as her spirit held up, there was not much change except that someone else had to cook. Now her spirit is flagging, and it's a pathetic thing. We expected the illness to make a difference and to have unpredictable after-effects, and as long as she was in the hospital she did too, but now she wants it to be the way it used to be, with her doing housework and driving the car – both entirely out of the question. She says the house is strange to her – naturally it is – and that she hates hearing other people doing her work. She cannot resign herself to being an invalid, and brooding and illness are making her, it almost seems, mentally disturbed. I don't know where it's going to end.

The intensity of Madzy's despair was such that she could no longer hide it. This was one of the rare occasions when she showed us her anguished inner self.

In January, still not recovered, she had a very bad flu. I wrote to Anne:

> It began with excruciating pain which stiffened all her joints so that Dad, trying to undress her and put her to bed, nearly cut the clothes off her. But she determined to move, and with great pain did. She had high fever but antibiotics coped with that, and, more or less, with the pain and stiffness, but then they affected her tender innards so that she had a day and a half

of vomiting and nausea and weakness and headache almost beyond enduring. That passed, but she was on a liquid diet for days and got terribly weak. Then she got an awful cough and head cold, which she is only now gradually overcoming.

By March, however, she was pottering about a little, doing small household tasks and helping Gerard with printing. But in April there was another setback. She had contracted shingles and been given cortisone; the cortisone was again withdrawn too quickly and the withdrawal led to a severe arthritis attack, which left her rigid and in appalling pain for two days. Bill had to come home from the office to look after her: phoning him was the last thing she could do before nearly blacking out with pain, and it was thirty-six hours before she could move enough to take off the sweater and bra she had been wearing when the attack began. The shingles affected her lower back down one thigh to the knee, so that she could neither sit nor lie comfortably.

By April 26, she was able to step out into the garden and even drive herself around the block. But this was only through an effort of will and determination; at other times she gave in, and her hands were so bad that she was unable to write more than a shopping list. Irene Prine came two mornings a week to do the housework. I was doing what I could from Toronto: phoning frequently, writing an occasional letter for her, making batches of meatballs to go into the freezer.

In early June I went to England on holiday. By then she was able to write me one of her diary-letters, sending it to my apartment so that I would find it when I returned. The first entries are short, telegraphic, and shaky, but both the writing and the content become more fluent and detailed.

She reports that at a rhododendron show at the Royal Botanical Gardens in Hamilton two of Bill's three entries won prizes. She and Gerard went to the show on the Sunday; when she writes on the Monday she has a painful nerve in her left leg, and her right eye is puffed and swollen from an insect sting. "Now (evening) grouse in tree, rabbit hopping around Paddy! Such a lovely rabbit!" She has been helping Gerard with printing.

On Wednesday she writes: "Today is one of my low days; probably did too much yesterday. So I left the housework to Irene." She is depressed because Bill was so busy all day that she hardly saw him. She is also missing me. "Somehow my heart bleeds, and I don't know why. I woke up crying in the middle of the night. I wondered how you were. My eyes are still poor, my good eye still puffed from the blackfly bite I got on Sunday, and reading bothers it."

The next day she amplifies on the events of that "low" day: "Yesterday ended kind of silly: when I got pan from cupboard (5 P.M.) I lost balance and fell on knees and hands. Not bad. But it was last straw. Ger came up [from his printing shop in the basement] and I even was not able to get frozen meat apart. I threw kitchen tools on sink, threw myself on couch and bawled. How melodramatic can you get! And that at my age! When Dad came home, Ger was already applying Brandstead's 'panacea,' a good glass of port!! And it excused me from cooking, dishwashing, sandwiches, etc."

On Sunday she writes: "I think so often of you, too much, I fear, and miss your near presence and phone calls." After I called her unexpectedly from England, she writes, "Your phone call! I was overwhelmed for a moment, to hear your voice, forgot what I wanted to say." All of us were crucially important parts of her world; any major absence was a rift in the fragile fabric of her life.

She is sad about a grouse that flew through a double-paned window into Gerard's flat and died of its injuries; Eva the guinea-pig had died a couple of weeks earlier. To cheer themselves up, she and Gerard went to the Hoeys' farm to see the new lambs. Visitors are expected. The weather is changeable: a killing frost on the night of 10–11 June, a few days of hot muggy weather, and then an arctic front. The mosquitoes are extremely bad. But when the weather is suitable all the (well-screened) windows of the house stand open, and the breeze blows through.

By then Madzy and Bill had made plans to go to Holland again in July–August – hoping that she would be well enough. In one entry in that diary-letter to me she says that she had an emotional tape from Hansje about the prospect of Madzy's coming: "I hope not too much emotion when arrival or departure in/from Holland. I'm not so poker-faced as I used to be!"

It is at this time that I wrote in a letter to Anne that Gerard and I had misgivings about how Madzy would manage the trip but that she was determined to go because she was miserable when Bill went alone.

The trip was too much for her. On 8 August, three or four days after returning, she wrote to me:

> My very own darling,
> May the peace that passeth all understanding be with you, now and for ever more ...
> First normal day at Brandstead: Dad to office, Ger getting Sophy [his first angora goat], dogs beside my couch. I turned off the radio in order to absorb the silence and vague sounds of this my place. I am weary, weary with the last shred of my body and spirit and mind.

But I know that this will pass when my body will be able to do some light work. In half an hour G. will come up for coffee and we will talk some desultory talk, since I am too weary for more.

Perhaps I'll add some later. When the shadows lengthen and evening falls ... Oh God, in thy mercy, grant us safe lodging and peace at the end ...

She does feel better later, as the postscript indicates: "I am less weary now, after my paper talk with you, and a nice coffee break with Ger. I begin to see things in the right perspective again. Try to do that, too, my very own girl and friend."

Three weeks later, in a tape to Tini Sandberg, she is cheerful. She made the trip, she tells Tini, because she was in need of a change. She reports that upon their return Bill bought her a wheelchair; she always opposed having one because it was such a sign that she would deteriorate, but now that she has a bad foot and cannot walk, she finds it handy. She will still walk whenever possible.

The wheelchair became like a normal piece of furniture in the house. While Madzy was lying down on the bed or couch, it stood nearby, and we would plop ourselves down on it when we came to talk to her. The dogs learned, more or less, to get out of its way. The first chair was not motorized, and because Madzy's hands were unable to turn the wheels, she propelled herself by keeping her feet on the floor and "walking" herself forwards; later she got a battery-powered one.

She was to go to Holland one more time, the following summer.

EARLIER I USED the phrase "the Brandstead world." It was that, and it deserves a closer look, not only because it was the world in which Madzy spent the last nineteen years of her life but because it fostered the talents of Gerard as wood engraver and bookwright, Jock as a film technician, and me as a writer. We are often asked how one family happened to produce three people so active in the arts and other creative fields. Genetics played a part, as did the favourable climate that Madzy and Bill always provided, but the world of Brandstead in those years was a major influence. It nourished us and we nourished it.

Madzy was at its heart: her creativity, extending beyond the arts into her surroundings and her life itself, was the spirit of Brandstead, just as Bill's practical abilities and attention to house and garden, barn and animals, created the setting, with Gerard's help. But the central position of Madzy –

her motivating spirit and our love and care for her, which drew us together – was shown by the completeness of its collapse after she died.

European influences blended with Canadian. There was always good music, an abundance of books, talk about intellectual and artistic matters. Hungry for stimulation, Madzy ordered books from the catalogues of a remainder firm; we brought her whatever we thought might interest her.

Gerard's work added to the richness of life at Brandstead. He and Madzy worked closely together; he discussed his work with her and showed her the proofs of his engravings; she proofread the printed sheets for the books. All of us kept informed about what he was doing, felt the influence of his creativity.

Jock, on his visits, talked about his life and work. When he bought the superannuated tugboat *Salvage Prince*, Madzy loved knowing that he lived on a boat. When she visited it in Toronto, cables were attached to her wheelchair, and the davit was used to lift and swing her over the gunwale.

I talked to her about my teaching, my writing, my reading. When her eyesight deteriorated, I made many tapes for her about English literature and history – the kind of thing I was teaching and researching – and put on tape the entire text of my book *The Quarter-Pie Window*.

The Brandstead world had two other important characteristics. Madzy and Bill believed in a life that in material terms was simple while at the same time being as rich as possible culturally and intellectually. The house was a plain wooden bungalow. The furniture that was not antique was home-made or bought inexpensively, some of it at junk stores, and it all blended comfortably. Food was simple, much of it home-grown, but there was always sherry and port served in good glasses.

We also practised as much self-sufficiency as reasonably possible, doing things ourselves, making things rather than buying them. Bill built a garage/barn/woodshed; the barn housed chickens, goats, sheep for a time, and briefly a pony. He kept bees, so there was always honey for the household and to give to friends. He had a large vegetable garden and some fruit trees and grape vines. Fruit and vegetables went into the freezer. Grapes – domestic ones from the vines Bill planted, and wild ones growing on the property – were made into wine. Milk from the goats was used to make yoghurt, and for a while the surplus milk was turned into cheese. Eggs came from our own hens; every year Bill bought a new batch of day-old chicks, and the two-year-old hens went to the abattoir and a few days later were returned to us ready for the freezer. When Bill needed fenceposts, he got them off our own property. When a larger tree had to be felled, the

Madzy, in wheelchair, being lifted on board the *Salvage Prince* by means of the davit, normally used for lifeboats

trunk was taken to a nearby old-fashioned sawmill and turned into lumber; I have a coffee table Bill made from it.

The living room had a fireplace, and the kitchen a small woodstove (in addition to an electric range). Later Bill installed several more woodstoves. The fuel came from the woodlot, mostly cut and hauled by Bill and Gerard and Jock. When the house needed a new roof, Jock helped put it on, just as he attended to things like TV aerials.

Bill and Gerard had small greenhouses where they started many plants themselves for the garden. Much of the fertilizer was manure from the barn and ashes from the fireplace and stoves.

Bill did the alterations to the house as needed. He added a bay window in the living room to accommodate a (home-made) sofa on which Madzy spent much of her time in later years. He combined two of the original tiny bedrooms into a larger one for Madzy and himself, with a huge window overlooking the garden and woods, and added a small greenhouse to the basement.

As Madzy became more handicapped, Bill constructed things to help her: a lower kitchen counter at which she could work from her wheelchair, a small lap desk, a box with compartments to hold pens, pencils, paper, a small dictionary and atlas, and a tape recorder and blank tapes – a tiny "office" that she could take with her as she moved in her wheelchair from her bedroom to the living-room couch and back. (It was typical of Madzy to want to have a dictionary and atlas close at hand.)

We made music ourselves, though not in a major way. For quite a while Gerard and I played recorder together. I had an accordion, dating from Terrace, which I played only at Christmas. Madzy had an auto-harp, a sound-box of lovely wood with strings across it. It lay on her lap and she played it softly with her maimed hands. Later she composed a few short pieces of music, playing the melody for Gerard to write down.

In many respects, Brandstead was the flowering of the vision that Madzy and Bill had brought with them from postwar Holland. The ideal of simplicity and as much self-sufficiency as possible had been achieved in Terrace, but life there had been too close to the struggle for bare survival to allow much development of intellectual and artistic elements. It was at Brandstead that this ideal was more nearly realized. With survival assured, there was energy left over to shape the surroundings to fit our vision, and to devote to the other arts of living. Without such a vision, a world like this does not come into being.

The creative and the practical blended: the readiness to do things for oneself combined with resourcefulness and creativity, and with the habit of taking initiative that is typical of most immigrants. For Gerard and Jock and me, some of the roots of our eccentric, self-directed careers are to be found in the family ethos and in its embodiment at Brandstead.

Gerard spun flax to weave into linen to make covers for some of his books. The homespun cloth was dyed using vegetation gleaned from Brandstead and from roadsides. He made paper, some of which had leaves and flowers embedded in it. All these processes had to be researched and learned; he largely taught himself. He sheared his own sheep (I helped him at least once); I spun some of the wool into yarn.

Jock took this combination of creativity and practical resourcefulness into his profession. He invented and for a time manufactured a device for hanging the lights on film-sets overhead instead of from stands on the floor. He used second-hand soft-drink trucks to transport film equipment: loading onto and unloading from outside compartments was much easier than into and out of a closed truck. He worked to produce a silent generator for on-location filming. Years later, getting involved in the lives of the people of Mali, in Africa, he invented a peanut-shelling device that the Malians could make themselves and which is now creating enthusiastic interest in many other third-world countries.

In a different area of creativity, he has since Madzy's death written a novel, *The Ship's Cat*, based on his experiences during the airlift of relief supplies into Biafra in 1969.

My work has been more intellectual than physical. In my university years, when I started becoming serious about writing, I learned how to write by reading, teaching myself first how to learn. When I began writing historical fiction I taught myself how to do the research, how to store and retrieve vast quantities of information, how to shape it into the books I wrote, how to use a computer.

Not all of the Brandstead projects worked. Madzy and Gerard tried to incubate eggs but the results were disappointing. Making maple syrup from our maple trees was not very successful either. Other projects lasted a year or two, perhaps because circumstances were favourable or the materials ready to hand, and were then abandoned. It was not so much the success or failure that mattered as the attitude: if it could be done yourself, there was satisfaction in figuring out how and learning the skills required, in starting with the raw materials and finding them, if possible, close to home.

IN THE SUMMER of 1972 our Dutch-Canadian friends Freek and Ina came to stay in Gerard's flat while he was in Europe for two months; Ina was there at the moment of Madzy's peritonitis attack, and her being on the spot may have saved Madzy's life. The following year they bought property across the road. Freek and Bill had met at UBC, and both Freek and Ina were now working at the Royal Botanical Gardens in Hamilton, Freek as the curator of collections and Ina as the botanical-horticultural librarian.

When they spent the summer of 1974 in Europe, on a sabbatical at the Freising agricultural campus of the University of Munich, Madzy and Ina engaged in a lively correspondence. Ina saved Madzy's letters and recently gave them to me. At times Madzy wrote almost daily, and the longest interval between letters is no more than two or three days. Altogether she wrote seventy-one pages, about 17,000 words. She saw it as a series of diary letters, so several days' entries might be sent off in one envelope. She wrote by hand, fluently, copiously, generously. Her chronicle of that summer at Brandstead with its amazing richness and detail, infused with warmth and love of the place and the people, provides a good counterpoint to her illness and occasional despair.

The letters are, again, autobiography, but they are so full of other people that they constitute a family portrait of the Brandstead world: the artist's eye seeing, the writer recording. But they are also directed to her friends: Madzy never forgets to whom she is writing – and I can see her mind reaching out to Ina and Freek, burnishing the fine filament that connected them and us.

In what she calls the "first report" she writes: "*Grüss Gott*, in case you have already forgotten your English. I'm cooling off after a nice shower." Then she gives the news: Gerard is hauling cement blocks from a house demolished next door; he will use them to build a small sheep barn. "Brandisses never will stop building, as you well know!" Madzy herself is using a borrowed incubator to try to hatch eggs of various kinds of poultry. From one of the guinea-fowl eggs had emerged "a lovely, sweet guinea-hen chick that converses with me; it is alone in my mini-greenhouse for the bantams don't like its lovely rosy-pink feet! ... All the rhodos are in bloom, gorgeous, a whole group of dark reds in front of my window."

On Saturday, 8 June: "Hectic weekend with an overload of visitors. On Sat. A.M., P.M., and in the evening, families with kids. On Sunday all afternoon, and while we had supper Jock, Barbara, 2 friends + laden truck + Daimler[10] all here! For lack of a dinner we fed them yoghurt, milk, and cheese sandwiches. It was all very cheerful and loud, for they had worked 4 weeks very hard, spent all their time in that hotel,[11] and just *loved* it here with all the flowers (now also broom, woad, mock-orange, etc)."

She cuts the letter short: "Sorry, I simply stick to the paper, *so* hot and humid, but there is a change in the air. Toronto got again a drenching rain, and here everything is powder dry and nothing is growing or sprouting ... Bill is getting his winter hay in."[12]

The letter of Saturday 15 June begins: "From a wild cherry branch over-hanging the driveway hangs an oriole's nest; it is hard to discover this hanging ball (like an old-fashioned, old lady's purse) but the parent birds are flying [to and fro], showing where the nest is and that there are little ones clamouring for food. It is fascinating to follow the exchange in feed-ing by the parents."

She tells about finding a home for the little buck born that spring to Belinda, one of the goats; Madzy and Bill drove to Norval, east of Toronto, to deliver it, the half-grown buck standing in the well between the car's front and back seats. "Mr A. and Bill put him with 5 nanny-goats where-upon he immediately elected one as Mama and began to suck! So then he was put with 5 goat-girls, of which he is now sire and master. No 'mèèèè' [of unhappiness] out of him nor out of Belinda or Daisy.[13] How easy it is to be a goat!"

On another day: "The sheep baa-ing, the wind rustling through the leaves while the evening sun is making deep shadows ... This afternoon Jock and Barb rumbled up on a motor-bike (English model!) fixed up by Jock out of hundreds of parts! It made a tremendous noise, vibrated accord-ing to Barb, but they both radiated happiness."

On Thursday the 27th:

> I have been very busy; day before yesterday I made strawberry jam, and now I have a recipe for "freezer jam" [she gives the recipe]. I'm going to experiment with that recipe today, for the strawberry crop is huge. Yesterday I baked peanut-butter cookies (such a success here that I bake them practically every other day) and a peanut-molasses bread ... On Saturday Ger and Marianne and Barbara will have their sale at Rod Steenbrugge's from 10–5, and M. will demonstrate spin-ning and G. will do the selling, while Jock and B. will help Bill with the fencing, for our neighbour has proposed to make a fence all along the line where the properties join ... the neighbour and 2 sons will work with Bill and 2 helpers, and share the costs. That means a fence of 660 feet.

Rod Steenbrugge had a fruit and vegetable store in the village, and the plan for the Saturday of the upcoming Canada Day weekend was for Gerard to show and sell his art and Barbara her pottery, and for me to demonstrate spinning using wool from Gerard's sheep – all out on the parking lot. It was very much a Brandstead kind of thing – the emphasis on crafts and on sharing them, showing them. I was by no means an expert spinner, but I could do it creditably and explain what I was doing.

The start of the event was delayed by rain, but the weather cleared after an hour or two. Madzy reports on it in her letter of Sunday, 30 June.

> After all, they did have their sale at Rod's: Marianne's demonstration drew enormous attention, sometimes 15 people at a time (especially also children who asked the most intelligent questions), Ger sold wood engravings for about $80.00 and talked to people, and Barbara's pottery was an enormous success. From the moment she arrived, and had not unpacked all her stuff nor price-tagged it, she sold continuously, and came home elated with $136.00, which will all go towards her electric kiln.

While writing this, Madzy was lying on the livingroom couch. We sat nearby, "talking about films, all very chummy." It was a typical family scene, all of us bringing our interests to Brandstead, the talk about our work creating a kind of cross-pollination.

"I *love* writing letters, I always did," Madzy wrote. "If only you can read them, for I write them on my lap on the couch, half askew because my wrist does not turn." A stiff wrist was not the only handicap. In the bundle is a letter from Gerard, undated but almost certainly from one of these days because when Ina had answered the letters, which was immediately, she filed them in chronological order.

Gerard reports: "Mam is not able to stand up [just now] because one knee will not hold her, but she is cheerful as usual." So the baking and the jam-making were done from the wheelchair. Later (19 July) she refers to "an odd painful bulge" in the middle of one heel, so she has to be "idle."

On 29 June, she told Ina not to feel obliged to answer all her letters:

> I do this writing because: 1/: I like writing "diary-letters," and 2/: I hope in this way to keep you posted with the daily unimportant happenings, so that, when you come home, you won't feel too strange and "outside-of-everything." – If you could see Nemo-View [their house] at this moment you would be pleasantly surprised: instead of sandy-stony-rubble everything is covered with hundreds of white daisies and other wild flowers and grasses. We will make a snapshot of it soon, and send it to you.

On 2 July:

> All of a sudden the house is so quiet that all the marvellous outdoor sounds come in: the rustling aspen-leaves in the wind, the sound of

some birds (cardinal, robins), and the chip-chip of the young birds born in your woodshed being fed in our front garden. We saw a sparrow frantically feeding a young cowbird (and you know why, but that is nature). It is warm and very humid today, but the fresh breeze blows through all the open windows. The two mock-oranges are at their prime, and their lovely smell comes in with the breeze. The roses are already very beautiful, so are the sweet-william, coreopsis; the male sumach proudly show off their green-golden torches.

On 3 July:

Of course, I had it coming to me when I said brazenly to Ina (who offered me the use of her washing machine [if needed]): "Oh, I don't think that will happen." Well, it did happen, and just now we are enmeshed in a pretty bad heat wave (88°[F], 99% rel. hum. yesterday, during night 74°) and we need several changes of clothes per day. While doing the laundry yesterday, the machine clicked off as usual when it had finished its cycle, but the water kept on spraying ... so that we had to turn off the main taps. And the repairman can't come before Thursday, that is, today week.

The heat brings to her mind a bit of Dutch doggerel verse, about seven people riding in a "diligence" (public stagecoach) on a boiling hot day. One lady says to the gentleman opposite: "Where you're sitting, it's not so bad. Here a person sweats to death. I have to say that the sweat from my hands is making a puddle in my lap." It is untranslatable; the original has not only the spice of dialect but subtly indecent overtones. "Oh, why do I remember the scandalous poems from my youth and not the beautiful ones?" Madzy asks. I would love to know where, in her youth, she was learning "scandalous" poems: from friends at school? From her father? Her brother Paul?

On 26 July she has been busy with the church bookkeeping: a mysterious mistake meant that she spent hours more on it than she would otherwise.

With Irene Prine on holiday, Madzy (with assistance from Bill and Gerard) does the housework herself: she says that she first thinks and plans how best to do it.

She reports watching the TV coverage of the impeachment of Richard Nixon; with her background in law and her interest in both history and current events it is a "breathtaking moment, a real experience in my life." She did not support Nixon, but she saw the drama in the proceedings and considered the human issues, imagined the state of mind of the members of the House Judiciary Committee as, one by one, they cast their vote.

On 3 July I had gone into hospital in Toronto for a sinus operation. On the 6th, Gerard writes to Freek and Ina that Madzy has been fretting about me and that fretting never did her any good; however, I will be coming to Brandstead to recuperate and then she will feel better.

Along with the bounty from Bill's vegetable garden, she says, they are eating purslane (a weed, delicious with cheese sauce) and are going to experiment with grape leaves boiled. It was a Brandstead thing to eat what was to hand – having checked, of course, that it was safe.

On 26 July Madzy is outraged to find that Irene is receiving less than the minimum wage from her other employers. "*Soit*, I shouldn't be so mad, for my handwriting becomes more illegible than before! ... Ger's sheep-cote is so far ready that the sheep + banties have moved into it. You will like it very much, I think. G. has worked like a slave for 2 weeks which he calls 'his vacation'! Now he is binding books again for he has many demands and doesn't want the people to wait too long."

By 9 August they are preparing vegetables for the freezer every day: french beans, green beans, peas. On the dinner table there are new potatoes, freshly dug.

A letter from Gerard on 29 August again reveals things she doesn't mention.

> Mam is generally all right, although she was always so easily tired. Now the doctor says that she is very anaemic, which she has often been before. I wish he had discovered this sooner and not let it go too far. She has great difficulty in digesting iron medicines, so we try to give it to her by choosing iron-rich foods, like raisins and liver [and purslane]. But it will be a slow building-up process.

He is publishing a little book containing one of my short stories and seven of his wood engravings, entitled *A Sense of Dust*; Ina is going to help with the binding; he himself has bound most of the copies but there are still a hundred to go. He is working on the binding of another book, though he cannot finish it until he weaves some more linen for the covers.

On 9 September, in the middle of a long letter, Madzy writes: "2 quickies: 1/ Paddy, our car, has something amiss with her innards and sounds like a police car or an ambulance so that every car draws to a halt at the side of the road to let her pass by; and 2/ there is a cricket in my plant room on the top shelf, bawling his head off all night and hidden in utter silence by day, and therefore untraceable!" A couple of aardvarks have been reported to have escaped from the Toronto Zoo and have not been seen since. The first prints from her new camera have come back: "a rather dismal result, partly my fault but partly the fault of the developer, for have you ever seen sky-blue chicks, or Bill with baby-pink trousers on? Picking blue peaches off a purple peach-tree?" The odd and amusing and mildly maddening things in daily life always delighted her: this was life.

Her sister, Hansje, had given her a subscription to the overseas weekly edition of a Dutch newspaper, so that Madzy could get a non-American perspective on world events and at the same time become better acquainted with the contemporary Dutch language, significantly different from the one she still used.

On 20 September she writes one of the last letters in this series.

> All is well here. Ger has put your houseplants indoors since there is danger of frost these nights. The sumac and birches start to colour. Ger cuts 6-foot tall weeds from your garden, to the great delight of goats and sheep. Bill picked all his peaches and we will bottle them, since the freezer space fills up rapidly. Rod Steenbrugge sells bushels of "fallen" apples and we are in for an "applesauce-bee" very soon. Autumn is in the air, summer is gone, and I feel somewhat sad. It was so lovely with all those windows open, and to be so much part of nature. Don't forget that nature, on whatever part of the globe it is, is wonderful if you accept it as it is. And Nemo-View, like Brandstead, has gained a special world of its own already, almost secretly and unnoticed. It is *settled*. And surely we are fortunate here. I love this piece of the world.

By 1 October it is really autumn. Bill goes to the office in warm tweed jacket and raincoat. On the Sunday morning he lights a fire in the fireplace. In that letter she writes about Gerard's work:

> G. is very busy for 2 shows, one in Kingston (small one) and the big Christmas show at Alice Peck's [in Burlington]. He has been working steadily at wood-engraving, and I find that his work has changed and he has some very good improvements in the way of conveying three-dimensional forms, depths, etc. It is a joy to study every new print he brings upstairs. I am sure Ina will love a dear, naughty rabbit, and a perky little mouse. But those are miniatures; he has made several large blocks as well.

Freek and Ina were back on 23 October. The friendship continued (and continues). Ina and Freek have been answering questions of mine, and in a recent e-mail Ina writes that in those years Brandstead became a second home to her and Freek:

> Madzy and I shared many interests; books we were both reading and discussed; the stamps we both collected; admiring stones, fossils, shells and interesting pieces or driftwood and roots I collected. It became a tradition to pot up a clump of the first snowdrops for Madzy, cut the first alder and pussy willows for a vase, take a cup with the first picked wild strawberries to her, and I made through the seasons smaller or larger bouquets for her ... In the early phases of her confinement [sic] Madzy used to sit in her little room drawing and painting and we had many a discussion there, often over a cup of tea.

IN DECEMBER 1973, when he was sixty-two, Bill was able to reduce his hours at Niagara Brand Chemicals so that he worked from nine to three; a year later he began working only in the mornings, and on 1 May 1975 he retired. By now Brandstead was a complex miniature farm, with the livestock, the large vegetable garden, the fruit trees, the firewood to be provided. He made alterations in the house and the barn-garage, attended to fences. Increasingly he took over the shopping and cooking and freezing and finally provided personal care for Madzy. In later years he had a pager so that when he was working outdoors she could reach him.

He and Madzy went to church together and he helped her with the book-keeping when necessary. Gerard was also there almost always. Along with the time spent on the many facets of his art and book-making, he helped with the work in the main house and garden and in caring for Madzy.

IN SPITE OF her impaired vision, Madzy did quite a lot of reading during this period. She read books connected with her research projects and had some access to scholarly books – those that came her way randomly from friends, and the ones she bought from remainder catalogues. I was always lending her books. Those she owned she used intensively, such as David Herlihy's *Mediaeval Culture and Society* and other history books. She owned a fair number of books in Latin and Greek, texts from her courses as well as others, an anthology of English literature, a biography of Samuel Pepys, and a condensed version of his diary. However, as her body in general deteriorated, she could no longer hold heavy books while lying down. Even paperbacks became a problem, with her frail hands and painful elbows. In the last few years, Bill cut up the thicker ones into sections so that she could manage them. Eventually, as her eyesight worsened, she used large-

Madzy and Bill in the living room at Brandstead

print books and talking books, though the limited range of subject matter frustrated her.

During the earlier part of the Brandstead period, her writing was side-lined – typing was now so painful – but she never stopped altogether. On 2 March 1966, at the end of their first winter there, she sent me an illustrated letter, much like the "*Dolphijn*" album that she had made as a girl. It is entitled "A Sunday on Brandstead," text and photos mounted on coloured paper. The photos had been taken the previous Sunday when – with the snow already gone from sunny slopes – she and Gerard decided "to open the cabin and have our coffee there." They lit the small stove and swept out the winter litter, surprising a few mice. She photographed Gerard, the dogs rooting around, Bill carrying a ladder after pruning the apple tree. One picture is of Madzy sitting on the steps of the cabin, in slacks, winter jacket, and boots; the text says that she was watching Gerard walk over from the main house with the tray of coffee. It was a delightful thing to find in my mail, and now, more than a third of a century later, with Brand-stead no longer in the family, it has all the appeal of warm memories.

Probably in the same year she wrote the account of the church bell that she arranged to bring from Holland to Terrace in 1949. She wrote it for a CBC Radio program called "Stories with John Drainie," but it was never submitted because (she says in a note accompanying the manuscript) Drainie died suddenly in October.[14] Revised more than ten years later, the piece is included in her last book, *The Scent of Spruce*.

In 1971 Gerard published a book on which he and Madzy had worked together, *Pekoo, the Cat Who Talks / Pikou, le chat qui parle*. Madzy's text, in English and French on facing pages, is designed to help children learn French; she said she used as many words as possible with similar forms in French and English, so that readers would recognize the resemblance between the two languages. Pekoo is the first-person narrator; the one human character, a girl called Mary, is fictional. Madzy describes Pekoo's habit, when she wanted to be let in, of scrambling up the outside of the door and hanging by her claws, looking in through the window. Pekoo dis-liked recorder music and made a nuisance of herself to register her protest. Gerard's lino-cut illustrations show her always in nearly solid black and the rest of the scene in black lines on white – except for one illustration near the end, in which Mary and Pekoo talk about the fact that there are white cats, and brown and yellow and white ones, as well as black ones like Pekoo. "And people?" Pekoo asks. "People also," Mary replies. The illus-tration shows the black cat accompanied by a cat of each of those colours; Madzy hand-tinted that page in each of the 250 copies of the book. Ina

Vrugtman, in a letter to Gerard (then in Europe) on 26 July 1971, writes: "Madzy has been trying to paint every day a few cats."

IN 1970 GERARD and I began writing down memories that Madzy recounted from her childhood. In those years Madzy told more stories about her and her family's past than she had done earlier. The project flagged after a while, but some important material was put on paper.

At about the same time, she wrote a short piece on the geology of Brandstead and its surroundings. She does not indicate her sources, simply referring to having done some "reading and research." Her interest in geology had expressed itself for years in the collection of fossils, and she later acquired a device for polishing particularly attractive small stones.

By 1972 she was using a tape recorder for some correspondence. Taping was to become a very important part of her life; not only did she make letter-tapes but by 1976 she was recording memories and family stories; the autobiographical drive emerged again direct and deliberate.

She began the first "memoir" tape, so far as I know, on 16 May 1976; it is the narrative based on her war diary.

> For years now I have promised to put my stories, the stories that I have told you during all those years, on paper and later, when I couldn't write any more, on tape; and I don't think I would have started it today if it had not happened that Gerald yesterday during our tea break said, "Well, you remember that you have always told us stories, and you always promised that you would put them on tape. Why don't you do it?" And I said to myself, "Yes, why don't I do it?" – because I cannot write any more. My hands are getting in a worse state than they have been and there are lots of things I cannot do and I have more time to make profitable in order to make me feel right, in order to make me feel that I still have a job to do in my life, and all these things combined make me think, "I am going to do it now." That was yesterday, the 15th of May, 1976, and that was by chance just thirty-four years after Dad was taken prisoner of war in Holland.

This account, memory rather than day-by-day experience, is quite different in slant and tone than the war diary; furthermore, she added information and explanations that I found useful when I was working with the diary itself. The typed transcript I prepared is twenty single-spaced pages, and the taping must have taken her some weeks, perhaps a couple of months.

The next year she and Gerard collaborated on another book. This was *April Snowstorm*, the account of a saw-whet owl – the smallest member of the owl family – that found refuge in the open-fronted part of the barn during a snowstorm. Unlike the cat in *Pekoo, the Cat Who Talks*, the bird is not anthropomorphized beyond being given the name "Little Owl." It observes the livestock occupying the barn: goats (one with a kid), sheep, chickens, bantams, a pony, Pekoo. There is no plot; it is a series of tableaux, and it beautifully captures the sense of quiet in barns when there are no humans to observe. I remember going into the barn in Terrace in early mornings and, as it were, surprising the creatures in just such a state of serenity. Gerard's wood engravings are exquisite, and the copy I have (number three of an edition of sixty) is printed on Gerard's own paper, printed and bound by hand. I can visualize them discussing the book at every stage and then carefully and lovingly creating it.

Also in 1977 she did watercolour paintings that Gerard bound into a small, beautiful, one-of-a-kind book, *Flowering Brandstead*. Each painting shows minute and careful observation, well-developed technique and use of the medium, and is executed with both control and poetic flair.

And this was the year as well in which she and Gerard produced *The Whatman 1873 Book* described earlier in this chapter.

IN LATE 1977 Madzy made contact through a newspaper advertisement with Barb Wintar, who did typing at home. They would work together until about 1982. This arrangement enabled Madzy to resume writing – that is, to record her work and have it transcribed. It marked a great liberation for her and brought about a resurgence of writing, though the limitations of the process led her to be sometimes (maybe always) dissatisfied with the results. It was during the next few years that she wrote the memories of her youth and the stories of her parents' lives in the Dutch East Indies that I used for earlier chapters of this book.

Barb described the process to me. Madzy would make the tape, spelling out the Dutch names and other difficult words and technical terms. Barb typed a rough draft that Madzy corrected by hand – the briefest of corrections only, because writing was a struggle. Sometimes she used block capitals to make sure that what she wrote was legible. When Barb could not make out a word, she phoned Madzy or left a space where Madzy could write it in. Sometimes Madzy herself instructed Barb to leave a space. If there was a major revision to make, Madzy would put that section on tape and indicate where it was to be inserted. Then Barb typed a neat copy.

For her handwritten revisions, Madzy mostly used felt-tip pens, and often did the work while lying on bed. More than once, an uncapped pen got lost among the bedclothes and left stains, but no one worried about that so long as the writing went on. Sometimes Barb and Madzy would work over a manuscript sitting side by side at the desk in Madzy's den; there is one that bears both their handwritings, and clearly at one moment Madzy picked up Barb's ball-point because there is a word written in her handwriting with Barb's pen. Barb says that Madzy occasionally consulted her on a matter of phraseology but that most of the time she knew exactly what she wanted to say. Revisions were the result of further thought, further information, or the recognition that what she had originally spoken into the tape recorder did not reflect her meaning.

During this period (1977–82) she wrote other work besides memoirs meant for the family: we have seven short pieces, all based on her experience, clearly intended for publication.

One appeared in *Early Canadian Life,* a periodical published in Milton, Ontario, not far from Carlisle. It was published in January 1980. A carbon copy has "sold" written in shaky writing on the first page; there must have been a great deal of satisfaction in that. Madzy was paid $20 for it. Entitled "Jim the Wheelwright," it tells the story of our arrival in Terrace and of a neighbour who, while Bill was preparing the house for occupancy, baked an apple for him every day at lunchtime.

Another, entitled "Riki," was sent to the *Atlantic Advocate* in April 1978 but so far as I know was not published. It recounts how Madzy acquired her beloved dog Riki. "Uncle Sebastian's Pet" deals with the turning in of the radios during the war, "Bacon on the Moors" with the Canadian soldiers giving her food immediately after the war. "Postwar Pioneers" brings together a few anecdotes from life in Terrace. "The Farmers' Meeting" describes the visit she and Bill made to the farmers' meeting in Nova Scotia. (I drew on most of these narratives in earlier chapters.)

One story, "Portrait of a Woman," deals with this period. It begins:

> In the middle of the hall my electric wheelchair stopped. The pilot light was off, which meant: no contact between the battery and the gear box mounted on the arm rest. I followed the wire connecting the two and noticed that the lower plug was loose. I could not reach it, so I was stuck on that very spot. I looked around for something to do or read but everything was beyond my reach.
>
> My glance fell on the portrait of a woman on the wall just above my right shoulder. A smile played around her closed full lips and she

was looking down upon me, as if saying, "You have lived with me for over half a century and this is the first time you take the trouble to look at me."

It was true! How many times had I passed her during those years?

The portrait came from her mother's house; Madzy describes in detail the subject depicted and the fine, delicate painting. "I know more about this woman than one usually knows about people in old family portraits. She was my great great grandmother." She goes on to tell the story of Mattha Cornelia van Stolk, born in 1794, who married Joan [a variant of Johan, I imagine] van Vollenhoven in 1813 and died in 1820. Madzy remarks that both she and her namesake in the portrait "crossed the Atlantic to weave a few threads in the cloth of Canada's multi-coloured tapestry."

IN 1978 SHE became absorbed in the research done by the Leakey family into the origins of the human race and prepared a synopsis of the book *Origins*, by Richard E. Leakey and Roger Lewin. The synopsis, another of her "educational" writings, is eighty-one double-spaced pages in length and incorporates a partial transcript of a CBC Radio program on the subject. She gave a copy to each of us at Christmas 1978. My copy is inscribed with a quotation: "An inquisitive mind is not soon daunted by a wayward body."

She also made a tape of notes on a book called *Tracking Fossil Man*. Earlier in her life she had made notes from a book entitled *The Amateur Scientist*, by C.L. Stong, including copying by hand some of the illustrations.

She researched the legend of St Nicholas, the eve of whose feast-day is an important holiday in the Netherlands; Madzy and her sister-in-law, Lies, exchanged information on tape and by letter about the origins of the saint's legend and the celebration. Madzy's main source was *The Golden Legend*, a thirteenth-century collection of saints' lives.

She became interested in early paper mills and in Dutch windmills. We have several tapes she made of notes from a book called *The Windmills of Holland*, by H. Besselaar. She records that when, as a girl, she went sailing with her father, she took the windmills for granted but now she finds them fascinating. The Besselaar book got her absorbed in their history and technology, the vanes and their construction, the lives of the people working in them. She is interested in the functional structure of the different kinds of mills and in the regulations that governed their operation in the middle ages. At about the same time I lent her a book entitled *The Medi-*

eval Machine: The Industrial Revolution of the Middle Ages, by Jean Gimpel, which has a mediaeval drawing of a windmill that she describes in detail.

One tape contains notes about Satsuma ware, a kind of Japanese porcelain of which we have some pieces, probably brought from the Dutch East Indies by Madzy's parents.

One consists of bird songs recorded, probably, through the open window.

On one she is reading French, in her beautiful accent – reading it slowly, then analyzing the grammar and idiom. Several times I went to a French bookstore in Toronto at her request to buy books for her, and I still have one that she annotated.

She made two tapes specifically for me. As she became more and more ill, I realized that with her death, information about my early health history would be lost. When I asked if she would put it on tape for me, she made a whole story of it, biography and autobiography both. She also made a tape labelled "Memories for you and me." At the end she says she will give it to me and we can discuss it if I wish. However, she never did. It first came into my hands when, collecting material for this book, I received from Bill a box of tapes she had made. It was a message in a bottle that arrived too late – or arrived just in time to be used in this book.

She begins by saying that I had asked her what kind of child I had been. She takes the question seriously, recognizing that this is a way of forming an image of one's own identity. Now aged sixty-seven, often alone and unable any longer to do many things with her hands and body, she spends some of her time thinking back over her varied life.

She begins my story from the time she married Bill, frequently interrupting the narrative to comment. She observes that as a child I much preferred the company of adults, and that I did not have a child's mind, so that she treated me more like a "grown-up child." She talks about the effect that the war must have had on me, not only psychologically but also physically in the form of inadequate nutrition. She says she worries about me and tries to think what she can do to help me deal with my tiredness and fearfulness. And there is much more – a long, quiet mulling over my situation past and present, in tone somewhere between thought and conversation.

For me, now, listening to this tape is a moving experience. Besides giving me insights into myself through her perception of me, it also tells a good deal about her. She refers to her own fear during the war, saying that as a small child I would have sensed that, and alludes to the anxieties of the time in Terrace. Some of the fearfulness and reluctant sociability that she ascribes to me were (as the evidence of her life indicates) also part of her nature.

Believing that the feelings of a pregnant mother influenced the unborn child, she talks about her intense loneliness when she and Bill were living in the United States. She identifies my state of mind and mood when Gerard was born and Bill imprisoned as anger – and surely she is also revealing her own anger at Bill's being taken captive. She talks about how close she and I were because of all we had gone through together, and how close I had been to my father before 1942, how safe I must have felt before Gerard was born and my father went away, how insecure after that. The impossibility of determining precisely what is biography and what is autobiography is itself revealing.

IN THE FALL of 1980 she began a major project, a history of Holland for her children. Like the history of Canada for Dutch immigrants, this was meant to bridge a gap between countries and cultures, and like the earlier work, it was told as a story. In a letter-tape made after completing the project, she says:

> When I planned to write a summary of Dutch history, I had mainly three objects in mind: first of all to make it as clear and short as possible; then to compare here and there the events in Holland with those in England, if possible chronologically; at the same time I wanted to use few difficult words and unpronounceable Dutch names which would only confuse the conciseness of the summary.
>
> I have enjoyed the work greatly, and it has shortened this cold winter of 1980/81 considerably. I knew very little of Dutch history and have learned much by studying it and putting it down on paper. There may be mistakes, but I have done my best to make it as pleasant reading as possible.

To prepare for the project, she asked someone in Holland to send her an up-to-date atlas of the country, if possible the kind that contains supplementary information. Tini Sandberg had given her a book about Dutch archaeology, which would be a great help. By now she was spending a large part of every day on the couch or her bed, books lying around or on top of her. With her weak and twisted hands, even holding and handling the books was painful and tiring. For years she had had vision in only one eye. Because she was unable to write more than a few words by hand, whatever material she wanted to remember from her reading had to be stored in her memory and sorted and shaped in her head.

In a letter-tape made in February, she tells her sister-in-law, Lies, "In the mornings I'm always busy with the project of the history of Holland and have more and more pleasure in it; from time to time I make changes in it, or begin anew from the start, and change what I covered in too much detail ... Frequently something new occurs to me, and therefore it will take the whole winter to finish the project, which is wonderful because that's something I can really be busy with."

On page 38 of the history itself she writes, "This is the end of my project. It has taken me about half a year to work at it. After five starts which I threw away because I didn't like them, I ended up with this result. I am not satisfied with it ... but finally I've learned the history of the country of my birth of which I knew very little[15] – far less than Dad. If I hadn't had Dad to ask questions of and to discuss subjects with, I don't know if this project would ever have been in the state it is now."

A subject about which Madzy was ignorant was always a challenge: the impulse to write came not from having her head full of knowledge but from the ardent desire to fill it.

At the end of the history is a map of Holland drawn by Bill (Madzy notes on it: "*Hoc fecit Pater*" – "Dad made this" – a phrase rich with the whole history of book production). Then there are sections on the present geography of Holland, its form of government (this she would know in detail from studying law), the history of the ruling House of Orange, the history of the national anthem, and information about the Most Excellent Order of the British Empire, of which her father had been made knight commander for his work in the First World War.

There are several personal touches. She gives details about her father's work in the First World War and, when dealing with the Dutch East Indies, talks about Willy Schüffner's malaria research. In connection with trade between the mother country and the colonies, she writes:

> From [Batavia, the Dutch trading settlement in Java] the Dutch brought great wealth to Holland, and Amsterdam became the centre of this activity. All the bales and chests full of riches were brought there from overseas. The large sea vessels moored in the harbour in Amsterdam and flat-bottomed barges pushed by men with poles carried the cargo through the canals to where the warehouses were. Now if we say "warehouses," we think of big square buildings. However, the Dutch at that time didn't know anything else but their way of building with brick. And so the warehouses were also tall buildings of brick, one against the other, and with a gabled roof while the

top beam was slightly longer so that they could attach a strong block and tackle underneath against that beam to haul up the crates and bales in order to put them in the various storerooms.

The barges were moored at the spot where the canal and the street surface met. The street was also paved with brick, and a sidewalk ran along the row of tall houses. The crates and bales were carried to the house and hoisted up, which brought them to the height where they had to be received by men to store them. I've seen this myself. As a child I was intrigued by these activities especially because it was then not any more a question of storage houses, but a similar procedure was done when someone lived in a canal house and was going to move in or out. The block-and-tackle was still used to get the furniture in and out of the houses. I remember watching with great intentness the hoisting up of a piano dangling on a hook but secured safely with heavy ropes until it reached the window of the room where it was to be placed. Then, gently, the piano was turned around and eased over the window sill (the window had been taken out) and hoisted into the room. I always wondered what would happen if one of the ropes gave way and the piano fell down – what kind of a noise would it make? Alas, it never happened when I was there.

By 2 April 1981 the history was all on tape, she told a correspondent; it would be typed, she would revise it, and then it would be retyped – it came out to fifty-four double-spaced pages. The project was complete in the fall of 1981.

DURING THE years when Barb Wintar's services were available, Madzy recorded substantial amounts of family history. One item is a translation and synopsis of a short book that her brother Paul had requested or commissioned Henri Sjollema, a distant cousin,[16] to research and write. This was the story of an ancestor of hers and Henri's named Isaac Rochussen (1631–?), who was a ship's captain.

During the third war between England and Holland (1672–74) Rochussen – no doubt along with other captains – was commissioned by the Dutch government to take any English ship he encountered on the high seas. The captured ship and its cargo would become the property of the Dutch government, and the captain would receive a portion of the proceeds. The fact that such captains were working on a commission from the government (the English term is "letter of marque") meant that they should properly be called corsairs rather than pirates or privateers.

Captain Rochussen captured an English treasure ship, the *Hawk*,[17] and, pursued by the English, sailed to Bergen, in Norway, and then to Germany before (a couple of months later) reaching Amsterdam. With his share of the proceeds he bought a shipyard and became a prosperous merchant and prominent citizen. The story delighted Madzy. She liked Rochussen's seafaring life and his enterprising (but very practical) spirit. The adventurous blood of Isaac Rochussen ran in her veins.

Other family stories that she recorded came from her own memories, some sparked by conversations during Hansje's five visits to Brandstead. Talking about their childhoods, they realized that Madzy, the elder by nine years, remembered much more of their early lives, especially things about their father, who died when Hansje was four. Accordingly, Madzy put some of those memories on tape, in Dutch, for Hansje's children. To friends in B.C., in December 1977, she reports that the tape she first made was such a success that Hansje asked her to do more. So she made four or five one-hour tapes for the family in Holland.

We asked her to make similar ones for us. The project is mentioned in a letter-tape of 31 May 1981 to Tini Sandberg, so she probably began it as soon as the history of Holland had gone to Barb Wintar for the first typing.

These memories – 124 double-spaced pages – are divided into essays ranging from four to twenty-eight pages. Each one is fairly unified, dealing with a particular person or topic or period. The whole thing is extremely readable; she is again the story-teller. There are two or three factual errors (spotted by a cousin of mine) in the sections where she is recording what other people told her, and one or two others that I found, but for the rest they are probably accurate as such memoirs go. For dates and specific career details of the people she dealt with, she drew on the "van Vollenhoven" volume in a series of publications of genealogical information about the gentry families of Holland,[18] and on the genealogy of the Rochussen family.

Chronologically, the account ends when Madzy was in her middle teens. It is a great pity that she went no further: there is no indication whether her stopping had to do with the wish to be reserved about her own life, or whether she ran out of time and energy, or whether she was too ill.

IN THE FALL of 1981 Madzy became interested in Norse mythology and Icelandic sagas. In one of her tapes she says she ordered a set of six paperback volumes of the sagas.

She had read *The Brendan Voyage*, by Tim Severin, the account of a modern-day crossing of the North Atlantic in a leather boat, a replica of the one used by the sixth-century Irish St Brendan. The crossing was successful and showed that the mediaeval accounts of Irish monks reaching North America could be true, whereas, with their encrustation of fabulous elements, they had been regarded as fiction. But if St Brendan's voyage was possible – if it could in fact have been what Madzy calls "pure history" – then what about the Icelandic sagas? She wonders about the concept of "pure history": after repeated copyings by scribes, what is pure history in the mediaeval narrative of St Brendan's voyage (or any such account) and what is embellishment? Where have later copyists made mistakes or omissions?

That led her to reflect on the extent to which family memories handed down orally, like those she recorded about the Dutch East Indies, were "pure history." Most of them are stories that she heard told by her parents and their friends from the Dutch East Indies, or stories she heard about her ancestors and their lives in Holland, rather than things she experienced herself. To what extent are they reliable?

We have two taped versions of this rumination; the first was apparently transcribed, because on the other side of the same tape appears much of the same material, often using identical words but with revisions and additions, as though she were reading aloud from a typescript and revising as she went.

Her interest in things Scandinavian had another facet. She obtained somewhere the "Nordic Issue" (number 18–19, 1980) of *Northward Journal: A Quarterly of Northern Arts*, published by Penumbra Press. It contained the text of a lecture given by J.E.H. MacDonald at the Art Gallery of Ontario in 1931 about an exhibition of Scandinavian art that he and Lawren Harris had seen in Buffalo, New York, in 1913. MacDonald describes how the Scandinavian artists' ways of relating to their subjects, including landscape, influenced the Group of Seven. This connected with Madzy's love of the art and literature of Scandinavia and the Canadian North (she had several little soapstone sculptures standing on the shelf above her bed) and also her own desire to link Europe and North America, to interpret each to the other.

I can picture her lying on her bed, closing her tired eyes and resting her always painful body, with her mind mulling over these things.

DURING THESE same years she was making letter-tapes that provide a vivid chronicle of her world in the late 1970s and early 1980s. She made hundreds, probably five or more in a good week. We have about two dozen that escaped erasure.

In a tape made in June 1977 she mentions that Gerard has just come up to ask her to read a proof of something he was printing. She has been doing this for years, she says, but is still uneasy lest she miss a typographical error. She reads "frontwards" first, then backwards, which removes the sense of the piece and reduces it to a series of individual words. By now she was no longer helping Gerard by inserting paper into the press: he had the local blacksmith make a treadle so that he could do the operation single-handed. She was doing a lot of reading and some cooking, and quite a lot of painting using watercolours or coloured inks.

By the summer of 1979 she had an electric wheelchair and could go into the garden by herself (there were ramps front and back) to do closeup photography of flowers. She had a good camera and a tripod. Cameras and film were probably among the things she discussed with Jock; she had always taken casual photographs of family, children, gardens, and animals, but in these years, while she was still sufficiently mobile, flower photography became quite a serious interest and we have some lovely examples of her work.

The summer and fall of 1981 were particularly busy in terms of visitors, as the tapes make clear. Her teenaged nephew Wiet came for three weeks, and her stewardess-niece Cathrien visited several times. A cousin and her husband arrived unexpectedly; fortunately the guest room was all ready for another visitor who was coming the following week. Old friends from Terrace came, and friends of friends. Other people dropped by to drink a cup of tea. "We aren't sitting forgotten in a corner," Madzy comments.

She knew people came to her because she could not go to them, and she appreciated it, but sometimes the noisy bustle was too much for her. When she was tired, she went to her bedroom to lie down. If she left the door open, it was a signal that a visitor could come in for a private talk, but if the door was closed, she preferred to be alone.

In a tape made on 5 July she reports that both knees are deplorable, and her right shoulder is very painful. In a tape to Jet (Bill's stepmother) in October 1981 she says that on the long weekend in August she had a bad arthritis attack; the doctor came on the holiday Monday to give her an injection and extra pills, but, as always, there was still a lot of pain.

Mostly the tapes were concerned with her activities and outward events. In one to members of Spuit Elf, she mentions having studied mediaeval Latin at UBC; she says she would have liked to go on with that, but now she is learning about the literature of Scandinavia. Mediaeval literature, including the sagas, was an area of interest that she and I shared; my postgraduate work had been in Old English literature, and as an undergraduate I had used a textbook from one of her courses. On the flyleaf, in her handwriting, is a list of the sections to be covered in the course, and the book is now annotated in both our handwritings.

THE LETTER-TAPES vary in the amount of insight they give into her inner life, depending on whom she was addressing and on her mood and physical condition. One of the people to whom she could be most open was Tini Sandberg. In a tape to Tini on 25 July 1977, Madzy said that there was less and less for her to do because her body was deteriorating. Her elbows were swollen and extremely painful. No medicine, apparently, could overcome the constant pain, though some amelioration was possible. Her knees "burn," while the elbows "gnaw." And, she points out, one uses one's arms all the time. Operating the tape recorder hurt, and so did drawing. She was depressed, but she fought it; she had always done that, but it took more effort now. She could keep herself busy, but what she was able to do was not enough to give her satisfaction. She is a person who does not often reveal what is happening inside her, she says, but sometimes it is good to talk about it if you can, and she can say anything to Tini.

In a tape of 1 January 1982 to Jet she says that the worst thing about ageing and ailing is that she is losing her autonomy. Decisions are taken out of her hands, and she can't stand it. Hearing this now, hearing her say it in her own voice, I wonder whether we were insensitive. Perhaps, rather, it was that she and we differed in our assessment of her needs – but that was partly because she did not tell us what she told Jet on this tape. In that tragic ruin of a body dwelt a lively, independent spirit; we did what we could to support and nourish it. But the body had very different needs than the spirit. It would have been difficult for any caregiver to have met all her needs adequately and at the same time.

On most of the tapes, the writer in her is present, setting the scene. In a tape for Tini on 25 July 1977 she mentions that it is two o'clock in the afternoon. A strong wind is blowing; the window is wide open and Tini can probably hear the wind in the trees. The sound reminds her of the waves of the sea; it is repetitive, like music. She is alone in the house. Gerard is in Spain in the course of his two-month trip to Europe; Bill, with a borrowed tractor and trailer, is bringing firewood in from the woods. She expects him to come in shortly for a cup of tea.

On another tape she describes how she has her hair cut. For a year or two Gerard had done it, but now she has found a hairdresser near McMaster University, "Mr Jens of Denmark," to whose shop Bill drives her. Mr Jens cuts Madzy's hair while she is sitting in her wheelchair, and by some arrangement she never has to wait.

She takes pleasure in the fact that Gerard is becoming well known as an engraver and maker of handmade books. *Flora*, the book he recently issued, is selling very well, to the surprise of everyone in view of its cost. She reports that Folly, the survivor of the two dogs she has had for years, has now also died; Tini, a dog-lover herself, had urged her to get another dog, but so far she hasn't. (The family gave her, for her birthday in August 1980, a West Highland terrier called Katie.) Lies will be arriving in a week, and Tini will come for a visit in the fall.

In December, after Tini's visit, Madzy makes a tape telling Tini that she gave her inner strength. When you're handicapped, she remarks, people regard you as being a bit special and treat you differently. She hates being called brave and special, and has to remind herself that she is an ordinary person with faults. To illustrate, she refers to a foolish thing she said when she and Tini were working in the kitchen. Tini had said the thermometer that Madzy used for making yoghurt was glass: Madzy maintained it was plastic. A few weeks later, Madzy accidentally broke the thermometer, and of course it *was* glass, as she should have known all along. But she thanks Tini for holding her peace, for her wise and warm friendship.

She told Tini that she always dreaded causing people grief; we in the family recognized that that was one of her guiding principles. She tended to feel that the frictions inevitable in family life were her fault – errors of omission if not of commission. She would sometimes lament, "I do so much my best!"

As her world narrowed physically, no doubt she felt all these things more; the life and personalities around her must have sent her delicately balanced seismograph fluctuating wildly. The narrower her life became in physical scope, the more sensitive she was to disturbances and the greater the need for the private space she created with her intellectual and creative work. She told me at that time that when she was alone, she was often in low spirits.

On the tape to Tini she describes the scene outside the window – snow on evergreens – with a painterly eye. When you bring the green into the foreground and ignore the white, you get one kind of pattern; when you focus on the white and regard the green as background, it is entirely different.

In the spring she reports that she is still able to work on her stamp collection, and talks about it at some length. (For her, stamp-collecting was a means of learning more about geography, and about developments such as the breaking up of the overseas empires of European nations.) Don, Gerard's partner, has gone to a stamp collectors' convention in Ottawa and brought back a few stamps for her. She explains the importance of New-

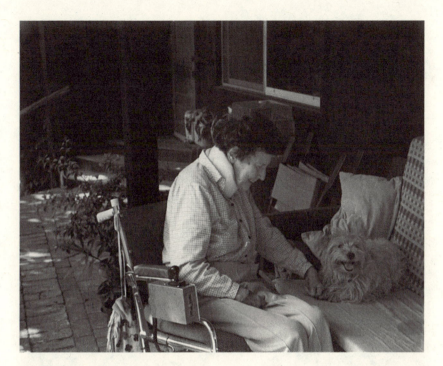

Madzy with Katie, her last dog

Winter scene

foundland stamps dating from before Newfoundland joined Confederation. Gerard and Don have built a small greenhouse onto their kitchen and are becoming interested in orchids. Marianne and Gerard are working on a book about pioneer life in Ontario. (*The Tinderbox* would be published by The Porcupine's Quill in August 1982.)

In October 1981 she makes a tape for the whole of Spuit Elf, who had made a joint tape for her at one of their gatherings. She reflects how, at the time of emigration, you don't realize the importance of some of the things you leave behind. She says that she is not severely homesick now; all the same, she will play their tape over and over again and is glad that there are still such strong bonds. Then she tells them about the taping of her memories, and about the Dutch history project, and about her interest in Norse sagas. She hasn't quite "gone to sleep."

She reports on her condition. She wears a neck brace, and she can't walk or stand but, in her electric wheelchair, can still do a lot of little chores in the house. She and Bill make it easy for themselves. Bill has reduced the size of the garden, which was producing more vegetables than they could handle. Every week they eat a chicken out of the freezer (as I recall, mostly as chicken à la king). They have their own fruit, eggs, milk. Five times a week after breakfast she makes yoghurt in a yoghurt maker. She makes both coffee and tea in the coffee maker (using different carafes). She works with a blender. Irene Prine comes once a week.

On 31 August 1982, she made a tape to her niece Cathrien, now married and no longer a stewardess and therefore no longer coming regularly to Brandstead. She reports that *The Tinderbox* came out the previous day and that everyone is busy preparing lists for invitations to the launching. Belinda the goat has had to be put down on account of age. Gerard has eight bantam ducks; he made a pond for them which they refuse to use. Don was in Newfoundland for three weeks; Gerard went to spend the last week there with him. Don is trying out new kinds of flowers in the garden and brings little bouquets to Madzy.

It is the texture of ordinary life; what is noticeable is her effort to stay connected to it. Her world was very small by now; she seldom left the house and was in touch with only as much of the outside world as she could see through the windows and what we brought to her. She watched TV only occasionally. She is right when she says that we treated her as someone special: she was special in her needs but also in her character and personality. She herself did all she could to keep her mind alive and we, respecting and valuing that effort for our sake as well as hers, did what we could to enrich her world, both the outer and the inner.

ABOUT THE end of 1981 I found for her what was called a Memowriter, a hand-held calculator that also had a small alphabet keyboard. On a narrow roll of paper, it would print three lines of text (about ten words) at a time. She was delighted with it; in a letter to me written on the Memowriter she says:

> When you found this writer for me, you did not know what you did for me; you gave my own words back to me! A particular word is formed by a very special mind and when that word looks at you, you recognize it as your very own. When you speak a word on a tape, it is lost in limbo and when you listen back to it, it does not belong to you any more. When you see it again, typed by someone, it looks a stranger to you, but my hands cannot make many corrections. Therefore I have to accept second-hands. But not anymore. Now I can look a word in the face and that comes straight from my brain on this paper like a special line or shading of a drawing. Thanks ever so much for all the trouble you took for me.

She phrases it a bit awkwardly – correcting on the Memowriter was impossible, and she was still learning its limitations – but her meaning is clear. I imagine her lying on the bed or couch, mulling this over with eyes closed, drawn into her inner world of ideas where she *could* be autonomous, and then painfully, her twisted and limp fingers picking the text out one letter at a time, recording her ideas in a form that I would receive in the mail a few days later – and, rereading it twenty years after that, feel again the close and vivid contact with her mind, her perceptions.

In 1982 she began a diary on the Memowriter, but stopped after a few days. What she wrote, however, gives the best glimpse we have into her inner life at this time.

> 29 April 1982.[19] Ever since I finished my latest project, the history of Holland compared to that of England, I have had a sad sense of loss, of emptiness. I was searching for a new subject that would fill my thoughts and my time, but the only project that would occur to me was a sort of diary, to put my thoughts down which whirl in my head constantly and keep on crying to be let out! Of course, I thought of my tape recorder, but I could never give them to a typist: they will be too private; moreover, it is so hard if you want to find something back that you want to correct. And then my eye fell on my Memo-writer. Would it be possible? By little bits? And by sticking them in

Madzy in old age, the signs of illness and pain clearly visible – and courage too

a scribbler? And in short bits so as not to get too tired? One can try at least!

Apr. 30. 82 This is the actual first day of my diary-product. I must as yet find my way, for my aim is to be as free + uninhibited in putting down my very inner thoughts knowing that noone will read them as long as I live. After my death I donot care what one thinks or knows of me; the more of me and my thoughts the better; for then they won't put me on an unearned piedestal.[20] Rather let my real self [appear]; something I so often try to hide. For they often think or pretend to think that I am a better or more honest person than I am. This really bothers or worries me. As I have promised myself to be as true to myself as humanly possible, though I think that no one can see himself as he really is, but always makes excuses for his actions, and truly believes in his self-deception or estimation. This project will have to cope with 2 obstacles: my arm soon tires and aches, and where can I hide it? The first one means that I have to be short or work in short periods; the second is absolutely necessary for my freedom of expression and this last one: freedom in movement, speech, actions, decisions. Much as he [Bill?] tries, I feel the vigilance, often expressed in loving care for me, or hidden disapproval and irritation and I give in. How many times I have silently given in I cannot say. It feels like a crushing mountain. Is it worth it? I cannot answer that; it is partly caused by my character, partly by the circumstances. There is one more obstacle to this project: where to put it hidden safely? I have so little privacy now I gave my den away.[21] I cannot yet solve it. Bathroom drawer? Still am searching.

She does not continue in this introspective vein; the entries for the next two days deal with the war in the Falkland Islands (having two sons of "fighting" age, she feared another world war) and then with a sudden and worrisome swelling of one of her legs. There it ends; the rest of the scribbler – in which she pasted the strips – is empty.

Her observation about being on a pedestal shows a remarkably clear and objective view of how others regarded her. (The verb tense is misleading, implying as it does that she thought she would be put on a pedestal after her death: in fact, she had been on one for much of her life, and I imagine she was thinking of that too.) People admired her and told her so. She was praised for her courage and endurance in the war, for the support and help she provided to others as well as her own children, for keeping the family together and alive. She was admired for the way she tackled emigration and pioneer farming. She was constantly admired for the way she lived with the handicaps and pain of arthritis. She was admired for her intellect, her ability to maintain the life of the mind through all the occupations and distractions of her life. She was respected – and very much loved – by almost all of the many people whose lives she touched. Despite her disclaimer, the pedestal was earned.

But a pedestal isolates. Her self-created image could only be achieved by mostly hiding considerable areas of her life, her total self. Glimpses of her "real self," which she regarded as weakness, were just the reality of being human; she, however, with the high standards she set for herself, always regarded them as lamentable, embarrassing lapses. We could not, with any assurance, guess at what lay behind the outer, public manner when it was securely in place. Often, no doubt, the optimistic and cheerful manner was genuine. We rarely questioned it: she had always been that way.

It appears from this passage as though she would have liked to climb down from the pedestal. She didn't want to be treated as someone special. She occasionally spoke of being lonely. One of her continuing worries about me was that I was or would be lonely; I have no doubt that she was transferring to me some of her own experience of isolation. In the last months of her life she remarked to Gerard that, confined to bed, she was lonely; accordingly, he began doing book stitching or some other portable work in her room. Her admission is remarkable; knowing her, that brief observation would be only the merest hint of the magnitude of what she was really feeling.

In her last months, in fact, she was no longer cheery, though she tried to be tranquil, and she made what must sometimes have been a great effort to be an easy patient. She faced dying with courage and resignation, outwardly calm. Everyone continued to admire her. Only she knew the exact dimensions of the pedestal.

SHE WROTE other things on the Memowriter. On the occasion of Gerard's birthday, probably in 1982, she wrote a poem to accompany the gift that she and Don were giving him:[22]

> Brandstead is, as someone says,
> A rather pleasant-enough place.
> And people come and like to stay
> As long as they aren't chased away!
> Alas, Don has one stone to throw:

Too many birthdays in a row![23]
Just recently he had to buy
More cakes and cookies, the poor guy!
And presents, too, on top of that!
His wallet never was so flat.
And Madzy had the same complaint:
Is there still money? No, there ain't!
So please don't tell it to a soul:
For Ger gets nothing ... but ... a ... hole!!
If he won't like it? *Soit!* In vain!
He can just go fill it again!
A hole is all he gets for sure;
Next year we might not be so poor.
With our best wishes and regrets
For this non-present he now gets!!

Gerard can not remember what the "hole" was; nor can Don.

The loss of autonomy, which she hated so much, showed itself in a poignant way in relation to money. Now almost everything was paid for by other people, though she did write cheques (for instance, for the books she ordered from remainder catalogues). But it felt wrong to her not to have some ready cash available. After she talked it over with me, I put $20 in small bills and coins in a drawer of the desk in my room at Brandstead. I don't believe she ever used it, but the important thing was knowing it was there.

Another glimpse into her inner life came from Gerard. He told me that she was afraid that, because of her deteriorating body, we would not want to touch her. To demonstrate that we did, he regularly brushed her hair, which was unaffected by the illness – still wavy, hardly grey – and she loved that.

IN OCTOBER 1980, Madzy's first grandchild (the only one she was to see) was born to Jock and Suzanna, a boy christened Darwin William Taylor. In a letter-tape on 8 May 1982 she tells Jet that on the previous day Suzanna had come with William to get plants for her garden. Madzy is enthusiastic about William. She can't remember precisely what her own children had been like at nineteen months of age, she says, but she is full of wonder at William. She admits that she may be rather a doting grandmother but says that she has always been fond of children and always enjoyed her own, was interested in them and their difficulties and studies. She is trying to figure out whether there is something that she can make for William: perhaps a jigsaw puzzle.

On other tapes she says that William has learned not to tamper with the electric wheelchair, and not to try to grab fish in the aquarium.

IN A TAPE to Jet in early September 1982 she gives another snapshot of her life. Jet had sent her the money for a very small TV set to have beside her bed, and Madzy thanks her. The screen is about 10 by 12 cm, Madzy says. She reports that she is becoming more and more "lazy," but that everyone encourages her to take it easy because it will spare her body a bit. She spends more time lying down, and has everything handy by her bed. On the shelves over the bed are her books. She has the Memowriter and "a little office."

She says that she has, hanging on the wall of her bedroom, a painting of a scene near Maarn in the snow, painted by a friend of those days, which makes her feel occasionally as though she is in Maarn. Beyond her windows are the trees of Brandstead, and sky, and sometimes the goats, which Bill brings to the lawn for her to see. She can still go outdoors, although the jolting of the wheelchair over the uneven ground hurts her. She says she enjoys everything, that Brandstead is a beautiful place, that all she misses are the people in Holland, but that they and everyone else spoil her. She ends the tape saying that she has to go and make lunch.

ON 5 SEPTEMBER 1982, she had another severe attack. I learned about it when Gerard phoned to tell me that her good eye had suddenly become misty and almost blind. She had been frightened and crying. Everyone was edgy: Gerard had a bad cold. Bill was facing a hernia operation. Don was ill with a stomach problem.

My teaching kept me from going to Brandstead immediately, but when I was able to talk to her on the phone, I found her exhausted and "rather depressed." She kept wanting to go to sleep. In my journal I wrote that I wondered if she meant "sleep" in a more profound way.

Some days after the attack, she was taken by ambulance to an eye specialist who diagnosed glaucoma, with complications. He said that it was not just a temporary condition and that the only known remedy was risky and uncertain. Instead of this drastic measure, she was given drops and pills; every two weeks from then on, she and Bill went by ambulance to the hospital in Hamilton so that her eyes could be checked and she could be given drops.

This episode marked a distinct setback in her overall condition. She was permanently in bed for the two years of life that remained to her. In a letter to Anne Eyolfson on 4 December, I say that we had been afraid that she might not pull through. But she did, only to suffer from an attack of gallstones in January that had her in the hospital for ten days. Bill told me that, when he kissed her goodnight during that time, she often said that she hoped she would not wake up the next morning.

Among her papers is a scrawled fragment on a page cut out of a scribbler. The handwriting is so shaky that some words are illegible. It is undated; I place it here because it refers to an occasion when her one good eye failed her.

This is the entire piece.

> When stretching on bed with a book I [illegible] to see it raining. But instead [illegible] impenetrable glass curtain blocking all vision I still had then I went to sleep. Thanks to a meeting I was brought in an ambulance and [illegible] the next day my same sight was back. I saw the alarm clock as before. Miracle. Today it is as before, but I must not use the eye. My body is poor, can't sit anymore [illegible] so my drawings are less and I shall try to practice on piano.
>
> The days are long and I have to improvise, all daily little chores. But to tell the truth, I [am] soon tired and long to lie [down], that I am [glad?] to be home. Also I still have forgotten to write without faults.

Her mind is confused, or she is unable to include details that would explain some of what seems obscure. The confusion could well be the result of the shock and the medications; her mind was to clear again later. Yet she is obstinately continuing to write, to record how it felt to be Madzy. Nothing could demonstrate more clearly how important the writing (and the writing of autobiography) was to her.

ONE PROJECT, undertaken about a year earlier, mainly by Bill and Gerard, was the putting together of some of her earlier writings for publication. This became a book called *The Scent of Spruce*, published in 1984 by the Netherlandic Press, a small publishing house operated in Windsor, Ontario, by Henny Ruger and Joan Magee. The book includes the story of the Dutch church bell, an excerpt from *Land for Our Sons*, and four of the stories published in the *Atlantic Advocate*. Gerard provided scratchboard illustrations. Madzy helped to choose the selections and wrote a letter on the Memowriter to Henny Ruger, and the book came out while she was still able to enjoy it.

SHE SPENT the last portion of her life at home, as she wished. Bill and Gerard cared for her with the assistance of VON nurses, and Jock and I did what we could with visits and phone calls and help. After the glaucoma attack of September 1982, her life narrowed further: she was unable to use her den any longer, so it became Bill's den. Her car was sold long after it had become evident that she would never drive again.

I spent the August long weekend of 1984 at Brandstead; Gerard and Don were away, and I went to be company for Madzy and Bill as well as to have a few quiet days away from Toronto. I was preparing for the fall's teaching; it was a hot, humid weekend. I had just finished a year's unpaid leave, during which (after years of research) I had written most of my book *Elizabeth, Duchess of Somerset*, and had put it aside to begin preparation for the academic year. I talked to Madzy about the book, my mind still full of the research and writing. She asked good questions. In my journal I recorded that when I leaned over to kiss her goodnight, "she was beautiful as old people are beautiful when age has pared them down." The next night, however, "that look was gone."

That weekend was the last time I had a real conversation with her; in the weeks that followed, her mind became slower; she gave the impression of withdrawing from us – not unnaturally, because by then her hearing had been failing for some time, as well as her vision. She was in as much pain as ever, and also had a large bedsore. I went to Brandstead most weekends, and did what I could by bringing supplies like linen and once a new pillow.

A few days before her death, according to Gerard's account, she asked for morphine. The doctor talked it over with her, pointing out that it would shorten her life, then talked to Bill and Gerard, then talked to Madzy again. She received morphine.

On the night of 4 October, her breathing became very deep and harsh, and she was in a coma. At one o'clock in the morning Bill phoned Gerard. When he entered the room, Gerard noticed that the catheter bag hanging beside her bed was not filling, so that probably her kidneys had stopped functioning. He and Bill sat with her, and in the early hours of 5 October 1984, she died without any visible signs of struggle or pain.

Blackberry leaves

MADZY IS off-stage now, insofar as she ever will be, and I am in front of the closed curtain speaking the epilogue. I have been with her, recreating something of her life, following her tracks, talking to people she talked to, reading books she read – above all, reading her own words and listening to her voice. The experience has enriched and enlarged me, and also saddened me because it is so much a story of ...

I was going to say of unrealized potential, handicap, and limitation, of a life that might have gone so differently. But whose is the life of which that cannot be said?

Unrealized potential? It is *almost* possible to imagine Madzy remaining unmarried, or working in the Arctic, or being an eminent linguist, researcher, professor, or sailing around the world single-handed. As a matter of fact, the war years, as survival tests go, were not so very different from solo sailing. Emigration and pioneer farming were as much adventures in their own way as any of these endeavours.

I can almost imagine these alternative lives, but they would not necessarily have been more fulfilling for her. Had she lived any of them, her aptitude for being wife, mother, and homemaker would have been less developed, or not at all, and that would have meant not realizing *that* potential.

As with so many people, her life was not "either/or" but both "a bit of this *and* a bit of that" – a collage of compromises, adaptations, inventiveness. It is a story of opportunities seized, recognized, or created where there appeared to be none, and, towards the end, of using a blank wall as a support for flowering plants.

I COME BACK again and again to her own words: "After my death I do not care what one thinks or knows of me; the more of me and my thoughts the better, for then they won't put me on an unearned pedestal. Rather let my real self appear, something I so often try to hide."

Why did she try to hide it? She was, in part, driven by the Victorian ideal of the wife and mother subordinating her needs and wishes to her family's – self-denial as duty, and as a way to earn self-esteem and the admiration of others, to make oneself important in spite of the self-denial (a neat paradox). The self-denial was, in fact, a more complicated thing than appeared on the surface, less conditioned, more analyzed and deliberate. She did not inherit it from her mother, who seems not to have been a self-denying woman. It came partly, I think, from Madzy's innate character. First articulated in the war diary, in some way – now obscure – it was connected with guilt and atonement. By the time she was writing the autobiographical fragments in Terrace in 1954, she was giving a good deal of thought to it, carefully considering the extent to which self-denial was a way of making her feel good.

At the end of the Terrace period, she began to try to satisfy more of her personal needs – taking a course, writing a book, returning to university. The inner world of writing became steadily more important, though she never neglected her family. The paid work she did, however, had probably at least as much to do with self-fulfilment as with earning money.

The issue of self-denial is connected with her separating her inner life from the outer, perhaps because both involve a playing of roles. She had an innate need for a private world. This was, I think, not just a matter of concealment but also creating a psychic space for herself. She cherished that world, because in it she did not have to deny her own needs and wishes.

Shutting us out of much of her inner life may also have been a way of protecting us. What she was hiding (though we caught glimpses, saw signs) was a woman who was independent, adventurous, exuberant, often naïve and insecure; who was frustrated, angry, sometimes depressed and desperately frightened – and who, had she emerged more frequently, would have upset the atmosphere of harmonious and cheerful busyness that was the family ideal.

Whatever her reasons for keeping us out, I regret it. Our lives might have been richer – though more turbulent – had her inner life been more visible. Her last writings show that she regretted it too, and knew that it could no longer be changed. She shared some of her intellectual enthusiasms with us, and a small portion of her pain and fear, not very much of her anger and anguish and despair, and only some of her thinking and her literary creativity. By limiting the areas where we could interact with her, she cut us all off from a deeper understanding and emotional connectedness. The times when she showed her anguish and despair at the moment of experiencing them – rather than putting them on tape, in small snippets, for people who were thousands of miles away, or on paper which no one would see in her lifetime – were rare and illuminating. A stiff upper lip was as much in her tradition as the British. At one level this can make life easier for everyone, but the cost of such self-control is incalculable. We were only ever relating to some parts of her. If she thought that we would not love her for what she really was, how mistrustful she was of us!

She was mistrustful in other ways too. She frequently expected other people to be less capable, especially of enduring boredom and stress, than she herself was. This was considerateness, but also arrogance: she felt that others were made of less stern stuff than she was and must be spared.

She was selective in her friendships, partly perhaps out of shyness and reserve, partly because she was able to meet many of her intellectual and emotional needs within the family and in books. She disliked small talk and superficial sociability; she preferred people who shared her interests and experiences, people with whom intellectual engagement was possible. She had little interest in talk about housekeeping, shopping, clothes – and, I suspect, a very limited one in stories of other people's children and pets.

Gerard suggested recently that perhaps she was so steeped in the past that she was looking for kinds of people who no longer existed – or were to be found only in books. Such people were always rare – she may not really have reckoned with the extent to which books, whether fiction or non-fiction, are selective in their reflection of "reality." It is very possible that she had a mental image of a society of artists and philosophers, of high-minded conversation about books and art and ideas – along with simple living close to nature. No doubt she realized that this was an extremely high ideal.

She retained a good deal that was Victorian, including the rebellion of late-Victorian women against the restrictions of their lives, their conviction that they could invent a new world for themselves, mainly through education. But if she looked backward in some ways, she was in advance of her time in others – in the vanguard, for example, in studying law. Her love of easy and casual ways would have led her to feel at home in later times than hers. She would, I think, have been totally at home in the environmental movement, partly but not completely in the women's movement.

Unquestionably she came to Canada with an unrealistic (and probably unexamined) image of the life she would encounter here: did she really expect to find a circle of kindred spirits like those she had found in Leiden, and those who had been her neighbours through the war? Women like that exist in Canada, and she met and made friends with some, but it did not prove easy to find them. In Canada such people are likely to be dispersed rather than – as is possible in tiny Holland – near enough for frequent contact.

Yet she was much loved by those who knew her – who interacted with her at whatever level. She had a strong desire to help others. She was mostly cheerful – and being cheerful requires courage, as she herself had remarked in the war diary. Her expectations of herself were high – and I don't know how often she felt that she lived up to them.

A sense of guilt was an important strand in her personality: for her as for the Victorians, a mistake was not just an error but a sin, because the mistaken choice or action came from one's weak and flawed character. She blamed herself for many of the things that went wrong in the family, especially in the relations among us. Her phrase "I do so much my best!" was couched as a lament but perhaps was sometimes a reproach: she was doing *her* best, and why were other people not responding as she expected?

Looking back, I'm astonished to realize again how varied she was in her character, her interests, her aptitudes, and how willing – *eager* – to change and adapt and evolve. A strong core sense of her identity must have helped. That identity was, I think, a good deal maimed and scarred by the war, though in some respects also strengthened. From then on she combined a painful vulnerability and dependence on the family with a continuing need for independence and privacy, for room to grow and develop and explore. Some stages of her life were more propitious for that than others, but the struggle between the need for space and the need for shelter – for both frontiers and sanctuaries – was perpetual, and only occasionally was she able to achieve some equilibrium.

She was decisive and certain about some things, unsure about many others. She had a joy in life, a zest for living, along with profound sadness and awareness of suffering. She yearned to be free but needed safety; she sought privacy but dreaded loneliness. She needed the space and natural surroundings of rural life but also the intellectual and cultural stimulus of cities. She needed both Canada and Europe. In fact, it is unlikely that she *could* have found anywhere a place where she would entirely fit and be rooted and content.

MADZY'S CREATIVITY cannot be assessed by looking only at the work she published, either its quantity or its quality. She focused on the content of what she wrote and considered few stylistic aspects beyond clarity – understandable especially when she was writing in her second language.

In published work, her intention to educate and/or entertain her readers was restricting. In *Land for Our Sons* she concentrates on the good aspects of immigration and life on the farm. Of the published fiction, only in one or two of the *Atlantic Advocate* stories has she included darker elements. Even in work meant for the family, she imposed this limitation on herself: in the tape based on the war diary, she says she wants to tell just the happy stories – though in fact she talks a good deal about the hardship and stress. It is in the war diary and other writings that we found after her death that the real darkness appears. Because of this difference between what her published and unpublished work reveal of her inner life, my access to diaries and autobiographical fragments has been essential.

Writing to be published affected what she wrote. If she wanted to see her work in print – and she did – she had to write for the market. At that time there were fewer opportunities for female and "ethnic" writers. She had no contacts in the literary world; her physical disabilities and the choices she made in her social life prevented her from making them.

She could have discussed her work with me, but she showed me only what was already in print. She never (to my recollection) raised questions about structure and other literary matters, only occasionally about historical data or the translation of a specific phrase or concept. Possibly she was shy about letting me read things with which she was dissatisfied. But I think the most important reason was simply that she wanted to do it her way.

Language was a factor in how she felt about her work: she was never as much at ease in English as in Dutch. Physical limitations were another: in later years, when she was having her taped work transcribed, she was unable to do more than the barest minimum of research, planning, and revision. What she did within those limits indicates the extent of her dedication and determination.

Gerard suggests she might be regarded as "a woman of letters," someone who valued and respected the written word and used it not merely as a way of chronicling events but also as a tool for exploration and dissemination of ideas. I agree. The need to write was, for her, probably more important than being published; by putting her thoughts on paper or tape, she constantly reasserted her identity and the existence of her private space.

Her other creative work, too, was mostly private. Her paintings hang on our walls but were only once, early on, publicly shown; her flower photography is in our albums and trays of slides. The vibrant creativity she expressed in life-making for herself and the family and others now exists mainly in our memories.

AS HER OWN world narrowed physically, her spirit reached outward; *The Brendan Voyage* no doubt appealed to her in part because it is a story of adventure and survival: the crew set off into the unknown, with their sailing experience and common sense and little more than a mediaeval manuscript as a guide. Similarly, every project she herself undertook was a voyage into the unknown. She was steering a vessel that had somehow to cope with devastating handicap and at times intolerable and maddening pain. She had no models, not even a mediaeval manuscript, for the vessel that would still give sufficient scope for her mind, her sense of adventure, her need to achieve something worthwhile; she was figuring it out as she went along. As long as possible, she maintained her identity and her inner and outer life, and as much normality as could be achieved. She was applying her creativity to the task of keeping her spirit alive. Her whole life was a journey of exploration and a test of character.

WHEN I began this project, I had misgivings about writing Madzy's biography: wasn't this a dreadful invasion? And yet the story gripped me, not only because I am her daughter and was her friend but also because I recognized a good yarn. As I worked with her papers, however, and realized that she had been writing autobiography all her life – fragmented, half-disguised, overt, detailed, fictionalized – my misgivings disappeared. Underneath the intensely private person, there was another Madzy who wanted to tell her story. Before long, I realized that I was working *with* her, in affectionate, respectful, and fascinated cooperation.

One of the curious and unexpected aspects of this work – of my double role as daughter and biographer – is that while Madzy was alive she "framed" me, but in the course of writing this book I have come to "frame" her. My framing of her is only partial; I'm aware of how much I don't know about her, how much will always remain private. But the reversal has been interesting and sometimes rather unsettling.

A biography of a writer deals with silences as well as words. Not only does the biographer sometimes have to guess about things not dealt with by the writer but she has to notice and reflect on the *fact* of silences. Some are accidental, a result of lost documents and information, or lack of time for writing diaries and other work, but quite a lot is deliberate. Even the autobiographical writings not meant for publication reveal only one more level, not the whole person, and I know that the dichotomy between outer and inner is not clear cut. Even the most "private" writings give no more than glimpses, but that is all that we ever have of each other at the best.

My earlier work as a historian and a writer of biography and autobiography had made me aware of the invisible things that lie behind and among what survives in the historical record. In this book I had more than the paper record; I drew on my own and my father's and brothers' memories of Madzy's spoken words, behaviour, tastes and choices, fears and wishes – the aspects of a life and personality that, if not recorded, are not found in the archives. I "read" her belongings. I still own a couple of sweaters of hers – men's sizes because of her long arms – and a pair of winter boots. I have hand-potted mugs and jugs that she bought, marked-up books, the small lap-desk that Bill made for her, a few things she wove on a small loom.

One night in the course of working on this project I had a dream that was probably about the limits of biography. In it I came across a book that had belonged to Madzy, with some annotations by her, and between the pages dozens of pieces of paper on which she had written. As I leafed back and forth through the book, I kept finding more. Finally I held up the book by its covers and shook, and even more slips of paper fell out. I had the sense that the book was the real life that she had led, and that I was not allowed to read it but was permitted to read the annotations and the notes on the loose scraps. I don't remember actually wanting to read the book; I know very well that it is impossible for any person to know and see and feel another person's life from the inside. But I was delighted to be allowed to read those fragments.

As for privacy – death is publicity, because what is left behind becomes the property of others. But it is also privacy. The last exposure, the last privacy.

Appendix 1
Sources, Dating, Translation, and the Use of Family Archives

This book is based to a considerable extent on Madzy's own writings, tapes, and photo albums, mentioned and quoted from in the text. What the text does not convey is the bulk of that material. The unpublished work fills a cardboard box (the kind designed for the storage of office files); outsize items like my baby book and the two volumes of the war diary – which is about 80,000 words in length – are stored separately. The family memories that Madzy taped and had transcribed fill a ring binder. The typed version of the translation of the war diary fills another. When I played the audio tapes (letters, research tapes, narrative tapes) I made notes or verbatim transcriptions, depending on the nature of the material; these notes would fill yet another binder.

Bill's writings on the genealogy of his and Madzy's families and on his youth and early adulthood are substantial. In addition, I asked him innumerable questions connected with this book, generating more paper. Gerard contributed memories in written and spoken form; Jock provided recollections and information, as did Madzy's other family and her friends.

In addition, I referred to the journal that I began writing in my late teens. The letters I wrote to Anne Eyolfson from 1971 to 1996, which she recently returned to me, contained invaluable details about Madzy during the latter part of her life and were a useful supplement to my journal.

Non-written sources were also important. Madzy's painting and photographs – the subjects chosen, the media used – reflected her interests and taste. Many of our family photos were taken by her, and she put together almost all the albums, so that the layout and captions reflect her interests, priorities, and idiom.

I took into account such of her belongings as we still have. Many of her books disappeared during the moves since her death, but we have several dozen, some with her annotations. We have pictures and ornaments that she bought, a couple of ceramic geese, small Inuit sculptures. The armchair in which she sat by the fireplace at Brandstead is in the room where I am writing, and the desk that she inherited from her mother is in my living room. I have her "third" typewriter. Gerard and I have tea-services that came from her mother to her and then to us. I have a tablecloth and napkins embroidered with an MV monogram, and some jewellery, including her father's signet ring, which she herself wore for years.

MADZY'S SERIOUSNESS about her writing is shown by the persistence with which she saved it, beginning when she was in the United States and continuing through emigration to Canada and many moves after that. We did not bring much furniture with us to Canada, and only a few books and paintings, but her writings came with us and were always preserved.

Some of her work has been lost. One item is a children's story about animals that she wrote during or just after the war, which she typed in instalments and put in a ring binder. I asked Hansje whether Madzy gave it to her children but was unable to trace it. Of the thousands of letters she wrote, we have only a few dozen.

A bigger loss is that of the diary she kept from 1947 until the time when she was no longer able to write – thirty years of the personal and family record, in small lockable volumes, five years per volume. She asked Bill to destroy them all. No one ever saw the contents. I deeply regret this loss – while respecting her wishes that it be destroyed. But the very fact that she wanted it destroyed and other writings kept is evidence that her other work was meant for people to see.

After her death, Bill handed me a cardboard box in which the surviving papers were roughly stacked, asking whether I thought they were worth keeping. I said I would look through them; the possibility of writing a biography crossed my mind, but it was years before I was able to begin thinking seriously about it. Bill and Gerard and I discussed it in February 1998; I was writing another book at the time but I began going through Madzy's papers, reading and filing.

I enjoyed the work. I liked handling the old onionskin carbons with their disintegrating edges and their rusty paperclips – one of which was circular, a design now extinct, so far as I know. I learned things about Madzy, met a woman and a person who had been in some ways nearly a stranger. I learned more than I had known about our ancestors, and about myself. My knowledge of Dutch improved greatly, and was further developed by the need to translate from Dutch into English.

I learned new ways of reading, and learned to put Madzy's early (and often naïve) writings into context. I benefited from the experience I had gained in my own writing, mainly historical fiction and memoirs, which involved a careful reconstruction, recreation, and reimagination of the past. But this time I explored new ways of interacting with documents without the mediation of scholars and editors.

Organizing the material was, at first, a matter of dividing it into fiction, non-fiction, and memoirs and other personal writings. But the more closely I read and reread her work, the more I realized that this classification was inadequate. In her newspaper columns there are glimpses of our family life, and in the fiction there are settings and characters that, in a more or less direct way, are pictures of what I know and remember. This gives her work unity as well as complexity, and enriches both "fact" and "fiction."

Dating manuscripts was a constant problem. I learned to look for references and allusions, to consider layout and type of paper, handwriting and kinds of pen used in revision. The light that one piece threw on another could indicate the order of composition. I made a close study of the three different typewriters Madzy had, irritating Bill and Gerard by poking about for any information that would tell me when she bought the second one.

Much of Madzy's work was in English, but for the first thirty-seven years – exactly half – of her life she lived and wrote in Dutch. Even during the two years she spent in the United States, all her writing was in Dutch. Bill roughly translated the war diary and, most important, identified places and people for me; I fine-tuned his translation of the passages that I needed, and did other translations where necessary, trying to reflect the tone and style of the original. Madzy was good at capturing Dutch idiom and also – especially in the writing not meant for publication – at conveying her own state of mind and mood. For the kind of writing I was doing, dealing with her inner life as well as the outer, it was essential to bring out those nuances. When quoting Madzy's work, I did minimal editing, because the tentativeness of the writing is part of the meaning, and the awkward expressions reveal the intensity of her focus.

The account of the war years is based on Madzy's and Bill's own writings, with only occasional reference to the large picture. Others who were in Holland at the time, or in POW camps, will no doubt have had different experiences, and research since then may have filled in parts of the picture that were to Madzy and Bill a blank. I did not attempt to deal with the war as a whole, or to put Madzy's account in a larger perspective. The important thing was to keep the immediacy of her experience and her day-by-day account of it. No doubt there are a few factual inaccuracies in her narratives about the war and about the Dutch East Indies. Except for the most obvious ones, or where there clearly was a problem caused by language or by the the process of recording, I did not correct them.

In everything, of course, I was both daughter and biographer, combining the material from the sources with my own memories, enriching each by merging it with the other.

AS I WORKED with the sources, I realized that I was witnessing how autobiography gets written, exploring the roots – usually invisible – of "finished" autobiography. What I had in front of me were various kinds of material, some published and some not, a mosaic of many thoughts and moods, of experiences and family narratives – every bit of it, to Madzy, important enough at that moment to be worth recording. I was working mostly with the first raw version, not smoothed, toned down, generalized, disguised, prepared for the public eye. There were many contradictions and inconsistencies.

I was especially aware of the significance of what I was seeing because I had just been writing autobiography myself in my chapbook *Singularity* and the book-length *Finding Words: A Writer's Memoir*. Now I was watching someone else going through the early stages, leaving what was to me the familiar litter of random jottings and fragments that contained her attempts at articulating, finding a voice, discovering meaning in the process of writing, working out the balance between private and public. I watched Madzy over the decades working out and recording her contradictory opinions and states of mind and mood – about immigration, for instance. I tuned my antenna for every sign of the autobiographical impulse, whether in a note scribbled on the back of a photo, a caption in an album, a sentence or image in a fictional story, an analogy or allusion in a historical work.

An example of materials turning into autobiography under my eyes, as it were, could be seen in the photo album that she began when she and Wim returned to Holland from the United States. The album contains captions, notes, and dates that make it more narrative than most photo albums are. Another is a tape, made at my request, in which she recounts my childhood ailments; she includes important autobiographical as well as biographical matter.

Even more significant is my baby book. She began this record in a functional foolscap-sized notebook with stiff covers. After four weeks she got a conventional baby book, decorated with wreaths of flowers and pictures of plastic-looking infants. (The big notebook was later used for the diary she wrote while Wim was in the POW camp.) Along with fragmentary notes about my acquisition of teeth and vocabulary, the baby book contains accounts of bombing, the fall of Singapore, and her and Wim's activities during the beginning of the war. It became – because of the way Madzy used it – a fragment of autobiography and the first surviving diary of hers that we have.

The writing of autobiography requires not just a recording of the facts but also commentary, analysis, an attention to patterns of (or conjectures about) cause and effect. It involves an awareness that not everything is of equal importance, though in the early stages anything may be put down on paper for later sorting. It requires an awareness of the importance of perception, the difference made by the angle of perception and mood, the possibility that memory is unreliable, the tendency to create myths and shape "factual" material into stories. In Madzy's unpublished writings, all of this was still in unrevised, unshaped form.

However diffident she often was in her manner, however much she appeared to be a private person, it is clear that she had the self-awareness and self-respect essential for the writing of autobiography. She considered that her story, inner and outer, was worth recording, in however fragmentary a way, and that what she wrote was worth preserving. Preservation involves decisions, judgments, priorities – a sense of the value of the record and of the self and life that it documents. Every act of preserving or destroying a document is revealing.

By using Madzy's own words wherever possible, I have taken the reader through some part of this process with me.

Appendix 2
Ancestry

Tracing genealogy in Madzy's family is not difficult, because in Holland there is an office for genealogical studies that has published genealogies of the "gentry" families of the country.[1] One volume traces the van Vollenhoven family. Madzy annotated this book, identifying the people who would be known to us through family portraits and her stories.

The genealogy of the Rochussen family, Madzy's mother's ancestors, was also published,[2] and it too was annotated by Madzy.

In the 1990s, my father put together the available information about his and Madzy's ancestry, using these and a few other sources, mostly published. Because the information is available in those forms, what I will give here is a simplified version of Bill's account of Madzy's ancestry. Like him, I will trace only the main line.

WHEN THEY first appear in the surviving records, the van Vollenhovens were prosperous merchants in Rotterdam. The earliest ancestor of whom there is a reliable record is Antoni Lubbertszn van Vollenhoven, 1617–1672. He and his son after him were owners of a fishing fleet. Cornelis (1690–1768), a grandson of the first Antoni, was a flax merchant. The grandson of that Cornelis, another Cornelis (1753–1835), became mayor of Rotterdam.

His son Jan (1774–1845) was a lumber merchant, as were his descendants for several generations. In Holland, being a lumber merchant did not mean having a lumber yard outside one's door. The country in the nineteenth century produced only hardwoods; all softwood had to be imported, mainly from Scandinavia, northern Russia, and North America. These lumber merchants, therefore, were owner-managers of large importing companies employing many workers in their wind-driven sawmills and holding important positions in their communities.

Jan's grandson Mari Rudolph Pieter van Vollenhoven (1839–1910) married another van Vollenhoven, Mattha Cornelia (1841–1906). They were Madzy's grandparents.

Mattha Cornelia's great-grandfather Joost (1754–1823) had been a lawyer, judge, and alderman. The occupation or profession of his son Joan (1784–1843) is unknown. He married Mattha Cornelia van Stolk (1794–1820).[3] Their son Joost (1814–1889) was mayor of Rotterdam and a member of the Upper Chamber (Senate) of the Netherlands. Mattha Cornelia van Vollenhoven, his daughter by his second wife, Catharina Maria Rochussen (1817–1893), married Mari Rudolph Pieter van Vollenhoven (see above).

Mari Rudolph Pieter was a lumber merchant; his son Joost, Madzy's father (1866–1923) at first worked in his father's business but, at the age of nineteen, went to the Dutch East Indies where, in 1904, he married Marie Louise Rochussen (1878–1963). They were Madzy's parents.

THE FIRST MEMBER of the Rochussen family of whom we have a record was Rochus Rochussen (1598–?). He was born in Rotterdam but was registered in early adulthood as a resident of Vlissingen (Flushing) in the province of Zeeland. It was his son Isaac (born 1631, died after 1690) who was the corsair;[4] with his share of the proceeds from the sale of the ship and cargo that he captured, he set up a shipyard, and from then on the family seems to have been prosperous and prominent. The name Isaac was used in the next four generations. During the first half of the eighteenth century the family moved back to Rotterdam.

The bearer of the name Isaac who was born in 1752 and died in 1822 had a daughter named Sara Cornelia (1781–1847); she married Jacobus Adrianus Roest van Limburg, who was a wine merchant. These were Bill's great-great-grandparents, so Bill and Madzy were related – not surprising, considering how these prominent Rotterdam families would have intermarried.

Sara's brother Hendrik (1779–1852) was a prosperous soap manufacturer and an artist; he and his wife were Madzy's great-grandparents on her mother's side. One of their sons was Charles Rochussen (1814–1894), who in his time was a very well-known painter, etcher, and engraver, mainly of historical subjects. His work was the subject of an important retrospective exhibition in Rotterdam in 1994.

One of Sara's sisters, Catharina Maria (1817–1893), married Joost van Vollenhoven, the mayor of Rotterdam (mentioned above); they were Madzy's great-grandparents on her father's side. Their son Jan Adolf (1819–1884) was a merchant in Rotterdam, and all three of his marriages were recorded there, but by 1877 he was living with his third wife in the small city of Lochem in the eastern part of Holland. This third wife was Anna Pauline von Natzmer (1842–1917), who had been born in Berlin to a family of the nobility. They had three daughters. It was in Lochem that Madzy's mother, Marie Louise, was born. Jan Adolf seems not to have been as prosperous as earlier generations, and after his death his widow and three daughters lived in fairly modest circumstances, though two of the daughters (and possibly the third) married men who were financially successful.

Marie Louise (always called Iete) married Captain Johannes Adama van Scheltema and went with him to the Dutch East Indies; their son Paul (Madzy's beloved half-brother) was three when Captain Adama van Scheltema died in a fall from a horse, and Iete married Joost van Vollenhoven. They returned to Holland very shortly before Madzy's birth on 25 August 1910.

Chapter One

1 Maxine Brandis, *Land for Our Sons* (London: Hurst & Blackett, 1958), 144.
2 Ibid., 145.
3 The date is given in D.G. van Epen, *Het Geslacht Rochussen: Genealogie met biografische aantekeningen* (*The Rochussen Family: Genealogy with Biographical Notes*) ('s-Gravenhage, 1928), 11.
4 In this and other passages I have set up the dialogue in conventional form; the typist, working from Madzy's dictation on tape, typed them as continuous paragraphs. The conventional dialogue format seems to me to reflect Madzy's intentions and her inner "replaying" of the scenes.
5 In late Victorian times it was not uncommon for the well-to-do to live for extended periods in hotels. See Katherine Grier, *Culture and Comfort: People, Parlours, and Upholstery, 1850–1930* (Rochester, N.Y.: Strong Museum, 1988).
6 *Land for Our Sons*, 112–14. Madzy changes the names of most of the characters; to avoid confusion, I have used the real names.
7 The "de" is part of the name of the street.
8 Madzy wrote several versions of this story, and they differ slightly in small details. I have used a version – the one in her history of Holland – that I know she wrote and edited with particular care.
9 The second highest of the five classes in the order.
10 It is not clear what Iete considered "horrible" – probably not the music itself but perhaps the children's singing and dancing or the invasion of the salon. She was likely to disapprove of anything she considered "common."
11 *Nederland's patriciaat: Genealogieën van vooraanstaande geslachten* (*The Patriciate of the Netherlands: Genealogies of Prominent Families*) ('s-Gravenhage: Centraal Bureau voor Genealogie, 1967) in fact names no husband and gives no date of marriage. She was born in 1880.
12 The second edition of the *OED* gives 1912 as the first date for the use of the word "vitamine."
13 Madzy recounts this in her unpublished history of Holland.

14 See chapter 11.

15 Her age is determined by the fact that her father, who died when she was thirteen, appears in the pictures.

Chapter Two

1 The website lists the years in the twentieth century in which the festivals were held, and this is the only year that fits.

2 According to the website, festivals actually occur "about every 22 years."

3 *Land for Our Sons*, 56.

4 "Jonkheer" was the lowest rank of the nobility.

5 In the Netherlands, mayors are appointed, not elected by popular vote.

6 Madzy calls this official (in two different versions of this account, both in English) "*amanuensis*" and "*registrar*." As these words have very different meanings in English, I am assuming that she was using terms current in Leiden in her time – and synonymous – and not translating them. The official seems to have been a sort of usher, and I have used that term.

7 In the Netherlands, being a magistrate is a career to plan for, not a matter of being appointed.

Chapter Three

1 Wim's grandmother was an artist as well as a botanist; her daughter Nanny (Hans's twin sister) inherited that talent, and we have paintings by Tante Nanny hanging in our various houses.

2 Johan Willem Hanrath (1867–1932) was an architect, based in Hilversum, specializing in country houses. His work was noted for its good proportions and careful attention to detail. In addition to de Hoogt, he also designed the more modest house belonging to an artist cousin of Wim's father. One of the specialties of houses he designed was the use of a type of wood that never lost its original fragrance. (The biographical information comes from the *Winkler Prins Encyclopedie*, 1951 edition.)

3 Virginia's grandson, Addison Worthington, has traced the connections and thinks that he and I are fourth cousins once removed.

4 "Het Prinselijk Huwelijk" ("The Royal Wedding"). The translation is mine.

5 The clipping does not include the date.

6 The story is entitled "Het Kruis Boven de Hudson" ("The Cross above the Hudson").

7 The clipping does not include the date.

8 *Land for Our Sons*, 13.

Chapter Four

1 Madzy evidently thought (mistakenly) that it was the husband who was the doctor.
2 My information about this incident, and Madzy's letters of this and later times, come from Addison Worthington, Virginia's grandson.
3 The passage quoted is from Bill's memoir. Information about the country's tiny air force and only slightly larger navy comes from Walter B. Maass, *The Netherlands at War: 1940–1945* (London, New York, and Toronto: Abelard Schuman, 1970), 16.
4 Ibid., 14–19.
5 Ibid., 24–5.
6 Ibid., 26.
7 Information about the larger picture comes from Maass and from *WWII: Time-Life Books History of the Second World War* (New York: Prentice Hall, 1989).
8 Maass, passim. Also Werner Warmbrunn, *The Dutch under German Occupation, 1940–1945* (Stanford: Stanford University Press, 1963), 11.
9 Madzy writes about this in her *Memories*: Paul, she explains, "had a very good job in Batavia as second-in-command ... of a shipbuilding concern ... Unfortunately he got caught by the Japanese when he tried to hide a new dry-dock ... When the Japanese were [known to be] coming, the shipbuilding concern had just built this new dry-dock. Paul wanted to save it and he, with many other people of course, towed the dry-dock around the island of Java to the southern coast in the hope that [it could be hidden] from the Japanese." The attempt failed, and Paul and his family were interned in Japanese prison camps until the end of the war.
10 Maass, passim.

Chapter Five

1 There actually was a bottle of champagne in the cellar. Later in the diary, on 21 December 1944, Madzy records that she is going to give it to her sister, Hansje.
2 Even before learning of Wim's imprisonment, she had been worried about the fact that on this occasion the officers had been told to report to a different location.
3 To avoid individual notes: Wendela van Tuyll van Serooskerken was a private nurse who was staying with Madzy for the confinement. She was a friend of a friend of Madzy's. Because there was no telephone at our cottage, she used the phone at the house of the van Nottens; the people she phoned in Amersfoort were Dick and Charlotte Kolff, who were close friends; Dick was a reserve officer and might therefore have information about what was going on. Moeder Iete, Madzy's mother, had been evacuated from her home in The Hague and

was living at de Hoogt with Wim's Tante Betsy, who was also a good friend of Iete's. In the diary Madzy always identifies her in this way to distinguish her from Moeder Hans, Wim's mother. "Pankie" was me; I was then three and a half years old. Throughout the diary Madzy refers to me by many forms of my real name and this nickname.

4 The servant, who lived close by and worked for Madzy whenever needed.

5 This was a printed card instructing relatives to send the imprisoned officers' uniforms and other personal effects to a specified address in Holland. On the card the prisoner was permitted to write only his home address, no personal message.

6 Madzy apparently thought (in the absence of reliable information, the country seethed with rumours) that the officers had been given a choice between their honour as officers and signing some "dishonourable" statement and being released. Wim, in his annotations to the diary, writes: "There was absolutely no choice; we were just put on the train to Germany." This is the first instance mentioned in the diary of the misinformation and guesswork that replaced accurate information and, for Madzy, confused and seriously aggravated the situation.

7 Because Willy Schüffner was German, he might, she hoped, have some influence with the occupying forces. Ede was the town between Maarn and Arnhem where Wim and the other Dutch officers had been taken captive.

8 Agriculture, with which Wim had a connection because of his work as estate manager, was a "privileged" occupation. Madzy's wording is convoluted; it was a delicate matter to ask for favours from the German occupying forces; she wrote obscurely in case the diary fell into German hands.

9 Madzy was still in bed after giving birth.

10 She writes as though this were an actual letter, which Wim would receive before the suitcase arrived. This is not a sign of mental confusion but an indication, I think, that in her extreme distress she found some comfort in the pretence that normal communications were possible.

11 It was apparently feared that labels from former travels might be dangerous.

12 Bill wrote in 2001: "The suitcase arrived in good shape some three to four weeks later. Most of the food I shared with friends, as they had done also. But the Germans had taken all the food from the suitcases at another assembly point. Madzy had included a small English bible which I read during the first month as there were no other books. It was of course marvellous to get all these things and also to get underwear, and being able to brush teeth and shave; besides, I had no coat with me."

13 Bill writes: "They were the owners of Broekhuizen, the very large estate in Leersum that I had managed for them during the [previous] year."

14 Presumably rumour said that that was where the POWs had been sent. In fact he was in Nüremberg.

15 She knew that Wim would be acquainted with a number of the officers in his camp because they had been serving together for several years.

16 D. Blijdenstein, unpublished diary, 17 February 1945.

17 This last point is documented by Maass in *The Netherlands at War*, passim.

18 The date is given in Maass, 143.

19 An entry (quoted below) in her diary suggests that these broadcasts were at nine o'clock, not ten o'clock. It is possible that at some point the time changed, or that after the lapse of decades she misremembered a few details.

20 This was her usual name for Wim.

21 Tante Ida was Wim's great-aunt by marriage.

22 It is likely that the mattress had been put there for someone in hiding from the Germans; if so, her silence about the details is another example of self-censorship. And of course Wim, for whom the diary was written, would have known the details.

23 Bill, in 2001, writes: "Because I buried them in the woods."

24 Bill (2001) explains that it was in order to get a minimum amount of poultry feed.

25 A member of the cabbage family; Bill translates it as mustard or turnip greens.

26 *Land for Our Sons*, 28.

27 This was Boy Ruijs de Perez, a friend who had tried to escape to England in a small boat with Carel Steensma and a third man. The boat was shot at by the Germans; Steensma eventually lost one leg but survived (and is still alive at the time of writing). Ruijs was, as Madzy says, executed. May was his wife and was known to many people in Maarn because she had grown up in Driebergen just a few kilometres away; Tante Anna was Anna de Gijselaar, wife of the former mayor of Leiden. Carel Steensma was married to Tienk de Veer, sister of Madzy's sister-in-law, Mita Adama van Scheltema. My information about the attempted escape comes from Frank Steensma, Carel's son. He consulted Peter Gerritse, *De Mei-vliegers* (Baarn, Bosch & Keuning, 1995).

28 Bill's note (2002): "Just around that time (mid-July) we had been moved from Nüremberg to Stanislau, where we stayed till January 1944." He explained to me that Stanislau was in an area which, during the war – when the Germans had seized it from the Russians – was "politically" Poland but actually in the Ukraine.

29 Maass, passim.

30 Bill's note (2001): "Probably she means cleaning moss off the bark, something which is needed in Holland."

31 It was necessary to be at the shops early, while there was still something to be obtained with the new ration coupons.

32 Her husband had been taken prisoner on the same day as Wim.

33 Mostly Madzy writes densely, leaving no margins or blank lines, but for this all-important passage she gives herself more room. There is a left-hand margin and she leaves occasional blank lines.

34 He wrote in English; I have edited slightly for clarity, focus, and length.

35 Maass writes: "The prisons were filled with men who were designated as 'death candidates' ... They were, so to speak, a reservoir for future executions. When

an act of sabotage occurred, a number of persons were chosen from their midst and executed, generally in public" (198–9).

36 *Encyclopedia Britannica*. It was the Geneva Conventions that founded the Red Cross in 1864.

37 Maass, 205.

38 Dientje Blijdenstein records in her diary that large numbers of trees in the woods on their estate were cut to provide fuel for the village.

39 Code for the radio.

40 To write down the news from the radio?

41 She had clearly been listening to the BBC broadcast.

42 Nando was the son of a cousin of Wim's.

43 She uses the Latin expression "*Hodie tibi cras mihi.*"

44 Her house, de Hoogt, was already entirely full.

45 These were homemade, I don't know by whom. The rabbits had been caught and eaten; the skins had not been adequately cured, and the slippers were stiff and awkward. Still, they were slippers.

46 Madzy, to encourage me to learn, had borrowed a desk from the school, which was shut down, and had made a "school corner" with a desk and a bookshelf where I did the schoolwork that she assigned. I also attended the little class for four children that was run by one of the unemployed teachers.

47 In English in the original. She is probably quoting a radio broadcast from England.

48 As opposed to the First World War, when Holland was neutral.

49 This is the clearest statement we have of the situation once it settled down. The Molhuizen family had moved on, and the West family were with us for the rest of the war.

50 Madzy means that at that point he did not have to take part in the compulsory labour – in Holland itself – for which the Germans conscripted many able-bodied Dutchmen.

51 The local police constable, now clearly cooperating with the Germans – a difficult choice that thousands of Dutch functionaries had had to make during the occupation. It is not clear why she did not recognize him at first; possibly she knew of him by name but had never had dealings with him before.

52 In a letter written later, she says that during the war we used a kind of soap made of clay.

53 Madzy is alluding to the fact that in the Dutch East Indies, in her father's time, one year of service counted for two on account of the strain for Europeans of working in the tropics.

54 Rika was Madzy's former maid, who had worked for her before the war in Amersfoort and was now married and living on a small farm.

55 This would be coffee substitute made with hot milk.

56 A cousin of Wim's father.

57 Sister of Wim's father.

58 Almost certainly some tea substitute.

59 In the last winter the services were held in private houses because the church was used to accommodate refugees.

60 A British plane.

61 One of the objects that Madzy or someone else found (we assumed that it had been left behind by the Germans) was a sleeveless, fur-lined, button-in lining from a long coat. It eventually came to me, and I wore it for many years in the house in cold weather as a kind of long vest.

62 I don't know how Madzy knew the date when the bread had been baked.

63 *Land for Our Sons*, 15–18. The unpublished short story, "Bacon on the Moors," written more than thirty years after the event, gives much the same account but instead of a basket on the bicycle she refers to saddlebags, and writes that they were "full to the lids with hard tack biscuits, chocolate bars, a tin with my dinner, a few more tins, and on top of all that a package of cigarettes." This is memory working, mythologizing, and turning real life into story. The incident must have resonated in her mind for the rest of her life.

64 Bill's comment in 2002: "Never received in the chaos."

65 The last remaining mini-truck of the gas works in The Hague, of which Wim's father was general manager; it ran on octane gas.

66 Actually Gerard had just turned three.

Chapter Six

1 Mak, *De Eeuw van mijn vader* (*My Father's Century*), Amsterdam/Antwerpen: Uitgeverij Atlas, 1999, 336 (my translation).

2 Ibid., 336–7.

3 J.J. Woltjer, *Recent Verleden: Nederland in de twintigste eeuw.* (*The Recent Past: The Netherlands in the Twentieth Century*). Original edition by Uitgeverij Balans, Amsterdam, 1992, 215. (Edition I used was Rainbow Pocketboeken, by Uitgeverij Maarten Muntinga bv, Amsterdam, 1994.)

4 Ibid., 216.

5 Information from Bill.

6 *Encyclopedia Britannica*.

7 Mak, 359.

8 This is clear from papers sent to me by Virginia Donaldson's grandson Addison Worthington.

9 It is significant that the narrator's name is "Atti": this was what Paul always called Madzy.

10 Madzy herself was pregnant during the summer of 1946, another autobiographical element.

11 *Land for Our Sons*, 188.

12 One remembers how many of his clothes had been bartered for food during the previous years and how impossible it still was to buy new clothing.

13 *Land*, 12.

14 Ibid., 14. Madzy changed most of the names: I have gone back to the real ones.

15 This was money that Wim had sent to a U.S. bank in September 1939 after the Germans invaded Poland.

Chapter Seven

1 Madzy wrote two different accounts of our arrival in Vancouver. This version is from the diary-letter.

2 *Land*, 21, 22–3.

3 Ibid., 22.

4 Ibid., 188.

5 Ibid., 9.

6 Ibid., 31.

7 Ibid., 32–3.

8 Ibid., 33.

9 Ibid., 34.

10 Nadine Asante, *The History of Terrace* (Terrace Public Library Association, 1972), 219.

11 Ibid., 221.

12 Other than *Land for Our Sons*, a "public" narrative, the only surviving writings for this period are a few letters to Virginia Donaldson, a few very brief and tentative "memoir" notes, and three or four short stories written for a creative writing course which she took towards the end of the period. There are photo albums with brief captions, which are of course "public."

From now until nearly the end of her life, Madzy kept a diary, using the small, lockable five-year volumes that give a space for each day's entry. She wrote in it regularly, so far as we can tell, but the contents were completely private. All we knew was that sometimes she would report on events that had happened on this date in previous years: storms, the first frost, the birth of farm animals. Shortly before her death she asked to have the whole set destroyed.

Besides the extant sources, I have relied on Bill's memories and Gerard's and my own, and contributions from some of the people who knew her.

13 He meant that it was "old" in Terrace terms; Nadine Asante, if I read her work correctly, says that Ed Eby moved to Terrace in 1912 (112).

14 *Land*, 39–40.

15 Ibid., 42.

16 Ibid., 47.

17 Ibid., 64–5.

18 Ibid., 59.

19 Ibid., 60–1.

20 This was not strictly true. She had done the cooking from the time she married, though the makeshift conditions of the last years of the war, while forcing her to be resourceful and ingenious, did not encourage a development of interest or skill in cooking.

21 *De Nederlandse Courant*, "Koffiepraatje" of 5 October 1963.

22 Enid is not named in the newspaper column, but in the comparable passage in *Land for Our Sons* Madzy says that it was she who "taught" her.

23 Havelaar, "Jumping and Landing," 38.

24 *Land*, 127–8.

25 Ibid., 126.

26 George Hendrick, *Mazo de la Roche* (New York: Twayne, 1970), 35.

27 *Land*, 66.

28 Ibid.

29 Madzy probably wrote this account in the late 1960s but the story was not published at that time. It was slightly revised and appeared in her last book, *The Scent of Spruce* (Windsor, Ont.: Netherlandic Press, 1984), 10–12.

30 This may be a pseudonym.

31 Some of the following information comes from an article by Vi Keenleyside, entitled "Bell a Ringing Endorsement of International Friendship," written for the *Islander* and published on Sunday, 16 June 1985. Madzy in her story does not name the donor of the bell. Vi Keenleyside notes that on the bell is the date of 1779 and the name Arendt Boolens – she conjectures that he may have been the bellcaster who made it.

32 From the letter quoted in the article.

33 Ed Harrison, "Dutch Bell Rings Out at Last from Knox United Church Tower," in *Terrace Review*, Wednesday, 16 May 1990.

34 *Land*, 143–4.

35 Ibid., 148.

36 Ibid.

37 Ibid., 53.

38 Ibid., 137.

39 Letter of 29 April 1947. I have translated her phrase verbatim because it seems to me to have a slightly mystical overtone, as though she and Wim had a sense that it was destined, that there was a course which, if not laid out for them by greater powers, was nevertheless "on the right road" for them.

40 I am not sure that we did look on it as "a disgrace," but if we did so it would have been the result of the near-silence concerning it that prevailed in the family in earlier years – a deliberate policy to make the "becoming Canadian" happen as quickly as possible – and the misunderstanding and occasional mockery that

we children encountered in school. At that time, no one apparently understood the magnitude and complexity of the issues involved in immigration.

41 Madzy uses quotation marks in the original: it is written as dialogue.

42 Actually great-great-grandmother.

43 *Land*, 150.

44 Ibid., 152.

45 Ibid., 152–3.

46 The birthmark under the left eye may have been suggested by the fact that I have one under my right eye.

47 E.H. Blakeney, *A Smaller Classical Dictionary* (London, J.M. Dent & Sons, 1913).

48 According to Bill. The fact that it was written in English – which Paul could read easily – does suggest, however, that she was thinking of her children as well.

49 *Land*, 68.

50 Ibid., 71–2.

51 Ibid., 72–3.

52 Translation by Edward Baxter.

53 *Land*, 19–20.

54 Ibid., 102.

55 Ibid., 110.

56 Ibid., 111.

57 His mother kept his letters and returned them to him, and he recently sent me "a free translation" of his own account of meeting us. Knowing that his translation would be included in this book, he presumably added brief explanations that would not have been needed for his mother. I have silently corrected one or two matters of punctuation, etc.

58 He isn't quite right about our ages.

59 *Land*, 178.

60 Ibid.

Chapter Eight

1 *Land*, 87.

2 Ibid., 188.

3 In the original, a rough draft with handwritten revisions, "was crippled with arthritis" is crossed out and replaced with "got trouble with my back." I have used the earlier version because that describes Madzy's actual situation before the fictional displacement and suggests that the original conception was very autobiographical.

4 This is how she put it in the first draft, which is all that we have; no doubt "bazaars" is shorthand, which she would have amplified or altered in revision.

5 Madzy used the word "spiritual" to refer not only to religious matters but to the whole life of the human spirit.

6 Russell, *History of Western Philosophy* (London: George Allen and Unwin, 1946), 11.

7 I am quoting from Madzy's essay: the letter from Russell did not turn up among her papers, though I know she kept it. Gerard said that she put it in a pocket pasted inside the cover of her copy of one of Russell's books. It is not in either of the two that I own now, so it must have been in another that was lent and never returned, or that disappeared in one of the moves following her death.

Chapter Nine

1 The information comes from an essay by Daniel Schugurensky on a website located by searching for "Antigonish Movement." I also consulted Anne Alexander, *The Antigonish Movement: Moses Coady and Adult Education Today* (Toronto: Thompson Educational Publishing, 1997) and M.M. Coady, *Masters of Their Own Destiny: The Story of the Antigonish Movement of Adult Education through Economic Cooperation* (New York: Harper & Brothers, 1939).

2 Schugurensky.

3 D. Kermode Parr, in the *Atlantic Advocate* of September 1958, 83. (For this review we have only the clipping. A later issue, vol. 49, no. 9, May 1959, says that the magazine was published by University Press of New Brunswick, Fredericton.)

4 Brandis, "Dusting the Shelves," *Maritime Co-operator*, 15 March 1959. In this column the number of books is given as "800"; in the next column (1 April) she says that that was a misprint: the actual number is "8,000").

5 Report of 3 March 1959 to the director of the Extension Department.

6 Quoted from the circular letter.

7 These would have been mostly those who came from third-world countries to learn about the Antigonish Movement.

8 "Dusting the Shelves," 15 February 1959.

9 Ibid., 6 January 1959.

10 "A Tour of the Extension Department," *The Casket*, n.d.

11 "Waste or Wealth?," ibid., 28 May 1959.

12 "Higher Education," ibid., n.d.

13 "Adult Education," ibid., n.d.

14 I quoted this passage in chapter 2. Bill and I have been unable to reconstruct when, in those three very busy weeks, she could have gone to Leiden, but she may have done so.

15 De Intergouvernementele Commissie voor Europese Migratie te Genève en de Nederlandse Emigratiedienst te Den Haag. The Emigratiedienst – a department of the Ministry of Social Affairs and Employment (Ministerie van Soci-

ale Zaken en Werkgelegenheid) – bought the rights and then apparently transferred them to Het Spectrum, which issued the book as a Prisma paperback.

16 When I discussed the story with Bill, he said that the woman mentioned in it was the only person they met who spoke only Gaelic.

Chapter Ten

1 The phrase comes from Gerard's personal communication.

2 The writer's initials are given in this form at the beginning of the article and as "P.G." at the end.

3 There is some uncertainty about the date: Mr Risseeuw says he came in October and, among quotations from the whole family, he quotes what I allegedly said during the visit – but I was in Holland then. So either he came earlier or later, or he fabricated what he reports me as saying. I appear in the pictures illustrating the article, but they were taken (as my journal records) on 21 January 1962 by Charlie Davis, a friend of ours, when I was back in Burlington.

4 She was fifty-three at the time of writing; if something happened to Bill and she did have to go into a care facility fairly soon, she could be facing many years of that life.

5 The quoted words are comments Bill made when he read this chapter in draft.

6 She had seen them five years earlier, but her mood might have contributed to her sense that they were all "fairly strange."

7 See appendix 2 on "Ancestry."

8 *Land voor onze zonen*, 6; *Land for Our Sons*, 10. Miles are converted into kilometres everywhere in the Dutch version.

9 *Land voor onze zonen*, 90. For someone in tiny Holland, the isolation of a town like Terrace, the hundreds of miles between hospitals, was unimaginable.

10 *Land voor onze zonen*, 11.

11 "Adult Student," *Atlantic Advocate*, May 1962, 43.

12 She must have regained at least some vision in the other eye as well, because during a foot operation in September 1972 she once again lost the vision in one eye, this time permanently, and then got glaucoma in the remaining eye.

13 Published by the Intergouvermentele Commissie voor Europese Migratie, 's-Gravenhage. Madzy's article appeared in the winter 1959–60 issue. (This was the same government department that commissioned and published *Land voor onze zonen*.)

14 Paul Sauvé was premier of Quebec from September 1959 until January 1960. In that short time, "he inaugurated a period of major political and social change" (*Canadian Encyclopedia*, 2nd ed.)

15 I have tried unsuccessfully to locate back copies of the newspaper to examine the context into which Madzy's first writings for the newspaper fitted.

16 Hyacinthe apparently did not return to Canada.

17 *De Nederlandse Courant voor Canada*, 13 October 1962.

18 31 August 1963.

19 Undatable column.

Chapter Eleven

1 Julius Lebow, besides being the owner of the Westdale Art Gallery through whom Gerard had first made contact with these artists, was a painter. Ann Suzuki was a painter and fabric artist. Lloyd Kinnee was an abstract painter. Fay Dubois did weaving and batik. Cal Whitehead was a former stage director, by now a teacher. Lorne Looker was a part-time sculptor. Aiko Suzuki was a painter. Don Nixon did collage, drawing, and painting.

2 This painting is reproduced at the end of chapter 6.

3 Gerard, after writing this, commented: "Writing that little piece about Mam's art was quite an experience. I saw much more than I had before, and for the first time in the context of her life." So both he and I have become reacquainted with our mother through her work.

4 University of British Columbia Archives, Cooke Family fonds, box 1.

5 He knew something about navigation because during his university years he had become a reserve officer in the navy, spending the summers in training at various naval installations.

6 Personal communication.

7 The family name for me, probably a shortening of the Dutch nickname "Pankie."

8 He had been asked to go to Antigonish, to help train the next group of workers going to the Caribbean and South America. He himself had been badly prepared for the work in Trenchtown; CUSO organizers realized this and asked him to come and talk about his experiences.

9 Not a light matter, because he had respiratory problems.

10 Jock had been given a Daimler by an actor he had met on one of his filming jobs; the car was, Jock says, "a nightmare under the hood," but Jock – who is extremely good with all things mechanical – was able to keep it running. When the actor left, he gave the car to Jock. Later, when their paths crossed again, Jock gave it back.

11 They had been filming somewhere on location.

12 Bill bought his hay from a nearby farmer.

13 The remaining Brandstead goats.

14 He died 30 October 1966, his daughter Jocelyn Drainie confirmed by phone in March 2002.

15 Her education in Holland had been focused on classics and ancient history.

16 Madzy refers to him as her distant cousin; I am not sure whether he was also related to Paul, Madzy's half-brother.

17 I have the book by Henri Sjollema (H.J. Sjollema, *Isaac Rochussen, 7 Juli 1672*, self-published, 1976), and it is of course in Dutch. It gives the correct name of the English ship as the *Falcon*. Sjollema says that in a book tracing the genealogy of the Rochussen family, it is incorrectly called the *Hawk*, or the *Golden Hawk*. In the Dutch records it is always called the *Valk* (*Falcon*).

18 *Nederland's patriciaat: Genealogieën van vooraanstaande geslachten* (*The Patriciate of The Netherlands: Genealogies of Prominent Families*).

19 I have silently corrected some of the most obvious mistakes here, the kinds of typos, spellings, and omissions that she would have corrected had she been able to. She corrected a few herself, on the printed version, but by this time writing was nearly impossible for her.

20 I have left some of the typos of this entry, including her spelling of "pedestal." She always used the French word in writing and speaking.

21 It had now become Bill's den.

22 I have set this up in verse form; the Memowriter's narrow strip of paper made that difficult and approximate, but the rhyming verse Madzy used indicated clearly what she intended.

23 Don's birthday was six days before Gerard's, and Bill's about two weeks before that.

Appendix Two

1 *Nederland's patriciaat: Genealogieën van vooraanstaande geslachten* (*The Patriciate of The Netherlands: Genealogies of Prominent Families*).

2 D.G. van Epen, *Het Geslacht Rochussen: Genealogie met biografische aantekeningen* (*The Rochussen Family: Genealogy with Biographical Notes*).

3 She is the subject of a fine portrait we have; Madzy wrote her story in "Portrait of a Woman."

4 See chapter 11.